THE NORTON SAMPLER

Seventh Edition

ALSO BY THOMAS COOLEY

Back to the Lake: A Reader for Writers

The Norton Guide to Writing

Adventures of Huckleberry Finn, A Norton Critical Edition
(Third Edition)

The Ivory Leg in the Ebony Cabinet:
Madness, Race, and Gender in Victorian America

Educated Lives: The Rise of Modern Autobiography in America

THE NORTON SAMPLER

SHORT ESSAYS FOR COMPOSITION

Seventh Edition

XXXXXXXXXXXXXXXXXXXXXXXXXXXXXXXXXXXXXXXXXXXXXXXXXXXXXXXXXXXXX

THOMAS COOLEY

THE OHIO STATE UNIVERSITY

W·W·NORTON & COMPANY

NEW YORK·LONDON

W. W. Norton & Company has been independent since its founding in 1923, when William Warder Norton and Mary D. Herter Norton first published lectures delivered at the People's Institute, the adult education division of New York City's Cooper Union. The firm soon expanded its program beyond the Institute, publishing books by celebrated academics from America and abroad. By midcentury, the two major pillars of Norton's publishing program—trade books and college texts—were firmly established. In the 1950s, the Norton family transferred control of the company to its employees, and today—with a staff of four hundred and a comparable number of trade, college, and professional titles published each year—W. W. Norton & Company stands as the largest and oldest publishing house owned wholly by its employees.

Manufacturing by Maple-Vail Book Manufacturing Group.
Book design by Martin Lubin and Jo Anne Metsch.
Production manager: Christine D'Antonio.

Library of Congress Cataloging-in-Publication Data
The Norton sampler : short essays for composition / [edited by]
Thomas Cooley.—7th ed.
p.   cm.
Includes bibliographical references and index.
ISBN 978-0-393-92935-5 (pbk.)
1. College readers. 2. English language—Rhetoric. 3. Essays.
I. Cooley, Thomas, 1942–
PE1417 .N6 2010
808'.0427—dc22   2009044731

Instructor's Edition ISBN: 978-0-393-93513-4

W. W. Norton & Company, Inc., 500 Fifth Avenue, New York, NY 10110
www.wwnorton.com
W. W. Norton & Company Ltd., Castle House, 75/76 Wells Street, London W1T 3QT
4 5 6 7 8 9 0

Contents

XXXXXXXXXXXXXXXXXXXXXXXXXXXXXXXXXXXXXXXXXXXXXXXXXXXXXXXX

INTRODUCTION   1

XXXXXXXXXXXXXXXXXXXXXXXXXXXXXXXXXXXXXXXXXXXXXXXXXXXXXXXX

Annie Dillard   ♠   *from* HOLY THE FIRM   2

And that is why I believe those hollow crisps on the bathroom floor are moths. I think I know moths, and fragments of moths, and chips and tatters of utterly empty moths, in any state. How many of you, I asked the people in my class, which of you want to give your lives and be writers?

Annie Dillard   ♠   HOW I WROTE THE MOTH ESSAY—
AND WHY   6

Walking back to my desk, where I had been answering letters, I realized that the burning moth was a dandy visual focus for all my recent thoughts about an empty, dedicated life. Perhaps I'd try to write a short narrative about it.

CHAPTER ONE: **ON WRITING AND READING** 19

CHAPTER TWO: **DESCRIPTION** 41

XXXXXXXXXXXXXXXXXXXXXXXXXXXXXXXXXXXXXXXXXXXXXXXXXXXXX

"He's mostly silver, but the silver is somehow made up of *all* the colors, if you know what I mean." I stopped. "Do you know what I mean by colors?"

Miss Dennis always wore a variation of one outfit—a dark-colored, flared woolen skirt, a tailored white blouse and a cardigan sweater, usually black, thrown over her shoulders and held together by a little pearl chain.

Can you see her? I can. And the image of her makes me smile. Still.

He looks almost like a young child buckled into a car seat, with his closed eyes and freshly shaved head, with the way the black restraints of the electric chair crisscross at his torso.

One girl stood by her llama and blew gently on its nose, and he looked lovingly into her eyes. A sort of conversation. If every teenager had his or her own llama, this would be a very different country.

As alarming as the Gaines-burgers were, their soy meal began to seem like an old friend when the time came to try some *canned* dog foods.

At first glance he looked like a snowman, except instead of snow he was covered in gray, asbestos-colored ash. . . . A small plume of dust drifted off the top of his head as he walked, echoing the larger plume of smoke drifting off of One World Trade behind him.

As the months pass, I remain miserably uncertain about all things but one: I would kill for a trashy American sweet. I do not miss cheese or pasta or even my friends, but I do miss, with a maddening intensity, that blast of sugar that only a glazed cruller can provide.

Affirmative Action programs had made it all possible. The disadvantages of others permitted my promotion; the absence of many Mexican-Americans from academic life allowed my designation as a "minority student."

Even my mother had an empty Tang bottle with a snug orange nylon net over it, a present from one of her fellow schoolteachers. She carried it from the office to the classroom and back again as if our family had also consumed a full bottle.

After several hours, I had more or less forgotten about my tent-sized, RWA jumpsuit when suddenly I heard someone laughing at me: "I wonder what she did to deserve that?!"

Most Americans have never had to live with terror. I had had to live with it all my life—the psychological terror of segregation, in which there was a special set of laws governing your movements. You violated them at your peril. . . .

In total, 347 individual acts of sin were committed at the bake sale, with nearly every attendee committing at least one of the seven deadly sins as outlined by Gregory the Great in the Fifth Century.

As I poked through the wreckage, suddenly there it was: my grandmother's ashtray, complete and unbroken. Delighted, I reached out to take it. And then its tongue came out.

My grandmother has bound feet. Cruelly tethered since her birth, they are like bonsai trees, miniature versions of what should have been.

If there are better images of the strength and selflessness of the American soldier, I can't think of any. It is easy to understand why newspapers and magazines around the country ran the photo big, making Private Dwyer an instant hero, back when the war was a triumphal tale of Iraqi liberation.

Sometimes you have to believe that all English speakers should be committed to an asylum for the verbally insane. In what other language do people drive in a parkway and park in a driveway? . . . In what other language can your nose run and your feet smell?

CHAPTER FIVE: **CLASSIFICATION** 165

XXXXXXXXXXXXXXXXXXXXXXXXXXXXXXXXXXXXXXXXXXXXXXXXXXXXX

I spend a great deal of my time thinking about the power of language—the way it can evoke an emotion, a visual image, a complex idea, or a simple truth. Language is the tool of my trade. And I use them all—all the Englishes I grew up with.

Help! I'm drowning. I have 112 unanswered e-mail messages. I'm a writer—imagine how many unanswered messages I would have if I had a real job. Imagine how much writing I could do if I didn't have to answer all this e-mail.

"Hitting the books," expressing oneself articulately, and, at times, displaying more than a modest amount of intelligence—these traits were derided as "acting white."

The world can be divided in many ways—rich and poor, democratic and authoritarian—but one of the most striking is the divide between the societies with an individualist mentality and the ones with a collectivist mentality.

All the mammals are divided into two subclasses. In one of these subclasses ("Protheria" or "first-beasts") are the duckbill and five species of the spiny anteater. In the other ("Theria" or just "beasts") are all the other 4,231 known living species of mammals.

CHAPTER SIX: **PROCESS ANALYSIS** 204

XXXXXXXXXXXXXXXXXXXXXXXXXXXXXXXXXXXXXXXXXXXXXXXXXXXXX

A BRIEF GUIDE TO WRITING A PROCESS ANALYSIS 209

EVERYDAY PROCESS ANALYSIS / ROZ CHAST RECIPES 214

Will Shortz ♠ HOW TO SOLVE SUDOKU 215

Solving a sudoku puzzle involves pure logic. No guesswork is needed—or even desirable. Getting started involves mastering just a few simple techniques.

Jon Katz ♠ HOW BOYS BECOME MEN 220

No. A chicken would probably have had the sense to get out of the way. This boy was already well on the road to becoming a *man*, having learned one of the central ethics of his gender: Experience pain rather than show fear.

Allegra Goodman ♠ SO, YOU WANT TO BE A WRITER? HERE'S HOW. 225

To begin, don't write about yourself. I'm not saying you're uninteresting. I realize that your life has been so crazy no one could make this stuff up. But if you want to be a writer, start by writing about other people.

Alexander Petrunkevitch ♠ THE SPIDER AND THE WASP 230

Meanwhile, the wasp, having satisfied itself that the victim is of the right species, moves off a few inches to dig the spider's grave. . . . Now and again the wasp pops out of the hole to make sure that the spider is still there.

Philip Weiss ♠ HOW TO GET OUT OF A LOCKED TRUNK 238

Every culture comes up with tests of a person's ability to get out of a sticky situation. . . . When they slam the [car] trunk, though, you're helpless unless someone finds you. You would think that such a common worry should have a ready fix, and that the secret of getting out of a locked trunk is something we should all know about.

And what, exactly, do I mean by "guys"? I don't know. I haven't thought that much about it. One of the major characteristics of guyhood is that we guys don't spend a lot of time pondering our deep innermost feelings. There is a serious question in my mind about whether guys actually *have* deep innermost feelings unless you count, for example, loyalty to the Detroit Tigers. . . .

The Spanish language was supposedly the glue that held the new Latino community together. But in my case it was what kept me apart. . . . I wanted to call myself Latina, to finally take pride, but it felt like a lie. So I set out to learn the language that people assumed I already knew.

Addiction does indeed discriminate. It "selects" for people who are bad at delaying gratification and gauging consequences, who are impulsive, who think they have little to lose, have few competing interests, or are willing to lie to a spouse.

The first shots of the Evo Devo revolution revealed that despite their great differences in appearance and physiology, all complex animals—flies and flycatchers, dinosaurs and trilobites, butterflies and zebras and humans—share a common "tool kit" of "master" genes that govern the formation and patterning of their bodies and body parts.

I want to eat what the kids at school eat: bologna, hot dogs, salami—foods my parents find repugnant because they contain pork and meat byproducts, crushed bone and hair glued together by chemicals and fat. . . . Indians, of course, do not eat such things.

CHAPTER NINE: **CAUSE AND EFFECT** 339

XXXXXXXXXXXXXXXXXXXXXXXXXXXXXXXXXXXXXXXXXXXXXXXXXXXXXXXXX

But what the Internet and its cult of anonymity do is to provide a blanket sort of immunity for anybody who wants to say anything about anybody else, and it would be difficult in this sense to think of a more morally deformed exploitation of the concept of free speech.

"Pauline," he said to my mother, his voice kindly but amused, "there's not a thing wrong with that child. The problem's psychosomatic. Your son's an overachiever."

That made me wonder, was I a cool person who smoked or a smoker who wanted to be cool? Either way, the problem with the theory is that it doesn't explain why the truly cool start to smoke.

Working at McDonald's has taught me a lot. . . . I'd like to have my own business someday, and working at McDonald's is what showed me I could do that.

This is how I became a Chilean poet who wrote in Spanish and lived in the southern United States. And then, one day, a poem of mine was translated and published in the English language. . . . My poem, expressed in another language, spoke for itself . . . and for me.

(Continued)

CHAPTER ELEVEN: **CLASSIC ESSAYS AND SPEECHES** 445

XXXXXXXXXXXXXXXXXXXXXXXXXXXXXXXXXXXXXXXXXXXXXXXXXXXXX

APPENDIX: **USING SOURCES IN YOUR WRITING** 487

XXXXXXXXXXXXXXXXXXXXXXXXXXXXXXXXXXXXXXXXXXXXXXXXXXXXXXX

THEMATIC CONTENTS

XXXXXXXXXXXXXXXXXXXXXXXX **HISTORY** XXXXXXXXXXXXXXXXXXXXXXXX

XXXXXXXXXXXXXXXX **HOME AND FAMILY** XXXXXXXXXXXXXXXX

XXXXXXXXXXXXXX **HUMOR AND SATIRE** XXXXXXXXXXXXXX

XXXXXXXXXXXX **LANGUAGE AND IDENTITY** XXXXXXXXXXXX

XXXXXXXXXXXXXX **LIFE AND DEATH** XXXXXXXXXXXXXXXXXXXX

✕✕✕✕✕✕✕✕✕✕✕✕✕✕✕✕✕✕✕ **MEDIA** ✕✕✕✕✕✕✕✕✕✕✕✕✕✕✕✕✕✕✕

✕✕✕✕✕✕✕✕✕✕✕✕✕ **MEMORIES OF YOUTH** ✕✕✕✕✕✕✕✕✕✕✕✕✕

⟩⟩⟩⟩⟩⟩⟩⟩⟩⟩⟩⟩⟩ MORALITY AND ETHICS ⟩⟩⟩⟩⟩⟩⟩⟩⟩⟩⟩⟩⟩

⟩⟩⟩⟩⟩⟩⟩⟩⟩ NATURE AND THE ENVIRONMENT ⟩⟩⟩⟩⟩⟩⟩⟩⟩

XXXXX **OVERCOMING HARDSHIP AND DISABILITY** XXXXX

XXXXXXXXXXXXXXXXXX **PUBLIC POLICY** XXXXXXXXXXXXXXXXXX

XXXXXXXXXXXX **SCHOOL AND EDUCATION** XXXXXXXXXXXX

XXXXXXXXXXX SCIENCE AND TECHNOLOGY XXXXXXXXXXX

XXXXXXXXX SOCIOLOGY AND ANTHROPOLOGY XXXXXXXXX

XXXXXXXXXXXXXX **SPORTS AND LEISURE** XXXXXXXXXXXXXX

XXXXXXXXXXXXXX **STUDENT WRITING** XXXXXXXXXXXXXX

XXXXXXXXXXXXXX **WRITERS AND WRITING** XXXXXXXXXXXXXX

PREFACE

The Norton Sampler is a collection of short essays for composition students. Like the cloth samplers in colonial America that schoolchildren made in order to practice their stitches—and their ABCs—*The Norton Sampler* assumes that writing is a practical art that can be learned by studying familiar, basic patterns.

The rhetorical patterns illustrated by the readings in this *Sampler* include description, narrative, example, classification, process analysis, comparison and contrast, definition, cause and effect, and argument. Each chapter focuses on one pattern and includes five or so short essays organized primarily around that pattern. Each essay is followed by a host of study questions and writing prompts.

Most of the model essays in *The Norton Sampler* are only two to four pages long, and even the longest can be easily read in one sitting. The essays are not only short but complete. As teachers, we cannot credibly ask students to study beginnings, middles, and endings or the shape of an argument if those forms and shapes are actually the work of an editor. Thus I have taken pains to select complete essays, or, in a few cases (indicated in the headnotes), complete chapters of books or sections of longer articles.

The chapters and essays in *The Norton Sampler* can be taken up in any order. However, the two essays by Annie Dillard in the Introduction show the processes that a professional writer typically goes through in order to capture her ideas on paper. (One of these, "How I Wrote the Moth Essay—and Why," was specially commissioned for the *Sampler*.) This chapter also introduces the four basic modes of writing—description, narration, exposition, and argument—and how they work together (or apart) to suit a writer's purpose and audience.

After a substantial chapter on the processes of writing and reading, the rest of the book takes up the modes of writing in greater detail. Chapters 2 and 3 are devoted, respectively, to the basic techniques of description and narration. These are followed by six chapters of exposition, ranging from the simpler techniques of exemplification and classification to the more complex strategies of process analysis, comparison, definition, and cause and effect. Then there is an extended chapter on argument, followed by a chapter of classic essays and speeches that show more about how the modes work in combination, an Appendix on using sources in writing, and a glossary.

HIGHLIGHTS

- **Great readings by good writers.** There are 61 readings in all—each one beautifully written—with half the readings new to this edition. The selections are on engaging topics that will interest students, from new readings such as Nora Ephron's analysis of the six stages of email and Barack Obama's Inaugural Address to old favorites from authors like Virginia Woolf, E. B. White, and Jonathan Swift.

- **More writing instruction,** including **templates** to help students get started, **a new chapter on writing and reading,** and **brief guides** in every chapter that lead students through the process of writing in each mode.

- **Expanded coverage of argument,** with two **clusters of readings on current issues:** the use of performance-enhancing drugs in sports and the role of the English language in multicultural American life.

- **Everyday examples** that show how the patterns taught in this book play an important role across media—from magazine covers and billboards to coffee mugs and cartoons.

- **More help for multilingual students,** with templates that show basic, sentence-level moves that students need to start writing in each mode and expanded glosses for unfamiliar terms and cultural allusions.

- **A new Appendix on doing research** (including a model student paper) that shows students how to find and use sources—and how to document them according to the **2009 MLA guidelines.**

• **Free and open resources on the Web.** Any student using *The Norton Sampler* has free access (no password required) to **wwnorton.com/write,** where students will find three easy-to-navigate sections: Writing and Rhetoric, Research and Documentation, Handbook and Exercises.

ACKNOWLEDGMENTS

There are three people above all whom I want to thank for their work and support on this new edition of *The Norton Sampler*: my wife, Barbara Cooley, a gifted technical writer, editor, and blogger; Marilyn Moller, editor extraordinaire, who has shaped a new generation of composition texts, including this one; and my wonderful hands-on editor at Norton, Ana Cooke. Then there is Barry Wade, original editor of the *Sampler*; Julia Reidhead, a subsequent editor and constant supporter of the book; and all the other people at Norton who have made possible this and earlier editions, including managing editor Marian Johnson, who has generously attended to matters both great and small; production manager Christine D'Antonio, who got the book out in good time and good form; Scott Berzon, who helped spread the word about the book; Megan Jackson, who cleared the permissions; Junenoire Mitchell, who located the photos; and Elizabeth Mullaney, who helped keep us all on track. I'm also grateful for the excellent work done by Judy Voss, our editor from out of town; to Mark Gallaher, for his work on the glosses and instructor's notes; and to Jo Anne Metsch for her work on the design.

I am also indebted to Richard Bullock of Wright State University for allowing me to draw from the fruits of his research and experience for the research appendix, and to Gerald Graff and Cathy Birkenstein, whose work inspired the writing templates in this book.

Among the teachers and composition experts across the country who reviewed this edition in progress and gave me advice on the selections and pedagogy, I wish especially to thank Fred C. Adams, Pennsylvania State University; Lauryn Angel-Cann, Tarrant County College; Dana Aspinal, Assumption College; Cynthia Becerra, Humphreys College; Dan Binkley, Hawaii Pacific University; Monica Bosson, City College of San Francisco; Jeffrey Brown, Pierce College; Mary Anne Brown,

Miami University Middletown; Carole Clark Papper, Hofstra University; William Coonfield, Pierce College; Bonnie Devet, College of Charleston; Michelle Ephraim, Worcester Polytechnic Institute; Amanda Estep Himes, John Brown University; Christine Evans, Lesley University; Anne Fearman, State University of New York Fredonia; Rebecca Fisher, Holyoke Community College; Kelly Fisher Lowe, Mount Union College; Mary Gossage, Dawson College; Kathryn Henkins, Mt. San Antonio College; Eileen Hermann-Miller, Dominican University; Carra Leah Hood, Stockton College; Chrisa Hotchkiss, Dominican University of California; Jennifer Jett, Bakersfield College; Helen Johannes, University of Wisconsin; Lynn Keeter, Gardner Webb University; John Kennedy, Rosemont College; Gloria Kerr, St. Vincent College; Daniel Lambert, East Los Angeles College; Ellen Lansky, Inver Hills Community College; R. E. Lee, State University of New York Oneonta; Aaron Lichtenstein, Borough of Manhattan Community College; Denise Lilley-Edgerton, Palo Verde College; Joe Lostracco, Austin Community College; Mary Mackey, California State College Sacramento; Marcia MacLennan, Kansas Wesleyan University; Kerry Moquett, San Joaquin Delta College; Nathan Nelson, Ferris State University; Troy Nordman, Butler Community College; Bronwyn O'Grady, Hampden-Sydney College; Michele Pajer, Gonzaga University; Marilyn Patton, De Anza College; Kelly Peinado, Ventura College; Christina Pinkston-Betts, Hampton University; Lou Ethel Roliston, Bergen Community College; Hephzibah Roskelly, University of North Carolina; Sister Marie Sagués, Dominican University of California; Mary Schiltz, University of Wisconsin; Martin Scott, Eastern Illinois University; Cheryl Smith, Baruch College; LuAnn Sorenson, Harvard University Institute for English Language; Dean Taciuch, George Mason University; Karen Tepfer, Bakersfield College; Christopher Trogan, Baruch College; Janet Rhett Iseman Trull, University of North Carolina; Ernest Tuft, San Joaquin Delta College; David Wee, Saint Olaf College; Karen Weyant, Jamestown Community College; Kathleen White, Bellevue Community College; and Patricia White, Norwich University.

Many thanks, too, to my colleagues in composition at Ohio State—including the late Edward P. J. Corbett, Sara Garnes, and Beverly Moss—and to Roy Rosenstein of the American University of Paris.

Thomas Cooley

THE NORTON SAMPLER

XXXXXXXXXXXXXXXXXXXXXXXXXXXXXXXXXXXXXXXXXXXXXXXXXXXXXXXXXXXXXXX

Seventh Edition

INTRODUCTION

Writing is a little like sewing or weaving. The end product may be a tight fabric of words, but you must construct it thread by thread. Since you usually don't know ahead of time exactly what you are going to say, it helps to have some patterns to work with. This is where *The Norton Sampler* comes in. As a collection of short essays for composition, this is a book of prose patterns, a sampler of basic stitches and forms that you can use to make finished designs of your own.

The two essays in this introduction are both written by the Pulitzer Prize-winning writer Annie Dillard, whose work has been compared to that of Henry David Thoreau and Emily Dickinson. The first essay, from *Holy the Firm* (1977), originally appeared in *Harper's* under the title "The Death of a Moth." As you will soon discover, it is not just about insects, but about writing; and it is the end product of a rigorous composing process that Dillard herself describes in the second selection, "How I Wrote the Moth Essay—and Why," written exclusively for *The Norton Sampler*.

These two essays, says Dillard, are "the most personal" ones she's ever written (25). They are her answer to the burning question all writers face when they begin the process of weaving words into a meaningful design: "How do you go from nothing to something? How do you face the blank page without fainting dead away?" (16) Taken together, these two essays will help you begin to answer that question for yourself by introducing you to the basic processes most writers follow to get from nothing to something. After you have studied these essays, we will then turn to specific patterns, or MODES OF WRITING,* that you can use in your own work.

---

*Words printed in SMALL CAPITALS are defined in the Glossary.

ANNIE DILLARD

FROM HOLY THE FIRM

⟨XXXXXXXXXXXXXXXXXXXXXXXXXXXXXXXXXXXXXXXXXXXXXXXXXXXX⟩

1   I live on northern Puget Sound, in Washington State, alone. I have a
gold cat, who sleeps on my legs, named Small. In the morning I joke
to her blank face, Do you remember last night? Do you remember? I
throw her out before breakfast, so I can eat.

2   There is a spider, too, in the bathroom, with whom I keep a sort
of company. Her little outfit always reminds me of a certain moth I
helped to kill. The spider herself is of uncertain lineage, bulbous at
the abdomen and drab. Her six-inch mess of a web works, works
somehow, works miraculously, to keep her alive and me amazed. The
web itself is in a corner behind the toilet, connecting tile wall to tile
wall and floor, in a place where there is, I would have thought, scant
traffic. Yet under the web are sixteen or so corpses she has tossed to
the floor.

3   The corpses appear to be mostly sow bugs, those little armadillo
creatures who live to travel flat out in houses, and die round. There is
also a new shred of earwig, three old spider skins crinkled and clenched,
and two moth bodies, wingless and huge and empty, moth bodies I drop
to my knees to see.

4   Today the earwig shines darkly and gleams, what there is of him: a
dorsal curve of thorax and abdomen, and a smooth pair of cerci[1] by
which I knew his name. Next week, if the other bodies are any indica-
tion, he will be shrunken and gray, webbed to the floor with dust. The
sow bugs beside him are hollow and empty of color, fragile, a breath
away from brittle fluff. The spider skins lie on their sides, translucent
and ragged, their legs drying in knots. And the moths, the empty moths,
stagger against each other, headless, in a confusion of arching strips of

---

1. Plural of cercus, the posterior "feeler" of an insect.

chitin like peeling varnish, like a jumble of buttresses for cathedral domes, like nothing resembling moths, so that I should hesitate to call them moths, except that I have had some experience with the figure Moth reduced to a nub.

Two summers ago I was camping alone in the Blue Ridge Mountains in Virginia. I had hauled myself and gear up there to read, among other things, James Ramsey Ullman's *The Day on Fire*, a novel about Rimbaud that had made me want to be a writer when I was sixteen;[2] I was hoping it would do it again. So I read, lost, every day sitting under a tree by my tent, while warblers swung in the leaves overhead and bristle worms trailed their inches over the twiggy dirt at my feet; and I read every night by candlelight, while barred owls called in the forest and pale moths massed round my head in the clearing, where my light made a ring.

Moths kept flying into the candle. They would hiss and recoil, lost upside down in the shadows among my cooking pans. Or they would singe their wings and fall, and their hot wings, as if melted, would stick to the first thing they touched—a pan, a lid, a spoon—so that the snagged moths could flutter only in tiny arcs, unable to struggle free. These I could release by a quick flip with a stick; in the morning I would find my cooking stuff gilded with torn flecks of moth wings, triangles of shiny dust here and there on the aluminum. So I read, and boiled water, and replenished candles, and read on.

One night a moth flew into the candle, was caught, burnt dry, and held. I must have been staring at the candle, or maybe I looked up when a shadow crossed my page; at any rate, I saw it all. A golden female moth, a biggish one with a two-inch wingspan, flapped into the fire, dropped her abdomen into the wet wax, stuck, flamed, frazzled and fried in a second. Her moving wings ignited like tissue paper, enlarging the circle of light in the clearing and creating out of the darkness the sudden blue sleeves of my sweater, the green leaves of jewelweed by my side, the ragged red trunk of a pine. At once the light contracted again and

2. French poet Arthur Rimbaud (1854–1891) himself began writing at age sixteen and produced his major work before he was twenty. Ullman's novel was published in 1958.

the moth's wings vanished in a fine, foul smoke. At the same time her six legs clawed, curled, blackened, and ceased, disappearing utterly. And her head jerked in spasms, making a spattering noise; her antennae crisped and burned away and her heaving mouth parts crackled like pistol fire. When it was all over, her head was, so far as I could determine, gone, gone the long way of her wings and legs. Had she been new, or old? Had she mated and laid her eggs, had she done her work? All that was left was the glowing horn shell of her abdomen and thorax—a fraying, partially collapsed gold tube jammed upright in the candle's round pool.

8 And then this moth-essence, this spectacular skeleton, began to act as a wick. She kept burning. The wax rose in the moth's body from her soaking abdomen to her thorax to the jagged hole where her head should be, and widened into flame, a saffron-yellow flame that robed her to the ground like any immolating monk. That candle had two wicks, two flames of identical height, side by side. The moth's head was fire. She burned for two hours, until I blew her out.

9 She burned for two hours without changing, without bending or leaning—only glowing within, like a building fire glimpsed through silhouetted walls, like a hollow saint, like a flame-faced virgin gone to God, while I read by her light, kindled, while Rimbaud in Paris burnt out his brains in a thousand poems, while night pooled wetly at my feet.

10 And that is why I believe those hollow crisps on the bathroom floor are moths. I think I know moths, and fragments of moths, and chips and tatters of utterly empty moths, in any state. How many of you, I asked the people in my class, which of you want to give your lives and be writers? I was trembling from coffee, or cigarettes, or the closeness of faces all around me. (Is this what we live for? I thought; is this the only final beauty: the color of any skin in any light, and living, human eyes?) All hands rose to the question. (You, Nick? Will you? Margaret? Randy? Why do I want them to mean it?) And then I tried to tell them what the choice must mean: you can't be anything else. You must go at your life with a broadax. . . . They had no idea what I was saying. (I have two hands, don't I? And all this energy, for as long as I can remember. I'll do it in the evenings, after skiing, or on the way home from the bank, or

after the children are asleep. . . .) They thought I was raving again. It's just as well.

I have three candles here on the table which I disentangle from the   11
plants and light when visitors come. Small usually avoids them, although once she came too close and her tail caught fire; I rubbed it out before she noticed. The flames move light over everyone's skin, draw light to the surface of the faces of my friends. When the people leave I never blow the candles out, and after I'm asleep they flame and burn.

XXXXXXXXXXXXXXXXXX For Discussion XXXXXXXXXXXXXXXXXX

1. What is Annie Dillard referring to in paragraph 10 when she says, "I'll do it in the evenings, after skiing, or on the way home from the bank . . . "?

2. What is the CLIMACTIC or most dramatic event of Dillard's NARRATIVE? How does she connect it with what she sees in her bathroom?

3. Dillard draws an extended ANALOGY between the burning moth and the writer. What does this analogy imply about the nature of the writer's calling as Dillard sees it?

4. What is "miraculous" about the spider's web in paragraph 2? How would you DESCRIBE Dillard's attitude toward nature and the natural world throughout her essay?

5. What would you say to George, the student who posted the following on bookcritics.org: "I need to know the significance of the butterfly in Annie Dillard's 'Death of a Moth.' This essay made absolutely no sense to me so I really need some help."

ANNIE DILLARD

How I Wrote the Moth Essay— and Why

1   It was November 1975. I was living alone, as described, on an island in Puget Sound, near the Canadian border. I was thirty years old. I thought about myself a lot (for someone thirty years old), because I couldn't figure out what I was doing there. What was my life about? Why was I living alone, when I am gregarious? Would I ever meet someone, or should I reconcile myself to all this solitude? I disliked celibacy; I dreaded childlessness. I couldn't even think of anything to write. I was examining every event for possible meaning.

2   I was then in full flight from success, from the recent fuss over a book of prose I'd published the previous year called *Pilgrim at Tinker Creek*. There were offers from editors, publishers, and Hollywood and network producers. They tempted me with world travel, film and TV work, big bucks. I was there to turn from literary and commercial success and to rededicate myself to art and to God. That's how I justified my loneliness to myself. It was a feeble justification and I knew it, because you certainly don't need to live alone either to write or to pray. Actually I was there because I had picked the place from an atlas, and I was alone because I hadn't yet met my husband.

3   My reading and teaching fed my thoughts. I was reading Simone Weil, *First and Last Notebooks*. Simone Weil was a twentieth-century French intellectual, born Jewish, who wrote some of the most interesting Christian theology I've ever read. She was brilliant, but a little nuts; her doctrines were harsh. "Literally," she wrote, "it is total purity or death." This sort of fanaticism attracted and appalled me. Weil had deliberately starved herself to death to call attention to the plight of French workers. I was taking extensive notes on Weil.

In the classroom I was teaching poetry writing, exhorting myself   4
(in the guise of exhorting my students), and convincing myself by my
own rhetoric: commit yourself to a useless art! In art alone is meaning!
In sacrifice alone is meaning! These, then, were issues for me at that
time: dedication, purity, sacrifice.

Early that November morning I noticed the hollow insects on the bath-   5
room floor. I got down on my hands and knees to examine them and
recognized some as empty moth bodies. I recognized them, of course,
only because I'd seen an empty moth body already—two years before,
when I'd camped alone and had watched a flying moth get stuck in a
candle and burn.

Walking back to my desk, where I had been answering letters, I   6
realized that the burning moth was a dandy visual focus for all my
recent thoughts about an empty, dedicated life. Perhaps I'd try to write a
short narrative about it.

I went to my pile of journals, hoping I'd taken some nice, specific   7
notes about the moth in the candle. What I found disappointed me at
first: that night I'd written a long description of owl sounds, and only an
annoyed aside about bugs flying into the candle. But the next night,
after pages of self-indulgent drivel, I'd written a fuller description, a
description of the moth which got stuck in candle wax.

The journal entry had some details I could use (bristleworms on the   8
ground, burnt moths' wings sticking to pans), some phrases (her body acted
as a wick, the candle had 2 flames, the moth burned until I blew it out),
and, especially, some verbs (hiss, recoil, stick, spatter, jerked, crackled).

Even in the journals, the moth was female. (From childhood read-   9
ing I'd learned to distinguish moths by sex.) And, there in the journal,
was a crucial detail: on that camping trip, I'd been reading about Rimbaud. Arthur Rimbaud—the French symbolist poet, a romantic, hot-
headed figure who attracted me enormously when I was sixteen—had
been young and self-destructive. When *he* was sixteen, he ran away from
home to Paris, led a dissolute life, shot his male lover (the poet Verlaine),
drank absinthe which damaged his brain, deranged his senses with
drunkenness and sleeplessness, and wrote mad vivid poetry which
altered the course of Western literature. When he was in his twenties, he

Jan

Kindling

while R out his fire blazing

Jan 2

Two summers ago I ~~went camped~~ was camping alone in the Blue Ridge mountains in Virginia. I had hauled myself and gear up there to read, ~~in peace~~ among other things, James Ramsey Ullman's ~~novel~~ The Day on Fire, a novel that had made ~~a writer~~ want to be a writer when I was sixteen; I was hoping it would do it again. So I read every ~~all~~ day sitting under a tree by my tent, ~~pausing to~~ eat four or five times and ~~walk once or twice, and I read all night~~ every ~~all night~~ while warblers sang in the leaves overhead and bristleworms trailed their inches over the twiggy ~~ground~~ dirt at my ~~(side)~~ feet, and I read every night by candlelight, while ~~the~~ barred owls called in the forest and pale ~~moths near me, when my light made~~ when my light made moths massed in the clearing. ~~singing the words~~ read, sing.

~~the mother flew on~~ Moths kept flying into the candle. They would hiss ~~and sputter~~ and recoil, lost upside down in the darkness shadows among my cooking pans. Or they would singe their wings and fall, and their ~~burnt~~ hot wings would stick, as if melted, to whatever they the first thing touched, a pan, a lid, a spoon, so that the moths snagged could struggle only in tiny arcs, unable to ~~flee~~ fly flutter free. These I could release ~~with~~ by a quick flip ~~by~~ with a stick; in the morning I would find my cooking stuff embossed with torn flecks of moth wings, little triangles of shiny dust here and there on the aluminum. So I read, and boiled water, and replenished candles, and read on.

One night one ~~moth~~ to female flew into the candle, ~~and burned so fast~~ sizzled, dropped ~~down~~ in ~~to~~ the wet wax, stuck, flamed and fried in a second. Her wings burnt right off and disappeared in a thin, foul smoke, her legs ~~crackled~~ spattered and curled, her head ~~jerked~~ crackled and jerked (like small arms fire)

~~Her wings fan wings~~ I must have been staring at the candle, or maybe I looked up when a shadow crossed my page; at any rate, I saw ~~the white thing~~ it fall

was caught, burned dry and ~~shield~~ burning

turned his back to the Western world and vanished into Abyssinia[1] as a gunrunner.

With my old journal beside me, I took up my current journal and scribbled and doodled my way through an account of my present life and the remembered moth. It went extraordinarily well; it was not typical. It seemed very much "given"—given, I think, because I'd asked, because I'd been looking so hard and so long for connections, meanings. The connections were all there, and seemed solid enough: I saw a moth burnt and on fire; I was reading Rimbaud hoping to rededicate myself to writing (this one bald statement of motive was unavoidable); I live alone. So the writer is like the moth, and like a religious contemplative: emptying himself so he can be a channel for his work. Of course you can reinforce connections with language: the bathroom moths are like a jumble of buttresses for cathedral domes; the female moth is like an immolating monk, like a hollow saint, a flame-faced virgin gone to God; Rimbaud burnt out his brains with poetry while night pooled wetly at my feet.

    I liked the piece enough to rewrite it. I took out a couple of paragraphs—one about why I didn't have a dog, another that ran on about the bathroom spider. This is the kind of absurdity you fall into when you write about anything, let alone about yourself. You're so pleased and grateful to be writing at all, especially at the beginning, that you babble. Often you don't know where the work is going, so you can't tell what's irrelevant.

    It doesn't hurt much to babble in a first draft, so long as you have the sense to cut out irrelevancies later. If you are used to analyzing texts, you will be able to formulate a clear statement of what your draft turned out to be about. Then you make a list of what you've already written, paragraph by paragraph, and see what doesn't fit and cut it out. (All this requires is nerves of steel and lots of coffee.) Most of the time you'll have to add to the beginning, ensuring that it gives a fair idea of what the point might be, or at least what is about to happen. (Suspense is for mystery writers. The most inept writing has an inadvertent element of

10

11

12

---

1. Historic, Arabic-derived name for Ethiopia, a country in eastern Africa.

OPPOSITE: *Page from the first draft of the essay from* Holy the Firm.

suspense: the reader constantly asks himself, where on earth is this going?) Usually I end up throwing away the beginning: the first part of a poem, the first few pages of an essay, the first scene of a story, even the first few chapters of a book. It's not holy writ. The paragraphs and sentences are tesserae—tiles for a mosaic. Just because you have a bunch of tiles in your lap doesn't mean your mosaic will be better if you use them all. In this atypical case, however, there were very few extraneous passages. The focus was tight, probably because I'd been so single-minded before I wrote it.

13 I added stuff, too, to strengthen and clarify the point. I added some speculation about the burning moth: had she mated and laid her eggs, had she done her work? Near the end I added a passage about writing class: which of you want to give your lives and become writers?

14 Ultimately I sent it to *Harper's* magazine, which published it. The early drafts, and the *Harper's* version, had a different ending, a kind of punch line that was a series of interlocking statements:

> I don't mind living alone. I like eating alone and reading. I don't mind sleeping alone. The only time I mind being alone is when something is funny; then, when I am laughing at something funny, I wish someone were around. Sometimes I think it is pretty funny that I sleep alone.

15 I took this ending out of the book version, which is the version you have. I took it out because the tone was too snappy, too clever; it reduced everything to celibacy, which was really a side issue; it made the reader forget the moth; and it called too much attention to the narrator. The new ending was milder. It referred back to the main body of the text.

16 Revising is a breeze if you know what you're doing—if you can look at your text coldly, analytically, manipulatively. Since I've studied texts, I know what I'm doing when I revise. The hard part is devising the wretched thing in the first place. How do you go from nothing to something? How do you face the blank page without fainting dead away?

17 To start a narrative, you need a batch of things. Not feelings, not opinions, not sentiments, not judgments, not arguments, but specific

objects and events: a cat, a spider web, a mess of insect skeletons, a candle, a book about Rimbaud, a burning moth. I try to give the reader a story, or at least a scene (the flimsiest narrative occasion will serve), and something to look at. I try not to hang on the reader's arm and bore him with my life story, my fancy self-indulgent writing, or my opinions. He is my guest; I try to entertain him. Or he'll throw my pages across the room and turn on the television.

I try to say what I mean and not "hide the hidden meaning." 18
"Clarity is the sovereign courtesy of the writer," said J. Henri Fabre, the great French entomologist, "I do my best to achieve it." Actually, it took me about ten years to learn to write clearly. When I was in my twenties, I was more interested in showing off.

What do you do with these things? You juggle them. You toss them 19
around. To begin, you don't need a well defined point. You don't need "something to say"—that will just lead you to reiterating clichés. You need bits of the world to toss around. You start anywhere, and join the bits into a pattern by your writing about them. Later you can throw out the ones that don't fit.

I like to start by describing something, by ticking off the five 20
senses. Later I go back to the beginning and locate the reader in time and space. I've found that if I take pains to be precise about *things*, feelings will take care of themselves. If you try to force a reader's feelings through dramatic writing ("writhe," "ecstasy," "scream"), you make a fool of yourself, like someone at a party trying too hard to be liked.

I have piles of materials in my journals—mostly information in 21
the form of notes on my reading, and to a lesser extent, notes on things I'd seen and heard during the day. I began the journals five or six years after college, finding myself highly trained for taking notes and for little else. Now I have thirty-some journal volumes, all indexed. If I want to write about arctic exploration, say, or star chemistry, or monasticism, I can find masses of pertinent data under that topic. And if I browse I can often find images from other fields that may fit into what I'm writing, if only as metaphor or simile. It's terrific having all these materials handy. It saves and makes available all those years of reading. Otherwise, I'd forget everything, and life wouldn't accumulate, but merely pass.

22   The moth essay I wrote that November day was an "odd" piece—
"freighted with heavy-handed symbolism," as I described it to myself
just after I wrote it. The reader must be startled to watch this apparently
calm, matter-of-fact account of the writer's life and times turn before his
eyes into a mess of symbols whose real subject matter is their own relationship. I hoped the reader wouldn't feel he'd been had. I tried to
ensure that the actual, historical moth wouldn't vanish into idea, but
would stay physically present.

23   A week after I wrote the first draft I considered making it part of the
book (*Holy the Firm*) I had been starting. It seemed to fit the book's
themes. (Actually, I spent the next fifteen months fitting the book
to *its* themes.) In order to clarify my thinking I jotted down some
notes:

>   moth in candle:
>
>   the poet—   materials of world, of bare earth at feet, sucked up,
>   transformed, subsumed to spirit, to air, to light
>
>   the mystic—not through reason
>   but through emptiness
>
>   the martyr—virgin, sacrifice, death with meaning.

I prefaced these notes with the comical word "Hothead."

24   It had been sheer good luck that the different aspects of the historical truth fit together so nicely. It had actually been on that particular solo
camping trip that I'd read the Rimbaud novel. If it hadn't been, I wouldn't
have hesitated to fiddle with the facts. I fiddled with one fact, for sure: I
foully slandered my black cat, Small, by saying she was "gold"—to
match the book's moth and little blonde burnt girl. I actually had a gold
cat at that time, named Kindling. I figured no one would believe it. It
was too much. In the book, as in real life, the cat was spayed.

25   This is the most personal piece I've ever written—the essay itself, and
these notes on it. I don't recommend, or even approve, writing personally. It can lead to dreadful writing. The danger is that you'll get
lost in the contemplation of your wonderful self. You'll include things

for the lousy reason that they actually happened, or that you feel strongly about them; you'll forget to ensure that the *reader* feels anything whatever. You may hold the popular view that art is self-expression, or a way of understanding the self—in which case the artist need do nothing more than babble uncontrolledly about the self and then congratulate himself that, in addition to all his other wonderfully interesting attributes, he is also an artist. I don't (evidently) hold this view. So I think that this moth piece is a risky one to read: it seems to enforce these romantic and giddy notions of art and the artist. But I trust you can keep your heads.

XXXXXXXXXXXXXXXXXX FOR DISCUSSION XXXXXXXXXXXXXXXXXXX

1. Why is Annie Dillard opposed, as a rule, to "writing personally" (25)? What dangers does she advise you to avoid when you write a personal essay? How well do you think she herself avoids these pitfalls? Point to specific passages in her two essays that support your opinion.

2. According to Dillard, what's the value to a writer of keeping a journal? Again, point to specific statements in her essays.

3. In which paragraphs does Dillard explicitly ANALYZE THE PROCESS of revising the moth essay? What did she omit in the second draft? How and when did she change the ending? What's the nature of the changes? Why did she make them?

4. Think about the ways you generally go about starting to write. Where do you start? What kind of research do you do? How much time do you spend revising? How does your writing process COMPARE with Dillard's?

THE MODES OF WRITING

In the two essays by Annie Dillard in this introduction, we watched as a professional writer worked her way through the basic processes of writing: first finding a subject to write about and taking notes on it; then, after mulling the subject over for a while, writing out a draft; and, afterward, revising it "coldly, analytically" (16). We will examine these processes more closely in the next chapter. First, let's look at the various modes of writing and how Dillard uses them.

Suppose that, in addition to keeping a journal and writing an essay about it, Dillard sent a letter to a friend about her camping trip and the moth that turned to flame. Her hypothetical letter might contain the following elements:

- *a description* of the campsite, surrounded by mountains, where "warblers swung in the leaves overhead and bristle worms trailed their inches over the twiggy dirt" (5)

- *a narrative* about her arrival in camp and what she did there: "hauled myself and gear up there to read"; "one night a moth flew into the candle, was caught, burnt dry, and held" (5, 7)

- *a comparison* between the burning moth and the religious ascetic: "like a hollow saint, like a flame-faced virgin gone to God" (9)

- *reasons* why the friend should join her: "when I am laughing at something funny, I wish someone were around" (14)

The four parts of this hypothetical letter are examples of the four traditional modes of writing that all writers use—description, narration, exposition, and argument.

DESCRIPTION tells how something looks, feels, sounds, smells, or tastes. It appeals directly to the senses. Chapter 2 focuses on description.

NARRATION is storytelling. It shows or tells "what happened." Whereas description focuses on sights, sounds, and other sensations, narration focuses on events, actions, adventures—and the NARRATOR's response to them. Chapter 3 focuses on narration.

EXPOSITION is informative writing. The part of our hypothetical letter that gives directions is exposition. It explains by *giving examples*

(Chapter 4), by *classifying* (Chapter 5), by *telling how something is made or works* (Chapter 6), by *comparing and contrasting* (Chapter 7), by *defining* (Chapter 8), or by *analyzing causes and effects* (Chapter 9).

Exposition gets more attention in this book than the other modes because it is the one you are likely to use most often. Examinations, term papers, insurance claims, job and graduate-school applications, sales reports, almost every scrap of practical prose you write over a lifetime, including your last will and testament, will demand expository skills.

ARGUMENT is writing that makes a CLAIM, advises, or moves the reader to action. The last part of our hypothetical letter is argument. In a sense, all writing aims to present an argument because the writer is always trying to convince readers that what he or she says deserves to be heard. Argument is discussed in Chapter 10.

MIXING THE MODES

If you look closely at examples of good writing, however, one thing about the modes becomes clear: they seldom occur alone. Almost all good writing mixes the modes together, although one mode will often dominate the others, as in the sample essays in the different sections of this book. For example, in the essay from *Holy the Firm*, Dillard uses description to help us visualize the cluttered scene in the writer's bathroom: "The spider skins lie on their sides, translucent and ragged, their legs drying in knots. And the moths, the empty moths, stagger against each other . . . like a jumble of buttresses for cathedral domes" (4).

Why is Dillard so minutely describing the dry carcasses of insects, particularly ones that catch on fire? Instead of exploring some strange bug fetish, Dillard's essay is working out a dramatic comparison between the writer and the moth drawn to the flame that consumes it "like a hollow saint, like a flame-faced virgin gone to God" (9). The point of this comparison is to explain what being a writer means to her. The writer's calling, she suggests, demands sacrifice and devotion, much as a saint or nun is devoted to her religion.

Describing the writer's raw materials and explaining the nature of the writer's calling are only part of what Dillard's first essay does, however. Besides describing and explaining, the essay also seeks to inspire young writers to take up the torch. "How many of you, I asked the people in my class, which of you want to give your lives and be writers?" (10) These words make an argument.

But here, again, argument is not the primary aim of Dillard's essay (from *Holy the Firm*) as a whole. It is first and foremost a personal narrative, like those you will encounter in Chapter 3. Its primary PURPOSE is to tell a story—the story of the moth that burns and of the writer who discovers the burning moth and what it signifies. Despite the apparent smallness of the game she hunts, Dillard's narrative is an intellectual adventure story with an emphasis on action, or PLOT, which is the soul of narrative.

Dillard's second essay is also primarily a personal narrative, although it, too, incorporates the other modes of writing. For example, she explains rather than narrates when she writes, "If you are used to analyzing texts, you will be able to formulate a clear statement of what your draft turned out to be about" (12). Much of Dillard's essay is written in this mode, which perhaps explains why she refers to her essay as "notes" (25).

To the extent that Dillard's essay explains how to write an essay, it may even be an example, in fact, of process analysis, the mode of exposition presented in Chapter 6. However, Dillard is not just explaining how to write here. She is writing a story about writing a story. The first essay tells what happened on the camping trip. The second tells what happened two years later in the writer's workshop. Like the first moth essay, in other words, the second one is also a personal narrative. It describes and explains, but its primary purpose is to tell about something that happened.

As you study and imitate the different kinds and techniques of writing illustrated by the model essays to follow, I hope you won't fall into the trap of trying to keep them entirely separate from one another—either in your reading or in your own writing. Incidentally, this book assumes that the two activities, reading and writing, are just as inextricably bound up together as are their respective modes and processes—as you'll read in Chapter 1, "On Writing and Reading."

A word about the doodles on page 8: they are facsimiles from the journal Dillard mentions in her two essays and which she graciously permitted the *Sampler* to copy. These artful scribblings afford an intimate visual glimpse into the mind and methods of the writer as she was actually drafting the moth essay. Look closely, and you will notice a cat peering out from the top of the page. This is Dillard's other cat, Kindling. Her name is discernible just to the right of the portrait. Dillard adopted the cat's golden color in her narrative but, in the interest of "truth," omitted the fact of her "incendiary" name. "I figured no one would believe it," she explains. "It was too much."

XXXXXXXXXXXXX **Understanding the Essays** XXXXXXXXXXXXX

1. Both the essay from *Holy the Firm* and "How I Wrote the Moth Essay—and Why" are, in part, personal NARRATIVES like the ones you will find in Chapter 3. How would you describe the NARRATOR, the person who is telling each story? Does she seem different in the two essays? If there are differences, how would you account for them?

2. Paragraph 7 of the essay from *Holy the Firm* is largely DESCRIPTIVE, like the essays in Chapter 2: "When it was all over, her head was, so far as I could determine, gone, gone the long way of her wings and legs. . . . All that was left was the glowing horn shell of her abdomen and thorax—a fraying, partially collapsed gold tube jammed upright in the candle's round pool." Point out other places in this essay where Dillard describes the physical world around her.

3. Paragraph 17 of "How I Wrote the Moth Essay and Why" is largely explanatory: "To start a narrative, you need a batch of things. Not feelings, not opinions, not sentiments, not judgments, not arguments, but specific objects and events." Where else in this essay does Dillard use EXPOSITION, especially to explain the processes of writing? Where is she primarily telling what happened?

4. Personal narratives are told from the POINT OF VIEW of a narrator. In paragraph 7 of the essay from *Holy the Firm*, for example, the narrator (Dillard) looks up "when a shadow crossed my page." How does Dillard give the impression in both of these essays that she is seeing and reporting on the natural world up close, almost as if she were looking through a magnifying glass? Refer to specific passages.

5. An ARGUMENT makes a CLAIM and supports it with EVIDENCE. In the essay from *Holy the Firm*, what claim is Dillard making about the life and work of a writer? What evidence does she use to support that claim? How convincing do you find that evidence? Explain.

XXXXXXXXXXXXXXXXXXX **For Writing** XXXXXXXXXXXXXXXXXXXXX

1. Recall a visit you made to a place where you felt especially close to the natural environment—the wilderness, a city park, or the beach, for example. Make a list of the physical details—objects, sounds, smells, tastes, colors, textures—that you remember most vividly from that experience.

2. Using your list of details as a basis, write a few paragraphs DESCRIBING the place you visited and telling what you did there. Be sure to explain why this experience made you feel especially close to the environment.

3. Write an essay explaining what you learned about the writing process from reading Dillard's two essays.

4. Write an essay explaining how you usually write. Include such information as where and when and under what conditions you work best, the supplies and materials you use, and the processes you go through, including your reading and research.

CHAPTER ONE

ON WRITING
AND READING

✗✗

To learn to do anything well, from making lasagna to hanging wall-paper, we usually break it down into a series of activities. Writing and reading are no exception. This chapter introduces the various stages of the writing process that will take you from a blank page to a final draft. It also explains the basic parts of the reading process—with tips for analyzing a text closely and critically.

THE WRITING PROCESS

Unlike flying from Tulsa to Miami, writing is not a linear process. We plan, we draft, we revise; we plan, we draft, we revise again. In addition, we tend to skip around as we write, perhaps going back and rewriting what we have already written. Often, in fact, we engage in the various activities of writing more or less at the same time.

PLANNING

Before you plunge headlong into any writing assignment, think about the nature of the assignment, the length and scope of the text you're supposed to write, and your PURPOSE* and AUDIENCE. To help budget your time, also keep in mind two things in particular: (1) *When the assignment is due.* As soon as you get an assignment, jot down the deadline. And remember that it's hard to write a good paper if you begin the

---

*Words printed in SMALL CAPITALS are defined in the Glossary.

night before it's due. (2) *What kind of research the assignment will require.* For many college papers, the research may take longer than the actual writing. Think about how much and what kind of research you will need to do, and allow plenty of time for it.

Considering Your Purpose and Audience

We write for many reasons: to organize and clarify our thoughts, express our feelings, remember people and events, solve problems, persuade others to act or believe as we think they should. As you think about *why* you're writing, however, you also need to consider *who* your readers are. The following questions will help you think about your intended purpose and audience:

- **What is your reason for writing?** Do you want to tell readers something they may not know? Entertain them? Change their minds?

- **Who is going to read (or hear) what you say?** Your classmates? Your teacher? Readers of a blog? Your supervisor at work?

- **How much does your audience already know about your subject?** If you are writing for a general audience, you may need to provide some background information and explain terminology that may be unfamiliar to them.

- **What should you keep in mind about the make-up and background of your audience?** Does the gender of your audience matter? How about their age, level of education, occupation, economic status, or religion? Are they likely to be sympathetic or unsympathetic to your position? Once you have sized up your audience, you're in a better position to generate ideas and EVIDENCE that will support what you have to say *and* appeal to that audience.

Coming Up with a Subject—and Focusing on a Topic

Before you can get very far into the writing process, you will need to come up with a subject and narrow it down to a workable topic. Though we often use the words interchangeably, a *subject*, strictly speaking, is a broad field of inquiry, whereas a *topic* is a specific area within that field. For example, if you are writing a paper on "the health care system in the United States," your teacher will still want to know just what approach you plan to take to that general subject. A good topic focuses in on a specific area of a general subject—such as the *causes* of waste in the health care system, or *why* more Americans need health insurance, or *how* to reform Medicare—that can be adequately covered in the time you have to write about it.

With many writing assignments, you will be given a specific topic, or choice of topics, as part of the assignment. In these instances, make sure you understand just what you are being asked to do. Look for key terms like *describe, define, analyze, compare and contrast, evaluate, argue.* Be aware that even short assignments may include more than one of these directives. For example, the same assignment may ask you not only to define Medicare and Medicaid but also to compare the two government programs.

For some assignments, you may have to find a topic yourself, perhaps after meeting with your teacher. Let your instructor know if you're already interested in a particular topic. Ask your instructor for suggestions—and start looking on your own. In each chapter in this book, you'll find ideas for finding a topic and for developing it into an essay by using the basic patterns of writing—DESCRIPTION, NARRATION, EXEMPLIFICATION, CLASSIFICATION, PROCESS ANALYSIS, COMPARISON, DEFINITION, CAUSE AND EFFECT, and ARGUMENT—that good writers use all the time.

GENERATING IDEAS

Once you have a topic to write about, where do you look for ideas? Over the years, writing teachers have developed a number of techniques to help writers generate ideas. All of the following techniques may come in handy at various points in the writing process, not just at the outset.

Freewriting

Simply put pen to paper (or fingers to keyboard) and jot down whatever pops into your head. Here are some tips for freewriting:

1. Write nonstop for five or ten minutes. If nothing comes to mind at first, just write: "Nothing. My mind is blank." Eventually the words *will* come—if you don't stop writing until time runs out.

2. Circle words or ideas that you might want to come back to, but don't stop freewriting. When your time is up, mark any passages that look promising.

3. Freewrite again, starting with something you marked in the previous session. Do this over and over until you find an idea you want to explore further.

Keeping Lists

Keeping lists is a good way to generate ideas—and to come up with interesting examples and details. Here are some tips for keeping a list:

- A list can be written any time and anywhere: on a computer, in a notebook, on a napkin. Always keep a pencil handy.
- If your lists start to get long, group related items into piles, as you would if you were sorting your laundry. Look for relationships not only *within* those piles but *between* them.

Brainstorming

When you brainstorm, you write down words and ideas in one sitting rather than over time. Here are a few tips for brainstorming:

- If you are brainstorming by yourself, first jot down a topic at the top of your page or screen. Then make a list of every idea or word that comes to mind.
- Brainstorming is often more effective when you do it collaboratively, with everyone throwing out ideas and one person acting as scribe. If you brainstorm with others, make sure everyone contributes—no one person should monopolize the session.

Asking Questions

Journalists and other writers ask *who, what, where, when, why,* and *how* to uncover the basic information in a story. Here is how you might use these questions if you were writing an essay about an argument in a parking lot:

- **Who** was involved in the argument? What should I say about my brother (one of the instigators) and his friends? The police officer who investigated? The witnesses?
- **What** happened? What did the participants say to one another? What did my brother do after he was struck by one of his friends?
- **Where** did the argument occur? How much of the parking lot should I describe?
- **When** did the argument take place? What time did my brother leave the party?
- **Why** did the argument occur? Did it have anything to do with my brother's girlfriend?
- **How** would my brother have reacted if he hadn't been drinking? Should I write about the effects of alcohol on anger management?

Keeping a Journal

As we learned from Annie Dillard in the Introduction, a personal journal can be a great source of raw material for your writing. Often, what you write in a journal today will help you with a piece of writing months or even years later. Here are some pointers for keeping a journal:

- Write as informally as you like, but jot down your observations as close in time to the event as possible.
- The observations in a journal do not have to deal with momentous events; record your everyday experiences.
- Make each journal entry as detailed and specific as possible; don't just write, "The weather was awful" or "I went for a walk." Instead, write, "Rained for an hour, followed by hail the size of mothballs" or "Walked from the wharf to Market St."

ORGANIZING AND DRAFTING

Once you have an abundance of facts, details, and other raw material, your next job is to organize that material and develop it into a draft. Generally, you will want to report events in chronological order—unless you are tracing the causes of a particular phenomenon or event, in which case you may want to work backward in time. Facts, statistics, personal experience, expert testimony, and other evidence should usually be presented in the order of their relative importance to your topic. But more than anything else, the order in which you present your ideas on any topic will be determined by exactly what you have to say about it.

Stating Your Point

Before you actually begin writing, think carefully about the main point you want to make—your THESIS. You may find that your thesis changes as you draft, but starting with a thesis in mind will help you identify the ideas and details you want to include—and the order in which you present them to the reader. Often you'll want to state your thesis in a single sentence as a THESIS STATEMENT.

What makes a good thesis statement? First, let's consider what a thesis statement is not. A simple announcement of your topic—"In this paper I will discuss what's wrong with the U.S. health-care system"—is not a thesis statement. A good thesis statement not only tells the reader what your topic is, it makes an interesting CLAIM *about* your topic, one that is open to further discussion. That's why statements of fact are not thesis statements, either: "More than forty-five million people in the United States have no health insurance." Facts may support your thesis, but the thesis itself should say something about your topic that requires further discussion. For example: "To fix health care in America, we need to develop a single-payer system of health insurance."

A thesis statement like this at the beginning of your essay clarifies your main point—and it helps to set up the rest of the essay. In this case, the reader might expect a definition of a single-payer insurance system, with an analysis of the effects of adopting such a system, and an argument for why those particular effects will provide the needed fix.

Making an Informal Outline

Once you have a thesis in mind, making an informal outline can also help you organize and develop your draft. Simply write down your thesis, and follow it with the main subpoints you intend to cover. Here is an informal outline that one student in a medical ethics class jotted down as she drafted a paper on the American health care system:

> THESIS: The costs of health care in America can be contained by paying for medical results rather than medical services.
>
> —what the current fee-for-services system is
>
> —problems with the system, such as unnecessary tests, high administrative costs
>
> —how to reform the system
>
> —how to pay for the new system

Using the Modes to Develop an Essay

As you draft, consider how to use the various MODES OF WRITING to develop your essay. Often you'll be assigned to write in one particular mode, but if not, you'll need to consider which mode (or modes) is most appropriate to your topic and purpose, and what other modes to integrate. Recall, for example, how Annie Dillard uses several modes, such as description and comparison, within her narrative essays in the Introduction. Here is a brief recap of each mode:

- Use DESCRIPTION to show how something looks, feels, smells, sounds or tastes: "The small waves were the same, chucking the rowboat under the chin as we fished at anchor, and the boat was the same boat, the same color green and the ribs broken in the same places, and under the floorboards the same freshwater leavings and debris—the dead helgramite, the wisps of moss, the rusty discarded fishhook, the dried blood from yesterday's catch." —E. B. WHITE, "Once More to the Lake"

- Use NARRATIVE to tell what happened to your subject: "We headed out to the street together, and, while I nervously fidgeted with the broom I carried, he calmly wheeled a bright blue trash can behind him. Seymour began sweeping the sidewalks, and I followed his lead."—ZOE SHEWER, "Ready, Willing, and Able"

- Use EXEMPLIFICATION to give specific instances of a general group or idea: "Sometimes you have to believe that all English speakers should be committed to an asylum for the verbally insane. In what other language do people drive in a parkway and park in a driveway? In what other language do people recite at a play and play at a recital? . . . In what other language can your nose run and your feet smell?"—RICHARD LEDERER, "English Is a Crazy Language"

- Use CLASSIFICATION to explain what categories your subject belongs to: "Is the duckbill platypus a mammal? A reptile? Or just a duckbill platypus?"—ISAAC ASIMOV, "What Do You Call a Platypus?"

- Use PROCESS ANALYSIS to tell how to do something, or how something works or is made: "To begin, don't write about yourself. I'm not saying you're uninteresting. I realize that your life has been so crazy no one could make this stuff up. But if you want to be a writer, start by writing about other people."
—ALLEGRA GOODMAN, "So You Want to Be a Writer? Here's How"

- Use COMPARISON AND CONTRAST to trace similarities and differences: "Each Ebenezer thrived. Middle-class whites drawn by a prosperous capital crowded into their church, and 1,200 blacks filled the other, the balconies creaking beneath the weight of worshipers."
—MICHAEL POWELL, "Two Churches, Black and White"

- Use DEFINITION to explain what your subject is or does: "One of the major characteristics of guyhood is that we guys don't spend a lot of time pondering our deep innermost feelings. There is a serious question in my mind about whether guys actually *have* deep innermost feelings, unless you count, for example, loyalty to the Detroit Tigers, or fear of bridal showers."—DAVE BARRY, "Guys vs. Men"

- Use CAUSE AND EFFECT to explain what caused something or what its effects are: "Destiny and the always ambiguous nature of history continued my family's enforced migration, and because of it I, too, became one who had to live and speak in translation."
—MARJORIE AGOSÍN, "Always Living in Spanish"

- Use ARGUMENT to make a case or justify a position: "Starting today, we must pick ourselves up, dust ourselves off, and begin again the work of remaking America."—BARACK OBAMA, "Inaugural Address"

Using each of these modes to draft and organize an essay is the focus of much of the rest of this book. In Chapters 2–10, you'll find templates to help you plot out the basic moves of each mode—moves that *all* writers rely on. And each chapter includes sample essays that show how various writers use the particular mode discussed in that chapter.

The Parts of an Essay

No matter what modes of writing you use, any essay you write should have a beginning, a middle, and an end. These three basic parts of an essay are usually referred to as the introduction, the body, and the conclusion.

In the *introduction*, you tell the reader exactly what you're writing about and state your thesis. Because it is the first thing the reader sees, the introduction needs to grab—and hold—your reader's attention. To do that, you can try one of these introductory strategies:

- ***Start with a quotation or dialogue.*** A brief bit of DIALOGUE or a pertinent quotation can spark your reader's interest. If you were writing an essay about your own development as a writer, for instance, you might begin by quoting comedian Steve Martin: "I think I did pretty well, considering I started out with nothing but a bunch of blank paper."

- ***Place your subject in a historical context.*** If your audience is your classmates, and your topic is the use of human subjects in psychological research, a brief summary of the lack of regulation in early college and university psych labs might help readers to understand the issue—and to see its relevance to their own lives.

- ***Open with an anecdote.*** A brief story that illustrates your main point can be a good way to begin an essay. If your thesis is "Working in customer service can help build patience and determination," you could start with an ANECDOTE about a time you dealt with an obnoxious customer.

- ***Shock or provoke the reader—mildly.*** You don't want to alarm your reader needlessly, but sometimes you may want to say "listen here" by being mildly provocative or controversial. In an essay about feminism, for example, Anna Quindlen begins with the following sentence: "Let's use the F word here."

- ***Start with a question.*** A good question can pique your readers' interest. In an essay about the physical benefits of laughter, a writer might open with this question: "Is laughter really the best medicine?"

In the *body* of your essay—which may run anywhere from a few paragraphs to many pages—you offer evidence in support of your main point. You can use many different kinds of evidence to develop the body of your essay: specific examples, facts and figures, the testimony of experts, your own personal experience. How much evidence will you need to include?

The amount of evidence you'll need will depend in part on how broad—or narrow—your thesis is. A broad thesis on how to combat global warming would require numerous facts, statistics, and examples to support it. However, to make the point that one campus-area bookstore is more expensive than another might require only a few examples of overpriced books or supplies.

Ultimately, it is the reader who determines whether or not your evidence is sufficient to support your thesis. So as you write, ask yourself these questions about the evidence you are presenting to the reader:

- *What is the best example I can give to illustrate my main point?* Is one example enough, or should I give several?

- *Of all the facts I could cite, which ones support my thesis best?* What additional facts will the reader expect or need to have?

- *Is my personal experience truly relevant to the point I'm making?* Or would I be better off staying out of the picture? Or citing someone whose experience or knowledge is even more compelling than mine?

- *Of everything I've read on my topic, which source (or sources) should I cite as absolutely indispensable?* What others were particularly clear or authoritative on the issue? How do I cite my sources appropriately? (For more information on using and citing sources, see the Appendix.)

In the *conclusion* of an essay, you wrap up what you have to say, often by restating the thesis—but with some variation based on the evidence you have just cited. The conclusion is your last chance to drive your point home with the reader—and to provide a sense of satisfaction and closure. Here are a few common approaches:

- **Restate your main point.** It is fine to remind your reader of what you've just said, but don't simply repeat your thesis. For example, after arguing for the benefits of a single-payer health insurance system, you might close by saying, "A single-payer system may not cure all the ills in the American health-care system, but it will put us firmly on the road to recovery with a fairer system in which we all receive the care we need—and deserve."

- **End with a recommendation.** To conclude an analysis showing that most home fires start in the kitchen, you might recommend that all kitchens be equipped with fire extinguishers.
- **Show the broader significance of your argument.** Say why your argument matters! After arguing that the use of human subjects in psychology experiments should be carefully regulated, you might observe that such experiments may give doctors the data they need to treat destructive personality disorders and serious mental illness.

Developing Paragraphs and Using Transitions

Within the main body of your essay, you will need to group your ideas into paragraphs. A paragraph is a group of sentences on the same topic or subtopic. Among those sentences, the one that tells the reader most clearly and directly what the paragraph is about—and where it's going (or has been)—is the *topic sentence.*

A good topic sentence should not only tell the reader precisely what the topic of the paragraph is ("preventing obesity in preschool"), it should also make a clear statement about that topic ("Preventing obesity in preschool-age children is more urgent than ever before because twice as many children are likely to be obese today as in the 1980s"). The following topic sentences, for example, propose something interesting—and arguable—about the topic:

> The democratization of addiction may be an appealing message, but it does not reflect reality.
>
> SALLY SATEL, "Addiction Doesn't Discriminate?"

> That the current testing regimen does not work to prevent doping is painfully obvious.
>
> BRIAN ALEXANDER, "Tour de Farce"

Both of these topic sentences appear at the beginning of a paragraph and tell the reader exactly where the paragraph is going. Occasionally, however, the topic sentence comes at the end and tells the reader where the paragraph has been:

> Ample food and resources exist to nourish man and all other creatures indefinitely into the future. This planet is indeed an Eden—to date our only Eden. Admittedly our Eden is plagued by pollution. Some of us have polluted the planet by reproducing too many of us. Too many people have made excessive demands on the long-range carrying-capacity of our garden; and during the last 200 years there has been dramatic, ever-increasing destruction of the web of life on earth. If we try to save the starving millions today, we will simply destroy what's left of Eden.
>
> JOHNSON C. MONTGOMERY, "Island of Plenty"

No matter where it comes in the paragraph, your topic sentence should be supported by every other sentence in the paragraph. The supporting sentences can give examples, introduce facts and figures, or even tell an illustrative story; but they all need to connect logically with the topic sentence in ways that are apparent to the reader.

To help you link one sentence or paragraph to another, you will want to use clear TRANSITIONS. Here are some transitional words and phrases that will help you tie ideas together for your reader:

To give examples: for example, for instance, in fact, in particular, namely, specifically, that is

To compare: also, as, in a similar way, in comparison, like, likewise

To contrast: although, but, by contrast, however, on the contrary, on the other hand

To indicate cause and effect: as a result, because, because of, consequently, so, then

To indicate logical reasoning: accordingly, hence, it follows, therefore, thus, since, so

To indicate place or direction: across, across from, at, along, away, behind, close, down, distant, far, here, in between, in front of, inside, left, near, next to, north, outside, right, south, there, toward, up

To indicate time: at the same time, during, frequently, from time to time, in 2007, in the future, now, never, often, meanwhile, occasionally, soon, then, until, when

To indicate sequence or continuation: also, and, after, before, earlier, finally, first, furthermore, in addition, last, later, next

To summarize or conclude: in conclusion, in summary, in the end, consequently, so, therefore, thus, to conclude

Using Visuals

Illustrations such as graphs and charts can be especially effective for presenting or comparing data, and photographs or drawings can help readers "see" things you describe in your written text. For example, if you were writing about the Civil War generals Grant and Lee, you might want to supply your readers with photographs like the ones on pp. 263–64 of the two men in uniform. But remember that visuals should never be mere decoration or clip art. When considering any kind of illustration, here are a few guidelines to follow:

- Visuals should be *directly relevant to your topic and must support your thesis* in some way. In this book, for example, you'll notice that most of the chapters include an illustrated example, such as a sign or cartoon, showing how the mode of writing discussed in that chapter is used in an everyday writing situation.

- Visual material *should be appropriate for your audience and purpose.* You might add a detailed medical drawing of a lung to an essay on the effects of smoking directed at respiratory specialists—but not to such an essay aimed at a general audience, who wouldn't necessarily need—or want—to see all the details.

- If you include visuals, *refer to them in the text* ("in the diagram below")—and, if necessary, number them so that your readers can find them ("see Fig. 1").

- *Position each visual close to the text it illustrates,* and consider adding a caption explaining the point of the visual.

- *If you use a visual you have not created yourself,* identify the source.

REVISING

Revising is a process of re-vision, of looking again at your draft and fixing problems in content, organization, or both. Sometimes revising requires some major surgery: adding new evidence, cutting out paragraphs or entire sections, rewriting the beginning, and so on.

Many writers try to revise far too soon. To avoid this pitfall, put aside your draft for a few hours—or better still, for a few days—before revising. Start by reading your draft yourself, and then try to get someone else to look it over—a classmate, a friend, your aunt. Whoever it is, be sure he or she is aware of your intended audience and purpose. Here's what you and the person with fresh eyes should look for:

- *Title.* Does the title pique the reader's interest and indicate the topic of the essay?
- *Thesis.* What is the main point? Is it clearly stated in a thesis statement? If not, should it be? Is the thesis sufficiently narrow?
- *Audience.* Is there sufficient background information for the intended readers? Are there clear definitions of terms and concepts they might not know? Will they find the topic interesting?
- *Support.* What evidence supports the thesis? Is the evidence convincing and the reasoning logical? Are more facts or specific details needed?
- *Organization.* Is the draft well organized, with a clear beginning, middle, and ending? Does each paragraph contribute to the main point, or are some paragraphs off the topic? Are the introduction and conclusion effective?
- *Modes of Writing.* What is the main mode the writer uses to develop the essay? For example, is the draft primarily a NARRATIVE? A DESCRIPTION? An ARGUMENT? Should other modes be introduced? For instance, would more EXAMPLES or a COMPARISON be beneficial?
- *Sources.* If there is material from other sources, how are those sources incorporated? Are they quoted? Paraphrased? Summarized? Is source material clearly cited following appropriate guidelines for documentation, so readers know whose words or ideas are being used? Does the source material effectively support the main point?

- **Paragraphs**. Does each paragraph focus on one main idea and have a clear topic sentence? Do your paragraphs vary in structure, or are they too much alike? Should any long or complex paragraphs be broken into two? Should short paragraphs be combined with other paragraphs, or developed more fully? How well does the draft flow from one paragraph to the next? If any paragraph seems to break the flow, should it be cut—or are transitions needed to help the reader follow the text?

- **Sentences.** If all of the sentences are about the same length, should some be varied? A short sentence in the middle of long sentences can provide emphasis. On the other hand, too many short sentences in a row can sound choppy. Some of them might be combined.

- **Visuals.** If the draft includes visuals, are they relevant to the topic and thesis? If there are no visuals, would any of the text be easier to understand if accompanied by a diagram or drawing?

After you analyze your own draft carefully and get some advice from another reader, you may decide to make some fairly drastic changes, such as adding more examples, writing a more effective conclusion, or dropping material that doesn't support your thesis. All such moves are typical of the revision process. In fact, it is not unusual to revise your draft more than once to get it to a near-final form. Recall, for instance, all of the revisions that Annie Dillard made in the moth essay, as she recounts in "How I Wrote the Moth Essay—and Why" in the Introduction. As Dillard puts it, "It doesn't hurt much to babble in a first draft, so long as you have the sense to cut out irrelevancies later."

EDITING AND PROOFREADING

When you finish revising your essay, you've blended all the basic ingredients, but you still need to put the icing on the cake. That is, you need to edit and proofread your final draft before presenting it to the reader.

When you edit, you add finishing touches and correct errors in grammar, sentence structure, punctuation, and word choice. When you proofread, you take care of misspellings, typos, problems with margins and format, and other minor blemishes. Here are some tips that can help you check your drafts for some common errors.

Editing Sentences

Check to be sure that each sentence expresses a complete thought—that it has a subject (someone or something) and a verb performing an action or indicating a state of being. (The Civil War started in 1861.)

Check capitalization and end punctuation. Be sure that each sentence begins with a capital letter and ends with a period, a question mark, or an exclamation point.

***Look for sentences that begin with* it *or* there.** Often such sentences are vague or boring, and they are usually easy to edit. For example, if you've written "There is a security guard on duty at every entrance," you could edit it to "A security guard is on duty at every entrance."

Check for parallelism. All items in a list or series should have parallel forms—all nouns (Lincoln, Grant, Lee), all verbs (dedicate, consecrate, hallow), all phrases (of the people, by the people, for the people), and so on.

Editing Words

There, their. Use *there* to refer to place or direction, or to introduce a sentence. (Was he there? There was no evidence.) Use *their* as a possessive. (Their plans fell apart.)

It's, its. Use *it's* to mean "it is." (It's often difficult to apologize.) Use *its* to mean "belonging to it." (Each dog has its own personality.)

Lie, lay. Use *lie* when you mean "recline." (She's lying down because her back hurts.) Use *lay* when you mean "put" or "place." (Lay the blanket on the bed.)

Use concrete words. If some of your terms are too ABSTRACT (Lake Michigan is so amazing and incredible), choose more CONCRETE terms (Lake Michigan is so cold and choppy that swimming in it often seems like swimming in the ocean).

***Avoid filler words like* very, quite, really, *and* truly.** You could write that "John Updike was truly a very great novelist," but it's stronger to say, "John Updike was a great novelist."

Editing Punctuation

Check for commas after introductory elements in a sentence.

> After that day, it was as if Miss Dennis and I shared something.
> ALICE STEINBACH, "The Miss Dennis School of Writing"

Check for commas before and, but, or, nor, so, *or* yet *in compound sentences.*

> Book sales are down, but creative writing enrollments are booming.
> ALLEGRA GOODMAN, "So You Want to Be a Writer? Here's How."

Check for commas in a series.

> It also had a flat rubbery bill, webbed feet, a broad flat tail, and a spur on each ankle that was clearly intended to secrete poison.
> ISAAC ASIMOV, "What Do You Call a Platypus?"

Put quotation marks at the beginning and end of a quotation.

> Finally he said, "Once you get to be thirty, you make your own mistakes."
> PHILIP WEIS, "How to Get Out of a Locked Trunk"

> "Dogs love real beef," the back of the box proclaimed loudly.
> ANN HODGMAN, "No Wonder They Call Me a Bitch"

Check your use of apostrophes with possessives. Singular nouns should end in *'s,* whereas plural nouns should end in *s'.* The possessive pronouns *hers, his, its, ours, yours,* and *theirs* should not have apostrophes.

> But to me, my mother's English is perfectly clear, perfectly natural.
> AMY TAN, "Mother Tongue"

> With these rulings and laws, whites' attitudes towards blacks have also greatly improved.
> ERIC A. WATTS, "The Color of Success"

> Theirs was the life I dreamt about during my vacation in eastern North Carolina.
> DAVID SEDARIS, "Remembering My Childhood on the Continent of Africa"

Proofreading and Final Formatting

Proofreading is the only stage in the writing process where you are *not* primarily concerned with meaning. Of course you should correct any substantive errors you find, but your main concern is the surface appearance of your text: misspellings, margins that are too narrow or too wide, unindented paragraphs, missing page numbers.

It is a good idea to slow down as you proofread. Use a ruler or piece of paper to guide your eye line by line; or read your entire text backward a sentence at a time; or read it out loud word by word. Use a spellchecker, too, but don't rely on it: a spellchecker doesn't know the difference, for example, between *their* and *there* or *human* and *humane.*

Also check the overall format of your document to make sure it follows any specific instructions that you may have been given. If your instructor does not have particular requirements for formatting, follow these standard guidelines:

Heading and title. Put your name, your instructor's name, the name and number of the course, and the date on separate lines in the upper-left-hand corner of your first page. Center your title on the next line, but do not underline it or put it in quotation marks. Double-space the heading and title.

Typeface and size. Use ten- or twelve-point type in an easy-to-read typeface, such as Times New Roman, Courier, or Palatino.

Spacing and margins. Double-space your document. Leave at least one-inch margins on each side and at the top and bottom of your text.

Paragraph indentation and page numbers. Indent the first line of each paragraph five spaces. Number your pages consecutively, and include your last name with each page number.

THE READING PROCESS

Like writing, reading is an active process. Even when you take a thriller to the beach and read for fun, your brain is at work translating words into mental images and ideas. When you read any text, then, you generally engage in several activities: previewing, reading, and responding. Let's take a look at each of these.

PREVIEWING A TEXT

Before you plunge into a text, take a few moments to survey the text as a whole. Try to get a sense of where the text is going and what you want to focus on. Here are some tips for previewing the readings in this book:

- **Look at the headnote** to learn about the author and the original context—the time, place, and circumstances in which the text was written and published.
- **Think about the title.** What does it reveal about the topic and TONE of the text? Are you expecting a serious argument, or an essay that pokes fun at its subject?
- **Skim the text for an overview,** noting headings, boldfaced words, and so on.
- **Skim the introduction and conclusion.** What insight do they give you into the purpose and message of the text?
- **Think about your own purpose for reading** Do you want to obtain information, fulfill an assignment? How will your purpose affect what you focus on?

READING A TEXT

Reading a text closely and critically is a little like investigating a crime scene. You look for certain clues; you ask certain questions. Your objective is to determine, as precisely and accurately as you can, both what the text has to say and how it says it. Your primary clues, therefore, are in the text itself—the actual words on the page.

If you've previewed the text, you already have some idea of what it's about. Now is the time to examine it closely. So pull out your pencil and highlighter, and annotate the text as you go along—jot down questions or comments in the margins, underline important points, circle key words, and mark places you may want to come back to. Here are some questions to ask yourself as you read:

- **What is the writer's main point?** Is it clearly stated in a thesis? If so, where? If the main point is not stated directly, is it clearly implied?

- **What is the primary purpose of the text?** To provide information? Sell a product or service? Argue a point of view? Make us laugh? Tell a story?

- **Who is the intended audience?** Readers who are familiar with the topic? Those who know little about it? People who might be inclined to agree—or disagree?

- **What is the tone and style of the text?** Serious, informal, inspirational, strident?

- **How and where does the writer support the main point?** Can you point out specific details, facts, examples, expert testimony, or other kinds of evidence?

- **Is the evidence sufficient?** Or does it fail to convince you? Are sources clearly identified so that you can tell where the material is coming from?

- **Has the writer fairly represented—and responded to—other points of view?** Has any crucial perspective been left out?

- **What is the text's larger historical and cultural context?** Who is the author? When was the text written? What other ideas or events does it reflect?

RESPONDING TO WHAT YOU'VE READ

When you read a text, you can agree, disagree—or both—or withhold judgment. In fact, it is not unusual to disagree with some statements in a text even if you think the author has done a good job overall.

After you have read and reread a text closely, think about and respond to it in writing. Here are a few tips for doing so:

- *Summarize what you've read in your own words.* If you can write a summary of the main point, you probably have a good grasp of what you've read.

- *Think about and record your own reactions.* Whether or not you agree with or like the text, did the writer accomplish what he or she set out to do?

- *Consider what you've learned about writing.* Note any techniques that you might want to try in your own writing, such as using a catchy introduction, unusual examples, or striking visuals.

WRITING FROM READING

Good writers are good readers. As you read the model essays in this book, examine them critically, using all the techniques of reading that we've been discussing. Those techniques are summed up in the study questions following each essay. Designed to help you write well from studying how accomplished writers do it, these questions ask you to approach reading and writing in basically four ways:

FOR DISCUSSION. These questions help you to look at the text as an exchange of ideas between a writer and a reader. With this approach, you read to understand what the text is saying—and to discover your own opinions about those ideas.

STRATEGIES AND STRUCTURES. These questions help you to understand the text as a verbal construction. With this approach, you learn techniques that writers commonly follow to organize ideas and present them to an audience in writing.

WORDS AND FIGURES OF SPEECH. These questions focus on the language and style of the text, an approach that helps you to sharpen your own choice of words and to expand their literal meanings.

FOR WRITING. These prompts help you consider the text you read as a source of inspiration, an approach that lets you use the text as a springboard to your own writing.

Good writers approach texts in all these ways when they read them closely and critically. The root meaning of the word *text* is something *woven* (like *textile*)—a fabric of words. When you read as a writer, you look for patterns and techniques in the text that you can use to construct designs of your own. The many study questions in this book will help you with this process. Every text is different, however. So while the study questions ask you to approach texts in the four general ways outlined above, they are also tailored to each individual text—to help you see the particular designs in that fabric of words.

CHAPTER TWO

DESCRIPTION

XXXXXXXXXXXXXXXXXXXXXXXXXXXXXXXXXXXXXXXXXXXXXXXXXXXXXXXX

D ESCRIPTION* is the mode of writing that appeals most directly to the
senses by showing us the physical characteristics of a subject—what
it looks like, or how it sounds, smells, feels, or tastes. A good description
shows us such characteristics; it doesn't just tell us about them. Description is especially useful for making an ABSTRACT or vague subject—such
as freedom or truth or death—more CONCRETE or definite.

For example, if you were describing an old cemetery, you might say
that it was a solemn and peaceful place. In order to show the reader
what the cemetery actually looked or sounded like, however, you would
need to focus on the physical aspects of the scene that evoked these more
abstract qualities—the marble gravestones, the earth and trees, and perhaps the mourners at the site of a new grave.

Such concrete, physical details are the heart of any description.
Those details can be presented either objectively or subjectively. Consider the following caption for a photograph from the website of Arlington National Cemetery:

> Six inches of snow blanket the rolling Virginia hillside as mourners gather at a fresh burial site in Arlington National Cemetery
> outside Washington, D.C. Rows of simple markers identify the
> more than 250,000 graves that make up the military portion of
> the cemetery. Visited annually by more than four million people,
> the cemetery conducts nearly 100 funerals each week.

In an OBJECTIVE description like this, the author stays out of the picture.
The description shows what a detached observer would see and hear—

---

*Words printed in SMALL CAPITALS are defined in the Glossary.

snow, rolling hills, graves, and mourners—but it does not say what the observer thinks or feels *about* those things.

A SUBJECTIVE description, on the other hand, presents the author's thoughts and feelings along with the physical details of the scene or subject, as in this description by novelist John Updike of a cemetery in the town where he lived:

> The stones are marble, modernly glossy and simple, though I suppose that time will eventually reveal them as another fashion, dated and quaint. Now, the sod is still raw, the sutures of turf are unhealed, the earth still humped, the wreaths scarcely withered. . . . I remember my grandfather's funeral, the hurried cross of sand the minister drew on the coffin lid, the whine of the lowering straps, the lengthening, cleanly cut sides of clay, the thought of air, the lack of air forever in the close dark space lined with pink satin. . . .
>
> JOHN UPDIKE, "Cemeteries"

This intimate description is far from detached. Not only does it give us a close-up view of the cemetery itself, it also reports the sensations that the newly dug graves evoke in the author's mind.

Whether the concrete details of a description are presented from a personal or an objective POINT OF VIEW, every detail should contribute to some DOMINANT IMPRESSION that the writer wants the description to make upon the reader. The dominant impression we get from Updike's description, for example, is of the "foreverness" of the place. Consequently, every detail in Updike's description—from the enduring marble of the headstones to the dark, satin-linked interior of his grandfather's coffin—contributes to the sense of airless eternity that Updike recalls from his grandfather's funeral.

Updike's references to the "raw" sod and to unhealed "sutures" in the turf show how such figures of speech as METAPHOR, SIMILE, and PERSONIFICATION can be used to make a description more vivid and concrete. This is because we often describe something by telling what it is like. A thump in your closet at night sounds like an owl hitting a haystack. A crowd stirs like a jellyfish. The seams of turf on new graves are like the stitches closing a wound.

As Updike's description narrows in on his grandfather's grave, we get a feeling of suffocation that directly supports the main point that the author is making about the nature of death. Death, as Updike conceives it, is no abstraction; it is the slow extinction of personal life and breath.

Updike's painful reverie is suddenly interrupted by his young son, who is learning to ride a bicycle in the peaceful cemetery. As Updike tells the story of their joyful afternoon together, the gloom of the cemetery fades into the background—as descriptive writing often does. Description frequently plays a supporting role within other MODES OF WRITING; it may serve, for example, to set the scene for a NARRATIVE (as in Updike's essay) or it may provide the background for an ARGUMENT about the significance of a national cemetery.

Almost as important as the physical details in a description is the order in which those details are presented. Beginning with the glossy stones of the cemetery and the earth around them, Updike's description comes to focus on the interior of a particular grave. It moves from outside to inside and from the general to the specific. A good description can proceed from outside in, or inside out, top to bottom, front to back, or in any other direction—so long as it moves systematically in a way that is in keeping with the dominant impression it is supposed to give, and that supports the main point the description is intended to make.

In the following description of a boy's room, the writer is setting the stage for the larger narrative—in this case, a fairy tale:

> The room was so spare one could see everything at a glance: a closet door with a lock on it, a long table with five perfect constructions—three ships, two dragons—nothing else on the table but a neat stack of stainless-steel razor-blades. What defined all the rest, of course, was that immense desk and chair. They made it seem that the room itself was from a picture book, or better yet, a stage-set, for across one end hung a dark green curtain. Beyond that, presumably, the professor's son crouched, hiding. My gaze stopped and froze on an enormous bare foot that protruded, unbeknownst to its owner, no doubt, from behind the curtain. It was the largest human foot I'd ever seen or imagined. . . .
>
> JOHN GARDNER, *Freddy's Book*

This description of the lair of a boy giant is pure fantasy, of course. What makes it appear so realistic is the systematic way in which Gardner presents the objects in the room. First we see the closet door, a feature we might find in any boy's bedroom. Next comes the lock. Even an ordinary boy might keep the contents of his closet under lock and key. The long table with the models and razor-blades is the first hint that something unusual may be at play. And when we see the oversized desk and chair, we truly begin to suspect that this is no ordinary room and no ordinary boy. But it is not until our gaze falls upon the enormous foot protruding from beneath the curtain that we know for sure we have entered the realm of make-believe.

Fanciful as the details of Gardner's description may be, his systematic method of presenting them is instructive for composing more down-to-earth descriptions. Also, by watching how Gardner presents the details of Freddy's room from a consistent VANTAGE POINT, we can see how he builds up to a dominant impression of awe and wonder.

A BRIEF GUIDE TO WRITING A DESCRIPTION

As you write a description, you need to identify who or what you're describing, say what your subject looks or feels like, and indicate the traits you plan to focus on. Cherokee Paul McDonald makes these basic moves of description in the beginning of his essay in this chapter:

> He was a lumpy little guy with baggy shorts, a faded T-shirt and heavy sweat socks falling down over old sneakers. . . . Covering his eyes and part of his face was a pair of those stupid-looking '50s-style wrap-around sunglasses.
>
> CHEROKEE PAUL McDONALD, "A View from the Bridge"

McDonald identifies what he's describing (a "little guy"); says what his subject looks like ("lumpy," "with baggy shorts, a faded T-shirt and heavy sweat socks"); and hints at characteristics (his "stupid-looking" sunglasses) that he might focus on. Here is one more example from this chapter:

> He looks almost like a young child buckled into a car seat, with his closed eyes and freshly shaved head, with the way the black restraints of the electric chair crisscross at his torso.
>
> DAN BARRY, "Chronicle of an American Execution"

The following guidelines will help you to make these basic moves as you draft a description—and to come up with your subject, consider your purpose and audience, state your point, and create a dominant impression of your subject by organizing and presenting the details of your description effectively.

Coming Up with a Subject

A primary resource for finding a subject is your own experience. You will often want to describe something familiar from your past—the lake in which you learned to swim, the neighborhood where you grew up, a person from your hometown. Also consider more recent experiences or less familiar subjects that you might investigate further, such as crowd behavior at a hockey game, an unusual T-shirt, a popular bookstore. Whatever subject you choose, be sure that you will be able to describe it vividly for your readers by appealing to their senses.

Considering Your Purpose and Audience

Your PURPOSE in describing something—whether to view your subject objectively, express your feelings about it, convince the reader to visit it (or not), or simply to amuse your reader—will determine the details you include. Before you start composing, decide whether your purpose will be primarily objective (as in a lab report) or subjective (as in a personal essay about your grandmother's cooking). Although both approaches provide information, an OBJECTIVE description presents its subject impartially, whereas a SUBJECTIVE description conveys the writer's personal response to the subject.

Whatever your purpose, you need to take into account how much your AUDIENCE already knows (or does not know) about your subject. For example, if you want to describe to someone who has never been on your campus the mad rush that takes place when classes change, you're going to have to provide some background: the main quadrangle with its sun worshipers, the brick-and-stone classroom buildings on either side, the library looming at one end. On the other hand, if you were to describe this same locale to fellow students, you could skip the background description and go directly to the mob scene.

Generating Ideas: Asking What Something Looks, Sounds, Feels, Smells, and Tastes Like

Good descriptive writing is built on CONCRETE particulars rather than ABSTRACT qualities. So don't just write, "It was a dark and stormy night"; try to make your reader see, hear, and feel the wind and the rain. To come up with specific details, observe your subject, ask questions, and take notes. Try to experience your subject as though you were a reporter on assignment or a traveler in a strange land.

One of your richest sources of ideas for a description—especially if you are describing something from the past—is memory. Ask friends or parents to help you remember details accurately and truthfully. Jog your own memory by asking, "What *did* the place (or object) look like exactly? What did it sound like? What did it smell or taste like?" Recovering the treasures of your memory is a little like fishing: think back to the spots you knew well; bait the hook by asking key questions; weigh and measure everything you pull up. Later on, you can throw back the ideas you can't use.

Templates for Describing

The following templates can help you to generate ideas for a description and then to start drafting. Don't take these as formulas where you just have to fill in the blanks. There are no easy formulas for good writing. But these templates can help you plot out some of the key moves of description and thus may serve as good starting points.

> ➤ The main physical characteristics of X are _____, _____, and _____.
>
> ➤ From the perspective of _____, however, X could be described as _____.
>
> ➤ In some ways, namely _____, X resembles _____; but in other ways, X is more like _____.
>
> ➤ X is not at all like _____ because _____.
>
> ➤ Mainly because of _____ and _____, X gives the impression of being _____.
>
> ➤ From this description of X, you can see that _____.

For more techniques to help you generate ideas and start writing, see Chapter 1.

Stating Your Point

We usually describe something to someone for a reason. Why are you describing bloody footprints in the snow? You need to let the reader know, either formally or informally. One formal way is to include an explicit THESIS STATEMENT: "This description of Washington's ragged army at Yorktown shows that the American general faced many of the same challenges as Napoleon in the winter battle for Moscow; but Washington turned them to his advantage."

Or your reasons can be stated more informally. If you are writing a descriptive travel essay, for example, you might state your point as a personal observation: "Chicago is an architectural delight in any season, but I prefer to visit from April through October because of the city's brutal winters."

Creating a Dominant Impression

Some descriptions appeal to several senses: the sight of fireflies, the sound of crickets, the touch of a hand—all on a summer evening. Whether you appeal to a single sense or several, make sure they all contribute to the DOMINANT IMPRESSION you want your description to make upon the reader. For example, if you want an evening scene on the porch to convey an impression of danger, you probably won't include details about fireflies and crickets. Instead, you might call the reader's attention to dark clouds in the distance, the rising wind, crashing thunder, and the sound of footsteps drawing closer. In short, you will choose details that play an effective part in creating your dominant impression: a sense of danger and foreboding.

Even though you want to create a dominant impression, don't begin your description with a general statement of what that impression is. Instead, start with descriptive details, and let your readers form the impression for themselves. Remember that a good description doesn't tell readers what to think or feel; it *shows* them point by point. The dominant impression that John Gardner creates in his systematic description of Freddy's room, for instance, is a growing sense of awe and wonder. But he does so by taking us step by step into unfamiliar territory. If you were describing an actual room or other place—and you wanted to create a similar dominant impression in your reader's mind—you would likewise direct the reader's gaze to more familiar objects first (table, chairs, fireplace) and then to increasingly unfamiliar ones (a shotgun, polar bear skins on the floor, an elderly lady mending a reindeer harness).

Using Figurative Language

Figures of speech can help to make almost any description more vivid or colorful. The three figures of speech you are most likely to use in composing a description are similes, metaphors, and personification.

SIMILES tell the reader what something looks, sounds, or feels like, using *like* or *as*: "Suspicion climbed all over her face like a kitten, but not so playfully" (Raymond Chandler).

METAPHORS make implicit comparisons, without *like* or *as*: "All the world's a stage" (William Shakespeare). Like similes, metaphors have two parts: the subject of the description (*world*) and the thing (*stage*) to which that subject is being implicitly compared.

PERSONIFICATION assigns human qualities to inanimate objects, as in Sylvia Plath's poetic description of a mirror: "I have no preconceptions. / Whatever I see I swallow immediately."

Arranging the Details from a Consistent Vantage Point

The physical configuration of whatever you're describing will usually suggest a pattern of organization. Descriptions of places are often organized by direction—north to south, front to back, left to right, inside to outside, near to far, top to bottom. If you were describing a room, for example, you might use an outside-to-inside order, starting with the door or the door knob.

An object or person can also suggest an order of arrangement. If you were describing a large fish, for instance, you might let the anatomy of the fish guide your description, moving from the body of the fish as a whole to its mouth, eyes, belly, and tail. When constructing a description, you can go from whole to parts, or parts to whole; from most important to least important features (or vice versa); from largest to smallest, specific to general, or concrete to abstract—or vice versa.

Whatever organization you choose, be careful to maintain a consistent VANTAGE POINT. In other words, be sure to describe your subject from one position or perspective—across the room, from the bridge, face-to-face, under the bed, and so on. Do not include details that you are unable to see, hear, feel, smell, or taste from your particular vantage point. Before you fully reveal any objects or people that lie outside the reader's line of sight—such as a boy giant behind a curtain—you will need to cross the room and fling open the door or curtain that conceals them. If your vantage point (or that of your NARRATOR) changes while you are describing a subject, be sure to let your reader know that you have moved from one location to another, as in the following description of a robbery: "After I was pushed behind the counter of the Quik-Mart, I could no longer see the three men in ski masks, but I could hear them yelling at the owner to open up the register."

EVERYDAY DESCRIPTION
A Calvin and Hobbes Cartoon

When you describe something, you tell what its main characteristics are. Usually, you should give the important physical characteristics of your subject before you get into its less tangible attributes. Calvin, for example, is more likely to find Hobbes if—instead of "a good companion"—he describes his lost tiger as a stuffed toy with black and orange stripes.

CHEROKEE PAUL McDONALD

A VIEW FROM THE BRIDGE

Cherokee Paul McDonald (b. 1949) is a fiction writer and journalist. His most recent book, *Into the Green* (2001), recounts his months of combat as an Army lieutenant in Vietnam. (One of the themes of the book, says McDonald, "is hate the war, but don't hate the soldier.") After Vietnam, McDonald served for ten years on the police force of Fort Lauderdale, Florida, an experience that he draws on in numerous crime novels and that he describes graphically in *Blue Truth* (1991). McDonald is also a fisherman and the father of three children, roles that come together in the following descriptive essay about a boy who helps the author see familiar objects in a new light. The essay was first published in 1990 in *Sunshine,* a Florida sporting magazine.

XXXXXXXXXXXXXXXXXXXXXXXXXXXXXXXXXXXXXXXXXXXXXXXXXXXXXXX

1   I was coming up on the little bridge in the Rio Vista neighborhood of Fort Lauderdale, deepening my stride and my breathing to negotiate the slight incline without altering my pace. And then, as I neared the crest, I saw the kid.

2   He was a lumpy little guy with baggy shorts, a faded T-shirt and heavy sweat socks falling down over old sneakers.

3   Partially covering his shaggy blond hair was one of those blue baseball caps with gold braid on the bill and a sailfish patch sewn onto the peak. Covering his eyes and part of his face was a pair of those stupid-looking '50s-style wrap-around sunglasses.

4   He was fumbling with a beat-up rod and reel, and he had a little bait bucket by his feet. I puffed on by, glancing down into the empty bucket as I passed.

5   "Hey, mister! Would you help me, please?"

6   The shrill voice penetrated my jogger's concentration, and I was determined to ignore it. But for some reason, I stopped.

With my hands on my hips and the sweat dripping from my nose 7
I asked, "What do you want, kid?"

"Would you please help me find my shrimp? It's my last one and 8
I've been getting bites and I know I can catch a fish if I can just find
that shrimp. He jumped outta my hand as I was getting him from the
bucket."

Exasperated, I walked slowly back to the kid, and pointed. 9

"There's the damn shrimp by your left foot. You stopped me for 10
that?"

As I said it, the kid reached down and trapped the shrimp. 11

"Thanks a lot, mister," he said. 12

I watched as the kid dropped the baited hook down into the canal. 13
Then I turned to start back down the bridge.

That's when the kid let out a "Hey! Hey!" and the prettiest tarpon 14
I'd ever seen came almost six feet out of the water, twisting and turning
as he fell through the air.

"I got one!" the kid yelled as the fish hit the water with a loud 15
splash and took off down the canal.

I watched the line being burned off the reel at an alarming rate. 16
The kid's left hand held the crank while the extended fingers felt for the
drag setting.

"No, kid!" I shouted. "Leave the drag alone . . . just keep that damn 17
rod tip up!"

Then I glanced at the reel and saw there were just a few loops of 18
line left on the spool.

"Why don't you get yourself some decent equipment?" I said, but 19
before the kid could answer I saw the line go slack.

"Ohhh, I lost him," the kid said. I saw the flash of silver as the fish 20
turned.

"Crank, kid, crank! You didn't lose him. He's coming back toward 21
you. Bring in the slack!"

The kid cranked like mad, and a beautiful grin spread across his face. 22

"He's heading in for the pilings," I said. "Keep him out of those 23
pilings!"

The kid played it perfectly. When the fish made its play for the pil- 24
ings, he kept just enough pressure on to force the fish out. When the

water exploded and the silver missile hurled into the air, the kid kept the rod tip up and the line tight.

25   As the fish came to the surface and began a slow circle in the middle of the canal, I said, "Whooee, is that a nice fish or what?"

26   The kid didn't say anything, so I said, "Okay, move to the edge of the bridge and I'll climb down to the seawall and pull him out."

27   When I reached the seawall I pulled in the leader, leaving the fish lying on its side in the water.

28   "How's that?" I said.

29   "Hey, mister, tell me what it looks like."

30   "Look down here and check him out," I said, "He's beautiful."

31   But then I looked up into those stupid-looking sunglasses and it hit me. The kid was blind.

32   "Could you tell me what he looks like, mister?" he said again.

33   "Well, he's just under three, uh, he's about as long as one of your arms," I said. "I'd guess he goes about 15, 20 pounds. He's mostly silver, but the silver is somehow made up of *all* the colors, if you know what I mean." I stopped. "Do you know what I mean by colors?"

34   The kid nodded.

35   "Okay. He has all these big scales, like armor all over his body. They're silver too, and when he moves they sparkle. He has a strong body and a large powerful tail. He has big round eyes, bigger than a quarter, and a lower jaw that sticks out past the upper one and is very tough. His belly is almost white and his back is a gunmetal gray. When he jumped he came out of the water about six feet, and his scales caught the sun and flashed it all over the place."

36   By now the fish had righted itself, and I could see the bright-red gills as the gill plates opened and closed. I explained this to the kid, and then said, more to myself, "He's a beauty."

37   "Can you get him off the hook?" the kid asked. "I don't want to kill him."

38   I watched as the tarpon began to slowly swim away, tired but still alive.

39   By the time I got back up to the top of the bridge the kid had his line secured and his bait bucket in one hand.

40   He grinned and said, "Just in time. My mom drops me off here, and she'll be back to pick me up any minute."

He used the back of one hand to wipe his nose. 41

"Thanks for helping me catch that tarpon," he said, "and for help- 42
ing me to see it."

I looked at him, shook my head, and said, "No, my friend, thank 43
you for letting *me* see that fish."

I took off, but before I got far the kid yelled again. 44

"Hey, mister!" 45

I stopped. 46

"Someday I'm gonna catch a sailfish and a blue marlin and a giant 47
tuna and all those big sportfish!"

As I looked into those sunglasses I knew he probably would. I 48
wished I could be there when it happened.

XXXXXXXXXXXXXXXXXX **For Discussion** XXXXXXXXXXXXXXXXXX

1. Which of the five senses does Cherokee Paul McDonald appeal to in his
DESCRIPTION of the tarpon in paragraph 35? In this essay as a whole?

2. How much does the jogger seem to know about fish and fishing? About boys?

3. What is the attitude of the jogger toward the "kid" before he realizes the boy
is blind? As one reader, what is your attitude toward the jogger? Why?

4. How does the jogger feel about the kid when they part? How do you feel
about the jogger? What, if anything, changes your view of him?

5. How does meticulously describing a small piece of the world help the
grumpy jogger to see the world anew?

XXXXXXXXXXXX **Strategies and Structures** XXXXXXXXXXXX

1. McDonald serves as eyes for the boy (and us). Which physical details in his
DESCRIPTION of the scene at the bridge do you find to be visually most effective?

2. McDonald's description is part of a NARRATIVE. At first, the NARRATOR seems
irritable and in a hurry. What makes him slow down? How does his behavior
change? Why?

3. The narrator does not realize the boy is blind until paragraph 31, but we figure it out much sooner. What descriptive details lead us to realize that the boy
is blind?

4. McDonald, of course, knew when he wrote this piece that the boy couldn't
see. Why do you think he wrote from the POINT OF VIEW of the jogger, who

doesn't know at first? How does he restrict the narrator's point of view in paragraph 6? Elsewhere in the essay?

5. How does the narrator's physical VANTAGE POINT change in paragraph 27? Why does this alter the way he sees the boy?

6. "No, my friend," says the jogger, "thank you for letting *me* see that fish" (43). So who is helping whom to see in this essay? How? Cite examples.

XXXXXXXXXXXXX **WORDS AND FIGURES OF SPEECH** XXXXXXXXXXXXX

1. METONYMY is a FIGURE OF SPEECH in which a word or object stands in for another associated with it. How might the blind boy's cap or sunglasses be seen as examples of metonymy?

2. Point out words and phrases in this essay—for example, "sparkle"—that refer to sights or acts of seeing (35).

3. What possible meanings are suggested by the word "view" in McDonald's title?

4. Besides its literal meaning, how else might we take the word "bridge" here? Who or what is being "bridged"?

XXXXXXXXXXXXXXXXXXX **FOR WRITING** XXXXXXXXXXXXXXXXXXXXXXX

1. Suppose you had to DESCRIBE a flower, bird, snake, butterfly, or other plant or animal to a blind person. In a paragraph, describe the object—its colors, smell, texture, movement, how the light strikes it—in sufficient physical detail so that the person could form an accurate mental picture of what you are describing.

2. Write an extended description of a scene in which you see a familiar object, person, or place in a new light because of someone else who brings a fresh viewpoint to the picture. For example, you might describe the scene at the dinner table when you bring home a new girlfriend or boyfriend. Or you might describe taking a tour of your campus, hometown, neighborhood, or workplace with a friend or relative who has never seen it before.

ALICE STEINBACH

THE MISS DENNIS SCHOOL
OF WRITING

Alice Steinbach (b. 1933) is a freelance writer whose essays and travel
sketches often deal with what she calls "lessons from a woman's life." As
a reporter for the *Baltimore Sun,* where she won a Pulitzer Prize for feature writing in 1985, Steinbach wrote a column about her ninth-grade
creative writing teacher. Revised as an essay—essays are "much more
complete" than columns, says Steinbach—it became the title piece in a
collection of personal essays, *The Miss Dennis School of Writing* (1996).
Here the "lesson" is both a writing lesson and a life lesson. Miss Dennis
taught that good descriptive writing (her specialty) makes the reader see
what the writer sees. She also taught her students to find their unique
personal voices. Steinbach's distinctive voice can be heard in her vivid
descriptions of her old teacher. It is a voice, she says, that "tends to look
at people with a child's eye."

XXXXXXXXXXXXXXXXXXXXXXXXXXXXXXXXXXXXXXXXXXXXXXXXXXXX

"What kind of writing do you do?" asked the novelist sitting to   1
my left at a writer's luncheon.

"I work for a newspaper in Baltimore," he was told.   2

"Oh, did you go to journalism school?"   3

"Well, yes."   4

"Columbia?" he asked, invoking the name of the most prestigious   5
journalism school in the country.

"Actually, no," I heard myself telling him. "I'm one of the lucky   6
ones. I am a graduate of the Miss Dennis School of Writing."

Unimpressed, the novelist turned away. Clearly it was a credential   7
that did not measure up to his standards. But why should it? He was not
one of the lucky ones. He had never met Miss Dennis, my ninth-grade

creative writing teacher, or had the good fortune to be her student. Which meant he had never experienced the sight of Miss Dennis chasing Dorothy Singer around the classroom, threatening her with a yardstick because Dorothy hadn't paid attention and her writing showed it.

8   "You want to be a writer?" Miss Dennis would yell, out of breath from all the running and yardstick-brandishing. "Then pay attention to what's going on around you. Connect! You are not Switzerland—neutral, aloof, uninvolved. Think Italy!"

9   Miss Dennis said things like this. If you had any sense, you wrote them down.

10   "I can't teach you how to write, but I can tell you how to look at things, how to pay attention," she would bark out at us, like a drill sergeant confronting a group of undisciplined, wet-behind-the-ears[1] Marine recruits. To drive home her point, she had us take turns writing a description of what we saw on the way to school in the morning. Of course, you never knew which morning would be your turn so—just to be on the safe side—you got into the habit of looking things over carefully every morning and making notes: "Saw a pot of red geraniums sitting in the sunlight on a white stucco porch; an orange-striped cat curled like a comma beneath a black van; a dark gray cloud scudding across a silver morning sky."

11   It's a lesson that I have returned to again and again throughout my writing career. To this day, I think of Miss Dennis whenever I write a certain kind of sentence. Or to be more precise, whenever I write a sentence that actually creates in words the picture I want readers to see.

12   Take, for instance, this sentence: Miss Dennis was a small, compact woman, about albatross height—or so it seemed to her students—with short, straight hair the color of apricots and huge eyeglasses that were always slipping down her nose.

13   Or this one: Miss Dennis always wore a variation of one outfit—a dark-colored, flared woolen skirt, a tailored white blouse and a cardigan sweater, usually black, thrown over her shoulders and held together by a little pearl chain.

---

1. Young and inexperienced.

Can you see her? I can. And the image of her makes me smile.   14
Still.

But it was not Miss Dennis's appearance or her unusual teaching   15
method—which had a lot in common with an out-of-control terrier—
that made her so special. What set her apart was her deep commitment
to liberating the individual writer in each student.

"What lies at the heart of good writing," she told us over and over   16
again, "is the writer's ability to find his own unique voice. And then to
use it to tell an interesting story." Somehow she made it clear that we
were interesting people with interesting stories to tell. Most of us, of
course, had never even known we had a story to tell, much less an interesting one. But soon the stories just started bubbling up from some
inner wellspring.

Finding the material, however, was one thing; finding the individ-   17
ual voice was another.

Take me, for instance. I arrived in Miss Dennis's class trailing all   18
sorts of literary baggage. My usual routine was to write like Colette on
Monday, one of the Brontë sisters on Wednesday, and Mark Twain[2] on
Friday.

Right away, Miss Dennis knocked me off my high horse.   19

"Why are you telling other people's stories?" she challenged me,   20
peering up into my face. (At fourteen I was already four inches taller
than Miss Dennis.) "You have your own stories to tell."

I was tremendously relieved to hear this and immediately pro-   21
ceeded to write like my idol, E. B. White.[3] Miss Dennis, however,
wasn't buying.

"How will you ever find out what you have to say if you keep try-   22
ing to say what other people have already said?" was the way she dis-

---

2. Mark Twain (1835–1910), American novelist and essayist known for his works of wit
and satire; Sidonie-Gabrielle Colette (1873–1954), French novelist known for her sophisticated depictions of female sexuality; Charlotte Brontë (1816–1855), Emily Brontë
(1818–1848), and Anne Brontë (1820–1849), British novelists known for their dramatic,
romantic novels.

3. American essayist and children's author (1899–1985), admired for his elegant style
and attention to detail.

pensed with my E. B. White impersonation. By the third week of class, Miss Dennis knew my secret. She knew I was afraid—afraid to pay attention to my own inner voice for fear that when I finally heard it, it would have nothing to say.

23   What Miss Dennis told me—and I have carefully preserved these words because they were then, and are now, so very important to me— was this: "Don't be afraid to discover what you're saying in the act of saying it." Then, in her inimitably breezy and endearing way, she added: "Trust me on this one."

24   From the beginning, she made it clear to us that it was not "right" or "wrong" answers she was after. It was thinking.

25   "Don't be afraid to go out on a limb," she'd tell some poor kid struggling to reason his way through an essay on friendship or courage. And eventually—once we stopped being afraid that we'd be chopped off out there on that limb—we needed no encouragement to say what we thought. In fact, after the first month, I can't remember ever feeling afraid of failing in her class. Passing or failing didn't seem to be the point of what she was teaching.

26   Miss Dennis spent as much time, maybe more, pointing out what was right with your work as she did pointing out what was wrong. I can still hear her critiquing my best friend's incredibly florid essay on nature. "You are a very good observer of nature," she told the budding writer. "And if you just write what you see without thinking so much about adjectives and comparisons, we will see it through your attentive eyes."

27   By Thanksgiving vacation I think we were all a little infatuated with Miss Dennis. And beyond that, infatuated with the way she made us feel about ourselves—that we were interesting people worth listening to.

28   I, of course, fancied I had a special relationship with her. It was certainly special to me. And, to tell the truth, I knew she felt the same way.

29   The first time we acknowledged this was one day after class when I stayed behind to talk to her. I often did that and it seemed we talked about everything—from the latest films to the last issue of the *New Yorker*. The one thing we did not talk about was the sadness I

felt about my father's death. He had died a few years before and, although I did not know it then, I was still grieving his absence. Without knowing the details, Miss Dennis somehow picked up on my sadness. Maybe it was there in my writing. Looking back I see now that, without my writing about it directly, my father's death hovered at the edges of all my stories.

But on this particular day I found myself talking not about the movies or about writing but instead pouring out my feelings about the loss of my father. I shall never forget that late fall afternoon: the sound of the vanilla-colored blinds flap, flap, flapping in the still classroom; sun falling in shafts through the windows, each ray illuminating tiny galaxies of chalk dust in the air; the smell of wet blackboards; the teacher, small with apricot-colored hair, listening intently to a young girl blurting out her grief. These memories are stored like vintage photographs.

The words that passed between the young girl and the attentive teacher are harder to recall. With this exception. "One day," Miss Dennis told me, "you will write about this. Maybe not directly. But you will write about it. And you will find that all this has made you a better writer and a stronger person."

After that day, it was as if Miss Dennis and I shared something. We never talked again about my father but spent most of our time discussing our mutual interests. We both loved poetry and discovered one afternoon that each of us regarded Emily Dickinson with something approaching idolatry. Right then and there, Miss Dennis gave me a crash course in why Emily Dickinson's poems worked. I can still hear her talking about the "spare, slanted beauty" in Dickinson's unique choice of words. She also told me about the rather cloistered life led by this New England spinster, noting that nonetheless Emily Dickinson[4] knew the world as few others did. "She found her world within the word," is the way I remember Miss Dennis putting it. Of course, I could be making that part up.

---

4. American poet (1830–1886) who wrote almost 1,800 poems and many letters but, in later years, seldom left her family home in Amherst, Massachusetts.

33   That night, propped up in bed reading Emily Dickinson's poetry, I wondered if Miss Dennis, a spinster herself, identified in some way with the woman who wrote:

> Wild nights–Wild nights!
> Were I with thee
> Wild Nights should be
> Our luxury!

34   It seems strange, I know, but I never really knew anything about Miss Dennis' life outside of the classroom. Oh, once she confided in me that the initial "M" in her name stood for Mildred. And I was surprised when I passed by the teachers' lounge one day and saw her smoking a cigarette, one placed in a long, silver cigarette holder. It seemed an exceedingly sophisticated thing to do and it struck me then that she might be more worldly than I had previously thought.

35   But I didn't know how she spent her time or what she wanted from life or anything like that. And I never really wondered about it. Once I remember talking to some friends about her age. We guessed somewhere around fifty—which seemed really old to us. In reality, Miss Dennis was around forty.

36   It was Miss Dennis, by the way, who encouraged me to enter some writing contests. To my surprise, I took first place in a couple of them. Of course, taking first place is easy. What's hard is being rejected. But Miss Dennis helped me with that, too, citing all the examples of famous writers who'd been rejected time and time again. "Do you know what they told George Orwell[5] when they rejected *Animal Farm?*" she would ask me. Then without waiting for a reply, she'd answer her own question: "The publisher told him, 'It is impossible to sell animal stories in the U.S.A.'"

37   When I left her class at the end of the year, Miss Dennis gave me a present: a book of poems by Emily Dickinson. I have it still. The spine is cracked and the front cover almost gone, but the inscription remains. On

---

5. British novelist and essayist (1903–1950). Much of his major work, including the satiric novel *Animal Farm* (1945), reflects his opposition to repressive governments.

the inside flyleaf, in her perfect Palmer Method handwriting,[6] she had written: "Say what you see. Yours in Emily Dickinson, Miss Dennis."

She had also placed little checks next to two or three poems. I took this to mean she thought they contained a special message for me. One of those checked began this way:

> Hope is the thing with feathers
> That perches in the soul . . .

I can remember carefully copying out these lines onto a sheet of paper, one which I carried around in my handbag for almost a year. But time passed, the handbag fell apart and who knows what happened to the yellowing piece of paper with the words about hope.

The years went by. Other schools and other teachers came and went. But one thing remained constant: My struggle to pay attention to my own inner life; to hear a voice that I would recognize finally as my own. Not only in my writing but in my life.

Only recently, I learned that Miss Dennis had died at the age of fifty. When I heard this, it occurred to me that her life was close to being over when I met her. Neither of us knew this, of course. Or at least I didn't. But lately I've wondered if she knew something that day we talked about sadness and my father's death. "Write about it," she said. "It will help you."

And now, reading over these few observations, I think of Miss Dennis. But not with sadness. Actually, thinking of Miss Dennis makes me smile. I think of her and see, with marked clarity, a small, compact woman with apricot-colored hair. She is with a young girl and she is saying something.

She is saying: "Pay attention."

6. A form of standardized handwriting that became popular around 1900 but is rarely taught today.

✕✕✕✕✕✕✕✕✕✕✕✕✕✕✕✕✕ FOR DISCUSSION ✕✕✕✕✕✕✕✕✕✕✕✕✕✕✕✕✕

1. When some teachers say, "Pay attention," they mean "Pay attention to what I am saying." According to her former pupil, Alice Steinbach, what did Miss Dennis mean when she told students to pay attention?

2. It was neither Miss Dennis's appearance nor her teaching methods that made her so special as a teacher of writing, says Steinbach, but "her deep commitment to liberating the individual writer in each student" (15). How did Miss Dennis accomplish this feat in Steinbach's case?

3. Steinbach poses a direct question to the reader in paragraph 14: "Can you see her?" Well, can you? And if so, what exactly do you see—and hear? For example, what color was Miss Dennis's hair?

4. Steinbach thinks of her old teacher whenever she writes a sentence "that actually creates in words the picture I want readers to see" (11). This is precisely what good DESCRIPTIVE writing does, although it may appeal to other senses as well as sight. How did Miss Dennis teach this kind of writing?

5. Writing about old teachers who die can be an occasion for sentimentality or excessively emotional writing. Do you think Steinbach's tribute to her former teacher is overly emotional, or does she successfully avoid sentimentality? If she avoids it, in your opinion, explain how she does so. If not, explain why you think she doesn't. Find places in her essay that support your view.

XXXXXXXXXXXXXX **STRATEGIES AND STRUCTURES** XXXXXXXXXXXXXX

1. Point out several DESCRIPTIVE passages in Steinbach's essay that follow her principle of creating in words what she wants the reader to see.

2. Why do you think Steinbach, looking back over her recollections of Miss Dennis, refers to them as "observations" (41)?

3. Description seldom stands alone. Often it shades into NARRATIVE, as here. Thus Miss Dennis, who greatly valued the writer's eye, urged the student, once she found her unique way of looking at the world, to use it "to tell an interesting story" (16). Besides Miss Dennis's, whose story is Steinbach telling? How interesting do you find *that* narrative?

4. What DOMINANT IMPRESSION of Miss Dennis do we get from Steinbach's description of her in paragraphs 12 through 14 and 41? Of Steinbach herself?

5. How informative do you find Steinbach's essay as a lesson on how to write, particularly on how to write good description? Where does Steinbach ANALYZE THE PROCESS?

✕✕✕✕✕✕✕✕✕✕✕✕ WORDS AND FIGURES OF SPEECH ✕✕✕✕✕✕✕✕✕✕✕✕

1. Which is more CONCRETE, to say that a woman has "hair the color of apricots" or to say that she is a redhead or blonde (12)? Which is more specific?

2. The orange-striped cat in young Steinbach's DESCRIPTION of her walk to school is "curled like a comma" beneath a van (10). Such stated COMPARISONS, frequently using *like* or *as*, are called SIMILES. Implied comparisons, without like or as, are called METAPHORS. What metaphoric comparison does Steinbach make in the same description? What is she comparing to what?

3. Steinbach compares Miss Dennis to an "albatross" and "an out-of-control terrier" (12, 15). Besides describing Miss Dennis, what do these fanciful comparisons tell you about her former writing pupil?

4. Steinbach arrived in Miss Dennis's class "trailing all sorts of literary baggage" (18). To what is she comparing herself here?

5. How would you describe the words that Steinbach uses in paragraph 30 to describe the afternoon? Concrete or ABSTRACT? Specific or general?

✕✕✕✕✕✕✕✕✕✕✕✕✕✕✕✕✕✕ FOR WRITING ✕✕✕✕✕✕✕✕✕✕✕✕✕✕✕✕✕✕✕

1. On your next walk to or around school, pay close attention to your surroundings. Take notes, as young Steinbach does in paragraph 10. DESCRIBE what you see in a paragraph that "creates in words the picture" you want your reader to see (11). Make it as free of literary or other baggage as you can, and try to select details that contribute to a single DOMINANT IMPRESSION.

2. Write a profile—a description of a person that not only tells but shows a piece of that person's life story—of one of your favorite (or most despised) teachers or coaches. Try to give your reader a clear sense of what that person looks like; of what he or she wears, says, and does; and of the dominant impression he or she makes on others. Be sure to show how you interact with that person and what he or she has (or has not) taught you.

DAN BARRY

Chronicle of an American Execution

Dan Barry (b. 1958) is a reporter and columnist for the *New York Times*. In 1994, Barry and his investigative team at the *Providence Journal-Bulletin* won a Pulitzer Prize for a series of articles about corruption in the Rhode Island court system. In 1995, Barry joined the staff of the *Times*, becoming a major contributor to the newspaper's award-winning coverage of 9/11 and Hurricane Katrina. "Chronicle of an American Execution," first published in 2007, is from Barry's "This Land" column in the *Times*. Reporting from Nashville, he gives a moment-by-moment description of an execution by electrocution—the first use of the electric chair in the state of Tennessee since 1960.

XXXXXXXXXXXXXXXXXXXXXXXXXXXXXXXXXXXXXXXXXXXXXXXXXXXXXXXXX

1   The window blinds to the execution chamber are raised shortly after 1 in the morning, in accordance with the Procedures for Electrocution in the State of Tennessee. And the condemned man is revealed.[1]

2   He looks almost like a young child buckled into a car seat, with his closed eyes and freshly shaved head, with the way the black restraints of the electric chair crisscross at his torso. He yawns a wide-mouthed yawn, as though just stirring from an interrupted dream, and opens his eyes.

3   He is moments from dying.

4   The cause of death will be cardiac arrest. Every step toward that end will follow those written state procedures, which strive to lend a

---

1. Family members of the prisoner and victim, prison and medical personnel, members of the clergy, witnesses officially designated by the state, and media representatives are permitted to witness executions.

kind of clinical dignity to the electrocution of a human being, yet read like instructions for jump-starting a car engine. Remember: "A fire extinguisher is located in the building and is near the electric chair as a precaution."

Behold Daryl Holton. He is 45. Ten years ago he shot his four young children in his uncle's auto-repair garage, two at a time, through the heart. He used their very innocence to kill them, telling them not to peek, daddy has a surprise. After he was done he turned himself in, saying he wanted to report a "homicide times four."

In seeking the execution of this Army veteran, now blinking in the cold, bright room, the state argued that Mr. Holton committed premeditated murder, times four, to punish his ex-wife for obtaining an order of protection and for moving away. He killed his children, so he must be killed.

In defending the life of this man—now pursing his lips, about all that he can move—his advocates argued that he believed his children were better off dead than living in a profoundly troubled home; that he actually felt relief after pulling a tarpaulin over those four small bodies. He killed his children, so he must be mentally ill.

All the while, Mr. Holton adhered to a peculiar code of conduct that vexed all sides. Those fighting for his life often did so against his will. Those seeking his remorse were unrewarded.

Just days ago he said the crimes for which he was convicted warranted the death penalty, but he pointedly removed himself from that equation. Perhaps to suggest the killings were justified; perhaps to keep things theoretical. No matter. Now, at 1:09 A.M. on Wednesday, September 12, 2007, at the Riverbend Maximum Security Institution, it is about to happen.

The warden, Ricky J. Bell, stands before him, supervising the first electrocution in Tennessee since 1960. Prison officials had hoped that Mr. Holton would choose to die by lethal injection, and had been gently reminding him of this option.[2] But he maintained that since electrocu-

---

2. Tennessee adopted lethal injection as its official method of capital punishment in 1999; those who committed capital crimes when electrocution was still the official form of punishment can choose to die by either method.

tion was the only form of capital punishment at the time of his crimes, then electrocution it should be.

11   Before the raising of those window blinds, Mr. Holton had started to hyperventilate, and Mr. Bell had sought to calm him by slightly loosening the straps. But now it is 1:10, the blinds are up, the clock is running. In accordance with procedures, the warden asks if the condemned has something to say.

12   The inmate's response is so slurred by his hyperventilating that he is asked to repeat what he has been planning to say for a long time. He says again, "Two words: I do."

13   This could be a joke of some kind, a cosmic conundrum, or maybe Mr. Holton's acceptance of whatever awaits him after life. It could be the use of his marital vow as a parting shot at his ex-wife, or perhaps a twisted reaffirmation of his belief in the sanctity of marriage and family.

14   The warden asks, "That it?" The inmate nods.

15   Two corrections officers step forward to place a sponge soaked in salted water on Mr. Holtons bald scalp to enhance conductivity. Next comes the headpiece, which the procedures describe as a "leather cranial cap lined with copper mesh inside." Finally, a power cable, not unlike the cable to your television, is attached to the headpiece.

16   The copper mesh pressing wet sponge sends salty water streaming down the inmate's ashen face, soaking his white cotton shirt to the pale skin beneath. When officers try to blot him dry with white towels, Mr. Holton says not to worry about it, "ain't gonna matter anyway."

17   After the white towels comes a black shroud to be attached to the headpiece. It is intended in part to protect the dignity of the inmate, now strapped, soaked and about to die before witnesses. His final expression, then, will be his own.

18   With the push of a button on a console labeled Electric Chair Control, 1,750 volts bolt through Mr. Holton's body, jerking it up and dropping it like a sack of earth. The black shroud offers the slightest flutter, and witnesses cannot tell whether they have just heard a machine's whoosh or a man's sigh.

19   Fifteen seconds later, another bolt, and Mr. Holton's body rises even higher, slumps even lower. His reddened hands remain gripped to

the arms of the chair, whose oaken pieces are said to have once belonged to the old electric chair, and before that, to the gallows.

It is 1:17. Procedures require a five-minute pause at this point. A prison official off to the side watches a digital clock on the wall while chewing something, perhaps gum, perhaps to calm his nerves. Two minutes, three, four, the only things moving in the room are his eyes and his jaw, five. The window blinds drop, and a physician begins a private examination. 20

Later, in the foggy darkness outside the prison, someone will read a statement from the ex-wife, Crystal Holton, in which she says that all the anger and hatred can finally leave her, to be replaced by a child's innocent love—"love times four." 21

Later, well after sunrise, Kelly Gleason, one of the lawyers who fought to keep Mr. Holton alive, will set aside her mourning for a friend and give in to fitful sleep. 22

Later, in the hot afternoon some fifty miles to the south, four polished tombstones will again cast shadows toward a playground at the bottom of a cemetery's hill. Arranged in order of age, the stones bear the names of the four Holton children: Stephen, 12, Brent, 10, Eric, 6, and Kayla, 4. 23

But first confirmation, in accordance with procedures. And now the disembodied voice of Tennessee: "Ladies and gentlemen, this concludes the legal execution of Daryl Holton. The time of death, 1:25. Please exit." 24

XXXXXXXXXXXXXXXXXX **For Discussion** XXXXXXXXXXXXXXXXXX

1. According to the state of Tennessee, why did Daryl Holton murder his four children? According to his defenders, why did he do it?

2. Why did Holton choose to be executed by electrocution rather than "lethal injection" (10)?

3. Dan Barry says Holton adhered to a "peculiar code of conduct" right up to the moment of his death (8). What "code of conduct" did Holton follow? Why does Barry call it "peculiar"?

4. Why did Kelly Gleason fight to prevent Holton's execution even though she and other "advocates" were acting against his will (7, 8)? Were they right to do so? Why or why not?

5. Barry DESCRIBES "an American execution" but does not ARGUE directly for or against capital punishment. Should he have? Why or why not?

XXXXXXXXXXXXX **STRATEGIES AND STRUCTURES** XXXXXXXXXXXXX

1. In many ways, Barry's eyewitness DESCRIPTION of the execution of Daryl Holton is a model of OBJECTIVE description. What are some of those ways? Point to specific passages in the text that support your answer.

2. Why do you think Barry begins his description of Holton by saying that the condemned man looks like a "child buckled into a car seat" (2)? Why does he wait so long to give the names and ages of Holton's four victims (23)? Point out other instances where, for all his objectivity, Barry may be seen as commenting on the proceedings he describes.

3. Barry refers to specific details of the official "Procedures for Electrocution in the State of Tennessee" (1) and describes the procedure itself in great detail. What does this indicate that Barry believes about his AUDIENCE? Would they be familiar with this procedure? If so, what's the PURPOSE of this detailed description?

4. How does Barry's use of verb tenses in paragraph 11 contribute to the immediacy and vividness of his description?

5. What DOMINANT IMPRESSION do you get from Barry's description of the execution of Daryl Holton? Which details contribute most directly to that impression? Explain.

6. Barry's description includes elements of NARRATION. How and how effectively, for example, does he use DIALOGUE and the FLASH FORWARD technique?

XXXXXXXXXXXXX **WORDS AND FIGURES OF SPEECH** XXXXXXXXXXXXX

1. A *chronicle* is a record of historical events in chronological order. Is this term appropriate to Barry's DESCRIPTION? Why or why not?

2. What difference, if any, would it make in Barry's description if he did not give the name of the condemned man—or of the warden, or of Holton's lawyer? Explain.

3. In his description of the execution chamber, Barry calls attention to the window "blinds" (1, 11, 20). What are the implications of this familiar term for a common form of window covering? In Barry's description, how do the blinds themselves serve as the curtain to a sort of stage?

4. Besides indicating the number of Holton's victims, why might the phrase "times four" be significant enough for Barry to repeat (5, 6, 21)? How do these words compare with the phrase "two words" (12)?

5. In his last paragraph, Barry quotes the "disembodied" voice of the state of Tennessee (24). How might this word describe Barry's own voice throughout his essay? Refer to specific examples in the text.

XXXXXXXXXXXXXXXXXXXXX **FOR WRITING** XXXXXXXXXXXXXXXXXXXXX

1. After rereading paragraph 20 in Barry's DESCRIPTION, write a paragraph of your own that describes a person who is anxiously passing the time by chewing something, playing with a pencil, adjusting his or her clothes, or engaging in some other unconscious nervous behavior.

2. Write an essay describing a solemn event that you have witnessed. Be sure to describe the physical scene in enough detail that the reader can see and hear it clearly, but focus on the people—the central figure, or figures, in the scene—and what they do and say.

GARRISON KEILLOR

A SUNDAY AT THE STATE FAIR

Garrison Keillor (b. 1942) is the father of public radio's *A Prairie Home Companion* and sole proprietor of the mythical Lake Wobegon, "where all the men are good looking, all the women are strong, and all the children are above average." "A Sunday at the State Fair" first appeared in the *International Herald Tribune* in 2008. It describes Keillor's visit to the Iowa State Fair, where he encountered, among the many booths and exhibits, a pork chop on a stick, U.S. Marines, a sauna salesman, a farm machinery auction, and teenagers exhibiting llamas.

XXXXXXXXXXXXXXXXXXXXXXXXXXXXXXXXXXXXXXXXXXXXXXXXXXXXXXXXXXXXXX

1 I got to go to the Iowa State Fair on Sunday and eat a very excellent pork chop on a stick as I stood by the U.S. Marines booth, where various civilians lined up to do chin-ups on a high bar, counted off by a Marine whose T-shirt said, "Pain Is Weakness Leaving The Body." I've seen many things at state fairs but never chin-ups. The look of chagrin on men's faces who had believed they could do chin-ups and then the truth dawned on them. One man looked as if he might blow out his aorta. A small, sharp memory of high school phys-ed. I had to turn away.

2 I passed up the novelty foods, the deep-fried pineapple on a stick, etc. A fair isn't about food, it is a carnival of ideas where the Lutheran booth sits between the "reverse osmosis" water purifier booth and the hot-tub booth. Here is an 8-foot-by-8-foot tub that seats four and reclines one, with water jets and a pedestal table for your champagne, which would feel awfully good after a day of combining Redemption By Faith Alone[1] versus Creaturely Comfort. Nearby you can learn about

---

1. In the Lutheran religion, divine salvation is possible only through faith in the sacrifice of Jesus Christ for humanity.

A man waving the state flag greets fairgoers at the entrance to the 2009 Iowa State Fair.

ethanol and hear the horn of a Model T,[2] which sounds like a terrified goose, or you can talk to a lawyer at the bar association booth. (He told me that most questions are about leases or divorces.)

Most fairgoers walk past like stunned sheep, but men are waiting in booths who'd be glad to explain about corn yield and herbicide or Republican principles or the advantages of vinyl siding. A kindly salesman told me all about an infrared "health cabin," which is sort of a sauna but without steam, just heat, up to 140 degrees, which "aids in the relief of chronic fatigue" and will detoxify you and "balance" your blood pressure. I didn't buy one, but I enjoyed the pitch. Salesmanship is basically a civil and

2. Popular and affordable automobile produced by Henry Ford from 1908 through 1927, now a prized collectible.

amiable profession. Fifty feet away are the Methodists[3] (Find Your Path, Share The Journey) and a display of bottled water (zero calories). And the anti-abortion people, and the natural latex mattress booth (80 percent less tossing and turning), and a booth selling a GPS gizmo that provides weather info and also local movie times.

4　　The beauty of a fair is conversation. You walk up to the Methodists and say, "What does that mean, 'find your path'? Is there more than one?" and you're good for fifteen minutes. Talk, talk, talk, everywhere. Witness the rare art of barking, which is the art of rising inflection, and here is a crowd of overheated people in shorts and sneakers watching a green pepper being sliced and minced by a barker who makes it seem thrilling. And next door, the hysteria of the auction ring, the old man in the big white hat and his bidibidibeebidyululation, the shouts of his spotters, the old man hollering, "Here we go!" and "It's only money! It'll only hurt for a little while!" and then "Sold for fifteen hundred dollars!"

5　　I saw acres of machinery where a man who took a wrong turn into the liberal arts can contemplate a life he'll never live and stuff he'll never own. A beautiful 29-foot flatbed trailer with pine flooring on which you could carry haybales or a tractor. A 4-by-4 double-cab pickup you could pull your trailer with. And beyond it an acre of FFA[4]-restored tractors that put an older Midwesterner in a very thoughtful mood. The green John Deeres and Olivers, the red Farmall and Allis-Chalmers, the yellow Minneapolis Moline. The steel bucket seats on a coiled spring, the exhaust stacks, the brake and clutch pedals. You could climb up in that seat and be 14 again. I was happy back then pulling a manure spreader across the corn stubble on a September day, big clots of matter flying through the air. I miss those days.

6　　And then I wound up at an open-air brick pavilion for the llama judging. Llamas are gentle, dignified beasts, and here were four of them being shown by teenagers. The animals' military bearing, heads high, their stately gait, their dark soulful eyes—they looked as if they'd walked

3. Practitioners of a Christian faith founded in the eighteenth century that values fellowship and individual spiritual responsibility.

4. Future Farmers of America, an extracurricular club popular in rural areas.

straight out of *Dr. Dolittle*,[5] and it was sweet to see them being handled lovingly by teenagers. Pigs are something else—you can see how a person might need to whack a pig. But nobody would ever whack a llama. According to a poster, they are raised for "fiber, showing, carting, guardians and companionship." One girl stood by her llama and blew gently on its nose, and he looked lovingly into her eyes. A sort of conversation. If every teenager had his or her own llama, this would be a very different country.

5. *The Story of Dr. Dolittle* (1920) is a British children's novel by Hugh Lofting, also adapted for film, whose title character can talk to and understand animals and is friends with a two-headed llama.

XXXXXXXXXXXXXXXXXXXXX **FOR DISCUSSION** XXXXXXXXXXXXXXXXXXXXX

1. In the first paragraph of his essay, Garrison Keillor DESCRIBES men doing chin-ups under the supervision of U.S. Marines. Why does he have to turn away from the sight? How serious do you think he is here? Explain.

2. Keillor apparently has no intention of buying a "health cabin" from the sauna salesman or of following the "path" of the Methodists (3, 4). So why does he spend time at their booths?

3. Why does the farm machinery that Keillor describes in paragraph 5 put him "in a very thoughtful mood?" What does he mean when he says he took a "wrong turn into the liberal arts" (5)? Do you think he is truly remorseful here? Why or why not?

4. "If every teenager had his or her own llama," Keillor concludes, "this would be a very different country" (6). Why? What effect does the llama have upon the young woman whom Keillor is describing? And vice versa?

XXXXXXXXXXXXX **STRATEGIES AND STRUCTURES** XXXXXXXXXXXXX

1. Is Keillor's DESCRIPTION of his visit to the Iowa State Fair more SUBJECTIVE or OBJECTIVE? Explain.

2. What is Keillor's main point in describing his visit to the fair? Where does he state it most directly?

3. What DOMINANT IMPRESSION of the fair do you get from Keillor's description? Which details contribute most directly to that impression?

4. "A fair," says Keilor, "isn't about food" (2). If taste is not the dominant sense in Keillor's description, what senses *does* he emphasize? Give several specific examples.

5. How does Keillor use his leisurely stroll through the fairgrounds to help organize his description?

6. Keillor's last stop is the pavilion where the llama judging takes place. The young woman he encounters there is having a "sort of conversation" with her llama (6). How does this particular description provide a fitting conclusion to Keillor's essay?

7. Point out elements of NARRATIVE in Keillor's description of his day at the fair. Does his story have a PLOT? Why or why not?

XXXXXXXXXXXXX **WORDS AND FIGURES OF SPEECH** XXXXXXXXXXXX

1. "Pain Is Weakness Leaving The Body" (1). Explain the implications of this METAPHOR—and of the word "chagrin" in the same paragraph.

2. In paragraph 2, is Keillor using the word "carnival" literally or metaphorically—or both? Explain.

3. The horn of a Model T Ford, says Keillor, sounds "like a terrified goose" (2). How effective do you find this SIMILE for DESCRIBING an old car horn and the noise it makes?

4. Why does Keillor describe some fairgoers as moving "like stunned sheep" (3)?

5. "Barking" and "bidibidibeebidyululation" are examples of ONOMATOPOEIA, or the use of words whose sounds echo their meanings (4). If the first is the sound a barker makes, what is the second? Explain.

6. Can an animal be accurately described as "soulful" (6)? Why or why not?

XXXXXXXXXXXXXXXXXXX **FOR WRITING** XXXXXXXXXXXXXXXXXXXXXXX

1. In a paragraph or two, DESCRIBE your favorite carnival ride, exhibit, or other attraction.

2. Write an essay describing a place or object (like the tractors in Keillor's essay) that puts you in "a very thoughtful mood," evokes your childhood, or makes you nostalgic. Try to give the reader a DOMINANT IMPRESSION of the place or object as it seemed to you.

ANN HODGMAN

No Wonder They Call
Me a Bitch

Ann Hodgman (b. 1956) is a freelance writer and former food critic for *Eating Well* magazine. Besides playing goalie on a women's hockey team, she is the author of more than forty children's books, several cookbooks, and the memoir *The House of a Million Pets* (2007). For reasons soon to be apparent, the following "tasteless" essay from 1990 did not appear in Hodgman's food column, "Sweet and Sour," but in the satiric magazine *Spy*, for which Hodgman was a contributing editor. A spoof on taste testing, it takes a blue ribbon for disgusting description that appeals to the grosser senses.

XXXXXXXXXXXXXXXXXXXXXXXXXXXXXXXXXXXXXXXXXXXXXXXXXXXXXXXX

I've always wondered about dog food. Is a Gaines-burger really like a hamburger? Can you fry it? Does dog food "cheese" taste like real cheese? Does Gravy Train actually make gravy in the dog's bowl, or is that brown liquid just dissolved crumbs? And exactly what *are* by-products?

Having spent the better part of a week eating dog food, I'm sorry to say that I now know the answers to these questions. While my dachshund, Shortie, watched in agonies of yearning, I gagged my way through can after can of stinky, white-flecked mush and bag after bag of stinky, fat-drenched nuggets. And now I understand exactly why Shortie's breath is so bad.

Of course, Gaines-burgers are neither mush nor nuggets. They are, rather, a miracle of beauty and packaging—or at least that's what I thought when I was little. I used to beg my mother to get them for our dogs, but she always said they were too expensive. When I finally bought a box of cheese-flavored Gaines-burgers—after twenty years of longing—I felt deliciously wicked.

4   "Dogs love real beef," the back of the box proclaimed proudly. "That's why Gaines-burgers is the only beef burger for dogs with real beef and no meat by-products!" The copy was accurate: meat by-products did not appear in the list of ingredients. Poultry by-products did, though—right there next to preserved animal fat.

5   One Purina spokesman told me that poultry by-products consist of necks, intestines, undeveloped eggs and other "carcass remnants," but not feathers, heads, or feet. When I told him I'd been eating dog food, he said, "Oh, you're kidding! Oh, *no!*" (I came to share his alarm when, weeks later, a second Purina spokesman said that Gaines-burgers *do* contain poultry heads and feet—but not undeveloped eggs.)

6   Up close my Gaines-burger didn't much resemble chopped beef. Rather, it looked—and felt—like a single long, extruded piece of redness that had been chopped into segments and formed into a patty. You could make one at home if you had a Play-Doh Fun Factory.

7   I turned on the skillet. While I waited for it to heat up I pulled out a shred of cheese-colored material and palpated it. Again, like Play-Doh, it was quite malleable. I made a little cheese bird out of it; then I counted to three and ate the bird.

8   There was a horrifying rush of cheddar taste, followed immediately by the dull tang of soybean flour—the main ingredient in Gainesburgers. Next I tried a piece of red extrusion. The main difference between the meat-flavored and cheese-flavored extrusions is one of texture. The "cheese" chews like fresh Play-Doh, whereas the "meat" chews like Play-Doh that's been sitting out on a rug for a couple of hours.

9   Frying only turned the Gaines-burger black. There was no melting, no sizzling, no warm meat smells. A cherished childhood illusion was gone. I flipped the patty into the sink, where it immediately began leaking rivulets of red dye.

10   As alarming as the Gaines-burgers were, their soy meal began to seem like an old friend when the time came to try some *canned* dog

foods. I decided to try the Cycle foods first. When I opened them, I thought about how rarely I use can openers these days, and I was suddenly visited by a long-forgotten sensation of can opener distaste. *This* is the kind of unsavory place can openers spend their time when you're not watching! Every time you open a can of, say, Italian plum tomatoes, you infect them with invisible particles of by-product.

I had been expecting to see the usual homogeneous scrapple inside, but each can of Cycle was packed with smooth, round, oily nuggets. As if someone at Gaines had been tipped off that a human would be tasting the stuff, the four Cycles really were different from one another. Cycle-1, for puppies, is wet and soyish. Cycle-2, for adults, glistens nastily with fat, but it's passably edible—a lot like some canned Swedish meatballs I once got in a care package at college. Cycle-3, the "lite" one, for fatties, had no specific flavor; it just tasted like dog food. But at least it didn't make me fat.

Cycle-4, for senior dogs, had the smallest nuggets. Maybe old dogs can't open their mouths as wide. This kind was far sweeter than the other three Cycles—almost like baked beans. It was also the only one to contain "dried beef digest," a mysterious substance that the Purina spokesman defined as "enzymes" and my dictionary defined as "the products of digestion."

Next on the menu was a can of Kal Kan Pedigree with Chunky Chicken. Chunky *chicken!* There were chunks in the can, certainly—big, purplish-brown chunks. I forked one chunk out (by now I was becoming more callous) and found that while it had no discernible chicken flavor, it wasn't bad except for its texture—like meat loaf with ground-up chicken bones.

In the world of canned dog food, a smooth consistency is a sign of low quality—lots of cereal. A lumpy, frightening, bloody, stringy horror is a sign of high quality—lots of meat. Nowhere in the world of wet dog foods was this demonstrated better than in the fanciest I tried—Kal Kan's Pedigree Select Dinners. These came not in a can but in a tiny foil packet with a picture of an imperious Yorkie. When I pulled open the container, juice spurted all over my hand, and the first chunk I speared was trailing a long gray vein. I shrieked and went instead for a plain chunk, which I was able to swallow only after taking a break to read some suddenly fascinating office equipment catalogues. Once again, though, it tasted no more alarming than, say, canned hash.

15   Still, how pleasant it was to turn to *dry* dog food! Gravy Train was the first I tried, and I'm happy to report that it really does make a "thick, rich, real beef gravy" when you mix it with water. Thick and rich, anyway. Except for a lingering rancid-fat flavor, the gravy wasn't beefy, but since it tasted primarily like tap water, it wasn't nauseating either.

16   My poor dachshund just gets plain old Purina Dog Chow, but Purina also makes a dry food called Butcher's Blend that comes in Beef, Bacon & Chicken flavor. Here we see dog food's arcane semiotics at its best: a red triangle with a *T* stamped into it is supposed to suggest beef; a tan curl, chicken; and a brown *S*, a piece of bacon. Only dogs understand these messages. But Butcher's Blend does have an endearing slogan: "Great Meaty Tastes—without bothering the Butcher!" *You know, I wanted to buy some meat, but I just couldn't bring myself to bother the butcher . . .*

17   Purina O.N.E. ("Optimum Nutritional Effectiveness") is targeted at people who are unlikely ever to worry about bothering a tradesperson. "We chose chicken as a primary ingredient in Purina O.N.E. for several reasonings," the long, long essay on the back of the bag announces. Chief among these reasonings, I'd guess, is the fact that chicken appeals to people who are—you know—*like us*. Although our dogs do nothing but spend eighteen-hour days alone in the apartment, we still want them to be *premium* dogs. We want them to cut down on red meat, too. We also want dog food that comes in a bag with an attractive design, a subtle typeface, and no kitschy pictures of slobbering golden retrievers.

18   Besides that, we want a list of the Nutritional Benefits of our dog food—and we get it on O.N.E. One thing I especially like about this list is its constant references to a dog's "hair coat," as in "Beef tallow is good for the dog's skin and hair coat." (On the other hand, beef tallow merely provides palatability, while the dried beef digest in Cycle provides palatability *enhancement*.)

19   I hate to say it, but O.N.E. was pretty palatable. Maybe that's because it has about 100 percent more fat than, say, Butcher's Blend. Or maybe I'd been duped by the packaging; that's been known to happen before.

As with people food, dog snacks taste much better than dog meals. They're better looking too. Take Milk-Bone Flavor Snacks. The loving-hands-at-home prose describing each flavor is colorful; the writers practically choke on their own exuberance. Of bacon they say, "It's so good, your dog will think it's hot off the frying pan." Of liver: "The only taste your dog wants more than liver—is even more liver!" Of poultry: "All those farm fresh flavors deliciously mixed in one biscuit. Your dog will bark with delight!" And of vegetable: "Gardens of taste! Specially blended to give your dog that vegetable flavor he wants—but can rarely get!"

Well, I may be a sucker, but advertising this emphatic just doesn't convince me. I lined up all seven flavors of Milk-Bone Flavor Snacks on the floor. Unless my dog's palate is a lot more sensitive than mine—and considering that she steals dirty diapers out of the trash and eats them, I'm loath to think it is—she doesn't detect any more difference in the seven flavors than I did when I tried them.

I much preferred Bonz, the hard-baked, bone-shaped snack stuffed with simulated marrow. I liked the bone part, that is; it tasted almost exactly like the cornmeal it was made of. The mock marrow inside was a bit more problematic: in addition to looking like the sludge that collects in the treads of my running shoes, it was bursting with tiny hairs.

I'm sure you have a few dog food questions of your own. To save us time, I've answered them in advance.

Q. *Are those little cans of Mighty Dog actually branded with the sizzling word* BEEF, *the way they show in the commercials?*

A. You should know by now that that kind of thing never happens.

Q. *Does chicken-flavored dog food taste like chicken-flavored cat food?*

A. To my surprise, chicken cat food was actually a little better—more chickeny. It tasted like inferior canned pâté.

Q. *Was there any dog food that you just couldn't bring yourself to try?*

A. Alas, it was a can of Mighty Dog called Prime Entree with Bone Marrow. The meat was dark, dark brown, and it was surrounded by gelatin that was almost black. I knew I would die if I tasted it, so I put it outside for the raccoons.

XXXXXXXXXXXXXXXXXX **FOR DISCUSSION** XXXXXXXXXXXXXXXXXX

1. Ann Hodgman's discourse on dog food may be a humorous, tongue-in-cheek play on conventional food reviews, but as DESCRIPTIVE writing do you agree that it is truly disgusting? Which do you find more effectively nauseating, her description of the tastes and textures of dry dog food or canned?

2. Most of Hodgman's "research" is done in her own laboratory kitchen. Where else does she go for information? Do you think her studies qualify her to speak expertly on the subject? How about vividly?

3. How do you suppose Hodgman knows what Play-Doh chews like after it's been "sitting out on a rug for a couple of hours"—that is, as opposed to fresh Play-Doh (8)?

4. What childhood fantasy does Hodgman fulfill by writing this essay? How does the reality COMPARE with the fantasy?

5. Do you find Hodgman's title in bad taste? Why or why not? How about her entire essay?

6. What question would you ask Hodgman about her research? For example, *Q: Why are you asking these unsavory questions?* A: Somebody has to honor those who do basic research in a new field.

XXXXXXXXXXXX **STRATEGIES AND STRUCTURES** XXXXXXXXXXXX

1. "When I pulled open the container, juice spurted all over my hand, and the first chunk I speared was trailing a long gray vein" (14). Can you see, smell, and taste it? Cite other examples of Hodgman's DESCRIPTIVE skills and her direct appeal (if that's the right word) to the senses.

2. Notice the major shift that occurs when the description moves from canned dog food to dry. Where does the shift occur? Why does she find the change so "pleasant"? When does she shift again—to snacks?

3. Why do you suppose Hodgman never tells us why she is describing the ingredients, tastes, and textures of dog food with such scrupulous accuracy and OBJECTIVITY? What is her PURPOSE in writing this piece, and how might her scrupulous objectivity be appropriate for that purpose?

4. Why do you think Hodgman shifts to a question-and-answer format at the end of her essay?

5. Hodgman is a professional food critic. What CONCRETE and specific words from her professional vocabulary does she use?

6. What is the DOMINANT IMPRESSION created by Hodgman's description of Bonz in paragraph 22?

7. Hodgman not only describes herself at work in her laboratory kitchen, she ANALYZES THE PROCESS of doing basic food research there. Besides tasting, what are some of the other steps in the process?

XXXXXXXXXXXXX **WORDS AND FIGURES OF SPEECH** XXXXXXXXXXXXX

1. Hodgman refers to "some suddenly fascinating office equipment catalogues" that divert her from tasting Kal Kan's best (14). Is this IRONY?

2. How does your dictionary DEFINE "dried beef digest" (12)? Where else does Hodgman use the technical language of the industry she is SATIRIZING?

3. Hodgman says her Gaines-burger, when fried and flipped into the sink, "began leaking rivulets of red dye" (9). Is this scientific detachment or HYPERBOLE?

4. The opposite of intentional exaggeration is UNDERSTATEMENT. In Hodgman's analysis of the simulated marrow in Bonz, would "problematic" qualify as an example (22)?

5. Hodgman says Kal Kan Pedigree with Chunky Chicken tasted "like meat loaf with ground-up chicken bones" (13). Is this a SIMILE, or do you suppose the chicken could be literally chunky because of the bones?

XXXXXXXXXXXXXXXXXXXXX **FOR WRITING** XXXXXXXXXXXXXXXXXXXXXX

1. While Hodgman gags her way through sample after sample of premium dog food, her dachshund, Shortie, looks on "in agonies of yearning" (2). DESCRIBE the "data" in Hodgman's taste experiment from Shortie's POINT OF VIEW. How might Gaines-burgers and Kal Kan Pedigree with Chunky Chicken taste to him? Is Hodgman right to say that Shortie cannot distinguish among the seven flavors of Milk-Bone Flavor Snacks? What would Shortie's palate tell us?

2. Conduct a program of research similar to Hodgman's but in the field of junk food. Write an unbiased description of your findings. Or, if you prefer, forget the taste tests, and follow Hodgman's lead in analyzing the claims of food advertisers. Choose a category of food products—gummy worms, breath mints, canned soup, frozen pizza, breakfast cereal, cookies—and study the packaging carefully. Write an essay in which you describe how the manufacturers of your samples typically describe their products.

CHAPTER THREE

Narrative

XXXXXXXXXXXXXXXXXXXXXXXXXXXXXXXXXXXXXXXXXXXXXXXXXXXXXXX

NARRATIVE* writing tells a story; it reports "what happened." All of the essays in this chapter are narratives, telling about what happened to one New York writer on September 11, for example, and to one African American man when he refused to give up his seat on a bus in North Carolina in the 1940s. There is a big difference, however, between having something "happen" and writing about it, between an event and telling about an event.

In real life, events often occur randomly or chaotically. But in a narrative, they must be told or shown in some orderly sequence (the PLOT), by a particular person (the NARRATOR), from a particular perspective (the POINT OF VIEW), within a definite time and place (the SETTING). Let's look more closely at each of these elements.

Suppose we wanted to tell a story about a young woman sitting alone eating a snack. Our opening line might go something like this:

Little Miss Muffet sat on a tuffet, eating her curds and whey.

Here we have the bare bones of a narrative because we have someone (Miss Muffet) who is doing something (eating) at a particular time (the past) in a particular place (on a tuffet). The problem with our narrative is that it isn't very interesting. We have a character and a setting, but we don't really have a plot.

A good plot requires more than just sitting and eating. Plot can be achieved by introducing a conflict into the action, bringing the tension to a high point (the CLIMAX), then releasing the tension—in other words, by giving the action of the story a beginning, middle, and end. In our

*Words printed in SMALL CAPITALS are defined in the Glossary.

story about Miss Muffet, we could achieve the necessary conflict in the action by introducing an intruder:

Along came a spider and sat down beside her

You know what's coming next, but I hope you can feel the tension building up and up before we resolve the conflict and release the rising tension in the final line of our story:

And frightened Miss Muffet away.

Well, that's better. We have a sequence of events now. Moreover, those events occur in our narrative in some sort of order—chronologically. But the events also have to be linked together in some meaningful way. In this case, the appearance of the intruder actually *causes* the departure of the heroine. There are many ways to connect the events in a narrative, but CAUSE AND EFFECT is one good approach (see Chapter 9).

We said earlier that a narrative must have a narrator. That narrator may be directly involved in the action of the narrative or may only report it. Do we have one here? Yes, we do; it is the narrator who refers to Miss Muffet as "her." But this narrator is never identified, and he or she plays no part in the action. Let's look at a narrator who does— Stephen King, in a passage from a narrative about an accident that almost killed him some years ago:

> Most of the sight lines along the mile-long stretch of Route 5 that I walk are good, but there is one place, a short steep hill, where a pedestrian heading north can see very little of what might be coming his way. I was three-quarters of the way up this hill when the van came over the crest. It wasn't on the road; it was on the shoulder. My shoulder. I had perhaps three-quarters of a second to register this.
> STEPHEN KING, "On Impact"

Notice that the "I" in this piece is King himself, and he is very much involved in the action of the story he is telling. In fact, he is about to be hit by the van coming over the crest of the hill. That would introduce a conflict into his walk along Route 5, wouldn't it?

By narrating this story from a first-person point of view, King is putting himself in the center of the action. If he had said instead, "The van was closing in on him fast," we would have a third-person narrative, and the narrator would be reporting the action from the sidelines instead of bearing the brunt of it. What makes a chilling story here is that King is not only showing us what happened to him, he is showing us what he was thinking as he suddenly realized that the van was almost on top of him: "It wasn't on the road; it was on the shoulder. My shoulder." We look in as the narrator goes, in a few swift phrases, from startled disbelief to horrified certainty.

Another way in which King creates a compelling story is by using direct speech, or DIALOGUE. When King tells about his first day back at work, he lets his wife speak to us directly: "I can rig a table for you in the back hall, outside the pantry. There are plenty of outlets—you can have your Mac, the little printer, and a fan." Quoting direct speech like this helps readers to imagine the characters as real people.

But why does King end his narrative back at the writing desk? Because he knows that stories serve a larger PURPOSE than just telling what happened. The larger purpose of King's story is to make a point about writing and the writer's life. The van almost killed him, but writing, King demonstrates, helped him to recover and keeps him going.

Well-told stories are almost always told for some reason. The searing tale you heard earlier about Miss Muffet, for example, was told to make a point about narrative structure. A brief, illustrative story like this is called an ANECDOTE. All stories should have a point, but anecdotes in particular are used in all kinds of writing to give examples and to illustrate the greater subject at hand—writing, for instance.

When you use a story to make a point, don't forget to remind the reader exactly what that point is. When Annie Dillard recounts her adventures with spiders and moths in the essay from *Holy the Firm*, she explicitly tells us that she is making a point about the profession of writing and the dedication of the writer. That "one bald statement of motive," as Dillard says, "was unavoidable." Don't keep your reader in the dark. When your purpose is to explain something, don't get so wound up in the web of telling a good story that you forget to say what the moral is.

A Brief Guide to Writing a Narrative

As you write a NARRATIVE, you need to say who or what the narrative is about, where it takes place, and what is happening. Mary Mebane makes these basic moves of narration in the following lines from her essay in this chapter:

> On this Saturday morning Esther and I set out for town for our music lesson. We were going on our weekly big adventure, all the way across town. . . . We walked the two miles from Wildwood to the bus line.
>
> MARY MEBANE, "The Back of the Bus"

Mebane says *who* her story is about ("Esther and I"), *where* it takes place (on the bus line), and *what* is happening as the story opens (the two teenagers are heading for a "big adventure").

The following guidelines will help you to make these basic moves as you draft a narrative—and to come up with a subject for your story, consider your purpose and audience, state your point, and organize the specific details and events of your story into a compelling plot by using chronology, transitions, verb tenses, and dialogue.

Coming up with a Subject

When you enjoy a well-told story, it is often because the author presents an everyday event in an interesting or even dramatic way. To come up with a subject for a story of your own, think of events, both big and small, that you have experienced. You might write a good story about a perfectly ordinary occurrence, such as buying a car, applying for a job, arguing with a friend—or even just doing your homework.

"No, no, no," the writer Frank McCourt, author of *Angela's Ashes*, used to say to his students when they complained that nothing had happened to them when they got home the night before. "What did you do when you walked in?" McCourt would ask. "You went through a door, didn't you? Did you have anything in your hands? A book bag? You didn't carry it with you all night, did you? Did you hang it on a hook? Did you throw it across the room and your mom yelled at you for it?"

Even mundane details like these can provide the material for a good story if you use them to show what people said and did—and exactly where, why, and how they said and did it.

Considering Your Purpose and Audience

As you compose a narrative, think hard about the AUDIENCE you want to reach and the PURPOSE your narrative is intended to serve. Suppose you are emailing a friend about a visit to a computer store in order to convince her to take advantage of the great deals you found there. You might tell your story this way: "When I walked into ComputerDaze, I couldn't believe my eyes. Printers everywhere! And the cheap prices! I went home with a printer under each arm." Or suppose you are writing a column in a computer magazine, and the purpose of your story is to show readers how to shop for a printer. You might write: "The first hurdle I encountered was the numbing variety of brands and models."

Whatever your purpose, think about how much your audience is likely to know about your subject so you can judge how much background information you need to give, what terms you need to DEFINE, and so on. If you are writing an ANECDOTE, make sure it is appropriate for your audience and illustrates your larger point.

Generating Ideas: Asking What Happened—and Who, Where, When, How, and Why

How do you come up with the raw materials for a narrative? To get started, ask yourself the questions that journalists typically ask when developing a story: who, what, where, when, how, and why? Your immediate answers will give you the beginnings of a narrative, but keep asking the questions over and over again. Try to recall lots of particular details, both visual and auditory. As the writer John Steinbeck once advised: "Try to remember [the situation] so clearly that you can see things: what colors and how warm or cold and how you got there . . . what people looked like, how they walked, what they wore, what they ate."

You will also want your readers to know *why* you're telling this particular story, so it's important to select details that support your point. For example, if you're trying to show why your sister is the funniest person in your family, your story might include specific, vivid details about the sound of her voice, her amusing facial expressions, and a practical joke she once pulled.

Templates for Narrating

The following templates can help you to generate ideas for a narrative and then to start drafting. Don't take these as formulas where you just have to fill in the blanks. There are no easy formulas for good writing. But these templates can help you plot out some of the key moves of narration and thus may serve as good starting points:

> ➤ This is a story about _____.
>
> ➤ My story takes place in _____ when _____.
>
> ➤ As the narrative opens, X is the act of _____.
>
> ➤ What happened next was _____, followed by _____ and _____.
>
> ➤ At this point, _____ happened.
>
> ➤ The climax of these events was _____.
>
> ➤ When X understood what had happened, he/she said, "_____."
>
> ➤ The last thing that happened to X was _____.
>
> ➤ My point in telling this story is to show that _____.

For more techniques to help you generate ideas and start writing, see Chapter 1.

Stating Your Point

If you are writing a personal story about your sister, you might reveal your point implicitly through the details of the story. However, in much of the narrative writing you do as a student, you will want to state your point explicitly. If you are writing about information technology for a communications class, for example, you might include the story about going to a computer store, and you would probably want to explain why in a THESIS STATEMENT like this: "Go into any computer store today, and you will discover that information technology is the main product of American business."

Developing a Plot Chronologically

As a general rule, arrange events in chronological order so your readers don't have to figure out what happened when. Chronology alone, however, is insufficient for organizing a good narrative. Events need to be related in such a way that one leads directly to, or causes, another. Taken together, the events should have a beginning, middle, and end. Then your narrative will form a complete action: a PLOT.

One of the best ways to plot a narrative is to set up a situation; introduce a conflict; build up the dramatic tension until it reaches a high point, or CLIMAX; then release the tension and resolve the conflict. Even the little horror story about Miss Muffet is satisfying because it's tightly plotted with a keen sense of completion at the close.

Using Transitions and Verb Tenses

When you write a narrative, you will often incorporate direct references to time: *first, last, immediately, not long after, next, while, then, once upon a time.* References like these can be boring in a narrative if they become too predictable, as in *first, second, third.* But used judiciously, such TRANSITIONS provide smooth links from one event to another, as do other connecting words and phrases like *thus, therefore, consequently, what happened next, before I knew it,* and so on.

In addition to clear transitions, your verb tenses can help you to connect events in time. Remember that all actions that happen more or less at the same time in your narrative should be in the same tense: "I *was* three-quarters of the way up this hill when the van *came* over the crest. It *wasn't* on the road; it *was* on the shoulder." Don't shift tenses needlessly; but when you *do* need to indicate that one action happened before another, be sure to change tenses accordingly—and accurately. If you need to shift out of chronological order altogether—you might shift back in time in a FLASHBACK or shift forward in time in a FLASH-FORWARD—be sure to make the leap clear to your readers.

Maintaining a Consistent Point of View

As you construct a narrative, you need to maintain a logical and consistent POINT OF VIEW. In a narrative written in the first person ("I" or "we"), like Stephen King's, the NARRATOR can be both an observer of the scene ("Most of the sight lines along the mile-long stretch of Route 5 that I walk are good") *and* a participant in the action ("I had perhaps three-quarters of a second to register this"). In a narrative written in the third person ("he," "she," "it," or "they"), as is the case in most articles and history books, the narrator is often merely an observer, though sometimes an all-knowing one.

Whether you write in the first or third person, don't attribute perceptions to yourself or your narrator that are physically impossible. If you are narrating a story from the front seat of your car, don't pretend to see what is going on three blocks away. If you do claim to see (or know) more than you reasonably can from where you sit, your credibility with the reader will soon be strained.

Adding Dialogue

You can introduce the points of view of other people into a story by using DIALOGUE. In a story about her childhood, for example, Annie Dillard lets her mother speak for herself: "Lie on your back," her mother tells young Dillard. "Look at the clouds and figure out what they look like."

As a first-person narrator, Dillard might have written, "My mother told me to look at the clouds and figure out what they look like." But these words would be a step removed from the person who said them and so would lack the immediacy of direct dialogue. If you let people in your narrative speak for themselves, your characters will come to life, and your whole narrative will have a greater dramatic impact.

When you write a narrative, you need to give your story a beginning, middle, and end—otherwise, it will have no plot. The narrative illustrated on this cover of the New Yorker magazine actually began when recently elected president Obama promised his daughters a new puppy as a reward for their patience during the 2008 campaign. Here we see the magazine's humorous rendering of the middle action of the story, as candidates for the position of first dog line up to be interviewed. How will the tale end? If you were writing a narrative about the hunt for a presidential dog, you would need to tell readers how the Obamas, a few months after the *New Yorker* "interviews," finally chose a six-month-old Portuguese water dog named Bo, a gift of Senator Edward M. Kennedy and his wife, Victoria.

THOMAS BELLER

THE ASHEN GUY: LOWER BROADWAY, SEPTEMBER 11, 2001

Thomas Beller is the author of a collection of short stories, *Seduction Theory* (1995); a novel, *The Sleep-Over Artist* (2000); and the essay collection *How to Be a Man: Scenes from a Protracted Boyhood* (2005). He is also the Web master of mrbellersneighborhood.com, a website where New Yorkers can publish "true stories" of life in the big city. Following the events of September 11, 2001, Beller collected many of those personal narratives in a book, *Before & After: Stories from New York* (2002). "The Ashen Guy," written by Beller himself, is an "after" story; it takes place just after the first World Trade Center tower falls down but while the second one is still standing.

XXXXXXXXXXXXXXXXXXXXXXXXXXXXXXXXXXXXXXXXXXXXXXXXXXXXXXXXXXX

A t Broadway and Union Square a woman moved with the crowd talking on her cell phone. "It's a good thing," she began. I biked south. At Tenth Street the bells of Grace Church pealed ten times. Everyone was moving in the same direction, orderly, but with an element of panic and, beneath that, a nervous energy. Their clothes were crisp and unrumpled, their hair freshly combed. Below Houston Street, a fleet of black shiny SUVs with sirens sped south, toward the smoky horizon somewhere south of Canal Street. A messenger biked beside me. I almost asked him if he was making a delivery.

At Thomas Street, about six blocks north of the World Trade Center, the nature of the crowd on the street changed. There was more urgency and less mirth. Cop cars parked at odd angles, their red sirens spinning. The policemen were waving their arms, shouting, and amidst the crowd was a guy who had been on the eighty-first floor of Two World Trade Center when the plane hit. It was just after 10 A.M. Two

World Trade had just collapsed, and One World Trade stood smoldering behind him.

3   At first glance he looked like a snowman, except instead of snow he was covered in gray, asbestos-colored ash. He was moving along with the crowd, streaming north, up Broadway. His head and neck and shoulders and about halfway down his chest were covered in gray ash. You could make out a pair of bloodshot eyes, and he was running his hand over his head. A small plume of dust drifted off the top of his head as he walked, echoing the larger plume of smoke drifting off of One World Trade behind him.

4   "There were about 230 people on the eighty-first floor and I was one of the last ones out. We took the stairs. There was smoke, but it wasn't fire smoke, it was dry wall smoke and dust. The fire was above us."

5   He was shaking. His eyes were red from dust and maybe tears. He didn't seem like the sort of man who cried. He had fair skin and a sandy-colored crew cut. He was wearing chinos and Docksiders and his shirt was a checked button-down.

6   He was walking with the crowd, but his body language was a little different. Everyone, even those who weren't looking back, had about them a certain nervous desire to look behind them, to see, to communicate to their neighbor, but this guy had no interest in anything but in getting away from where he had just been. It radiated from every muscle in his body. To get away.

7   "I was almost out. I got down to the lobby, right near the Borders book store. And then there was this explosion. I don't know, I just got thrown to the ground and all this stuff fell on top of me."

8   By now he had dusted his head off and you could see his skin. It was pale and ashen, one of his eyes was very red. At first I thought maybe it was the dust and perhaps tears that had made his eyes bloodshot; looking closer I saw that one eye was badly inflamed.

9   He was joined by another man, a blue oxford shirt with a tie, midforties, lawyerly, who worked in the building across the street.

10   "I watched the whole thing. I saw the second plane hit, the explosion. No one told us to evacuate, and then the building just collapsed and I thought I better get out of here because my building could go too."

On Franklin Street the police were screaming: "There's a package!   11
There's a package! Keep moving!"

They were herding everyone to the left, towards West Broadway.   12
"People! Trust me! Let's go! People let's go! There's an unidentified
package across the street!"

The view on West Broadway and Franklin was very good. One   13
tower, gray sky billowing, the sky darkening.

"Do you know which way the tower fell?" a woman asked. A tall   14
man stood behind her, scruffy beard and longish hair, his hand on her
shoulder.

"It fell straight down!" someone said.   15

"Because we live one block away and . . . does anyone know which   16
way the building fell?"

The man behind her, her husband, I assumed, had this very sad   17
look on his face, as though he understood something she didn't. It was
as if that consoling hand on her shoulder was there to make sure she
didn't try and make a run for it.

"I don't know what happened," said the ashen guy. "I just hit the   18
ground, don't know if something hit me or . . . "

"It was the force of the building collapsing," said the lawyer.   19

"I got up and just started walking," said the ashen guy.   20

There was a huge rumbling sound accompanied by the sound of   21
people shrieking. Everyone who wasn't already looking turned to see the
remaining building start to crumble in on itself, a huge ball of smoke
rising out from beneath it, a mushroom cloud in reverse. The whole
street paused, froze, screamed, some people broke into tears, many people brought their hands up to their mouths, everyone was momentarily
frozen, except for the ashen guy, who just kept walking.

ⅩⅩⅩⅩⅩⅩⅩⅩⅩⅩⅩⅩⅩⅩⅩⅩ **FOR DISCUSSION** ⅩⅩⅩⅩⅩⅩⅩⅩⅩⅩⅩⅩⅩⅩⅩⅩ

1. Who is telling this story? How does he identify himself in his NARRATIVE?
How is he getting around?

2. Why does the NARRATOR single out the ashen guy from the rest of the crowd?
Where was the ashen guy when the first plane hit? When did he get covered
with ash?

3. The ashen guy is walking along with the crowd, "but his body language," says the narrator, "was a little different" from everyone else's (6). How and where does the narrator DESCRIBE the ashen guy's body? What does it "say"?

4. The identity of the ashen guy is never specified. Who might he be? What might he stand for?

5. The people in Thomas Beller's narrative walk as if they were in a dream. How appropriate do you find this dreamlike account of the events of September 11, 2001?

XXXXXXXXXXXXX **STRATEGIES AND STRUCTURES** XXXXXXXXXXXXX

1. This is a NARRATIVE about mass movement. In which direction is the NARRATOR himself moving at first? When and where does he come closest to ground zero before moving back with the crowd? What role do the police play to move the narrative along?

2. When does the ashen guy first appear? How does the narrator create the impression in paragraph 8 that he is getting closer to this mysterious man who is the focal point of his narrative? In which paragraphs, before and after this close-up, does the narrator give a long perspective to the scene by looking back toward ground zero?

3. DIALOGUE is one of the most dramatic or playlike elements of narrative, introducing multiple POINTS OF VIEW, thus enabling the narrator to show us what other characters are thinking instead of just telling us about their thoughts. How many different speakers does Beller identify? What does each contribute to this narrative?

4. Dialogue also enables the narrator to convey new information to the reader. What crucial details does the ashen guy give us through what he says?

5. Why do you think Beller ends this tale of near mass hysteria with the fall of the second tower? What is the significance of his ending with the ashen guy "who just kept walking" (21)?

6. Beller's narrator seldom refers directly to himself. Why might Beller want his narrator to recede into the background? What's the focus of his story?

7. "At first glance he looked like a snowman, except instead of snow he was covered in gray, asbestos-colored ash" (3). Is this DESCRIPTION or NARRATION? Find some other passages in Beller's narrative where these two MODES OF WRITING shade into one another.

XXXXXXXXXXXX **Words and Figures of Speech** XXXXXXXXXXX

1. What are the implications of Beller's use of the word "ashen" in the story of a national nightmare?

2. Why do you suppose Beller calls the person at the center of his NARRATIVE a "guy," rather than a man or a gentleman or a citizen?

3. "A small plume of dust drifted off the top of his head as he walked, echoing the larger plume of smoke drifting off of One World Trade behind him" (3). What do you think of Beller's use of the word "echoing" in this sentence? What are the CONNOTATIONS of "plume"?

4. What are some other examples of Beller's figurative linking of "the ashen guy" with the tower? At the end of the narrative, the second World Trade Center tower falls. What happens to the ashen guy?

XXXXXXXXXXXXXXXXXXX **For Writing** XXXXXXXXXXXXXXXXXXXXXXX

1. In the days and months following the attacks on the World Trade Center, stories of survivors and eyewitnesses abounded. Of all the stories you heard, which one affected you most? In a brief NARRATIVE, tell what that survivor or witness did or saw on that fateful day.

2. People often recall their whereabouts at the time of significant events in a nation's history—such as where they were on September 11, 2001. Choose a significant event in recent history and write a narrative in which you recount where you were and tell what you and others did and felt. Try to remember the gist of what was said, and quote it directly as DIALOGUE in your NARRATIVE.

HEIDI JULAVITS

TURNING JAPANESE

Heidi Julavits (b. 1968) is a novelist, freelance journalist, and founding editor of *The Believer*, a monthly magazine about books and culture. Her novels include *The Mineral Palace* (2000) and *The Uses of Enchantment* (2006). Julavits graduated from Dartmouth College in 1990, a time of global recession and imminent war in the Persian Gulf. With an unsure future and little in the way of marketable skills, Julavits decided to live in Japan and "reach a higher plane of existence while eating amazing food." First published in the *New York Times Magazine* in 2006, "Turning Japanese" tells the story of Julavits's "post-college limbo" and the understanding of Zen Buddhism she gained by eating a bean cake dessert.

XXXXXXXXXXXXXXXXXXXXXXXXXXXXXXXXXXXXXXXXXXXXXXXXXXXXXXXXXXXXXX

1   I graduated from college in 1990, an uncertain time indeed. Recession. Gulf war imminent. In keeping with the shaky global mood, I haven't a clue what to do with my life. So I decide to move to Japan to teach the only thing I can confidently claim to know after four years of college: English. In America, I reason, the only thing more shameful than not knowing what you want is knowing, with absolute certainty, that stuffed animals turn you on. In Japan I'll be immersed in a culture that nurtures uncertainty as a form of enlightenment.[1] I remind myself of the Zen-like quotation: "Emotional freedom comes with being aware of the certainty of uncertainty." I will go to Japan, I will be certainly uncertain and I will reach a higher plane of existence while eating amazing food.

2   I find a sublet in a functional-blah apartment building off Shijo Street in Kyoto, and two things happen: I remain unenlightened by my

---

1. From Zen Buddhism, an influential belief system in Japan, the idea that self-awareness of any sort is a fundamental goal.

uncertainty, and I eat amazing food. A typical on-the-cheap lunch bowl, offered in local spots displaying dusty plastic food in the window, is katsu-don, a fried pork cutlet with scrambled eggs, served with rice and a sweet donburi sauce; or tekka-don, strips of raw tuna and pressed dried seaweed over rice. A Japanese family invites me to dinner each week for shabu shabu: a pot of water and enoki mushrooms, set on an electric tabletop coil, in which we poach very thin slices of beef or hacked-up Alaskan king crab; after the meat is finished, we dump our rice into the broth and slurp the resulting porridgy soup.

As the months pass, I remain miserably uncertain about all things but one: I would kill for a trashy American sweet. I do not miss cheese or pasta or even my friends, but I do miss, with a maddening intensity, that blast of sugar that only a glazed cruller can provide. Plenty of Japanese bakeries offer deceptively Western-looking cakes and cookies, which reveal themselves to be gaggingly dry and possessing a slight aftertaste of fish, as if whatever fat the baker used came not from a cow or a pig but from a hake. I patronize a previously disdained restaurant called Spaghetti and Cake (Kyoto has a number of these "Western" establishments; another is Coffee and Golf) and am disappointed—huge shock. The best of the lousy bunch is ring cake, a rolled-up yellow sponge cut into slices. But one day while working as a movie extra in a period film (1850s Yokohama[2] being the period), I am forced to wear a bonnet and eat slice after slice of ring cake because the lead, a Japanese pop star, can't remember her three short lines. I come to hate ring cake. When another American tells me about a Western breakfast restaurant, I bike ten miles through a downpour and order French toast as an excuse to deluge my plate with dyed-brown corn syrup, which I eat until I am headachingly ill.

I orchestrate my own intervention. I remind myself that everybody knows that ersatz American food, or ersatz any food, is a doomed proposition. You must play to a culture's strengths and not order a

---

2. Japanese town that developed as a major shipping port after the arrival of Westerners in the mid-nineteenth century.

cataplana[3] of paella when in Green Bay, Wisconsin. Yet my first encounters with the native sweets are alienating. Gummy lime green bean blobs dusted in a flavorless white flour, for example, are not only not sweet, but they also do not appeal to any of my tongue's five regions and are all the more disappointing for appearing so pretty.

5   One dusky evening I am biking through Gion, Kyoto's geisha district,[4] examining the window displays with their meticulously wrapped I-don't-know-what. (Jewelry? Art supplies? Stew meat?) One helpfully exhibits what's concealed beneath the wrapping: a bloated Fig Newton look-alike bisected to reveal a dense and grainy maroon center. I buy what I learn, decades later, is called manju. The filling is a paste made from red azuki beans and sugar. I call it a bean cake. I bike to Gion every day and buy two.

6   And so it is that I come to grapple with that oldest of Zen mysteries: the bean-cake conundrum. Of course I've been paddling around this riddle for months, but it's not until I encounter the bean cake that it assumes its most potent form. While eating a bean cake, I reach a moment when I don't need, or want, another bite. I experience what I believe is contentment (rather than "no thought," think "no appetite"), and despite what my layman's notion of Zen Buddhist nongoal goals leads me to expect, it is no blissfest. My American relationship to sugar is always to want more of it; to encounter a sweet that doesn't court abuse in order to be enjoyed destabilizes my entire concept of craving-cruller-gluttony-happiness. I feel these moments of so-called contentment when I have no pointed desires—not a petit four to follow the chocolates to follow the tarte Tatin, not even a salt-funky cheese course as counterbalance—to be physically unbearable and thus, by quick extrapolation, existentially crippling. Does this mean that contentment is anathema to my person? That contentment is a punishing mind-bender (to be content is to be less content than when you weren't content)? That this period of post-college limbo has been encapsulated, in all its dumb, stereotypical hand-wringing, by a bean cake?

3. Cooking dish used for preparing a Portuguese seafood specialty.

4. An area with many establishments featuring elaborately dressed women who are trained in traditional arts such as dance and music and who entertain male clientele.

Two months later I am spiritually annihilated by contentment. I   7
haven't had a craving in months, and I'm so worried that I won't desire
anything ever again that I forget to worry about my uncertain future. I
pack my things, and within twenty-four hours I am on a dawn bus to
Phuket, Thailand. Suddenly I am seized by a familiar sense of specific
urgency, a hunger disconnected from appetite: I want tekka-don for breakfast. I am on a bus in the south of Thailand, and I want—no, must have—
a bowl of Japanese rice and raw tuna. While I'm beside myself with relief,
I'm simultaneously aware of the bear hug of my iffy future (no job, no
place to live, running out of money) tightening around my chest again with
an intensity I interpret as affection. My uncertain future missed me, too. I
get off the bus at the beach and stare at the aptly blank horizon. I am broke
and aimless, I am racked by doubt and worry, I crave a food that's three
thousand miles away and I've never experienced such bliss in my life.

✕✕✕✕✕✕✕✕✕✕✕✕✕✕✕✕ FOR DISCUSSION ✕✕✕✕✕✕✕✕✕✕✕✕✕✕✕✕

1. When Heidi Julavits graduated from college, she was "confident" of her
knowledge of only one subject (1). Which one? Does her essay show that her
confidence is justified?

2. Besides having a job there, why did Julavits go to Japan? Explain.

3. What did Julavits miss most about life back in America? How and how successfully did she attempt to make up for that loss?

4. How and when did Julavits realize that she had "turned Japanese"?

5. Why is Julavits so full of "bliss" at the end of her NARRATIVE (7)? Explain.

✕✕✕✕✕✕✕✕✕✕✕✕✕ STRATEGIES AND STRUCTURES ✕✕✕✕✕✕✕✕✕✕✕✕✕

1. Almost all the events in Julavits's NARRATIVE pertain to food. How well do these
adventures in eating support the Zen-like point that Julavits is making, namely that
"emotional freedom comes with being aware of the certainty of uncertainty" (1)?

2. Even though the events of Julavits's narrative took place in the past, many of
her verbs are in the present tense. Point out several examples, and explain how
and what they contribute to her narrative.

3. Should Julavits have said more about the other things (besides eating) that
she did in Japan, such as her teaching or her work "as a movie extra" (3)? Why
or why not?

4. In the last paragraph of her narrative, Julavits travels from Japan to Thailand. Instead of bandits or pirates, she is suddenly "seized" by a hunger for "a bowl of Japanese rice and raw tuna" (7). How does this event serve as a CLIMAX to the main PLOT of Julavits's narrative? Explain.

5. How and how well does Julavits's narrative also serve as a DESCRIPTION of "post-college limbo" (6)?

XXXXXXXXXXXXX **WORDS AND FIGURES OF SPEECH** XXXXXXXXXXXXX

1. In Japan, Julavits knows that she will be "certainly uncertain" (1). Explain the implications of this OXYMORON for her NARRATIVE as a whole.

2. In Kyoto, Julavits finds an apartment in a "functional-blah" building (2). What does she mean by "functional-blah"? Point out other places in her narrative where she invents hyphenated words to convey concepts. How effective do you find this device? Explain.

3. Why would the Japanese name a restaurant "Spaghetti and Cake" or "Coffee and Golf" (3)? How apt do you find such names for supposedly "Western" establishments (3)?

4. At one point in her narrative, Julavits decides to "orchestrate my own intervention" (4). Why does she use such ABSTRACT language to say that she is trying the local desserts?

5. In Catholic and other western theologies, "limbo" is a border state where some souls remain until they can enter heaven. How is Julavits DEFINING the term, and why does she use it here (6)?

6. A "conundrum" is a difficult and fascinating problem (6). How and why does eating bean cake pose such a problem for Julavits?

XXXXXXXXXXXXXXXXXXX **FOR WRITING** XXXXXXXXXXXXXXXXXXXXX

1. Write a paragraph about the first time you tried a food from another country or culture. Explain what insights—if any—you gained about that culture through its food.

2. Write a NARRATIVE about a time when you became so wrapped up in the affairs and adventures of the moment that you forgot to worry about the uncertainties of the future.

RICHARD RODRIGUEZ

None of This Is Fair

Richard Rodriguez (b. 1944) is an editor for Pacific News Service in his native San Francisco and a contributing editor for *Harper's, U.S. News & World Report*, and the *Los Angeles Times*. He is the author of *Hunger of Memory: The Education of Richard Rodriguez* (1982), from which this personal narrative is adapted; *Days of Obligation* (1992); and *Brown: The Last Discovery of America* (2002), a reflection on race in American life. Although Rodriguez holds a Ph.D. in English from Berkeley, he has never been an academic. In "None of This Is Fair" he touches on his reasons for becoming a writer and journalist instead of a university professor.

✕✕✕

My plan to become a professor of English—my ambition during long years in college at Stanford, then in graduate school at Columbia and Berkeley—was complicated by feelings of embarrassment and guilt. So many times I would see other Mexican-Americans and know we were alike only in race. And yet, simply because our race was the same, I was, during the last years of my schooling, the beneficiary of their situation. Affirmative Action programs[1] had made it all possible. The disadvantages of others permitted my promotion; the absence of many Mexican-Americans from academic life allowed my designation as a "minority student."

For me opportunities had been extravagant. There were fellowships, summer research grants, and teaching assistantships. After only two years in graduate school, I was offered teaching jobs by several col-

---

1. Programs initiated in the 1960s by government entities, schools, employers, and others to provide greater opportunities for minorities.

leges. Invitations to Washington conferences arrived and I had the chance to travel abroad as a "Mexican-American representative." The benefits were often, however, too gaudy to please. In three published essays, in conversations with teachers, in letters to politicians and at conferences, I worried the issue of Affirmative Action. Often I proposed contradictory opinions. Though consistent was the admission that—because of an early, excellent education—I was no longer a principal victim of racism or any other social oppression. I said that but still I continued to indicate on applications for financial aid that I was a Hispanic-American. It didn't really occur to me to say anything else, or to leave the question unanswered.

3   Thus I complied with and encouraged the odd bureaucratic logic of Affirmative Action. I let government officials treat the disadvantaged condition of many Mexican-Americans with my advancement. Each fall my presence was noted by Health, Education, and Welfare department statisticians. As I pursued advanced literary studies and learned the skill of reading Spenser and Wordsworth and Empson,[2] I would hear myself numbered among the culturally disadvantaged. Still, silent, I didn't object.

4   But the irony cut deep. And guilt would not be evaded by averting my glance when I confronted a face like my own in a crowd. By late 1975, nearing the completion of my graduate studies at Berkeley, I was so wary of the benefits of Affirmative Action that I feared my inevitable success as an applicant for a teaching position. The months of fall—traditionally that time of academic job-searching—passed without my applying to a single school. When one of my professors chanced to learn this in late November, he was astonished, then furious. He yelled at me: Did I think that because I was a minority student jobs would just come looking for me? What was I thinking? Did I realize that he and several other faculty members had already written letters on my behalf? Was I going to start acting like some other minority students he had known? They struggled for success and then, when it was almost within reach, grew strangely afraid and let it pass. Was that it? Was I determined to fail?

2. William Empson (1906–1984), British literary critic; Edmund Spenser (1522–1599), British poet; William Wordsworth (1770–1850), British poet.

I did not respond to his questions. I didn't want to admit to him, 5
and thus to myself, the reason I delayed.

I merely agreed to write to several schools. (In my letter I wrote: "I 6
cannot claim to represent disadvantaged Mexican-Americans. The very
fact that I am in a position to apply for this job should make that
clear.") After two or three days, there were telegrams and phone calls,
invitations to interviews, then airplane trips. A blur of faces and the
murmur of their soft questions. And, over someone's shoulder, the sight
of campus buildings shadowing pictures I had seen years before when I
leafed through Ivy League catalogues with great expectations. At the
end of each visit, interviewers would smile and wonder if I had any
questions. A few times I quietly wondered what advantage my race had
given me over other applicants. But that was an impossible question for
them to answer without embarrassing me. Quickly, several persons
insisted that my ethnic identity had given me no more than a "foot
inside the door"; at most, I had a "slight edge" over other applicants.
"We just looked at your dossier with extra care and we like what we saw.
There was never any question of having to alter our standards. You can
be certain of that."

In the early part of January, offers arrived on stiffly elegant sta- 7
tionery. Most schools promised terms appropriate for any new assistant
professor. A few made matters worse—and almost more tempting—by
offering more: the use of university housing; an unusually large starting
salary; a reduced teaching schedule. As the stack of letters mounted, my
hesitation increased. I started calling department chairmen to ask for
another week, then 10 more days—"more time to reach a decision"—to
avoid the decision I would need to make.

At school, meantime, some students hadn't received a single job 8
offer. One man, probably the best student in the department, did not
even get a request for his dossier. He and I met outside a classroom one
day and he asked about my opportunities. He seemed happy for me.
Faculty members beamed. They said they had expected it. "After all, not
many schools are going to pass up getting a Chicano with a Ph.D. in
Renaissance literature," somebody said laughing. Friends wanted to
know which of the offers I was going to accept. But I couldn't make up
my mind. February came and I was running out of time and excuses.

(One chairman guessed my delay was a bargaining ploy and increased his offer with each of my calls.) I had to promise a decision by the 10th; the 12th at the very latest.

9   On the 18th of February, late in the afternoon, I was in the office I shared with several other teaching assistants. Another graduate student was sitting across the room at his desk. When I got up to leave, he looked over to say in an uneventful voice that he had some big news. He had finally decided to accept a position at a faraway university. It was not a job he especially wanted, he admitted. But he had to take it because there hadn't been any other offers. He felt trapped, and depressed, since his job would separate him from his young daughter.

10   I tried to encourage him by remarking that he was lucky at least to have found a job. So many others hadn't been able to get anything. But before I finished speaking I realized that I had said the wrong thing. And I anticipated his next question.

11   "What are your plans?" he wanted to know. "Is it true you've gotten an offer from Yale?"

12   I said that it was. "Only, I still haven't made up my mind."

13   He stared at me as I put on my jacket. And smiling, then unsmiling, he asked if I knew that he too had written to Yale. In his case, however, no one had bothered to acknowledge his letter with even a postcard. What did I think of that?

14   He gave me no time to answer.

15   "Damn!" he said sharply and his chair rasped the floor as he pushed himself back. Suddenly, it was to *me* that he was complaining. "It's just not right, Richard. None of this is fair. You've done some good work, but so have I. I'll bet our records are just about equal. But when we look for jobs this year, it's a different story. You get all of the breaks."

16   To evade his criticism, I wanted to side with him. I was about to admit the injustice of Affirmative Action. But he went on, his voice hard with accusation. "It's all very simple this year. You're a Chicano. And I am a Jew. That's the only real difference between us."

17   His words stung me: there was nothing he was telling me that I didn't know. I had admitted everything already. But to hear someone else say these things, and in such an accusing tone, was suddenly hard to take. In a deceptively calm voice, I responded that he had simplified the

whole issue. The phrases came like bubbles to the tip of my tongue: "new blood"; "the importance of cultural diversity"; "the goal of racial integration." These were all the arguments I had proposed several years ago—and had long since abandoned. Of course the offers were unjustifiable. I knew that. All I was saying amounted to a frantic self-defense. I tried to find an end to a sentence. My voice faltered to a stop.

"Yeah, sure," he said. "I've heard all that before. Nothing you say really changes the fact that Affirmative Action is unfair. You see that, don't you? There isn't any way for me to compete with you. Once there were quotas to keep my parents out of certain schools; now there are quotas to get you in and the effect on me is the same as it was for them." 18

I listened to every word he spoke. But my mind was really on something else. I knew at that moment that I would reject all of the offers. I stood there silently surprised by what an easy conclusion it was. Having prepared for so many years to teach, having trained myself to do nothing else, I had hesitated out of practical fear. But now that it was made, the decision came with relief. I immediately knew I had made the right choice. 19

My colleague continued talking and I realized that he was simply right. Affirmative Action programs *are* unfair to white students. But as I listened to him assert his rights, I thought of the seriously disadvantaged. How different they were from white, middle-class students who come armed with the testimony of their grades and aptitude scores and self-confidence to complain about the unequal treatment they now receive. I listen to them. I do not want to be careless about what they say. Their rights are important to protect. But inevitably when I hear them or their lawyers, I think about the most seriously disadvantaged, not simply Mexican-Americans, but of all those who do not ever imagine themselves going to college or becoming doctors: white, black, brown. Always poor. Silent. They are not plaintiffs before the court or against the misdirection of Affirmative Action. They lack the confidence (my confidence!) to assume their right to a good education. They lack the confidence and skills a good primary and secondary education provides and which are prerequisites for informed public life. They remain silent. 20

21   The debate drones on and surrounds them in stillness. They are distant, faraway figures like the boys I have seen peering down from freeway overpasses in some other part of town.

XXXXXXXXXXXXXXXXXXX **For Discussion** XXXXXXXXXXXXXXXXXXX

1. His ambition to become a university professor, says Richard Rodriguez in this NARRATIVE of his graduate school days, "was complicated by feelings of embarrassment and guilt" (1). What did he feel guilty about? Why, after all that schooling and other training, do you suppose he decided not to take a job in a university?

2. Rodriguez's story leads up to an ARGUMENT between himself and another graduate student. What position does his opponent take on the issue of Affirmative Action? How convincing do you find the opponent's reasoning?

3. What does Rodriguez say he is thinking during this debate? How does he respond to his opponent's argument?

4. Rodriguez ends with a reference to the boys he has seen "peering down from freeway overpasses" (21). Who are these boys? Why do they come to his mind?

5. Do you think someone in Rodriguez's position should have allowed himself to be "guilted" into changing his plans for his life? Why or why not?

6. "Affirmative Action programs *are* unfair to white students" (20), says Rodriguez. Do you agree or disagree? What else is "unfair," in his opinion?

XXXXXXXXXXXXX **Strategies and Structures** XXXXXXXXXXXXX

1. How does Rodriguez's NARRATIVE of his search for an academic job use the calendar to build suspense? Where does he resolve that suspense?

2. We might say that the PLOT of this story is about an internal struggle that Rodriguez is trying to resolve. How do his interactions with his professors and potential employers help to advance this plot?

3. A key moment in this narrative is when the two fellow graduate students argue. How does Rodriguez show that his own mind is divided and that he struggles with a debate within himself?

4. In the snippets of DIALOGUE that punctuate Rodriguez's text, various articulate speakers give good reasons both for and against Affirmative Action. What do we hear from the "seriously disadvantaged" (20) in this debate? Why?

5. Rodriguez never explicitly tells us why he decides to give up on becoming a university professor, instead leaving us to DEDUCE the reasons. Why doesn't he just tell us outright? Does choosing to show rather than tell us make his narrative more or less dramatic? Why?

6. How, in the last two paragraphs, does Rodriguez keep his narrative from turning into a speech about the inequities and moral ambiguities of Affirmative Action?

7. What ARGUMENT about Affirmative Action is Rodriguez making in the last two paragraphs? Is this the main point of his narrative? If not, what is?

XXXXXXXXXXXX **WORDS AND FIGURES OF SPEECH** XXXXXXXXXXXX

1. What does the pronoun "this" refer to in Rodriguez's title?

2. Rodriguez speaks of the "logic" of Affirmative Action as both "bureaucratic" and "odd" (3). Why do you think he pairs these two adjectives?

3. What are the CONNOTATIONS of the word "drones" (21)? For whom, according to Rodriguez, are the niceties of academic debate over Affirmative Action a droning, essentially meaningless sound?

4. To whom is Rodriguez COMPARING the boys in his last paragraph? What does this SIMILE tell us about those people?

XXXXXXXXXXXXXXXXXXXX **FOR WRITING** XXXXXXXXXXXXXXXXXXXX

1. Have you or anyone you know ever experienced racial, gender, ethnic, or other forms of profiling—whether "affirmative" or negative? If so, write a brief NARRATIVE about that experience.

2. Write a personal narrative about your internal struggle to make some important decision in your life. Lead up to and then focus sharply on the moment of clarity when your mind was made up and you suddenly knew what you were going to do or say or be.

YIYUN LI

ORANGE CRUSH

Yiyun Li (b. 1972) is a Chinese American writer who grew up in Beijing, China. In 1996, after attending Peking University, Li moved to the United States to study medicine at the University of Iowa, earning master's degrees in both immunology and the writing of creative nonfiction. Li's first collection of short stories, *A Thousand Years of Good Prayers* (2005), won numerous literary awards, and in 2009 she published her first novel, *The Vagrants*. "Orange Crush" first appeared in the food and culture section of the *New York Times Magazine* in 2006. It tells the story of Li's encounter, as a teenager in China, with a new space-age drink imported from America—Tang.

XXXXXXXXXXXXXXXXXXXXXXXXXXXXXXXXXXXXXXXXXXXXXXXXXXXXXXXXX

1   During the winter in Beijing, where I grew up, we always had orange and tangerine peels drying on our heater. Oranges were not cheap. My father, who believed that thrift was one of the best virtues, saved the dried peels in a jar; when we had a cough or cold, he would boil them until the water took on a bitter taste and a pale yellow cast, like the color of water drizzling out of a rusty faucet. It was the best cure for colds, he insisted.

2   I did not know then that I would do the same for my own children, preferring nature's provision over those orange- and pink- and purple-colored medicines. I just felt ashamed, especially when he packed it in my lunch for the annual field trip, where other children brought colorful flavored fruit drinks—made with "chemicals," my father insisted.

3   The year I turned sixteen, a new product caught my eye. Fruit Treasure, as Tang[1] was named for the Chinese market, instantly won

---

1. An orange-flavored powdered drink mix first marketed in the United States in 1959.

everyone's heart. Imagine real oranges condensed into a fine powder! Equally seductive was the TV commercial, which gave us a glimpse of a life that most families, including mine, could hardly afford. The kitchen was spacious and brightly lighted, whereas ours was a small cube—but at least we had one; half the people we knew cooked in the hallways of their apartment buildings, where every family's dinner was on display and their financial states assessed by the number of meals with meat they ate every week. The family on TV was beautiful, all three of them with healthy complexions and toothy, carefree smiles (the young parents I saw on my bus ride to school were those who had to leave at six or even earlier in the morning for the two-hour commute and who had to carry their children, half-asleep and often screaming, with them because the only child care they could afford was that provided by their employers).

The drink itself, steaming hot in an expensive-looking mug that   4
was held between the child's mittened hands, was a vivid orange. The mother talked to the audience as if she were our best friend: "During the cold winter, we need to pay more attention to the health of our family," she said. "That's why I give my husband and my child hot Fruit Treasure for extra warmth and vitamins." The drink's temperature was the only Chinese aspect of the commercial; iced drinks were considered unhealthful and believed to induce stomach disease.

As if the images were not persuasive enough, near the end of the   5
ad an authoritative voice informed us that Tang was the only fruit drink used by NASA for its astronauts—the exact information my father needed to prove his theory that all orange-flavored drinks other than our orange peel water were made of suspicious chemicals.

Until this point, all commercials were short and boring, with   6
catchy phrases like "Our Product Is Loved by People Around the World" flashing on screen. The Tang ad was a revolution in itself: the lifestyle it represented—a more healthful and richer one, a Western luxury—was just starting to become legitimate in China as it was beginning to embrace the West and its capitalism.

Even though Tang was the most expensive fruit drink available, its   7
sales soared. A simple bottle cost seventeen yuan, a month's worth of lunch money. A boxed set of two became a status hostess gift. Even the

sturdy glass containers that the powder came in were coveted. People used them as tea mugs, the orange label still on, a sign that you could afford the modern American drink. Even my mother had an empty Tang bottle with a snug orange nylon net over it, a present from one of her fellow schoolteachers. She carried it from the office to the classroom and back again as if our family had also consumed a full bottle.

8   The truth was, our family had never tasted Tang. Just think of how many oranges we could buy with the money spent on a bottle, my father reasoned. His resistance sent me into a long adolescent melancholy. I was ashamed by our lack of style and our life, with its taste of orange peel water. I could not wait until I grew up and could have my own Tang-filled life.

9   To add to my agony, our neighbor's son brought over his first girl-friend, for whom he had just bought a bottle of Tang. He was five years older and a college sophomore; we had nothing in common and had not spoken more than ten sentences. But this didn't stop me from having a painful crush on him. The beautiful girlfriend opened the Tang in our flat and insisted that we all try it. When it was my turn to scoop some into a glass of water, the fine orange powder almost choked me to tears. It was the first time I had drunk Tang, and the taste was not like real oranges but stronger, as if it were made of the essence of all the oranges I had ever eaten. This would be the love I would seek, a boy unlike my father, a boy who would not blink to buy a bottle of Tang for me. I looked at the beautiful girlfriend and wished to replace her.

10   My agony and jealousy did not last long, however. Two months later the beautiful girlfriend left the boy for an older and richer man. Soon after, the boy's mother came to visit and was still outraged about the Tang. "What a waste of money on someone who didn't become his wife!" she said.

11   "That's how it goes with young people," my mother said. "Once he has a wife, he'll have a better brain and won't throw his money away."

12   "True. He's just like his father. When he courted me, he once invited me to an expensive restaurant and ordered two fish for me. After we were married, he wouldn't even allow two fish for the whole family for one meal!"

That was the end of my desire for a Tangy life. I realized that every dream ended with this bland, ordinary existence, where a prince would one day become a man who boiled orange peels for his family. I had not thought about the boy much until I moved to America ten years later and discovered Tang in a grocery store. It was just how I remembered it—fine powder in a sturdy bottle—but its glamour had lost its gloss because, alas, it was neither expensive nor trendy. To think that all the derams of my youth were once contained in this commercial drink! I picked up a bottle and then returned it to the shelf.

13

XXXXXXXXXXXXXXXXXX **FOR DISCUSSION** XXXXXXXXXXXXXXXXXXX

1. Yiyun Li was sixteen when she first heard about Tang, or "Fruit Treasure," as the American drink mix was marketed in her native China (3). How significant is the author's age to her story? Explain.

2. Why was Li's father against spending family money on the prestigious new drink? Was his position justified? Why or why not?

3. What happened to Li when she tasted Tang for the first time?

4. Why does Li change her mind about the importance of Tang in her life? What brings an end to her "agony and jealousy" (10)?

5. What life lesson does Li take from her early experience? How is her perspecive on her experience influenced by her later life in America? Explain.

XXXXXXXXXXXXX **STRATEGIES AND STRUCTURES** XXXXXXXXXXXX

1. Why does Li begin her story with a DESCRIPTION of the orange and tangerine peels that her father saves to treat family coughs and colds—and of the water that results when he boils them (1)? What role does this "orange peel water" play throughout her NARRATIVE?

2. What is the function of the TV commercial in Li's narrative (3–6)? Why does she describe it in such detail?

3. How does Li's crush on the neighbor's son contribute to the PLOT of her story?

4. Where and how effectively does Li use DIALOGUE? Explain.

5. In the last paragraph of her narrative, Li jumps ahead ten years in time. What is the PURPOSE of this FLASH FORWARD? How does she anticipate this ending in the second paragraph of her story?

6. In her personal coming-of-age story, what point is Li making about the dreams of youth in general? How does she use CAUSE-AND-EFFECT analysis to help her make that point?

XXXXXXXXXXXX **WORDS AND FIGURES OF SPEECH** XXXXXXXXXXXX

1. Li gives her NARRATIVE the name of an American soft drink. Why? How does she connect this and the other "vivid orange" crush in her narrative to the "painful crush" she experienced as an adolescent (4, 9)?

2. How effective is Li's choice of a powdery American drink as a METAPHOR for the changes in her life and in the "lifestyle" of her native country (6)? Explain.

3. Explain the PUN in Li's reference to a "Tangy life" (13).

4. The Tang ad, says Li, was "a revolution" (6). What are the implications of this term, especially in a Communist culture such as China's?

5. What cultural differences do you find reflected in the different names for Tang in America and in China? Explain.

XXXXXXXXXXXXXXXXXX **FOR WRITING** XXXXXXXXXXXXXXXXXXXXX

1. Have you or anyone you know ever purchased a product because you thought it would change your life? In a paragraph or two, tell about your encounter with this product and whether or not it met your expectations.

2. Write a NARRATIVE about an infatuation you've had with a particular person or lifestyle—or perhaps a person who represented a lifestyle. Tell what you did to act on your infatuation—and/or how you got over it.

3. Write a coming-of-age narrative about someone—such as a sibling, friend, or neighbor—whom you have seen change and grow over a period of time. Focus on specific actions and events that show your subject in the process of maturing.

ZOE SHEWER

READY, WILLING, AND ABLE

Zoe Shewer (b. 1990) grew up in New York City and is currently studying at Vanderbilt University, where she plans to major in English and
Art History. When Shewer is not in school or doing community service,
she works at a stable in North Carolina and rides competitively on her
favorite horse, Mr. Happy. "Ready, Willing, and Able" takes its title
from the name of a social program, sponsored by the Doe Fund, that
helps formerly homeless or incarcerated men and women to obtain housing and job skills. Written as part of Shewer's college application, it tells
the story of the day she "shadowed" an inspiring street sweeper on the
sidewalks of Manhattan.

XXXXXXXXXXXXXXXXXXXXXXXXXXXXXXXXXXXXXXXXXXXXXXXXXXXXXX

Wearing a canvas jumpsuit zipped up to my neck, I must have   1
looked as though I was stepping onto the set of *ET: The Extra-
Terrestrial*, but my actual destination was Madison Avenue, home to
some of the fanciest boutiques in New York City. The bright blue jumpsuit I wore was far from high fashion: it was sized for a full-grown man,
and it ballooned about my slender frame. My blonde hair was pulled
back in a ponytail, and the only label I displayed was the bold-lettered
logo on my back: Ready, Willing & Able. I was suited up to collect trash
from the sidewalks of New York.

July is stifling in New York City, and I was not looking forward to   2
wearing the oversized jumpsuit in the ninety-degree heat. As I made my
way through the Ready, Willing & Able (RWA) headquarters, I passed
colorfully decorated bulletin boards bearing smiley-faced reminders:
"Drug testing is on Monday!" "Curfew is midnight!" Most full-time
employees of RWA are ex-convicts or former addicts for whom street
cleaning is the work-for-housing component of a transitional lifestyle

program. For me, street cleaning was day 1 of Camp Robin Hood, a hands-on summer crash course in New York nonprofit organizations. As I selected a broom from the supply closet, I reminded myself that I had volunteered to do this. Feeling like a new kid on the first day of school, I stood nervously next to the program supervisor, who would be introducing me to the street-cleaning attendant I would be helping.

3   If I was the awkward new kid, the street-cleaning attendant to whom I was assigned, a tall man named Seymour, was undoubtedly the Big Man on Campus. Seymour wore his RWA cap slightly askew, and, as he reached out to shake my hand, I caught a glimpse of a tattoo under his sleeve. We headed out to the street together, and, while I nervously fidgeted with the broom I carried, he calmly wheeled a bright blue trash can behind him. Seymour began sweeping the sidewalks, and I followed his lead. He not only showed me how to drain the gutters, he also taught me how to "read" the back stories in the litter. To Seymour, a torn hemp bracelet on the curb was a schoolgirl's temper tantrum; a Twinkie wrapper in the street was a closet eater's discarded evidence. Though I have lived in New York my entire life, I began to see my surroundings in a new light. The streets that had always felt so familiar seemed full of surprises. As our afternoon continued, Seymour also told me stories about his sister, his desire to get his life back on track after some time on the wrong side of the law, his love of Central Park, and his aspiration to travel across the country.

4   After several hours, I had more or less forgotten about my tent-sized RWA jumpsuit when suddenly I heard someone laughing at me: "I wonder what she did to deserve that?!"

5   I looked up and saw a group of girls my age looking in my direction and laughing as they walked past. My stomach tightened. They obviously thought I was being punished, perhaps serving a juvenile court sentence. Ordinarily I might have laughed at the idea that I could be mistaken for a juvenile delinquent, but on this day I felt a jumble of feelings—panic, shame, sadness, and admiration for a man whose history is suggested by his jumpsuit and the logo on his back. I will admit that a few hours earlier I had been embarrassed about my ill-fitting uniform. Halfway through the work day, however, the girls' rude comments caused an entirely different kind of shame: What if

Seymour thought I was anything like those girls? What if he thought that I was faking a smile and counting down the minutes until the day was over?

I suddenly wanted to thank Seymour for this experience. I wanted to tell him that he was probably the best guide through these streets I had ever had, and that I knew I could not possibly understand what he does by shadowing him for a day in a borrowed uniform. I wanted to explain to him that I volunteer regularly in New York: I am committed to working with at-risk children, and have done so for years at an after-school program in Harlem. I wanted to share how much I relate to his closeness with his family, his desire to travel, and his love of Strawberry Fields in Central Park,[1] But the girls' mocking comments and laughter had left us in an uncomfortable silence, and I felt that anything I might say would make us feel even more awkward.

6

It was Seymour who broke this silence. As I stood next to the trash can and tried to avoid staring off in the direction of the latte-carrying girls, Seymour caught my eye, smiled, and nodded toward my broom with one excellent piece of advice: "Put some muscle in it, Goldilocks."

7

1. Landscaped area honoring slain rock star John Lennon (1940–1980); it is named for The Beatles' song "Strawberry Fields Forever."

ⅩⅩⅩⅩⅩⅩⅩⅩⅩⅩⅩⅩⅩⅩⅩⅩⅩⅩ **FOR DISCUSSION** ⅩⅩⅩⅩⅩⅩⅩⅩⅩⅩⅩⅩⅩⅩⅩⅩⅩⅩⅩ

1. Why was Zoe Shewer sweeping the streets of New York City on a hot July day under the guidance of a man who has spent time "on the wrong side of the law" (3)?

2. What does Shewer learn from Seymour—aside from "how to drain the gutters" (3)?

3. Why is Shewer embarrassed by the "group of girls" who stop to watch as she and Seymour ply their brooms (5)?

4. Do you think Shewer's admiration for her street-sweeping mentor is justified? Why or why not?

5. How effective, in your opinion, are nongovernment programs like Ready, Willing, & Able for dealing with homelessness, drug addiction, and other social problems? Explain.

XXXXXXXXXXXXXX **STRATEGIES AND STRUCTURES** XXXXXXXXXXXXXX

1. What point is Shewer making by telling the story of the day she volunteered at the RWA headquarters?

2. What is the CLIMAX of Shewer's NARRATIVE? How does this event bring the tension in her story to a high point? How and when is that tension resolved?

3. In paragraph 6, Shewer has a moment of insight. About what? How necessary is this revelation to her PLOT?

4. Shewer incorporates DIALOGUE in only two places in her narrative. Where? Why do you think she chose these two instances of speech to relate directly? Explain what these words contribute to her story.

5. Shewer's essay was written as part of her application to college. Which aspects of her narrative do you find particularly suitable for this PURPOSE? How so?

6. How does Shewer's physical DESCRIPTION of herself in the first paragraph help to prepare the reader for the ending of her narrative?

XXXXXXXXXXXX **WORDS AND FIGURES OF SPEECH** XXXXXXXXXXXX

1. Why does Shewer choose "Ready, Willing, and Able" for the title of her NARRATIVE? To whom do these words apply? Explain.

2. In what sense is Shewer's mentor teaching her to "read" the litter that they sweep up (3)? What does she mean by "back stories" (3)?

3. Having first DESCRIBED her jumpsuit as "tent-sized" and "ill-fitting" (4, 5), Shewer says in paragraph 6 that it is simply "borrowed." How does Shewer's choice of adjectives help to indicate her change in perspective toward her experience?

4. "Latte-carrying" is an *epithet,* or term that characterizes the person or thing it identifies. What does this particular epithet tell us about the "girls" to whom it is applied—other than that they are drinking coffee (7)?

5. What is the effect of Shewer's ALLUSION to "Goldilocks and the Three Bears" (7)?

XXXXXXXXXXXXXXXXXXX **For Writing** XXXXXXXXXXXXXXXXXXXXX

1. Find an object that someone has lost or discarded—perhaps something from a lost-and-found box or an object someone has left in a classroom or on the street. Write a short NARRATIVE in which you "read" the back story behind that object.

2. Write a narrative about a time when, instead of following convention or listening to your peers, you followed the advice and example of an unusual mentor or guide. Try to recall any specific advice that he or she gave you, and include it in your narrative as DIALOGUE.

MARY MEBANE

THE BACK OF THE BUS

Mary Mebane (1933–1992) was the daughter of a dirt farmer who sold junk to raise cash. She earned a Ph.D. from the University of North Carolina and became a professor of English. In 1971 on the Op-Ed page of the *New York Times*, Mebane told the story of a bus ride from Durham, North Carolina, to Orangeburg, South Carolina, during the 1940s that "realized for me the enormousness of the change" since the Civil Rights Act of 1964. That bus ride was the germ of two autobiographical volumes, *Mary* (1981) and *Mary Wayfarer* (1983). The essay printed here is a complete chapter from the first book. It is a personal narrative of another, earlier bus ride that Mebane took when the segregation laws were still in place. Mebane said she wrote this piece because she "wanted to show what it was like to live under legal segregation *before* the Civil Rights Act of 1964."

XXXXXXXXXXXXXXXXXXXXXXXXXXXXXXXXXXXXXXXXXXXXXXXXXXXXXXXXXX

1   Historically, my lifetime is important because I was part of the last generation born into a world of total legal segregation[1] in the Southern United States. When the Supreme Court outlawed segregation in the public schools in 1954, I was twenty-one. When Congress passed the Civil Rights Act of 1964, permitting blacks free access to public places, I was thirty-one. The world I was born into had been segregated for a long time—so long, in fact, that I never met anyone who had lived during the time when restrictive laws were not in existence, although some people spoke of parents and others who had lived during the

---

1. Government-endorsed policy that barred African Americans from white neighborhoods, schools, and other facilities, and required that African Americans sit in separate sections from whites in public spaces like buses and movie theaters.

"free" time. As far as anyone knew, the laws as they then existed would stand forever. They were meant to—and did—create a world that fixed black people at the bottom of society in all aspects of human life. It was a world without options.

Most Americans have never had to live with terror. I had had to live with it all my life—the psychological terror of segregation, in which there was a special set of laws governing your movements. You violated them at your peril, for you knew that if you broke one of them, knowingly or not, physical terror was just around the corner, in the form of policemen and jails, and in some cases and places white vigilante mobs formed for the exclusive purpose of keeping blacks in line.

It was Saturday morning, like any Saturday morning in dozens of Southern towns.

The town had a washed look. The street sweepers had been busy since six o'clock. Now, at eight, they were still slowly moving down the streets, white trucks with clouds of water coming from underneath the swelled tubular sides. Unwary motorists sometimes got a window-ful of water as a truck passed by. As it moved on, it left in its wake a clear stream running in the gutters or splashed on the wheels of parked cars.

Homeowners, bent over industriously in the morning sun, were out pushing lawn mowers. The sun was bright, but it wasn't too hot. It was morning and it was May. Most of the mowers were glad that it was finally getting warm enough to go outside.

Traffic was brisk. Country people were coming into town early with their produce; clerks and service workers were getting to the job before the stores opened at ten o'clock. Though the big stores would not be open for another hour or so, the grocery stores, banks, open-air markets, dinettes, were already open and filling with staff and customers.

Everybody was moving toward the heart of Durham's downtown, which waited to receive them rather complacently, little knowing that in a decade the shopping centers far from the center of downtown Durham would create a ghost town in the midst of the busiest blocks on Main Street.

8   Some moved by car, and some moved by bus. The more affluent used cars, leaving the buses mainly to the poor, black and white, though there were some businesspeople who avoided the trouble of trying to find a parking place downtown by riding the bus.

9   I didn't mind taking the bus on Saturday. It wasn't so crowded. At night or on Saturday or Sunday was the best time. If there were plenty of seats, the blacks didn't have to worry about being asked to move so that a white person could sit down. And the knot of hatred and fear didn't come into my stomach.

10   I knew the stop that was the safety point, both going and coming. Leaving town, it was the Little Five Points, about five or six blocks north of the main downtown section. That was the last stop at which four or five people might get on. After the stop, the driver could some-times pass two or three stops without taking on or letting off a passen-ger. So the number of seats on the bus usually remained constant on the trip from town to Braggtown. The nearer the bus got to the end of the line, the more I relaxed. For if a white passenger got on near the end of the line, often to catch the return trip back and avoid having to stand in the sun at the bus stop until the bus turned around, he or she would usually stand if there were not seats in the white section, and the driver would say nothing, knowing that the end of the line was near and that the standee would get a seat in a few minutes.

11   On the trip to town, the Mangum Street A&P was the last point at which the driver picked up more passengers than he let off. These peo-ple, though they were just a few blocks from the downtown section, pre-ferred to ride the bus downtown. Those getting on at the A&P were usually on their way to work at the Duke University Hospital—past the downtown section, through a residential neighborhood, and then past the university, before they got to Duke Hospital.

12   So whether the driver discharged more passengers than he took on near the A&P on Mangum was of great importance. For if he took on more passengers than got off, it meant that some of the newcomers would have to stand. And if they were white, the driver was going to have to ask a black passenger to move so that a white passenger could sit down. Most of the drivers had a rule of thumb, though. By custom the seats behind the exit door had become "colored" seats, and no matter

how many whites stood up, anyone sitting behind the exit door knew that he or she wouldn't have to move.

The disputed seat, though, was the one directly opposite the exit door. It was "no-man's-land." White people sat there, and black people sat there. It all depended on whose section was fuller. If the back section was full, the next black passenger who got on sat in the no-man's-land seat; but if the white section filled up, a white person would take the seat. Another thing about the white people: they could sit anywhere they chose, even in the "colored" section. Only the black passengers had to obey segregation laws.   13

On this Saturday morning Esther[2] and I set out for town for our music lesson. We were going on our weekly big adventure, all the way across town, through the white downtown, then across the railroad tracks, then through the "colored" downtown, a section of run-down dingy shops, through some fading high-class black neighborhoods, past North Carolina College, to Mrs. Shearin's house.   14

We walked the two miles from Wildwood to the bus line. Though it was a warm day, in the early morning there was dew on the grass and the air still had the night's softness. So we walked along and talked and looked back constantly, hoping someone we knew would stop and pick us up.   15

I looked back furtively, for in one of the few instances that I remembered my father criticizing me severely, it was for looking back. One day when I was walking from town he had passed in his old truck. I had been looking back and had seen him. "Don't look back," he had said. "People will think that you want them to pick you up." Though he said "people," I knew he meant men—not the men he knew, who lived in the black community, but the black men who were not part of the community, and all of the white men. To be picked up meant that something bad would happen to me. Still, two miles is a long walk and I occasionally joined Esther in looking back to see if anyone we knew was coming.   16

Esther and I got to the bus and sat on one of the long seats at the back that faced each other. There were three such long seats—one on   17

2. Mebane's sister.

each side of the bus and a third long seat at the very back that faced the front. I liked to sit on a long seat facing the side because then I didn't have to look at the expressions on the faces of the whites when they put their tokens in and looked at the blacks sitting in the back of the bus. Often I studied my music, looking down and practicing the fingering. I looked up at each stop to see who was getting on and to check on the seating pattern. The seating pattern didn't really bother me that day until the bus started to get unusually full for a Saturday morning. I wondered what was happening, where all these people were coming from. They got on and got on until the white section was almost full and the black section was full.

18   There was a black man in a blue windbreaker and a gray porkpie hat sitting in no-man's-land, and my stomach tightened. I wondered what would happen. I had never been on a bus on which a black person was asked to give a seat to a white person when there was no other seat empty. Usually, though, I had seen a black person automatically get up and move to an empty seat farther back. But this morning the only empty seat was beside a black person sitting in no-man's-land.

19   The bus stopped at Little Five Points and one black got off. A young white man was getting on. I tensed. What would happen now? Would the driver ask the black man to get up and move to the empty seat farther back? The white man had a businessman's air about him: suit, shirt, tie, polished brown shoes. He saw the empty seat in the "colored" section and after just a little hesitation went to it, put his briefcase down, and sat with his feet crossed. I relaxed a little when the bus pulled off without the driver saying anything. Evidently he hadn't seen what had happened, or since he was just a few stops from Main Street, he figured the mass exodus there would solve all the problems. Still, I was afraid of a scene.

20   The next stop was an open-air fruit stand just after Little Five Points, and here another white man got on. Where would he sit? The only available seat was beside the black man. Would he stand the few stops to Main Street or would the driver make the black man move? The whole colored section tensed, but nobody said anything. I looked at Esther, who looked apprehensive. I looked at the other men and women, who studiously avoided my eyes and everybody else's as well, as they maintained a steady gaze at a far-distant land.

Just one woman caught my eye; I had noticed her before, and I had been ashamed of her. She was a stringy little black woman. She could have been forty; she could have been fifty. She looked as if she were a hard drinker. Flat black face with tight features. She was dressed with great insouciance in a tight boy's sweater with horizontal lines running across her flat chest. It pulled down over a nondescript skirt. Laced-up shoes, socks, and a head rag completed her outfit. She looked tense.

21

The white man who had just gotten on the bus walked to the seat in no-man's-land and stood there. He wouldn't sit down, just stood there. Two adult males, living in the most highly industrialized, most technologically advanced nation in the world, a nation that had devastated two other industrial giants in World War II[3] and had flirted with taking on China in Korea. Both these men, either of whom could have fought for the United States in Germany or Korea, faced each other in mutual rage and hostility. The white one wanted to sit down, but he was going to exert his authority and force the black one to get up first. I watched the driver in the rearview mirror. He was about the same age as the antagonists. The driver wasn't looking for trouble, either.

22

"Say there, buddy, how about moving back," the driver said, meanwhile driving his bus just as fast as he could. The whole bus froze— whites at the front, blacks at the rear. They didn't want to believe what was happening was really happening.

23

The seated black man said nothing. The standing white man said nothing.

24

"Say, buddy, did you hear me? What about moving on back." The driver was scared to death. I could tell that.

25

"These is the niggers' seats!" the little lady in the strange outfit started screaming. I jumped. I had to shift my attention from the driver to the frieze of the black man seated and white man standing to the articulate little woman who had joined in the fray.

26

"The government gave us these seats! These is the niggers' seats." I was startled at her statement and her tone. "The president said that these are the niggers' seats!" I expected her to start fighting at any moment.

27

3. The United States and its allies defeated "industrial giants" Germany and Japan, as well as Italy, in World War II (1939–45).

28   Evidently the bus driver did, too, because he was driving faster and faster. I believe that he forgot he was driving a bus and wanted desperately to pull to the side of the street and get out and run.

29   "I'm going to take you down to the station, buddy," the driver said.

30   The white man with the briefcase and the polished brown shoes who had taken a seat in the "colored" section looked as though he might die of embarrassment at any moment.

31   As scared and upset as I was, I didn't miss a thing.

32   By that time we had come to the stop before Main Street, and the black passenger rose to get off.

33   "You're not getting off, buddy. I'm going to take you downtown." The driver kept driving as he talked and seemed to be trying to get downtown as fast as he could.

34   "These are the niggers' seats! The government plainly said these are the niggers' seats!" screamed the little woman in rage.

35   I was embarrassed at the use of the word "nigger" but I was proud of the lady. I was also proud of the man who wouldn't get up.

36   The bus driver was afraid, trying to hold on to his job but plainly not willing to get into a row with the blacks.

37   The bus seemed to be going a hundred miles an hour and everybody was anxious to get off, though only the lady and the driver were saying anything.

38   The black man stood at the exit door; the driver drove right past the A&P stop. I was terrified. I was sure that the bus was going to the police station to put the black man in jail. The little woman had her hands on her hips and she never stopped yelling. The bus driver kept driving as fast as he could.

39   Then, somewhere in the back of his mind, he decided to forget the whole thing. The next stop was Main Street, and when he got there, in what seemed to be a flash of lightning, he flung both doors open wide. He and his black antagonist looked at each other in the rearview mirror; in a second the windbreaker and porkpie hat were gone. The little woman was standing, preaching to the whole bus about the government's gift of these seats to the blacks; the man with the brown shoes practically fell out of the door in his hurry; and Esther and I followed the hurrying footsteps.

We walked about three doors down the block, then caught a bus to the black neighborhood. Here we sat on one of the two long seats facing each other, directly behind the driver. It was the custom. Since this bus had a route from a black neighborhood to the downtown section and back, passing through no white residential areas, blacks could sit where they chose. One minute we had been on a bus in which violence was threatened over a seat near the exit door; the next minute we were sitting in the very front behind the driver. 40

The people who devised this system thought that it was going to last forever. 41

XXXXXXXXXXXXXXXXXXX **For Discussion** XXXXXXXXXXXXXXXXXXX

1. Why does the bus driver threaten to drive to the police station? What was his official duty under segregation?

2. Why does the businessman with the briefcase and brown shoes take the separate seat in the back of the bus instead of the place on the bench across from the exit? Was he upholding or violating segregation customs by doing so?

3. What is the main confrontation of the NARRATIVE? What emotion(s) does it arouse in young Mary Mebane and her sister as witnesses?

4. Who are the "people" to whom Mebane refers in paragraph 41?

5. Why does Mebane claim a national significance for the events of her private life as narrated here? Is her CLAIM justified? How does this claim relate to her PURPOSE for writing?

XXXXXXXXXXXXX **Strategies and Structures** XXXXXXXXXXXXX

1. In which paragraph does Mebane begin telling the story of the bus ride? Why do you think she starts with the routine of the street sweepers and the homeowners doing yard work?

2. List several passages in Mebane's text that seem to be told from young Mary's POINT OF VIEW. Then list others that are told from the point of view of the adult author looking back at an event in her youth. Besides time, what is the main difference in their perspectives?

3. Why does Mebane refer to the black passenger who confronts the bus driver as "the windbreaker and porkpie hat" (39)? Whose point of view is she capturing? Is she showing or telling here—and what difference does it make in her essay?

4. How does Mebane use the increasing speed of the bus to show rather than tell about the precariousness of the segregation system?

5. Mebane interrupts her NARRATIVE of the events of that Saturday morning in paragraphs 10 through 13. What is she explaining to her AUDIENCE, and why is it necessary that she do so? Where else does she interrupt her narrative with EXPOSITION?

XXXXXXXXXXXXX **WORDS AND FIGURES OF SPEECH** XXXXXXXXXXXXX

1. Why does Mebane refer to the seat across from the exit as a "no-man's land" (13)? What does this term mean?

2. Mebane COMPARES the seated black man and the standing white man to a "frieze," a decorative horizontal band, often molded or carved, along the upper part of a wall (26). Why is the METAPHOR appropriate here?

3. Look up "insouciance" in your dictionary (21). Does the use of this word prepare you for the rebellious behavior of the "stringy" little woman (21)? How?

4. What are the two possible meanings of "scene" (19)? How might Mebane's personal NARRATIVE be said to illustrate both kinds?

5. Which of the many meanings of "articulate" in your dictionary best fits the woman who screams back at the bus driver (26)?

XXXXXXXXXXXXXXXXXXX **FOR WRITING** XXXXXXXXXXXXXXXXXXXXX

1. In a brief ANECDOTE, recount a bus, train, plane, roller coaster, boat, or other ride you have taken. Focus on the vehicle itself and the people who were on it with you.

2. Write a personal NARRATIVE about an experience you had with racial tension in a public place. Be sure to DESCRIBE the physical place and tell what you saw and heard and did there.

CHAPTER FOUR

EXAMPLE

XXXXXXXXXXXXXXXXXXXXXXXXXXXXXXXXXXXXXXXXXXXXXXXXXXX

E XAMPLES* are used in all kinds of writing. In the *Nuclear Waste Primer: A Handbook for Citizens* (revised 1993), the League of Women Voters makes the following statement about our exposure to nuclear radiation:

> Most people have received only small amounts of radiation from nuclear weapons production and testing. Some activities, occupations, and geographic areas, however, expose a person to greater-than-average radiation. For example, a person living at an altitude of 5,000 feet in Denver, Colorado, receives nearly twice as much cosmic radiation from outer space as a person living at sea level in Washington, D.C.

In this paragraph, Denver and Washington, D.C., are particular examples of "geographic areas" where, according to the League of Women Voters, people receive differing degrees of cosmic radiation. Examples like these help to explain a subject by giving particular instances of it. They are individuals (in this case, individual American cities) taken out of a general group ("geographic areas") to represent the whole group. Such examples help to make general statements more specific—and ABSTRACT statements more CONCRETE.

Good examples also help to make a subject more vivid in the reader's mind. The League of Women Voters is not actually suggesting that the inhabitants of Denver leave their homes and migrate to Washington. As the League acknowledges, the increased risk of harm from nuclear radiation that could result from living in Denver as opposed to Washington isn't great. But the two cities are good examples for show-

---

*Words printed in SMALL CAPITALS are defined in the Glossary.

ing that different places expose inhabitants to different levels of radiation—which is the League's main point in citing them. And they grab the reader's attention before the *Nuclear Waste Primer* goes on to cite other places and activities that are truly dangerous, such as living near a nuclear dump or test site.

Good examples are not only concrete and vivid, they also truly *representative* of the group they exemplify. That is, they exhibit all of the main characteristics of the group. To see how an example stands for, or represents, an entire group—such as the victims of indiscriminate nuclear testing—let's look at some residents of the state of Utah in the 1950s as described by Kori Quintana:

> Apparently, the atmospheric bomb tests of the 1950s were performed only when winds were blowing away from Las Vegas toward Utah. Subsequent studies of residents of towns with high nuclear fallout showed that various illnesses, especially leukemia, had stricken people who had no family history of them.
>
> KORI QUINTANA, "The Price of Power: Living in the Nuclear Age"

Two overlapping groups are identified here: residents of towns in Utah with a high incidence of nuclear fallout in the 1950s and Utah residents mysteriously stricken with such illnesses as leukemia even though they "had no family history of them."

Quintana herself was diagnosed at age seventeen with lupus, a disease of the autoimmune system. But she is not a good representative of the "mysteriously stricken" group because, by the time her generation came along, her family had developed a "history" of illnesses with unknown causes. And while Quintana was born and raised in Utah, she is not a good representative of the group that experienced fallout during the 1950s either, since she was born well after that.

Unlike Quintana, her mother and grandmother were both residents of Utah in the fifties, when nuclear weapons were being tested, and they both lived downwind of the Nevada test site. Thus both of them would make good, representative examples of the first group because they possess all the features that define that group. Since they have also been diagnosed with mysterious illnesses—her mother with allergies and thyroid problems, her grandmother with bone cancer—the two women would also qualify as representatives of the second group because, again, they possess all of the distinguishing characteristics of the group.

As solid, representative examples of both groups, Quintana's mother and grandmother also support a broader point that Quintana is trying to make—that those exposed to nuclear radiation run a greater risk of developing a variety of illnesses, specifically those resulting from genetic mutations. But while they may be representative, are Quintana's relatives really *sufficient* to make the case for the severe dangers of nuclear radiation?

To help convince readers that groups exposed to high levels of nuclear radiation are at a greater risk for illness, Quintana gives several more examples: of animals and humans in areas around the Chernobyl nuclear plant that have developed deformities, of high rates of miscarriage around nuclear plants, of illnesses among Japan's bomb survivors, and so on. And while these examples alone might be sufficient to convince some readers of the dangers of radiation, Quintana also uses careful CAUSE-AND-EFFECT analysis to clarify the link between radiation and the genetic mutations in the examples she cites—to support her ARGUMENT that "Millions of innocent people have paid the price of nuclear power through their suffering and untimely deaths." Ultimately, whether or not your examples are sufficient to make your point will depend on your AUDIENCE—and your PURPOSE in writing.

Sometimes a single example can serve as the focal point for an entire essay, or even a book—if it is sufficiently specific, vivid, and representative. Take the example of J. P. Morgan's nose, for instance. In her introduction to *Morgan, American Financier* (1999), the prize-winning biographer Jean Strouse discusses the difficulties she faced in writing a life of the banker who almost single-handedly ran the American economy a hundred years ago. In addition to the sheer bulk of biographical material to be pulled together, there were also countless stories and legends that had grown up around Morgan.

Strouse did not solve the problem of organizing all this material by focusing on Morgan's unusual nose; but she did use it effectively to introduce the legendary nature of her subject to her readers:

> Even Morgan's personal appearance gave rise to legend. He had a skin disease called rhinophyma that in his fifties turned his nose into a hideous purple bulb. One day the wife of his partner Dwight Morrow reportedly invited him to tea. She wanted her daughter Anne to meet the great man, and for weeks coached the girl about what would happen. Anne would come into the room and say good afternoon; she would not stare at Mr. Morgan's nose, she would not say anything about his nose, and she would leave.

The appointed day came, as Strouse tells the story, and the Morrows' young daughter, Anne, played her part flawlessly. Mrs. Morrow herself, however, had more difficulty:

> Mrs. Morrow and Mr. Morgan sat on a sofa by the tea tray. Anne came in, said hello, did not look at Morgan's nose, did not say anything about his nose, and left the room. Sighing in relief, Mrs. Morrow asked, "Mr. Morgan, do you take one lump or two in your nose?"

The usefulness of this story as an example of how examples can help to organize and focus our writing is only enhanced by the fact that it never happened.

When she grew up, Anne Morrow went on to become the writer Anne Morrow Lindbergh, wife of aviator Charles Lindbergh, who made the first solo transatlantic flight. "This ridiculous story has not a grain of truth in it," Mrs. Lindbergh told Morgan's biographer many years later; but "it is so funny I am sure it will continue."

Brief NARRATIVES, or ANECDOTES, such as the story of Mrs. Morrow and J. P. Morgan's nose, often make good, organizing examples because they link generalities or abstractions—populations at risk from nuclear radiation, principles of biography—to specific people and concrete events. By citing just this one story among the many inspired by Morgan's appearance and personality, Strouse accomplishes several things at a stroke: she paints a clear picture of how his contemporaries regarded the man whose life story she is introducing; she shows how difficult it was to see her controversial subject through the legends that enshrouded him; and she finds a focal point for organizing the introduction to her entire book. Evidently, Strouse has a good nose for examples.

A Brief Guide to Writing an Exemplification Essay

For most of us, it is easier to digest a piece of pie than the whole pie at once. The same goes for examples. They make general concepts easier to grasp (and swallow), and they give the flavor of the whole in a single bite.

As you write an essay based on examples, you need to identify your subject, say what its main characteristics are, and give specific instances that exhibit those characteristics. Laurence Gonzales makes these basic moves of exemplification in the following passage from his essay in this chapter:

> Without ever considering it, I had been harboring a mistaken mental model of a rattlesnake. It was my grandmother's ashtray; it was ceramic and not real; it was not harmful. The nostalgic emotional attachment I had for it made it a strong and persistent model, difficult to displace.
>
> Laurence Gonzales, "My Grandmother's Ashtray: Why Smart People Do Stupid Things"

Gonzales identifies his subject ("mistaken mental model[s]"), says what the main characteristics of these models are (emotionally "strong and persistent," "difficult to displace"), and gives a specific instance that exhibits these characteristics (his mental model of his grandmother's ceramic ashtray shaped like a rattlesnake).

The following guidelines will help you to make these basic moves as you draft an exemplification essay. They will also help you to ensure that your examples fit your purpose and audience, are sufficient to make your point, are truly representative of your subject, and are effectively organized with appropriate transitions.

Coming Up with a Subject

To come up with a subject for your essay, take any subject you're inter-ested in—the presidency of Abraham Lincoln, for example—and con-sider whether it can be narrowed down to focus on a specific aspect of the subject (such as Lincoln's humor in office) for which you can find a reasonable number of examples. Then choose examples that show the characteristics of that narrower topic. In this case, a good example of the presidential humor might be the time a well-dressed lady visited the White House and inadvertently sat on Lincoln's hat. "Madame," the president is supposed to have responded, "I could have told you it wouldn't fit."

If you have personal knowledge of your topic, you may already have a store of exemplary facts or stories about it. Or you may need to do some research. (For suggested sources and procedures, see the Appendix.) As you look for examples, choose ones that truly represent the qualities and characteristics you're trying to illustrate—and that are most likely to appeal to your AUDIENCE.

Considering Your Purpose and Audience

Before you begin writing, think about your PURPOSE. Is it to entertain? inform? persuade? For instance, the purpose of "All Seven Deadly Sins Committed at Church Bake Sale" on page 139 is to entertain, so the writer offers humorous examples of incidents at the bake sale. But if you were writing about the bake sale in order to persuade others to participate next time, you might offer examples of the money earned at various booths, how much fun participants had, and the good causes the money will be used for. In every case, your purpose determines the kinds of examples you use.

Before you can select effective examples, you need to take into account how much your audience already knows about your topic and how sympathetic they are likely to be to your position. If you are writ-ing to demonstrate that the health of Americans has declined over the past decade, and your audience consists of doctors and nutritionists, a few key examples would probably suffice. For a more general audience, however, such as your classmates, you would need to give more back-ground information and cite more (and more basic) examples. And if your readers are unlikely to view your topic as you do, you will have to work even harder to come up with sufficient examples.

Generating Ideas: Finding Good Examples

Try to find examples that display as many of the typical characteristics of your topic as possible. Suppose you were writing an essay on the seven deadly sins, and you decided to focus on gluttony. One characteristic of gluttony is overeating, so you might look for examples of people who overeat. Great athletes eat large quantities of food, however, and we don't consider them gluttons because they're fit and energetic. In this case, you would need to consider other characteristics of gluttony: obesity and lethargy. Perhaps Jabba the Hutt, the obese alien of *Star Wars* fame, would make a good example of gluttony because he not only overeats but also is fat and lazy.

Templates for Exemplifying

The following templates can help you to generate ideas for an exemplification essay and then to start drafting. Don't take these as formulas where you just have to fill in the blanks. There are no easy formulas for good writing. But these templates can help you plot out some of the key moves of exemplification and thus may serve as good starting points.

> ➤ About X, it can generally be said that _____; a good example would be _____.
>
> ➤ The main characteristics of X are _____ and _____, as exemplified by _____, _____, and _____.
>
> ➤ For the best example(s) of X, we can turn to _____.
>
> ➤ Additional examples of X include _____, _____, and _____.
>
> ➤ From these examples of X, we can conclude that _____.

For more techniques to help you generate ideas and start writing, see Chapter 1.

Stating Your Point

In an exemplification essay, you usually state your point directly in a THESIS STATEMENT in your introduction. For example:

> College teams depend more on teamwork than on star athletes for success.
>
> In general, the health of Americans has declined in the last ten years.
>
> John McCain's 2008 campaign for the U.S. presidency made a number of tactical errors.

Each of these thesis statements calls for specific examples to support it. How many examples do you need—and what kinds?

Using Sufficient Examples

As you select examples to support a thesis, you can use either multiple brief examples or one or two extended examples. The approach you take will depend, in part, on the kind of generalization you're making. Multiple examples work well when you are dealing with different aspects of a large topic (the McCain presidential campaign strategy) or with trends involving large numbers of people (Americans' declining health, college athletes). Extended examples work better when you are writing about a particular case, such as a single scene in a novel.

Keep in mind that sufficiency isn't strictly a matter of numbers. Often a few good examples will suffice, which is what sufficiency implies: enough to do the job, and no more. In other words, whether or not your examples are sufficient to support your thesis is not determined by the number of examples but by how persuasive those examples seem to your readers. Choose examples that you think they will find vivid and convincing.

Using Representative Examples

Be sure that your examples fairly and accurately support the point you're making. In an essay on how college athletic teams depend on teamwork, for instance, you would want to choose examples from several teams and sports. Similarly, if you are trying to convince readers that John McCain made many tactical errors in his presidential campaign, you would need to show a number of errors from different points in the campaign. And if you're exemplifying an ABSTRACT concept, such as gluttony, be sure to choose CONCRETE examples that possess all of its distinguishing characteristics.

Another way to make sure that your examples are representative is to steer clear of highly unusual examples. In an essay about the benefits of swimming every day, for instance, Michael Phelps might not be the best example since he is not a typical swimmer. Better to cite several swimmers who can demonstrate a variety of benefits.

Organizing Examples and Using Transitions

Once you have stated your thesis and chosen your examples, you need to put them in some kind of order. You might present them in order of increasing importance or interest, perhaps saving the best for last. Or if you have a large number of examples, you might organize them into categories. Or you might arrange them chronologically, if you are citing errors made during a campaign, for example.

Regardless of the organization you choose, you need to relate your examples to each other and to the point you're making by using clear TRANSITIONS and other connecting words and phrases. You can always use the phrases *for example* and *for instance*. But consider using other transitions as well, such as *more specifically, exactly, precisely, thus, namely, indeed, that is, in other words, in fact, in particular*: "Obesity, in fact, has caused a dramatic increase in the incidence of diabetes." Or try using a RHETORICAL QUESTION, which you then answer with an example: "So what factor has contributed the most to the declining health of Americans?"

Everyday Exemplification
A Lighted Billboard

By illuminating only one of the spotlights on this billboard, a utility company sets a good example for consumers—and gives a "for instance" of the general point it is making here. You can use examples to shed light on almost any subject by making abstract concepts (energy conservation) more concrete (turning off extra lights) and by focusing the reader's attention on a particular instance or illustration of your subject.

THE ONION

ALL SEVEN DEADLY SINS COMMITTED AT CHURCH BAKE SALE

The *Onion* is a SATIRICAL newspaper that originated in Madison, home of the University of Wisconsin. In a typical issue, the paper pokes fun at everything from politics ("Obama Practices Looking-Off-Into-Future Pose") and American lifestyles ("TV Helps Build Valuable Looking Skills") to medicine ("Colonoscopy Offers Non-Fantastic Voyage through Human Body") and religion (which is what this selection is about—sort of). According to the Catholic Church, there are basically two types of sins: "venial" ones that are easily forgiven and "deadly" ones that, well, are not. In the fifth century, Pope Gregory the Great identified what he, and the Church ever since, took to be the seven worst of the worst: pride, envy, wrath, sloth, avarice (or greed), gluttony, and lust. As originally conceived, the seven deadlies are highly abstract concepts. In this tongue-in-cheek news release from a church bake sale in Gadsden, Alabama, the roving *Onion* reporter, who knows sin when he sees it, finds concrete, specific examples of each of them. The down-to-earth acts of sin reported here actually took place. In accordance with *Onion* editorial policy, however, the names of the sinners have been changed to protect the not-so-innocent. Additional examples can be reported to theonion.com.

XXXXXXXXXXXXXXXXXXXXXXXXXXXXXXXXXXXXXXXXXXXXXXXXXXXXXXXXX

G ADSDEN, AL—The seven deadly sins—avarice, sloth, envy, lust, gluttony, pride, and wrath—were all committed Sunday during the twice-annual bake sale at St. Mary's of the Immaculate Conception Church.   1

In total, 347 individual acts of sin were committed at the bake sale, with nearly every attendee committing at least one of the seven deadly sins as outlined by Gregory the Great in the Fifth Century.   2

Patti George (far right) commits the sin of envy as she eyes fellow parishioner Mary Hoechst's superior strawberry rhubarb pie.

3   "My cookies, cakes, and brownies are always the highlight of our church bake sales, and everyone says so," said parishioner Connie Barrett, 49, openly committing the sin of pride. "Sometimes, even I'm amazed by how well my goodies turn out."

4   Fellow parishioner Betty Wicks agreed.

5   "Every time I go past Connie's table, I just have to buy something," said the 245-pound Wicks, who commits the sin of gluttony at every St. Mary's bake sale, as well as most Friday nights at Old Country Buffet. "I simply can't help myself—it's all so delicious."

6   The popularity of Barrett's mouth-watering wares elicited the sin of envy in many of her fellow vendors.

7   "Connie has this fantastic book of recipes her grandmother gave her, and she won't share them with anyone," church organist Georgia Brandt said. "This year, I made white-chocolate blondies and thought they'd be a

big hit. But most people just went straight to Connie's table, got what they wanted, and left. All the while, Connie just stood there with this look of smug satisfaction on her face. It took every ounce of strength in my body to keep from going over there and really telling her off."

While the sins of wrath and avarice were each committed dozens of times at the event, Barrett and longtime bake-sale rival Penny Cox brought them together in full force.   8

"Penny said she wanted to make a bet over whose table would make the most money," said Barrett, exhibiting avarice. "Whoever lost would have to sit in the dunk tank at the St. Mary's Summer Fun Festival. I figured it's for such a good cause, a little wager couldn't hurt. Besides, I always bring the church more money anyway, so I couldn't possibly lose."   9

Moments after agreeing to the wager, Cox became wrathful when Barrett, the bake sale's co-chair, grabbed the best table location under the pretense of having to keep the coffee machine full. Cox attempted to exact revenge by reporting an alleged Barrett misdeed to the church's priest.   10

"I mentioned to Father Mark [O'Connor] that I've seen candles at Connie's house that I wouldn't be surprised one bit if she stole from the church's storage closet," said Cox, who also committed the sin of sloth by forcing her daughter to set up and man her booth while she gossiped with friends. "Perhaps if he investigates this, by this time next year, Connie won't be co-chair of the bake sale and in her place we'll have someone who's willing to rotate the choice table spots."   11

The sin of lust also reared its ugly head at the bake sale, largely due to the presence of Melissa Wyckoff, a shapely 20-year-old redhead whose family recently joined the church. While male attendees ogled Wyckoff, the primary object of lust for females was the personable, boyish Father Mark.   12

Though attendees' feelings of lust for Wyckoff and O'Connor were never acted on, they did not go unnoticed.   13

"There's something not right about that Melissa Wyckoff," said envious and wrathful bake-sale participant Jilly Brandon, after her husband Craig offered Wyckoff one of her Rice Krispie treats to "welcome   14

[her] to the parish." "She might have just moved here from California, but that red dress of hers should get her kicked out of the church."

15   According to St. Mary's treasurer Beth Ellen Coyle, informal church-sponsored events are a notorious breeding ground for the seven deadly sins.

16   "Bake sales, haunted houses, pancake breakfasts . . . such church events are rife with potential for sin," Coyle said. "This year, we had to eliminate the 'Guess Your Weight' booth from the annual church carnival because the envy and pride had gotten so out of hand. Church events are about glorifying God, not violating His word. If you want to do that, you're no better than that cheap strumpet Melissa Wyckoff."

XXXXXXXXXXXXXXXXXXXX **For Discussion** XXXXXXXXXXXXXXXXXXXX

1. The *Onion* reporter gives bake-sale-specific EXAMPLES for each of the Deadly Sins. How well do you think these examples represent the sins they're meant to illustrate?

2. Statistics is the science of analyzing numerical examples. In all, says the *Onion* reporter, parishioners at the St. Mary's bake sale committed "347 individual acts of sin" (2). Anything suspicious about these stats? How do you suppose they were determined?

3. All of the seven deadly sins are identified in the first paragraph of the *Onion*'s spoof. In what order are they explained after that? Which one does the watchful reporter come back to at the end?

4. Which specific deadly sin is the only one unacted upon at the bake sale? Who inspired it?

XXXXXXXXXXXXXX **Strategies and Structures** XXXXXXXXXXXXXX

1. Pope Gregory might object that the *Onion*'s EXAMPLES are a bit trivial. But how CONCRETE and specific are they?

2. SATIRE is writing that makes fun of vice or folly for the PURPOSE of exposing and correcting it. To the extent that the *Onion* is satirizing the behavior of people at "church-sponsored events," what less-than-truly-deadly "sins" is the paper actually making fun of (15)?

3. A *spoof* is a gentle parody or mildly satirical imitation. What kind of writing or reporting is the *Onion* spoofing here? Who is the AUDIENCE for this spoof?

4. As a Catholic priest, "boyish Father Mark" would probably say that all the other deadly sins are examples of pride (12). How might pride be thought of as the overarchingly general "deadly sin"?

5. As a "news" story, this one has elements of NARRATIVE. What are some of them, specifically?

XXXXXXXXXXXX **WORDS AND FIGURES OF SPEECH** XXXXXXXXXXXX

1. What, exactly, is a "strumpet" (16)?

2. *Deadly* (or *mortal*) sins are to be distinguished from *venial* sins. According to your dictionary, what kind of sins would be venial sins? Give several EXAMPLES.

3. Give a SYNONYM for each of the following words: "avarice," "sloth," "gluttony," and "wrath" (1).

4. Another word for *pride* is *hubris*. What language does it derive from? What's the distinction between the two?

5. *Hypocrisy* is not one of the seven deadly sins, but how would you DEFINE it? Which of the St. Mary's parishioners might be said to commit *this* sin?

XXXXXXXXXXXXXXXXXXX **FOR WRITING** XXXXXXXXXXXXXXXXXXXXX

1. Imagine a strip mall called the Seven Deadly Sins Shopping Center, where each item on Pope Gregory's list is represented by a store selling ordinary products and services. Draw up a list of store names that would EXEMPLIFY each of the seven deadlies—for example, Big Joe's Eats. You might also compose some signs or other advertising to place in the windows of each shop.

2. Using examples, write an essay entitled "All Seven Deadly Sins Committed at _____." Fill in the blank with any venue you choose—"School Cafeteria," for example, or "College Library." Give at least one example for each offense.

3. According to somebody's critical theory, the characters on Gilligan's Island each represent one of the seven deadly sins. If you've seen enough reruns of the show to have an opinion, write an essay either questioning or supporting this reading.

LAURENCE GONZALES

MY GRANDMOTHER'S ASHTRAY: WHY SMART PEOPLE DO STUPID THINGS

Laurence Gonzales (b. 1947) is an editor and columnist for *National Geographic Adventure* magazine who has researched and written widely on the psychology of accidents. In his best-selling book *Deep Survival* (2003), Gonzales examined the mental and physical traits that enable some people to survive under extreme conditions—plane wrecks, avalanches, forest fires, lost in the wilderness—while others perish. In this selection from *Everyday Survival* (2008), a book that focuses on more familiar situations, Gonzales uses himself as an example of how we sometimes mistakenly believe ourselves to be safe because we are working from a "mental model" that blinds us to the real danger around us.

XXXXXXXXXXXXXXXXXXXXXXXXXXXXXXXXXXXXXXXXXXXXXXXXXXXXXXXXXXXXXXX

1   When I was a child in San Antonio, Texas, my grandmother had an ashtray that I loved. She had bought it in old Mexico. It was ceramic rattlesnake, and its coiled body formed the tray for the ashes, while its raised head provided a menacing decoration. It was dark and dusty and very realistic. As I grew up, I always wondered what had become of that ashtray.

2   Decades later, I was hiking in the Santa Monica Mountains above Los Angeles. As I bushwhacked along a stream, I came across the ruin of a stone house. Everything was shattered and broken and overrun by thistles and weeds. Only the chimney remained standing. I thought I'd see if I could find a souvenir to take home, a bit of broken dish with a design on it or some old tool. As I poked through the wreckage, suddenly there it was: my grandmother's ashtray, complete and unbroken. Delighted, I reached out to take it. And then its tongue came out. I froze. Its tongue came out again. The serpent was smelling me. With the hair standing up on my neck, I carefully backed away.

This is an example of how our scripts and mental models can   3
betray us. I had both a strong mental model and a familiar behavioral
script working against me and blinding me to the obvious. Without ever
considering it, I had been harboring a mistaken mental model of a rattlesnake. It was my grandmother's ashtray; it was ceramic and not real;
it was not harmful. The nostalgic emotional attachment I had for it
made it a strong and persistent model, difficult to displace. My lack of
experience with real rattlesnakes made for a much weaker competing
model. During that split second (about one-twentieth of a second) in
which seeing becomes recognition, my brain had selected the strongest
mental model, the ashtray.

The second process working against me was a behavioral script for   4
what I was doing. I had told myself that I was looking for an interesting
artifact to take home. That circumscribed and defined what I was doing.
It formed the boundaries of my illusion, blinding me to what I knew
intellectually to be true. If someone had magically snatched me out of
there and questioned me, I could have articulated what I knew. I was in
the dry mountain wilderness of California, where rattlesnakes are common. I was in a rock ruin, where rattlesnakes like to go because mice live
there. Moreover, I could have stated one other obvious fact. The chance
of finding an ashtray identical to my grandmother's anywhere in the
world was close to zero. I didn't have any strong model or script (that is,
direct experience) to support that intellectual knowledge. I had a strong
script associated with the fun of finding something cool to take home
from a hiking trip, because I'd done it many times. I had been rewarded
in the past for following that script. Some of my favorite objects are
found objects. . . . I was operating as if under a spell, in a vacation state
of mind.

This kind of coupling of mental models and scripts leads to intelli-   5
gent mistakes in all walks of life. When I reached out to the rattlesnake,
I was exhibiting a flaw that attends many of our bad decisions: a fundamental lack of curiosity about the world around me. I was not paying
deliberate attention. I wasn't intentionally pushing myself to gather new
information. My behavioral script was sending a strong signal that said,
"The world you see before you is a familiar one. Relax. You've got this
wired." But as the acronym for behavioral script suggests, that message

is often wrong. And this failure represented nothing more than the natural workings of the human brain. Over the eons, it has been good for survival to assume that what has happened before will happen again, and that what has not happened yet never will.

6   This assumption comes from the fact that the human brain classifies everything we encounter—along with the outcomes of our interactions with those things—and labels them good, bad, or indifferent. This system generalizes from previous experience. When things are similar, we lump them together into categories. We also tend to average things, ignoring special cases. We sketch out crude images for quick reference to tell us what we're perceiving and what its value is to us, if any. We create rules to go with those images, so that we know how things ought to behave, and we write scripts so that we can respond in a way that worked before.

7   When one of those scripts doesn't work and we are punished for our behavior, we revise our learning (if we survive) because we're smart. So when I at last comprehended that I was reaching for a real rattlesnake—in that moment of recognition, charged with adrenaline—I instantly created a new mental model for rattlesnakes and a new script for my behavior. The model of my grandmother's ashtray was gone, lost forever. And poking around in ruins would never be quite the same enjoyable pastime. Too bad. On the other hand, I'll probably survive longer, because I'd never try to pick up a rattlesnake again. The experience was a gift, because it awakened my curiosity about the world. I had an opportunity to cast off the mental models and behavioral scripts and explore what's really there.

XXXXXXXXXXXXXXXXXXX **FOR DISCUSSION** XXXXXXXXXXXXXXXXXXX

1. Why did Laurence Gonzales almost pick up a live rattlesnake while looking for artifacts in the mountains above Los Angeles?

2. According to Gonzales's explanation of his life-threatening behavior on this particular occasion, what's a "mental model" (3)? What about a "behavioral script" (4)? What's the difference between the two?

3. How accurate and convincing do you find Gonzales's explanation for "why smart people do stupid things?" Explain.

4. Should Gonzales have known better than to do what he (almost) did? Why or why not?

XXXXXXXXXXXXX **Strategies and Structures** XXXXXXXXXXXXX

1. What main point about mental models and behavioral scripts is Gonzales EXEMPLIFYING by telling about his experience with the rattlesnake? Where does he state it most directly?

2. Is Gonzales's single, extended example of his own experience with the "ashtray" in the ruined house sufficient to illustrate the psychological phenomenon he DESCRIBES? Why or why not?

3. Why does Gonzales begin his essay by telling about his grandmother's ashtray and wondering what happened to it—instead of explaining right away what he means by "a strong mental model and a familiar behavioral script" (3)? Is this organization effective? Where else does Gonzales include elements of NARRATIVE in his essay?

4. What AUDIENCE does Gonzales appear to have in mind when he refers to "our bad decisions" (5)? Explain.

5. In the last paragraph of his essay, Gonzales says that his life-threatening experience "was a gift" (7). What is he exemplifying now? Explain.

6. Where and how does Gonzales use CLASSIFICATION to help explain the phenomenon he is exemplifying?

XXXXXXXXXXXXX **Words and Figures of Speech** XXXXXXXXXXXXX

1. An "artifact" is something made or produced, usually by human workmanship (4). How and how well do an old ashtray or "a bit of broken dish . . . or some old tool" fit this DEFINITION (2)?

2. A "script" can be defined as both a form of writing and a plan of action (3–7). Which definition do you think Gonzales intends—or does his use of "script" include both? What are the implications of using this term to define forms of human behavior? What is Gonzales suggesting about how the human brain works?

3. Why do you think Gonzales refers to the state of mind that led him try to pick up a rattlesnake as "a vacation state of mind" (4)?

4. What kind of "rules" is Gonzales referring to in paragraph 6?

5. What are some of the CONNOTATIONS of the word *survivor*?

❌❌❌❌❌❌❌❌❌❌❌❌❌❌❌❌ **FOR WRITING** ❌❌❌❌❌❌❌❌❌❌❌❌❌❌❌❌❌

1. In a paragraph or two, DESCRIBE an object from your childhood that had a special significance for you. Be sure to say what it EXEMPLIFIED and how.

2. Write an essay using yourself (or someone else) as an example of a smart person who did something really stupid because you were "harboring a mistaken mental model" and a "flawed" behavioral script—but survived anyway (3, 5).

JANET WU

HOMEWARD BOUND

Janet Wu (b. 1960), a reporter for Boston television, was twelve years old when she first met her Chinese grandmother. Wu's father had escaped China during the communist revolution at the end of World War II, and for the next twenty-five years, because of strained relations between China and the United States, Chinese Americans were not allowed to return to their homeland. "Homeward Bound," first published in the *New York Times Magazine* in 1999, is about Wu's visits with a relative she did not know she had. In this essay, Wu looks at the vast differences between two cultures through a single, extended example—the ancient practice, now outlawed, of breaking and binding the feet of upper-class Chinese girls. These "lotus feet" were a symbol of status and beauty.

XXXXXXXXXXXXXXXXXXXXXXXXXXXXXXXXXXXXXXXXXXXXXXXXXXXXXXXXXXX

M y grandmother has bound feet. Cruelly tethered since her birth, they are like bonsai trees, miniature versions of what should have been. She is a relic even in China, where foot binding was first banned more than 80 years ago when the country could no longer afford a population that had to be carried. Her slow, delicate hobble betrays her age and the status she held and lost.   1

My own size 5 feet are huge in comparison. The marks and callouses they bear come from running and jumping, neither of which my grandmother has ever done. The difference between our feet reminds me of the incredible history we hold between us like living bookends. We stand like sentries on either side of a vast gulf.   2

For most of my childhood, I didn't even know she existed. My father was a young man when he left his family's village in northern China, disappearing into the chaos of the Japanese invasion and the   3

Communist revolution[1] that followed. He fled to Taiwan and eventually made his way to America, alone. To me, his second child, it seemed he had no family or history other than his American-born wife and four children. I didn't know that he had been writing years of unanswered
4   letters to China.

I was still a young girl when he finally got a response, and with it the news that his father and six of his seven siblings had died in those years of war and revolution. But the letter also contained an unexpected blessing: somehow his mother had survived. So 30 years after he left home, and in the wake of President Nixon's visit,[2] my father gathered us
5   up and we rushed to China to find her.

I saw my grandmother for the very first time when I was 12. She was almost 80, surprisingly alien and shockingly small. I searched her wrinkled face for something familiar, some physical proof that we belonged to each other. She stared at me the same way. Did she feel cheated, I wondered, by the distance, by the time we had not spent together? I did. With too many lost years to reclaim, we had everything and nothing to say. She politely listened as I struggled with scraps of formal Chinese and smiled as I fell back on "Wo bu dong" ("I don't understand you"). And yet we communicated something strange and beautiful. I found it easy to love this person I had barely
6   met.

The second time I saw her I was 23, arriving in China on an indulgent post-graduate-school adventure, with a Caucasian boyfriend in tow. My grandmother sat on my hotel bed, shrunken and wise, looking as if she belonged in a museum case. She stroked my asymmetrically cropped hair. I touched her feet, and her face contorted with the memory of her

1. The Japanese invasion of China began in the late 1930s and lasted until Japan surrendered to the Allied forces at the close of World War II. In the years following this surrender, the Chinese Nationalist and Communist parties battled for control, with the Communists seizing power in 1949.

2. In 1972, Richard Nixon became the first U.S. president to meet with Communist leaders on Chinese soil, opening relations between countries that had been enemies since the revolution.

childhood pain. "You are lucky," she said. We both understood that she was thinking of far more than the bindings that long ago made her cry. I wanted to share even the smallest part of her life's journey, but I could not conceive of surviving a dynasty and a revolution, just as she could not imagine my life in a country she had never seen. In our mutual isolation of language and experience, we could only gaze in wonder, mystified that we had come to be sitting together.

I last saw her almost five years ago. At 95, she was even smaller, and her frailty frightened me. I was painfully aware that I probably would never see her again, that I would soon lose this person I never really had. So I mentally logged every second we spent together and jockeyed with my siblings for the chance to hold her hand or touch her shoulder. Our departure date loomed like some kind of sentence. And when it came, she broke down, her face bowed into her gnarled hands. I went home, and with resignation awaited the inevitable news that she was gone.

But two months after that trip, it was my father who died. For me, his loss was doubly cruel: his death deprived me of both my foundation and the bridge to my faraway grandmother. For her, it was the second time she had lost him. For the 30 years they were separated, she had feared her son was dead. This time, there was no ambiguity, no hope. When she heard the news, my uncle later wrote us, she wept quietly.

When I hear friends complain about having to visit their nearby relatives, I think of how far away my grandmother is and how untouched our relationship remains by the modern age. My brief handwritten notes are agonizingly slow to reach her. When they do arrive, she cannot read them. I cannot call her. I cannot see, hear or touch her.

But last month my mother called to tell me to brush up on my Chinese. Refusing to let go of our tenuous connection to my father's family, she has decided to take us all back to China in October for my grandmother's 100th birthday. And so every night, I sit at my desk and study, thinking of her tiny doll-like feet, of the miles and differences that separate us, of the moments we'll share when we meet one last time. And I beg her to hold on until I get there.

XXXXXXXXXXXXXXXXX **For Discussion** XXXXXXXXXXXXXXXXX

1. Janet Wu's feet are calloused from exercise. What does this difference between her feet and her grandmother's show about the differences in their lives?

2. Why does Wu touch her grandmother's feet in paragraph 6? What is her grandmother's response? What has happened to the "vast gulf" between them (2)?

3. What is the CONCRETE EXAMPLE Wu's essay is organized around? How does this example illustrate the differences between her and her grandmother, and their connection as family? Refer to particular passages.

XXXXXXXXXXXXX **Strategies and Structures** XXXXXXXXXXXXX

1. Where does Wu mention her grandmother's feet for the last time in her essay? How does this mention serve as an EXAMPLE of bridging two disparate thoughts?

2. Wu is separated from her grandmother by culture, physical distance, and *time*. Point out several of the many references to time and the passage of time in her essay. How do these references help Wu to organize her essay?

3. Wu's NARRATIVE takes an unexpected turn in paragraph 8. What is it? How does the physical frailty of her grandmother contribute to the IRONY of this turn of events?

4. A big part of the cultural difference that separates Wu and her grandmother is *language*. List some of the examples Wu gives of this separation. Why do you think Wu says, in the last paragraph of her essay, that "every night, I sit at my desk and study" (10)?

5. Wu uses the example of her grandmother's bound feet as the basis of an extended COMPARISON AND CONTRAST. Besides feet, what is she comparing to what? What specific similarities and differences does she touch on? What other examples does she use?

XXXXXXXXXXXXX **Words and Figures of Speech** XXXXXXXXXXXXX

1. Explain the PUN(s), or play(s) on words, in Wu's title.

2. Wu COMPARES her grandmother's feet to "bonsai trees" (1). What is a bonsai, and what do the grandmother's feet have in common with one?

3. Wu says her wrinkled, shrunken grandmother looks like she belongs in "a museum case" (6). Why? To what is she comparing her grandmother?

4. If Wu and her grandmother are "living bookends," what do they hold between them (2)? What connection(s) between books and "history" does Wu's use of this METAPHOR imply (2)?

5. When is Wu using her grandmother's bound feet as a metaphor, and when are the feet simply serving her as a literal EXAMPLE? Please cite specific passages.

XXXXXXXXXXXXXXXXXXXXX **FOR WRITING** XXXXXXXXXXXXXXXXXXXXX

1. In a paragraph or two, give several EXAMPLES of distinctive traits, gestures, or physical features shared by members of your family.

2. Write a personal NARRATIVE about a meeting between you and a relative or family friend that exemplifies both the differences separating you and the ties binding you together. Use lots of examples to illustrate those similarities and differences.

LAWRENCE DOWNES

LOSING PRIVATE DWYER

Lawrence Downes (b. 1965) is a reporter and editorial writer for the *New York Times*. After graduating from Fordham University in 1986, Downes attended the University of Missouri School of Journalism. He joined the *Times* staff in 1993 as a copyeditor, rising through the ranks to become a member of the newspaper's editorial board in 2004. "Losing Private Dwyer," which appeared in the *Times* in 2008, was inspired by a battlefield photograph of a U.S. Army medic carrying a wounded boy to safety in Iraq. The heroic medic was Pfc. Joseph Dwyer of El Paso, Texas. A shining example of "the strength and selflessness" of the American soldier, according to Downes, Private Dwyer also came to exemplify the "bitter" side of the Iraqi conflict.

XXXXXXXXXXXXXXXXXXXXXXXXXXXXXXXXXXXXXXXXXXXXXXXXXXXXXXXXXX

1   The photo below captures everything that Americans wanted to believe about the Iraq war in the earliest days of the invasion in 2003. Pfc.[1] Joseph Dwyer, an Army medic whose unit was fighting its way up the Euphrates[2] to Baghdad, cradles a wounded boy. The child is half-naked and helpless, but trusting. Private Dwyer's face is strained but calm.

2   If there are better images of the strength and selflessness of the American soldier, I can't think of any. It is easy to understand why newspapers and magazines around the country ran the photo big, making Private Dwyer an instant hero, back when the war was a triumphal tale of Iraqi liberation.

3   That story turned bitter years ago, of course. And the mountain of sorrows keeps growing: Mr. Dwyer died last month in North Carolina.

1. Private first class, the third-lowest rank in the U.S. Army.
2. River that runs the length of central Iraq.

He was 31 and very sick. For years he had been in and out of treatment for post-traumatic stress disorder and addiction. He was seized by fearful delusions and fits of violence and rage. His wife left him to save herself and their young daughter. When the police were called to Mr. Dwyer's apartment on June 28, he was alone. They broke down the door and found him dying among pill bottles and cans of cleaning solvent that friends said he sniffed to deaden his pain.

He had been heading for a disastrous end ever since he came home. 4

Two of his best friends were Angela Minor and Dionne Knapp, 5 fellow medics at Fort Bliss, near El Paso, Texas. For a while, they were part of a small, inseparable group that worked together, ate out, went to movies and called one another by their first names, which is not the military habit.

Joseph was a rock, Ms. Minor said, a guy who would change your 6 oil and check your tires unasked and pick you up by your broken-down car at 3 A.M. Ms. Knapp said he was like an uncle to her son, Justin, who was having trouble in kindergarten and brightened whenever Mr. Dwyer went there to check on him.

7   Ms. Knapp was called up to Iraq, but Mr. Dwyer insisted on taking her place, because she was a single mom. He had no children at the time, and besides, he had enlisted right after 9/11 just for this. He went and stunned everybody by getting his picture all over the newspapers and TV.

8   A few months later, he was home. He was shy about his celebrity. He was also skinny and haunted. Ms. Minor said he was afraid. Ms. Knapp said paranoid was more like it.

9   It didn't help that El Paso looked a lot like Iraq. Once he totaled his car. He said he had seen a box in the road and thought it was a bomb. He couldn't go to the movies anymore: too many people. In restaurants, he sat with his back to the wall.

10   He said that Iraqis were coming to get him. He would call Angela and Dionne at all hours, to talk vaguely about the "demons" that followed him all day and in his dreams. He became a Baptist, doggedly searching Scripture on his lunch hour—for solace. His friends knew he was also getting high with spray cans bought at computer stores.

11   "He would call me in the middle of the day," Ms. Minor said. "I'd be like: 'Why are you at Best Buy? Why aren't you at work?' I could tell he'd been drinking and huffing again."

12   His friends tried an intervention, showing up at his door in October 2005 and demanding his guns and cans of solvent. He refused to give them up.

13   Hours later, gripped by delusions, he shot up his apartment. He was glad when the SWAT team[3] arrived, Ms. Knapp said, because then he could tell them where the Iraqis were. He was arrested and discharged, and later moved to Pinehurst, North Carolina. His parents tried to get him help, but nothing worked. "He just couldn't get over the war," his mother, Maureen, told a reporter. "Joseph never came home."

---

3. Special weapons and tactics team, an elite group of police officers trained to handle particularly dangerous situations.

It's not clear what therapy and medication could have saved Mr.   14
Dwyer. He admitted lying on a post-deployment questionnaire about
what he had seen and suffered because he just wanted to get back to his
family. Ms. Minor said he sometimes skipped therapy appointments in
El Paso. One thing that did seem to help, Ms. Knapp and Ms. Minor
said, was peer counseling from a fellow veteran, a man who had been
ambushed in Iraq and knew about fear and death. But that was too little, too late, and both women say they are frustrated with the military
for letting Mr. Dwyer slip away.

Private Dwyer, who survived rocket-propelled grenades and shock-   15
ing violence, made his way back to his family and friends. But part of
him was also stuck forever on a road in Iraq, helpless and terrified, with
nobody to carry him to safety.

✕✕✕✕✕✕✕✕✕✕✕✕✕✕✕✕✕✕✕ FOR DISCUSSION ✕✕✕✕✕✕✕✕✕✕✕✕✕✕✕✕✕✕✕

1. Lawrence Downes says the widely circulated photograph of Private Dwyer
cradling a wounded child captured "everything that Americans wanted to
believe about the Iraq war" at the beginning of the conflict in 2003 (1). Is he
right? Why or why not?

2. The American newspapers and magazines hailed Private Dwyer as a "hero"
(2). Was he, in your opinion? Explain.

3. What did Dwyer's mother mean when she told reporters that "Joseph never
came home" (13)?

4. Whom do Angela Minor and Dionne Knapp blame for letting Pfc. Joseph
Dwyer "slip away" (14)? Why?

✕✕✕✕✕✕✕✕✕✕✕✕✕ STRATEGIES AND STRUCTURES ✕✕✕✕✕✕✕✕✕✕✕✕✕

1. How and how effectively does Downes use the photograph of Private Dwyer
to illustrate what he has to say? How well does it support his PURPOSE? Explain.

2. What main point is Downes making by citing the EXAMPLE of Private Dwyer
after he returns home? Point out passages where he states that point directly.

3. Is the example of Private Dwyer sufficient to support Downes's main point?
Should Downes have included additional examples of "casualties" of the war in
Iraq? Why or why not?

4. How does Downes tie the ending of his essay back to the photograph at the beginning? Is this an effective strategy? Why or why not?

5. Downes's NARRATIVE of Private Dwyer's life begins with his "disastrous end" (3–4). Why? Would this essay be just as effective if the events of Private Dwyer's life were presented in chronological order? Why or why not?

XXXXXXXXXXXXX **WORDS AND FIGURES OF SPEECH** XXXXXXXXXXXXX

1. Explain the ALLUSION in the title of Downes's essay.

2. What are some of the main symptoms of a "paranoid" personality (8)? Is Downes right to say that Pfc. Dwyer exhibited those symptoms? Explain.

3. In military language, what is an "intervention" (12)? Why does Downes use the term here?

4. As Downes uses it in paragraph 14, is "too little, too late" a CLICHÉ? Why or why not?

XXXXXXXXXXXXXXXXXXXX **FOR WRITING** XXXXXXXXXXXXXXXXXXXXXX

1. Look again at the photograph of Pfc. Joseph Dwyer on p. 155. Write a paragraph or two explaining what *you* think it EXEMPLIFIES.

2. Write an essay about someone who exemplifies the virtues of "strength and selflessness" or who was "lost" and "never came home"—or both.

RICHARD LEDERER

ENGLISH IS A CRAZY LANGUAGE

Richard Lederer (b. 1938) taught for many years at St. Paul's, a boarding school in New Hampshire. He retired in 1989 to carry on his "mission as a user-friendly English teacher" by writing extensively and humorously about the peculiarities of the English language. Lederer is the author of *Anguished English* (1987) and *Adventures of a Verbivore* (1994), among many other books. This essay, made up of one rapid-fire example after another, is the opening chapter of his best-selling *Crazy English* (1989).

XXXXXXXXXXXXXXXXXXXXXXXXXXXXXXXXXXXXXXXXXXXXXXXXXXXXXXXXXXXXX

English is the most widely spoken language in the history of our planet, used in some way by at least one out of every seven human beings around the globe. Half of the world's books are written in English, and the majority of international telephone calls are made in English. English is the language of over 60 percent of the world's radio programs, many of them beamed, ironically, by the Russians, who know that to win friends and influence nations, they're best off using English. More than 70 percent of international mail is written and addressed in English, and 80 percent of all computer text is stored in English. English has acquired the largest vocabulary of all the world's languages, perhaps as many as two million words, and has generated one of the noblest bodies of literature in the annals of the human race.

Nonetheless, it is now time to face the fact that English is a crazy language.

In the crazy English language, the blackbird hen is brown, blackboards can be blue or green, and blackberries are green and then red before they are ripe. Even if blackberries were really black and blueberries really blue, what are strawberries, cranberries, elderberries, huckleberries, raspberries, boysenberries, mulberries, and gooseberries supposed to look like?

4   To add to the insanity, there is no butter in buttermilk, no egg in eggplant, no grape in grapefruit, neither worms nor wood in wormwood, neither pine nor apple in pineapple, neither peas nor nuts in peanuts, and no ham in a hamburger. (In fact, if somebody invented a sandwich consisting of a ham patty in a bun, we would have a hard time finding a name for it.) To make matters worse, English muffins weren't invented in England, french fries in France, or danish pastries in Denmark. And we discover even more culinary madness in the revelations that sweetmeat is candy, while sweetbread, which isn't sweet, is made from meat.

5   In this unreliable English tongue, greyhounds aren't always grey (or gray); panda bears and koala bears aren't bears (they're marsupials); a woodchuck is a groundhog, which is not a hog; a horned toad is a lizard; glowworms are fireflies, but fireflies are not flies (they're beetles); ladybugs and lightning bugs are also beetles (and to propagate, a significant proportion of ladybugs must be male); a guinea pig is neither a pig nor from Guinea (it's a South American rodent); and a titmouse is neither mammal nor mammaried.

6   Language is like the air we breathe. It's invisible, inescapable, indispensable, and we take it for granted. But when we take the time, step back, and listen to the sounds that escape from the holes in people's faces and explore the paradoxes and vagaries of English, we find that hot dogs can be cold, darkrooms can be lit, homework can be done in school, nightmares can take place in broad daylight, while morning sickness and daydreaming can take place at night, tomboys are girls, midwives can be men, hours—especially happy hours and rush hours—can last longer than sixty minutes, quicksand works *very* slowly, boxing rings are square, silverware can be made of plastic and tablecloths of paper, most telephones are dialed by being punched (or pushed?), and most bathrooms don't have any baths in them. In fact, a dog can go to the bathroom under a tree—no bath, no room; it's still going to the bathroom. And doesn't it seem at least a little bizarre that we go to the bathroom in order to go to the bathroom?

7   Why is it that a woman can man a station but a man can't woman one, that a man can father a movement but a woman can't mother one,

and that a king rules a kingdom but a queen doesn't rule a queendom? How did all those Renaissance men reproduce when there don't seem to have been any Renaissance women?

A writer is someone who writes, and a stinger is something that stings. But fingers don't fing, grocers don't groce, hammers don't ham, and humdingers don't humding. If the plural of *tooth* is *teeth*, shouldn't the plural of *booth* be *beeth*? One goose, two geese—so one moose, two meese? One index, two indices—one Kleenex, two Kleenices? If people ring a bell today and rang a bell yesterday, why don't we say that they flang a ball? If they wrote a letter, perhaps they also bote their tongue. If the teacher taught, why isn't it also true that the preacher praught? Why is it that the sun shone yesterday while I shined my shoes, that I treaded water and then trod on soil, and that I flew out to see a World Series game in which my favorite player flied out?

8

If we conceive a conception and receive at a reception, why don't we grieve a greption and believe a beleption? If a horsehair mat is made from the hair of horses and a camel's hair brush from the hair of camels, from what is a mohair coat made? If a vegetarian eats vegetables, what does a humanitarian eat? If a firefighter fights fire, what does a freedom fighter fight? If a weightlifter lifts weights, what does a shoplifter lift? If *pro* and *con* are opposites, is congress the opposite of progress?

9

Sometimes you have to believe that all English speakers should be committed to an asylum for the verbally insane. In what other language do people drive in a parkway and park in a driveway? In what other language do people recite at a play and play at a recital? In what other language do privates eat in the general mess and generals eat in the private mess? In what other language do men get hernias and women get hysterectomies? In what other language do people ship by truck and send cargo by ship? In what other language can your nose run and your feet smell?

10

How can a slim chance and a fat chance be the same, "what's going on?" and "what's coming off?" be the same, and a bad licking and a good licking be the same, while a wise man and a wise guy are opposites? How can sharp speech and blunt speech be the same and *quite a lot* and *quite a few* the same, while *overlook* and *oversee* are opposites? How can the weather be hot as hell one day and cold as hell the next?

11

12   If *button* and *unbutton* and *tie* and *untie* are opposites, why are *loosen* and *unloosen* and *ravel* and *unravel* the same? If *bad* is the opposite of *good*, *hard* the opposite of *soft*, and *up* the opposite of *down*, why are *badly* and *goodly*, *hardly* and *softly*, and *upright* and *downright* not opposing pairs? If harmless actions are the opposite of harmful actions, why are shameless and shameful behavior the same and pricey objects less expensive than priceless ones? If appropriate and inappropriate remarks and passable and impassable mountain trails are opposites, why are flammable and inflammable materials, heritable and inheritable property, and passive and impassive people the same and valuable objects less treasured than invaluable ones? If *uplift* is the same as *lift up*, why are *upset* and *set up* opposite in meaning? Why are *pertinent* and *impertinent*, *canny* and *uncanny*, and *famous* and *infamous* neither opposites nor the same? How can *raise* and *raze* and *reckless* and *wreckless* be opposites when each pair contains the same sound?

13   Why is it that when the sun or the moon or the stars are out, they are visible, but when the lights are out, they are invisible, and that when I wind up my watch, I start it, but when I wind up this essay, I shall end it?

14   English is a crazy language.

XXXXXXXXXXXXXXXXXX **For Discussion** XXXXXXXXXXXXXXXXXX

1. Most of the time, Richard Lederer is illustrating his main point that "English is a crazy language" (2). But what does he say about its widespread influence? What EXAMPLES does he give?

2. Do you think English is as crazy as Lederer says it is? Why or why not? Give several examples to support your opinion.

3. How seriously do you think Lederer actually intends for us to take the general proposition of his essay? Why do you think he gives so many crazy examples?

4. Linguists hold that the meanings of words are arbitrary, determined by convention rather than by any innate qualities. Do you think the examples in Lederer's essay represent this principle? Refer to specific passages in his essay that support your position.

5. List several examples of your own of the craziness of the English language.

XXXXXXXXXXXXX **STRATEGIES AND STRUCTURES** XXXXXXXXXXXXX

1. What is the PURPOSE of the opening paragraph of Lederer's essay? How does the opening paragraph color the rest of what he says about the craziness of the English language?

2. Lederer's essay is made up almost entirely of clusters of EXAMPLES. What do the examples in paragraph 3 have in common? Are the examples in paragraph 4 more like those in paragraph 3 or paragraph 5? Explain.

3. In paragraph 8, Lederer pretends to be upset with irregular verbs and irregular plurals of nouns. Which are examples of which? Make a list of his examples for both categories.

4. Which examples have to do primarily with gender? What connects all the examples in paragraph 12?

5. In paragraph 6, Lederer refers to two related aspects of the English language that all of his examples might be said to illustrate. What are these aspects? Where else in his essay does Lederer actually name the aspects of English he is exemplifying?

6. Lederer gives his essay the form of a logical ARGUMENT. The proposition he intends to prove is stated in paragraph 2. Where does he state it again as a conclusion? Is the argument in between primarily INDUCTIVE (reasoning from specific examples to a general conclusion) or DEDUCTIVE (reasoning from general principles to a more specific conclusion)? Explain.

XXXXXXXXXXXXX **WORDS AND FIGURES OF SPEECH** XXXXXXXXXXXXX

1. In American English (speaking of contradictions), a *rant* is a form of vehement speech; in British English (speaking of redundancies), a *rant* can also mean an outburst of wild merriment. Which meaning or meanings apply to Lederer's essay?

2. A *misnomer* is a term that implies a meaning or interpretation that is actually untrue or inaccurate—"koala bear," for example. Choose one of the following misnomers that Lederer mentions and explain why you think the object it refers to has this inaccurate name—and why the name persists: "eggplant," "peanut," "french fries," "horned toad," "firefly," "guinea pig" (4, 5).

3. How does your dictionary DEFINE the word "vagaries" (6)? How is it related to the word *vagabonds*?

4. Lederer "winds up" his essay in paragraph 13. Could he be said, just as accurately, to "wind it down"?

1. Write an essay illustrating the craziness of some language other than English—one you speak and/or have studied. For example, one way to say you're welcome in French is "Je vous en prie," which means, literally, "I beg of you."

2. For all its "craziness," Lederer asserts that "English is the most widely spoken language in the history of our planet" (1). Write an essay that supports or contests this proposition. Be sure to include sufficient EXAMPLES of who uses the language, where, and for what purposes.

CHAPTER FIVE

CLASSIFICATION

XXXXXXXXXXXXXXXXXXXXXXXXXXXXXXXXXXXXXXXXXXXXXXXXXXXXXXXXX

When we CLASSIFY* things, we say what categories they belong to. Dogs, for instance, can be classified as collies, Great Danes, Labrador retrievers, Chihuahuas, and so on. A category is a group with similar characteristics. Thus, to be classified as a Labrador, a dog must be sturdily built, have soft jaws for carrying game, and have a yellow, black, or chocolate coat because these are the characteristics, among others, that distinguish the Labrador group—or breed.

Dogs, like anything else, can be classified in more than one way. We can also classify dogs as working dogs, show dogs, and mutts that make good family pets. Or simply as small, medium, and large dogs—or as males and females. The categories into which we divide any subject will depend upon the basis on which we classify it. In the case of dogs, our principle of classification is often by breed, but it can also be by role, size, sex, or some other principle.

No matter your subject or your principle of classification, the categories in your system must be inclusive and not overlap. You wouldn't classify dogs as hunting dogs, show dogs, and retrievers, for example, because some dogs, such as most family pets, would be left out—while others, such as Irish setters, would belong to more than one category, since setters are both hunting dogs and retrievers.

The categories in any classification system will vary with who is doing the classifying and for what PURPOSE. A teacher divides a group of thirty students according to grades: A, B, C, D, and F. A basketball coach might divide the same group of students into forwards, guards, and centers. The director of a student drama group would have another

*Words printed in SMALL CAPITALS are defined in the Glossary.

set of criteria. Yet all three systems are valid for the purposes they are intended to serve. And classification must serve some larger purpose, or it becomes an empty game.

Systems of classification can help us organize our thoughts about the world around us. They can also help us organize our thoughts in writing, whether in a single paragraph or a whole essay. For example, you might organize a paragraph by introducing your subject, dividing it into types, and then giving the distinguishing features of each type. Here is a paragraph that follows such a pattern. The subject is lightning:

> There are several types of lightning named according to where the discharge takes place. Among them are intracloud lightning, by far the most common type, in which the flash occurs within the thundercloud; air-discharge lightning, in which the flash occurs between the cloud and the surrounding air; and cloud-to-ground lightning, in which the discharge takes place between the cloud and the ground.
>
> RICHARD ORVILLE, "Bolts from the Blue"

This short paragraph could be the opening of an essay that goes on to discuss each of the three types of lightning in order, devoting a paragraph or more to each type. If the author's purpose were simply to help us understand the different types, he would probably spend more time on the first kind of lightning—perhaps coming back to it in detail later in his essay—because "intracloud lightning" is the most common variety.

In this case, however, Richard Orville, a meteorologist at Texas A&M University, chose to develop his essay by writing several additional paragraphs on the third type of lightning, "in which the discharge takes place between the cloud and the ground." Why emphasize this category?

Meteorologists classify storms—especially hurricanes, tornadoes, and thunderstorms—not only to understand them but also to predict where they are most likely to occur. As Orville says, his main point in classifying lightning is to "tell what parts on the ground will be most threatened by the lightning activity." Based on this information, the meteorologist can then warn people to take shelter. He can also alert the power companies, so they can deploy power crews more effectively, or reroute electricity away from a power plant even before it is hit.

Given this purpose—to predict weather activity so he can issue accurate weather warnings and advisories—Orville first classifies his subject into types based on the location of the electrical discharge, or "flash." He then devotes most of his essay to the third type of lightning (cloud-to-ground) because it is the most dangerous kind—to property, to natural resources such as forests, and to people.

Meteorologists divide the subject of lightning into groups or kinds— intracloud, air-discharge, cloud-to-ground. This is the equivalent of classifying dogs by dividing them into distinct breeds. Meteorologists also sort individual bolts of lightning according to the group or kind they belong to: "The bolt of lightning that just destroyed the oak tree in your yard was the cloud-to-ground kind." This is the equivalent of saying that a particular dog is a Lab or a husky or a Portuguese water dog. In this chapter, we will use the term *classification* whether we are dividing a subject into groups or sorting individuals according to the group they belong to— because in either case we are organizing a subject into categories.

A Brief Guide to Writing a Classification Essay

As you write a classification essay, you need to identify your subject and explain the basis on which you're classifying it. David Brooks makes these basic moves of classification in the first paragraph of his essay in this chapter:

> The world can be divided in many ways—rich and poor, democratic and authoritarian—but one of the most striking is the divide between the societies with an individualist mentality and the ones with a collectivist mentality.
>
> David Brooks, "Harmony and the Dream"

Brooks identifies his subject (societies of the world) and explains the basis on which he is classifying it (their basic philosophies, or "mentalities").

The following guidelines will help you to make these basic moves as you draft a classification essay. They'll also help you to come up with your subject and to select categories that fit your purpose and audience, are effectively organized, support your main point, and are sufficiently inclusive yet don't overlap.

Coming Up with a Subject

Almost any subject—lightning, convertibles, TV dramas—can be classified in some way. As you consider subjects to classify, think about what you might learn from doing so—your PURPOSE for classifying. For example, you might want to classify something in order to evaluate it (Which dog breeds are appropriate for families with young children?); to determine causes (Was the crash due to mechanical failure, weather, or pilot error?); or to make sense of events (What kinds of economic recessions has the United States historically experienced?). Choose a subject that interests you, but also ask yourself, "Why is this subject worth classifying?"

Considering Your Purpose and Audience

The specific traits you focus on and the categories you divide your subject into will be determined largely by your purpose and AUDIENCE. Suppose the roof of your town's city hall blows off in a hurricane, and your purpose is to determine—and write an article for your neighborhood newsletter explaining—what kind of roof will stay on best in the next hurricane. In this case, you'd look closely at such traits as weight and wind resistance and pay less attention to traits such as color or energy efficiency.

Once you've determined the kind of roof that has the highest wind rating, you probably will not have a hard time convincing your readers (many of whom also lost their roofs) that this is the kind to buy. However, since your audience of homeowners may not be experts in roofing materials, you'll want to DEFINE any technical terms and use language they're familiar with. Keep in mind that readers will not always agree with the way you classify a subject. So you may need to explain why they should accept the criteria you've used.

Generating Ideas: Considering What Categories There Are

Once you have a subject in mind and a reason for classifying it, consider what categories there are and choose the ones that best suit your purpose and audience. For example, if your purpose is to evaluate different kinds of movies for a film course, you might classify them by genre—drama, comedy, romance, horror, thriller, musical. But if you are reviewing movies for the campus newspaper, you would probably base your classification on quality, perhaps dividing them into these five categories: "must see," "excellent," "good," "mediocre," and "to be avoided at all costs."

When you devise categories for a classification essay, make sure they adhere to a consistent principle (or basis) of classification. For example, if the basis of your movie classification is "movies appropriate for young children," you might use categories such as "good for all ages," "pre-school," "six and up," and "not suitable for children." But you should avoid mixing such categories with those based on genre or quality. In other words, you wouldn't use "drama," "excellent," and "not suitable for children" as the categories in your classification system.

Templates for Classifying

The following templates can help you to generate ideas for a classification essay and then to start drafting. Don't take these as formulas where you just have to fill in the blanks. There are no easy formulas for good writing. But these templates can help you plot out some of the key moves of classification and thus may serve as good starting points.

> ➤ X can be classified on the basis of _____.
>
> ➤ Classified on the basis of _____, some of the most common types of X are _____, _____, and _____.
>
> ➤ X can be divided into two basic types, _____ and _____.
>
> ➤ Experts in the field typically divide X into _____, _____, and _____.
>
> ➤ This particular X clearly belongs in the _____ category, since it is _____, _____, and _____.
>
> ➤ _____ and _____ are examples of this type of X.
>
> ➤ By classifying X in this way, we can see that _____.

For more techniques to help you generate ideas and start writing, see Chapter 1.

Organizing a Classification Essay

In the opening paragraphs of your essay, tell the reader what you're classifying and why, and explain your classification system. If you were writing an essay classifying types of environmentally friendly cars, for example, you might use an introduction like this:

> If you are considering buying an environmentally friendly car, you need to know which types of fueling are available in order to find a car that meets your goals for a green lifestyle. Green cars can best be divided into the following categories: petrol cars, diesel cars, electric cars, hybrid cars, and biofuel cars. If you understand these five basic types and the differences among them, you can make an informed decision for the good of both the environment and your wallet.

Typically, the body of a classification essay is devoted to a point-by-point discussion of each of the categories that make up your classification system. Thus if you are classifying green cars, you would spend a paragraph, or at least several sentences, explaining the most important characteristics of each type.

Once you've laid out the categories in some detail, remind the reader of the point you are making. The point of classifying cars by fuel type, for example, is to help readers choose the green car that best meets their goals for an environmentally friendly lifestyle.

Stating Your Point

When you compose a classification essay, you should have in mind what you learned about your subject by classifying it in a particular way. Tell the reader in a THESIS STATEMENT what your main point is and why you're dividing up your subject as you do. Usually, you'll want to state your main point in the introduction of your essay as you explain your classification system. In the opening paragraph of the essay on green cars, for instance, the writer states her main point in the last sentence: "If you can understand these five basic types . . . you can make an informed decision."

Choosing Significant Characteristics

Whatever classification system you use, base your categories on the most significant characteristics of your subject—ones that explain something important about it. For example, you probably would not discuss color when classifying environmentally friendly cars because this attribute does not tell the reader what environmentally significant kind of car it is. After all, every kind of car comes in different colors. Instead, you would probably use such attributes as fuel type, miles-per-gallon, and types of emissions—traits that differentiate, say, a hybrid car from other kinds of green cars.

Choosing Categories That Are Inclusive and Don't Overlap

When you divide your subject into categories, those categories must be inclusive enough to cover most cases, and they must not overlap. For example, classifying ice cream into chocolate and vanilla alone isn't very useful because this system leaves out many other important kinds, such as strawberry, pistachio, and rum raisin. The categories in a good classification system include all kinds: for instance, no-fat, low-fat, and full-fat ice cream. And they should not overlap. Thus, chocolate, vanilla, homemade, and Ben and Jerry's do not make a good classification system because the same scoop of ice cream could fit into more than one category.

EVERYDAY CLASSIFICATION
United States of Obesity Map

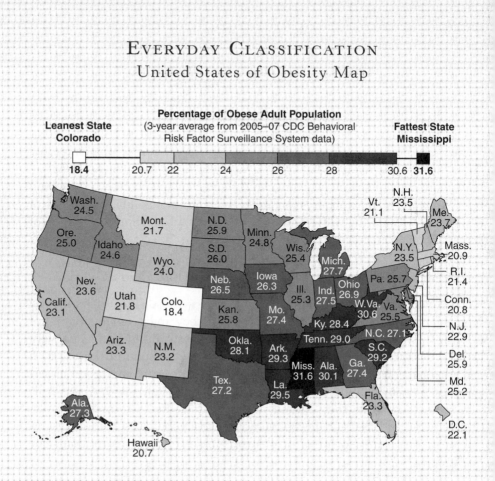

Percentage of Obese Adult Population
(3-year average from 2005–07 CDC Behavioral
Risk Factor Surveillance System data)

Leanest State
Colorado

Fattest State
Mississippi

18.4   20.7 22   24   26   28   30.6 31.6

Wash. 24.5
Ore. 25.0
Idaho 24.6
Mont. 21.7
N.D. 25.9
Minn. 24.8
Vt. 21.1
N.H. 23.5
Me. 23.7
Nev. 23.6
Wyo. 24.0
S.D. 26.0
Wis. 25.4
Mich. 27.7
N.Y. 23.5
Mass. 20.9
R.I. 21.4
Calif. 23.1
Utah 21.8
Colo. 18.4
Neb. 26.5
Iowa 26.3
Ill. 25.3
Ind. 27.5
Ohio 26.9
Pa. 25.7
Conn. 20.8
Ariz. 23.3
N.M. 23.2
Kan. 25.8
Mo. 27.4
W.Va. 30.6
Va. 25.5
N.J. 22.9
Ky. 28.4
Okla. 28.1
Ark. 29.3
Tenn. 29.0
N.C. 27.1
S.C. 29.2
Del. 25.9
Tex. 27.2
Miss. 31.6
Ala. 30.1
Ga. 27.4
Md. 25.2
La. 29.5
Fla. 23.3
Ala. 27.3
Hawaii 20.7
D.C. 22.1

"How Fat Is Your State?" asks the nutrition website CalorieLab.com. When you classify things, you divide them into categories. In this map of the United States from 2008, the calorie counters at CalorieLab classify the states according to the "Percentage of Obese Adult Population." Classified on this basis, the leanest state is Colorado (18.4 percent) and the fattest is Mississippi (31.6 percent). There are many ways to classify states, people, or almost any other subject. Whatever your system, you should have a good reason for classifying your subject in that way. For the nutritionists at CalorieLab, the purpose is not only to find out which states are leaner or heavier than others, but also to encourage overweight adults in every state to reduce their numbers—and their calorie intake.

AMY TAN

MOTHER TONGUE

Amy Tan (b. 1952) is a native of California. In her best-selling first
novel, *The Joy Luck Club* (1989), Tan used all of the different forms of
the English language she had spoken since childhood with her mother,
whose native language was Chinese. In "Mother Tongue," which first
appeared in the *Threepenny Review* (1990), Tan not only *uses* her family's
different "Englishes," she classifies them into their various kinds and
explains how each type lends itself to a different form of communication. Tan's other novels include *The Bonesetter's Daughter* (2001) and
Saving Fish from Drowning (2006).

XXXXXXXXXXXXXXXXXXXXXXXXXXXXXXXXXXXXXXXXXXXXXXXXXXXXXXX

I am not a scholar of English or literature. I cannot give you much more   1
than personal opinions on the English language and its variations in
this country or others.

I am a writer. And by that definition, I am someone who has   2
always loved language. I am fascinated by language in daily life. I spend
a great deal of my time thinking about the power of language—the way
it can evoke an emotion, a visual image, a complex idea, or a simple
truth. Language is the tool of my trade. And I use them all—all the
Englishes I grew up with.

Recently, I was made keenly aware of the different Englishes I do   3
use. I was giving a talk to a large group of people, the same talk I had
already given to half a dozen other groups. The nature of the talk was
about my writing, my life, and my book, *The Joy Luck Club*. The talk
was going along well enough, until I remembered one major difference
that made the whole talk sound wrong. My mother was in the room.
And it was perhaps the first time she had heard me give a lengthy
speech, using the kind of English I have never used with her. I was saying things like, "The intersection of memory upon imagination" and

"There is an aspect of my fiction that relates to thus-and-thus"—a speech filled with carefully wrought grammatical phrases, burdened, it suddenly seemed to me, with nominalized forms, past perfect tenses, conditional phrases, all the forms of standard English that I had learned in school and through books, the forms of English I did not use at home with my mother.

4   Just last week, I was walking down the street with my mother, and I again found myself conscious of the English I was using, the English I do use with her. We were talking about the price of new and used furniture and I heard myself saying this: "Not waste money that way." My husband was with us as well, and he didn't notice any switch in my English. And then I realized why. It's because over the twenty years we've been together I've often used the same kind of English with him, and sometimes he even uses it with me. It has become our language of intimacy, a different sort of English that relates to family talk, the language I grew up with.

5   So you'll have some idea of what this family talk I heard sounds like, I'll quote what my mother said during a recent conversation which I videotaped and then transcribed. During this conversation, my mother was talking about a political gangster in Shanghai who had the same last name as her family's, Du, and how the gangster in his early years wanted to be adopted by her family, which was rich by comparison. Later, the gangster became more powerful, far richer than my mother's family, and one day showed up at my mother's wedding to pay his respects. Here's what she said in part:

6   "Du Yusong having business like fruit stand. Like off the street kind. He is Du like Du Zong—but not Tsung-ming Island people. The local people call putong, the river east side, he belong to that side local people. That man want to ask Du Zong father take him in like become own family. Du Zong father wasn't look down on him, but didn't take seriously, until that man big like become a mafia. Now important person, very hard to inviting him. Chinese way, came only to show respect, don't stay for dinner. Respect for making big celebration, he shows up. Mean gives lots of respect. Chinese custom. Chinese social life that way. If too important won't have to stay too long. He come to my wedding. I didn't see, I heard it. I gone to boy's side, they have YMCA dinner. Chinese age I was nineteen."

You should know that my mother's expressive command of English belies how much she actually understands. She reads the *Forbes*[1] report, listens to *Wall Street Week,* converses daily with her stockbroker, reads all of Shirley MacLaine's[2] books with ease—all kinds of things I can't begin to understand. Yet some of my friends tell me they understand 50 percent of what my mother says. Some say they understand 80 to 90 percent. Some say they understand none of it, as if she were speaking pure Chinese. But to me, my mother's English is perfectly clear, perfectly natural. It's my mother tongue. Her language, as I hear it, is vivid, direct, full of observation and imagery. That was the language that helped shape the way I saw things, expressed things, made sense of the world.

Lately, I've been giving more thought to the kind of English my mother speaks. Like others, I have described it to people as "broken" or "fractured" English. But I wince when I say that. It has always bothered me that I can think of no way to describe it other than "broken," as if it were damaged and needed to be fixed, as if it lacked a certain wholeness and soundness. I've heard other terms used, "limited English," for example. But they seem just as bad, as if everything is limited, including people's perceptions of the limited English speaker.

I know this for a fact, because when I was growing up, my mother's "limited" English limited *my* perception of her. I was ashamed of her English. I believed that her English reflected the quality of what she had to say. That is, because she expressed them imperfectly her thoughts were imperfect. And I had plenty of empirical evidence to support me: the fact that people in department stores, at banks, and at restaurants did not take her seriously, did not give her good service, pretended not to understand her, or even acted as if they did not hear her.

My mother has long realized the limitations of her English as well. When I was fifteen, she used to have me call people on the phone to pretend I was she. In this guise, I was forced to ask for information or even to

7

8

9

10

---

1. Business magazine popular with corporate executives and investors.
2. American film actress (b. 1934) who has written a number of memoirs.

complain and yell at people who had been rude to her. One time it was a call to her stockbroker in New York. She had cashed out her small portfolio and it just so happened we were going to go to New York the next week, our very first trip outside California. I had to get on the phone and say in an adolescent voice that was not very convincing, "This is Mrs. Tan."

11   And my mother was standing in the back whispering loudly, "Why he don't send me check, already two weeks late. So mad he lie to me, losing me money."

12   And then I said in perfect English, "Yes, I'm getting rather concerned. You had agreed to send the check two weeks ago, but it hasn't arrived."

13   Then she began to talk more loudly. "What he want, I come to New York tell him front of his boss, you cheating me?" And I was trying to calm her down, make her be quiet, while telling the stockbroker, "I can't tolerate any more excuses. If I don't receive the check immediately, I am going to have to speak to your manager when I'm in New York next week." And sure enough, the following week there we were in front of this astonished stockbroker, and I was sitting there red-faced and quiet, and my mother, the real Mrs. Tan, was shouting at his boss in her impeccable broken English.

14   We used a similar routine just five days ago, for a situation that was far less humorous. My mother had gone to the hospital for an appointment, to find out about a benign brain tumor a CAT scan had revealed a month ago. She said she had spoken very good English, her best English, no mistakes. Still, she said, the hospital did not apologize when they said they had lost the CAT scan and she had come for nothing. She said they did not seem to have any sympathy when she told them she was anxious to know the exact diagnosis, since her husband and son had both died of brain tumors. She said they would not give her any more information until the next time and she would have to make another appointment for that. So she said she would not leave until the doctor called her daughter. She wouldn't budge. And when the doctor finally called her daughter, me, who spoke in perfect English—lo and behold—we had assurances the CAT scan would be found, promises that a conference call on Monday would be held, and apologies for any suffering my mother had gone through for a most regrettable mistake.

I think my mother's English almost had an effect on limiting my pos-   15
sibilities in life as well. Sociologists and linguists probably will tell you that
a person's developing language skills are more influenced by peers. But I do
think that the language spoken in the family, especially in immigrant families which are more insular, plays a large role in shaping the language of the
child. And I believe that it affected my results on achievement tests, IQ
tests, and the SAT. While my English skills were never judged as poor,
compared to math, English could not be considered my strong suit. In
grade school I did moderately well, getting perhaps B's, sometimes B-
pluses, in English and scoring perhaps in the sixtieth or seventieth percentile on achievement tests. But those scores were not good enough to
override the opinion that my true abilities lay in math and science, because
in those areas I achieved A's and scored in the ninetieth percentile or higher.

This was understandable. Math is precise; there is only one correct   16
answer. Whereas, for me at least, the answers on English tests were
always a judgment call, a matter of opinion and personal experience.
Those tests were constructed around items like fill-in-the-blank sentence
completion, such as, "Even though Tom was _____, Mary thought he
was _____." And the correct answer always seemed to be the most bland
combinations of thoughts, for example, "Even though Tom was shy,
Mary thought he was charming," with the grammatical structure "even
though" limiting the correct answer to some sort of semantic opposites,
so you wouldn't get answers like, "Even though Tom was foolish, Mary
thought he was ridiculous." Well, according to my mother, there were
very few limitations as to what Tom could have been and what Mary
might have thought of him. So I never did well on tests like that.

The same was true with word analogies, pairs of words in which   17
you were supposed to find some sort of logical, semantic relationship—
for example, "*Sunset* is to *nightfall* as _____ is to _____." And here you
would be presented with a list of four possible pairs, one of which
showed the same kind of relationship: *red* is to *stoplight, bus* is to *arrival,
chills* is to *fever, yawn* is to *boring.* Well, I could never think that way. I
knew what the tests were asking, but I could not block out of my mind
the images already created by the first pair, "*sunset* is to *nightfall*"—and
I would see a burst of colors against a darkening sky, the moon rising,
the lowering of a curtain of stars. And all the other pairs of words—red,

bus, stoplight, boring—just threw up a mass of confusing images, making it impossible for me to sort out something as logical as saying: "A sunset precedes nightfall" is the same as "a chill precedes a fever." The only way I would have gotten that answer right would have been to imagine an associative situation, for example, my being disobedient and staying out past sunset, catching a chill at night, which turns into feverish pneumonia as punishment, which indeed did happen to me.

18   I have been thinking about all this lately, about my mother's English, about achievement tests. Because lately I've been asked, as a writer, why there are not more Asian Americans represented in American literature. Why are there few Asian Americans enrolled in creative writing programs? Why do so many Chinese students go into engineering? Well, these are broad sociological questions I can't begin to answer. But I have noticed in surveys—in fact, just last week—that Asian students, as a whole, always do significantly better on math achievement tests than in English. And this makes me think that there are other Asian-American students whose English spoken in the home might also be described as "broken" or "limited." And perhaps they also have teachers who are steering them away from writing and into math and science, which is what happened to me.

19   Fortunately, I happen to be rebellious in nature and enjoy the challenge of disproving assumptions made about me. I became an English major my first year in college, after being enrolled as pre-med. I started writing nonfiction as a freelancer the week after I was told by my former boss that writing was my worst skill and I should hone my talents toward account management.

20   But it wasn't until 1985 that I finally began to write fiction. And at first I wrote using what I thought to be wittily crafted sentences, sentences that would finally prove I had mastery over the English language. Here's an example from the first draft of a story that later made its way into *The Joy Luck Club*, but without this line: "That was my mental quandary in its nascent state." A terrible line, which I can barely pronounce.

21   Fortunately, for reasons I won't get into today, I later decided I should envision a reader for the stories I would write. And the reader I decided upon was my mother, because these were stories about moth-

ers. So with this reader in mind—and in fact she did read my early drafts—I began to write stories using all the Englishes I grew up with: the English I spoke to my mother, which for lack of a better term might be described as "simple"; the English she used with me, which for lack of a better term might be described as "broken"; my translation of her Chinese, which could certainly be described as "watered down"; and what I imagined to be her translation of her Chinese if she could speak in perfect English, her internal language, and for that I sought to preserve the essence, but neither an English nor a Chinese structure. I wanted to capture what language ability tests can never reveal: her intent, her passion, her imagery, the rhythms of her speech and the nature of her thoughts.

Apart from what any critic had to say about my writing, I knew I had succeeded where it counted when my mother finished reading my book and gave me her verdict: "So easy to read."

22

✗✗✗✗✗✗✗✗✗✗✗✗✗✗✗✗✗✗ FOR DISCUSSION ✗✗✗✗✗✗✗✗✗✗✗✗✗✗✗✗✗✗

1. Into what two basic categories does Amy Tan CLASSIFY all the Englishes that she uses in writing and speaking?

2. How many Englishes did Tan learn at home from conversing with her mother, a native speaker of Chinese? How does she distinguish among them?

3. According to Tan, what are the significant characteristics of "standard" English (3)? How and where did she learn standard English?

4. Tan tells us that she envisions her mother as the AUDIENCE for her stories, using "all the Englishes I grew up with" in writing them (21). For what audience did Tan write this essay? How would you classify the English she uses in it?

✗✗✗✗✗✗✗✗✗✗✗✗✗✗ STRATEGIES AND STRUCTURES ✗✗✗✗✗✗✗✗✗✗✗✗✗✗

1. Why do you think Tan begins her essay with the disclaimer that she is "not a scholar" of the English language (1)? How does she otherwise establish her authority on the subject? Does she do it well, in your opinion?

2. Tan first gives EXAMPLES of "family talk" and only later CLASSIFIES them (4, 21). Why do you think she follows this order? Why not give the categories first, then the specific examples?

3. What specific kind of English, by Tan's classification, is represented by paragraph 6 of her essay?

4. Besides classifying Englishes, Tan also includes NARRATIVES about using them. What do the narratives contribute to her essay? How would the essay be different without the stories?

5. In which paragraphs is Tan advancing an ARGUMENT about achievement tests? What is her point here, and how does she use her different Englishes to support that point?

XXXXXXXXXXXXX **WORDS AND FIGURES OF SPEECH** XXXXXXXXXXXXX

1. Explain the PUN in Tan's title. What does it tell us about the essay?

2. By what standards, according to Tan, is "standard" English to be established and measured (3)?

3. What are some of the implications of using such terms as "broken" or "fractured" to refer to "nonstandard" forms of speech or writing (8)?

4. Do you find "simple" to be better or worse than "broken"? How about "watered down" (21)? Explain.

5. Tan does not give a term for the kind of English she uses to represent her mother's "internal language" (21). What name would you give it? Why?

XXXXXXXXXXXXXXXXXXX **FOR WRITING** XXXXXXXXXXXXXXXXXXXXX

1. Many families have private jokes, code words, gestures, even family whistles. In a paragraph or two, give EXAMPLES of your family's private speech or language. How does each function within the family? In relation to the family and the outside world?

2. How many different Englishes (and other languages) do you use at home, at school, among friends, and elsewhere? Write an essay CLASSIFYING them, giving the characteristics of each, and explaining how and when each is used.

NORA EPHRON

THE SIX STAGES OF E-MAIL

Nora Ephron (b. 1941) is a journalist and film writer and director. Well-known for her humorous writing and romantic comedies, Ephron has been nominated for Academy Awards for the original screenplays of *Silkwood* (1983), *When Harry Met Sally* (1989), and *Sleepless in Seattle* (1993). She is also the author of the essay collection *I Feel Bad about My Neck: And Other Thoughts on Being a Woman* (2006). In "The Six Stages of E-Mail," which appeared in the *New York Times* in 2007, Ephron chronicles her personal struggle with a subject that she dramatized in the film *You've Got Mail* (1998). The categories in Ephron's classification system are loosely based on the "five stages of grief" experienced by people facing terminal illness or cataclysmic loss, which Elisabeth Kübler-Ross identified in her 1969 book, *On Death and Dying*.

XXXXXXXXXXXXXXXXXXXXXXXXXXXXXXXXXXXXXXXXXXXXXXXXXXXXXXXXXX

Stage One: Infatuation

I just got e-mail! I can't believe it! It's so great! Here's my handle. Write me! Who said letter writing was dead? Were they ever wrong! I'm writing letters like crazy for the first time in years. I come home and ignore all my loved ones and go straight to the computer to make contact with total strangers. And how great is AOL? It's so easy. It's so friendly. It's a community. Wheeeee! I've got mail!

Stage Two: Clarification

O.K., I'm starting to understand—e-mail isn't letter-writing at all, it's something else entirely. It was just invented, it was just born, and overnight it turns out to have a form and a set of rules and a language all its own. Not since the printing press. Not since television. It's revolutionary. It's life-altering. It's shorthand. Cut to the chase. Get to the point.

3   And it saves so much time. It takes five seconds to accomplish in an e-mail message something that takes five minutes on the telephone. The phone requires you to converse, to say things like hello and good-bye, to pretend to some semblance of interest in the person on the other end of the line. Worst of all, the phone occasionally forces you to make actual plans with the people you talk to—to suggest lunch or dinner— even if you have no desire whatsoever to see them. No danger of that with e-mail.

4   E-mail is a whole new way of being friends with people: intimate but not, chatty but not, communicative but not; in short, friends but not. What a breakthrough. How did we ever live without it? I have more to say on this subject, but I have to answer an Instant Message from someone I almost know.

Stage Three: Confusion

5   I have done nothing to deserve any of this:

6   Viagra!!!!! Best Web source for Vioxx. Spend a week in Cancún. Have a rich beautiful lawn. Astrid would like to be added as one of your friends. XXXXXXXVideos. Add three inches to the length of your penis. The Democratic National Committee needs you. Virus Alert. FW: This will make you laugh. FW: This is funny. FW: This is hilarious. FW: Grapes and raisins toxic for dogs. FW: Gabriel García Márquez's Final Farewell. FW: Kurt Vonnegut's Commence-ment Address. FW: The Neiman Marcus Chocolate Chip Cookie recipe. AOL Member: We value your opinion. A message from Hillary Clinton. Find low mortgage payments, Nora. Nora, it's your time to shine. Need to fight off bills, Nora? Yvette would like to be added as one of your friends. You have failed to establish a full con-nection to AOL.

Stage Four: Disenchantment

7   Help! I'm drowning. I have 112 unanswered e-mail messages. I'm a writer—imagine how many unanswered messages I would have if I had a

real job. Imagine how much writing I could do if I didn't have to answer all this e-mail. My eyes are dim. I have a mild case of carpal tunnel syndrome. I have a galloping case of attention deficit disorder because every time I start to write something, the e-mail icon starts bobbing up and down and I'm compelled to check whether anything good or interesting has arrived. It hasn't. Still, it might, any second now. And yes it's true—I can do in a few seconds with e-mail what would take much longer on the phone, but most of my messages are from people who don't have my phone number and would never call me in the first place. In the brief time it took me to write this paragraph, three more messages arrived. Now I have 115 unanswered messages. Strike that: 116.

Stage Five: Accommodation

Yes. No. No :). No :(. Can't. No way. Maybe. Doubtful. Sorry. So Sorry. Thanks. No thanks. Not my thing. You must be kidding. Out of town. O.O.T. Try me in a month. Try me in the fall. Try me in a year. NoraE@aol.com can now be reached at NoraE81082@gmail.com. 8

Stage Six: Death

Call me. 9

For Discussion

1. What is Nora Ephron CLASSIFYING here—her email or her attitudes toward her email? What principle of classification does she base her distinctions on? Explain.

2. According to Ephron, what's "revolutionary" about email (2)? How does it differ from older forms of communication?

3. Why does Ephron experience "disenchantment"? Do you think this is an appropriate title for this stage, as Ephron identifies it? Why or why not?

4. How does Ephron attempt to cope with the rising tide of unanswered messages? Does it work?

Strategies and Structures

1. Except for the title, Ephron's essay has no introduction. Does it need one?

2. "Help!" Ephron implores in the fourth stage. To whom is she speaking? Where else in her essay does Ephron address her readers directly? Why?

3. In *On Death and Dying* (1969), Elisabeth Kübler-Ross identified "five stages" of grief: denial, anger, bargaining, depression, and acceptance. How and where does Ephron borrow from that classification system?

4. Ephron gives highly ABSTRACT names to each of her categories, followed by CONCRETE examples from her own experience. Is this an effective strategy for a humorous CLASSIFICATION essay? Why or why not?

5. Are the categories in Ephron's classification system mutually exclusive? Do they cover all the likely instances without overlapping? Explain.

6. Where and in what ways does Ephron's classification essay include elements of PROCESS ANALYSIS?

XXXXXXXXXXXXX **WORDS AND FIGURES OF SPEECH** XXXXXXXXXXXX

1. Why does Ephron use the word "stages" (instead of, say, *types* or *kinds*) to identify the different categories in her classification system?

2. Why does Ephron use the phrase "I've got mail!" in paragraph 1? What ALLUSION is she making here?

3. How and how well do the brief entries in the "Accommodation" stage of Ephron's essay (8) illustrate what she says about email having rules and "a language all its own" (2, 8)?

XXXXXXXXXXXXXXXXXXX **FOR WRITING** XXXXXXXXXXXXXXXXXXXXXX

1. Choose one of Ephron's categories and write a paragraph or two illustrating it with EXAMPLES from your own emailing experience.

2. Using Ephron's CLASSIFICATION system as a model but changing the categories as you like, write a classification essay—humorous *or* serious—about your experience with instant messaging, text messaging, Twitter, Facebook, YouTube, or some other form of electronic communication.

ERIC A. WATTS

The Color of Success

Eric A. Watts grew up in Springfield, Massachusetts, and attended
Brown University, graduating in 1995. He wrote this essay about racial
typing for the Brown *Alumni Monthly* when he was a sophomore. In it,
Watts argues that African Americans who criticize each other for "acting
white" and who say that success based on academic achievement is "not
black" are making a false distinction because they are misclassifying
themselves as victims. Responding to an article on campus diversity in
the Brown *Daily Herald* in 2000, Watts added that the real question for
him was not whether his alma mater and other schools encouraged
diversity, but whether they encouraged "harmony and understanding
among the diverse communities [already] in place there."

XXXXXXXXXXXXXXXXXXXXXXXXXXXXXXXXXXXXXXXXXXXXXXXXXXXXX

When I was a black student at a primarily white high school, I occa-   1
sionally confronted the stereotypes and prejudice that some
whites aimed at those of my race. These incidents came as no particular
surprise—after all, prejudice, though less prevalent than in the past, is
ages old.

What did surprise me during those years was the profound disap-   2
proval that some of my black peers expressed toward my studious
behavior. "Hitting the books," expressing oneself articulately, and, at
times, displaying more than a modest amount of intelligence—these
traits were derided as "acting white."

Once, while I was traveling with other black students, a young   3
woman asked me what I thought of one of our teachers. My answer,
phrased in what one might call "standard" English, caused considerable discomfort among my audience. Finally, the young woman
exploded: "Eric," she said, "stop talking like a white boy! You're with
us now!"

4   Another time, again in a group of black students, a friend asked how I intended to spend the weekend. When I answered that I would study, my friend's reaction was swift: "Eric, you need to stop all this studying; you need to stop acting so white." The others laughed in agreement.

5   Signithia Fordham's[1] 1986 ethnographic study of a mostly black high school in Washington, D.C., *Black Students' School Success*, concluded that many behaviors associated with high achievement—speaking standard English, studying long hours, striving to get good grades—were regarded as "acting white." Fordham further concluded that "many black students limit their academic success so their peers won't think they are 'acting white'."

6   Frankly, I never took the "acting white" accusation seriously. It seemed to me that certain things I valued—hard work, initiative, articulateness, education—were not solely white people's prerogative.

7   Trouble begins, however, when students lower their standards in response to peer pressure. Such a retreat from achievement has potentially horrendous effects on the black community.

8   Even more disturbing is the rationale behind the "acting white" accusation. It seems that, on a subconscious level, some black students wonder whether success—in particular, academic success—is a purely white domain.

9   In his essay "On Being Black and Middle Class," in *The Content of Our Character* (1990), Shelby Steele, a black scholar at San Jose State University, argues that certain "middle-class" values—the work ethic, education, initiative—by encouraging "individualism," encourage identification with American society, rather than with race. The ultimate result is integration.

10   But, Steele argues, the racial identification that emerged during the 1960s, and that still persists, urges middle-class blacks to view themselves as an embattled minority: to take an adversarial stance toward the mainstream. It emphasizes ethnic consciousness over individualism.

---

1. African American scholar (b. 1955), currently a professor of anthropology at the University of Rochester.

Steele says that this form of black identification emerged in the 11
civil-rights effort to obtain full racial equality, an effort that demanded
that blacks present themselves (by and large) as a racial monolith: a single mass with the common experience of oppression. So blackness
became virtually synonymous with victimization and the characteristics
associated with it: lack of education and poverty.

I agree with Steele that a monolithic form of racial identification 12
persists. The ideas of the black as a victim and the black as inferior have
been too much entrenched in cultural imagery and too much enforced by
custom and law not to have damaged the collective black psyche.

This damage is so severe that some black adolescents still believe that 13
success is a white prerogative—the white "turf." These young people view
the turf as inaccessible, both because (among other reasons) they doubt
their own abilities and because they generally envision whites as, if not out-
spoken racists, people who are mildly interested in "keeping blacks down."

The result of identifying oneself as a victim can be, "Why even 14
try? It's a white man's world."

Several years ago I was talking to an old friend, a black male. He 15
justified dropping out of school and failing to look for a job on the basis
of one factor: the cold, heartless, white power structure. When I suggested that such a power structure might indeed exist, but that opportunity for blacks was at an unprecedented level, he laughed. Doomed, he
felt, to a life of defeat, my friend soon eased his melancholy with crack.

The most frustrating aspect of the "acting white" accusation is that its 16
main premise—that academic and subsequent success are "white"—is
demonstrably false. And so is the broader premise: that blacks are the
victims of whites.

That academic success is "not black" is easily seen as false if one 17
takes a brisk walk through the Brown University campus and looks at
the faces one passes. Indeed, the most comprehensive text concerning
blacks in decades, *A Common Destiny* (1989), states, "Despite large gaps
. . . whether the baseline is the 1940s, 1950s, or 1960s, the achievement
outcomes . . . of black schooling have greatly improved." That subsequent success in the world belongs to blacks as well as whites is exemplified today by such blacks as Jesse Jackson, Douglas Wilder, Norman

Rice, Anne Wortham, Sara Lawrence Lightfoot, David Dinkins, August Wilson, Andrew Young. . . . [2]

18   The idea of a victimized black race is slowly becoming outdated. Today's black adolescents were born after the *Brown v. Board of Education* decision of 1954; after the passage of the Civil Rights Act; after the Economic Opportunity Act of 1964.[3] With these rulings and laws, whites' attitudes toward blacks have also greatly improved. Although I cannot say that my life has been free of racism on the part of whites, good racial relations in my experience have far outweighed the bad. I refuse to apologize for or retreat from this truth.

19   The result of changes in policies and attitudes has been to provide more opportunities for black Americans than at any other point in their history. As early as 1978, William Julius Wilson,[4] in *The Declining Significance of Race*, concluded that "the recent mobility patterns of blacks lend strong support to the view that economic class is clearly more important than race in predetermining . . . occupational mobility."

20   There are, of course, many factors, often socioeconomic, that still impede the progress of blacks. High schools in black neighborhoods receive less local, state, and federal support than those in white areas; there is evidence that the high school diplomas of blacks are little valued by employers.

21   We should rally against all such remaining racism, confronting particularly the economic obstacles to black success. But we must also

---

2. Andrew Young (b. 1932), civil rights activist, former U.S. congressman and Atlanta mayor; Jesse Jackson (b. 1941), civil rights activist; Douglas Wilder (b. 1931), former governor of Virginia; Norman Rice (b. 1943), two-term mayor of Seattle; Anne Wortham (b. 1942), professor of sociology at Illinois State University; Sara Lawrence Lightfoot (b. 1941), professor at the Harvard Graduate School of Education; David Dinkins (b. 1927), former mayor of New York; August Wilson (1945–2005), prize-winning playwright.

3. The Economic Opportunity Act initiated programs to promote the welfare of poor Americans; *Brown v. Board of Education* is a Supreme Court decision that struck down long-standing legal precedent allowing separate public schools for whites and African Americans; the Civil Rights Act of 1964 made racial discrimination in public places illegal and required employers to provide equal opportunities for minorities.

4. African American scholar (b. 1935) and director of the Joblessness and Urban Poverty Research Program at Harvard University.

realize that racism is not nearly as profound as it once was, and that opportunities for blacks (where opportunity equals jobs and acceptance for the educated and qualified) have increased. Furthermore, we should know that even a lack of resources is no excuse for passivity.

As the syndicated columnist William Raspberry (who is black) says, it is time for certain black adolescents to "shift their focus": to move from an identity rooted in victimization to an identity rooted in individualism and hard work.   22

Simply put, the black community must eradicate the "you're-acting-white" syndrome. Until it does, black Americans will never realize their potential.   23

XXXXXXXXXXXXXXXXXXX **FOR DISCUSSION** XXXXXXXXXXXXXXXXXXX

1. In his high school, what specific behaviors did Eric A. Watts's black peers associate with "acting white" (2, 5)?

2. Watts says that he personally never took the accusation of "acting white" too seriously when he was in high school (2). Why not? Did he change his mind when he went to college?

3. According to Watts (and the columnist William Raspberry, whom he quotes), what is the worst potential danger of "identifying oneself as a victim" (14)?

4. Watts lists several successful African Americans at the end of paragraph 17. Why? What other names can you think of that might be added to this list?

XXXXXXXXXXXXX **STRATEGIES AND STRUCTURES** XXXXXXXXXXXXX

1. As an essay that CLASSIFIES (or, rather, declassifies), is "The Color of Success" about race or success or both? How?

2. Watts does not deny that people come in different colors. How, then, do his frequent references to color help him to call into question stereotypical ways of CLASSIFYING human beings?

3. Why do you think Watts refers to the work of such scholars and researchers as Signithia Fordham and Shelby Steele?

4. What, according to Watts, is the color of success? What alternate system of classifying people does he suggest to replace "black and white" distinctions?

5. Watts makes an ARGUMENT against the validity of classifying human behavior based on race, identifying two false premises behind the idea that someone can "act white." What two false premises does he identify? What EVIDENCE does he use to show they're invalid?

XXXXXXXXXXX **WORDS AND FIGURES OF SPEECH** XXXXXXXXXXX

1. One of Watts's key terms is "success." How does he DEFINE it?

2. What does Watts mean by "standard" English (3)? Cite several of his phrases that help to define "standard."

3. How does Watts's own use of language in this essay confirm (or deny) what he is saying about acting "white" or "black"?

4. What is a "syndrome" (23)? How well does the term fit the feelings of being victimized that Watts DESCRIBES?

XXXXXXXXXXXXXXXXXXX **FOR WRITING** XXXXXXXXXXXXXXXXXXXXX

1. "Success" is a relative term. What different kinds are there? Make a list of the different kinds that occur to you and of the traits that distinguish each kind.

2. Watts is especially concerned with racial stereotyping, but race is only one of the grounds on which people can falsely CLASSIFY each other's behavior. In an all-girls' school, for example, female students frequently do better in math and science than female students in schools with a mixed student body. Apparently, acting "feminine" and acting "masculine" are socially conditioned. Write an essay about your own high school experience in which you classify the socially acceptable and socially unacceptable ways in which students pressured one another to behave.

DAVID BROOKS

Harmony and the Dream

David Brooks (b. 1961) is a political columnist for the *New York Times* and a regular commentator on National Public Radio. He is the author of *Bobos in Paradise* (2000), a book of cultural commentary about wealth in the United States, and *On Paradise Drive* (2004), which focuses on the future of the American middle class. In "Harmony and the Dream," an Op-Ed column published in the *Times* in 2008, Brooks takes a more global view, classifying the societies of the world, particularly China and the United States, as either "collectivist" or "individualistic." Brooks wrote this essay in Chengdu, China, while on assignment at the 2008 Olympic Games.

XXXXXXXXXXXXXXXXXXXXXXXXXXXXXXXXXXXXXXXXXXXXXXXXXXXXXXXXX

The world can be divided in many ways—rich and poor, democratic and authoritarian—but one of the most striking is the divide between the societies with an individualist mentality and the ones with a collectivist mentality.   1

This is a divide that goes deeper than economics into the way people perceive the world. If you show an American an image of a fish tank, the American will usually describe the biggest fish in the tank and what it is doing. If you ask a Chinese person to describe a fish tank, the Chinese will usually describe the context in which the fish swim.   2

These sorts of experiments have been done over and over again, and the results reveal the same underlying pattern. Americans usually see individuals; Chinese and other Asians see contexts.   3

When the psychologist Richard Nisbett[1] showed Americans individual pictures of a chicken, a cow and hay and asked the subjects to   4

----

1. Professor of social psychology (b. 1940) and co-director of the Culture and Cognition program at the University of Michigan.

pick out the two that go together, the Americans would usually pick out the chicken and the cow. They're both animals. Most Asian people, on the other hand, would pick out the cow and the hay, since cows depend on hay. Americans are more likely to see categories. Asians are more likely to see relationships.

5   You can create a global continuum with the most individualistic societies—like the United States or Britain—on one end, and the most collectivist societies—like China or Japan—on the other.

6   The individualistic countries tend to put rights and privacy first. People in these societies tend to overvalue their own skills and overestimate their own importance to any group effort. People in collective societies tend to value harmony and duty. They tend to underestimate their own skills and are more self-effacing when describing their contributions to group efforts.

7   Researchers argue about why certain cultures have become more individualistic than others. Some say that Western cultures draw their values from ancient Greece, with its emphasis on individual heroism, while other cultures draw more on tribal philosophies. Recently, some scientists have theorized that it all goes back to microbes. Collectivist societies tend to pop up in parts of the world, especially around the equator, with plenty of disease-causing microbes. In such an environment, you'd want to shun outsiders, who might bring strange diseases, and enforce a certain conformity over eating rituals and social behavior.

8   Either way, individualistic societies have tended to do better economically. We in the West have a narrative that involves the development of individual reason and conscience during the Renaissance and the Enlightenment,[2] and then the subsequent flourishing of capitalism. According to this narrative, societies get more individualistic as they develop.

9   But what happens if collectivist societies snap out of their economic stagnation? What happens if collectivist societies, especially those in

---

2. During the Enlightenment, which began in the late 1600s, European philosophers questioned conventional ways of thinking about morality, social systems, religion, and individual freedom. The Renaissance refers to a rebirth in learning and the arts in the fifteenth century.

Asia, rise economically and come to rival the West? A new sort of global conversation develops.

The opening ceremony in Beijing was a statement in that conversa- 10
tion. It was part of China's assertion that development doesn't come only through Western, liberal means, but also through Eastern and collective ones.

The ceremony drew from China's long history, but surely the most 11
striking features were the images of thousands of Chinese moving as one—drumming as one, dancing as one, sprinting on precise formations without ever stumbling or colliding. We've seen displays of mass conformity before, but this was collectivism of the present—a high-tech vision of the harmonious society performed in the context of China's miraculous growth.

If Asia's success reopens the debate between individualism and col- 12
lectivism (which seemed closed after the cold war[3]), then it's unlikely that the forces of individualism will sweep the field or even gain an edge.

For one thing, there are relatively few individualistic societies on 13
earth. For another, the essence of a lot of the latest scientific research is that the Western idea of individual choice is an illusion and the Chinese are right to put first emphasis on social contexts.

Scientists have delighted to show that so-called rational choice is 14
shaped by a whole range of subconscious influences, like emotional contagions[4] and priming effects[5] (people who think of a professor before taking a test do better than people who think of a criminal). Meanwhile, human brains turn out to be extremely permeable (they naturally mimic the neural firings of people around them). Relationships are the key to happiness. People who live in the densest social networks tend to flourish, while people who live with few social bonds are much more prone to depression and suicide.

---

3. A period of intense hostility between the United States and the communist-led Soviet Union that lasted from the mid-1940s until the fall of the Soviet Union in 1991.

4. Concept that people subconsciously mimic the emotions of others they interact with.

5. Concept that a previous stimulus can prompt the human brain to perform in certain ways.

15   The rise of China isn't only an economic event. It's a cultural one. The ideal of a harmonious collective may turn out to be as attractive as the ideal of the American Dream.[6]

16   It's certainly a useful ideology for aspiring autocrats.

6. American ideal that through hard work, persistence, and good moral character, anyone can succeed, even from humble beginnings.

XXXXXXXXXXXXXXXXXXXX **For Discussion** XXXXXXXXXXXXXXXXXXXX

1. Why, according to David Brooks, does the "divide" between China and the United States go "deeper than economics" (2)?

2. What does Brooks mean when he says that "the debate between individualism and collectivism . . . seemed closed after the cold war" (12)? In his view, what would reopen the "global conversation" (9) between the two types of societies? Explain.

3. In what ways does recent scientific research suggest that "the Chinese are right to put first emphasis on social contexts" (13)?

4. How does this same research suggest that "the American Dream" might be an "illusion" (15, 13)? Explain.

XXXXXXXXXXXXXX **Strategies and Structures** XXXXXXXXXXXXXX

1. What is Brooks's main point in dividing the world into "collectivist societies" and "individualistic societies" (5)? Where does he state it most directly?

2. On what basis is Brooks classifying the societies of the world into these two categories? What's his main principle of classification here?

3. According to Brooks, what are some of the main characteristics of collectivist societies? Of individualistic societies?

4. How effective is Brooks's EXAMPLE of the fish tank (2) for explaining the differences between the two categories that he examines? Point to other similar examples throughout his essay. How and how well do they help explain the characteristics that distinguish each of the groups he discusses?

5. Brooks's classification system is made up of two basic categories, which he places at opposite ends of a "global continuum" (5). Is this an effective strategy for enlarging the scope of his classification system? What problems might arise from this strategy, and what are the benefits of it?

6. Who does Brooks assume is his main AUDIENCE for this essay? What cultural background does this audience share? Point to specific passages in the text that support your answer.

7. What possible CAUSES does Brooks give for the development of collectivist societies? How about individualistic societies? What do his explanations contribute to his essay?

XXXXXXXXXXX **WORDS AND FIGURES OF SPEECH** XXXXXXXXXXX

1. What does Brooks mean by "mentality" (1)? How does his use of this term fit with his later references to psychology and the human brain?

2. Brooks chooses the word "harmony" to DESCRIBE the ideology of collectivism (6). What alternate terms might he have chosen? Why do you think he chose this one?

3. What are the implications of describing the "economic stagnation" of collectivist societies as a condition they can "snap out" of (9)?

4. Why do you think Brooks refers to a new global "conversation" rather than a new global *standoff*, *conflict*, or *confrontation* (9)?

5. Explain the different CONNOTATIONS of the following words: "idea," "ideal," and "ideology" (13, 15, 16).

6. What is an "autocrat," and why might he or she find the ideology of a collective society to be "useful" (16)?

XXXXXXXXXXXXXXXXX **FOR WRITING** XXXXXXXXXXXXXXXXXXXX

1. Have you ever been in a situation where a group of people exhibited signs of "mass conformity" (11)? DESCRIBE that situation or event in a paragraph or two. Be sure to say what was "collectivist" about it.

2. Using Brooks's categories of individualistic and collectivist groups, write an essay CLASSIFYING the clubs and other student organizations in your school. Be sure to account for groups that share characteristics of both categories, and consider adding additional categories to your system, if necessary.

ISAAC ASIMOV

WHAT DO YOU CALL A PLATYPUS?

Isaac Asimov (1920–1992) was born in Petrovichi, Russia, entered the United States at age three, and became a naturalized citizen in 1928. He wrote almost 500 books dealing with an astounding range of subjects: biochemistry, the human body, ecology, mathematics, physics, astronomy, genetics, history, the Bible, and Shakespeare—to name only a few. Asimov is best known, however, for his science fiction, including *I, Robot* (1950) and the *Foundation* trilogy (1951–53). "What Do You Call a Platypus?" (1973) is an essay in taxonomy, the science of classifying plants and animals. Is the duckbill platypus (*Ornithorhynchus anatinus*) to be classified as a mammal? A reptile? A bird? There are good anatomical reasons for placing it in any of these categories, and Asimov's playful exercise in scientific classification shows both the limitations of classification systems and how they can help us to organize our knowledge of the world—or even to discover new knowledge.

XXXXXXXXXXXXXXXXXXXXXXXXXXXXXXXXXXXXXXXXXXXXXXXXXXXXX

1   In 1800, a stuffed animal arrived in England from the newly discovered continent of Australia.

2   The continent had already been the source of plants and animals never seen before—but this one was ridiculous. It was nearly two feet long, and had a dense coating of hair. It also had a flat rubbery bill, webbed feet, a broad flat tail, and a spur on each hind ankle that was clearly intended to secrete poison. What's more, under the tail was a single opening.

3   Zoologists stared at the thing in disbelief. Hair like a mammal! Bill and feet like an aquatic bird! Poison spurs like a snake! A single opening in the rear as though it laid eggs!

4   There was an explosion of anger. The thing was a hoax. Some unfunny jokester in Australia, taking advantage of the distance and

strangeness of the continent, had stitched together parts of widely different creatures and was intent on making fools of innocent zoologists in
England.

Yet the skin seemed to hang together. There were no signs of arti-   5
ficial joining. Was it or was it not a hoax? And if it wasn't a hoax, was it
a mammal with reptilian characteristics, or a reptile with mammalian
characteristics, or was it partly bird, or *what?*

The discussion went on heatedly for decades. Even the name   6
emphasized the ways in which it didn't seem like a mammal despite its
hair. One early name was *Platypus anatinus* which is Graeco-Latin[1] for
"Flat-foot, ducklike." Unfortunately, the term, platypus, had already
been applied to a type of beetle and there must be no duplication in scientific names. It therefore received another name, *Ornithorhynchus paradoxus*, which means "Birdbeak, paradoxical."

Slowly, however, zoologists had to fall into line and admit that the   7
creature was real and not a hoax, however upsetting it might be to zoological notions. For one thing, there were increasingly reliable reports from people in Australia who caught glimpses of the creature alive. The paradoxus
was dropped and the scientific name is now *Ornithorhynchus anatinus.*

To the general public, however, it is the "duckbill platypus," or   8
even just the duckbill, the queerest mammal (assuming it is a mammal)
in the world.

When specimens were received in such condition as to make it   9
possible to study the internal organs, it appeared that the heart was just
like those of mammals and not at all like those of reptiles. The egg-
forming machinery in the female, however, was not at all like those of
mammals, but like those of birds or reptiles. It seemed really and truly
to be an egg-layer.

It wasn't till 1884, however, that the actual eggs laid by a creature   10
with hair were found. Such creatures included not only the platypus, but
another Australian species, the spiny anteater. That was worth an
excited announcement. A group of British scientists were meeting in

1. Combination of Greek and Latin; many scientific names put Latin endings on the
Greek roots.

Montreal at the time, and the egg-discoverer, W. H. Caldwell, sent them a cable to announce the finding.

11   It wasn't till the twentieth century that the intimate life of the duckbill came to be known. It is an aquatic animal, living in Australian fresh water at a wide variety of temperatures—from tropical streams at sea level to cold lakes at an elevation of a mile.

12   The duckbill is well adapted to its aquatic life, with its dense fur, its flat tail, and its webbed feet. Its bill has nothing really in common with that of the duck, however. The nostrils are differently located and the platypus bill is different in structure, rubbery rather than duckishly horny. It serves the same function as the duck's bill, however, so it has been shaped similarly by the pressures of natural selection.

13   The water in which the duckbill lives is invariably muddy at the bottom and it is in this mud that the duckbill roots for its food supply. The bill, ridged with horny plates, is used as a sieve, dredging about sensitively in the mud, filtering out the shrimps, earthworms, tadpoles and other small creatures that serve it as food.

14   When the time comes for the female platypus to produce young, she builds a special burrow, which she lines with grass and carefully plugs. She then lays two eggs, each about three quarters of an inch in diameter and surrounded by a translucent, horny shell.

15   These the mother platypus places between her tail and abdomen and curls up about them. It takes two weeks for the young to hatch out. The new-born duckbills have teeth and very short bills, so that they are much less "birdlike" than the adults. They feed on milk. The mother has no nipples, but milk oozes out of pore openings in the abdomen and the young lick the area and are nourished in this way. As they grow, the bills become larger and the teeth fall out.

16   Yet despite everything zoologists learned about the duckbills, they never seemed entirely certain as to where to place them in the table of animal classification. On the whole, the decision was made because of hair and milk. In all the world, only mammals have true hair and only mammals produce true milk. The duckbill and spiny anteater have hair and produce milk, so they have been classified as mammals.

17   Just the same, they are placed in a very special position. All the mammals are divided into two subclasses. In one of these subclasses

("Prototheria" or "first-beasts") are the duckbill and five species of the spiny anteater. In the other ("Theria" or just "beast") are all the other 4,231 known species of mammals.

But all this is the result of judging only living species of mammals. 18 Suppose we could study extinct species as well. Would that help us decide on the place of the platypus? Would it cause us to confirm our decision—or change it?

Fossil remnants exist of mammals and reptiles of the far past, but 19 these remnants are almost entirely of bones and teeth. Bones and teeth give us interesting information but they can't tell us everything.

For instance, is there any way of telling, from bones and teeth 20 alone, whether an extinct creature is a reptile or a mammal?

Well, all living reptiles have legs splayed out so that the upper part 21 above the knee is horizontal (assuming they have legs at all). All mammals, on the other hand, have legs that are vertical all the way down. Again, reptiles have teeth that all look more or less alike, while mammals have teeth that have different shapes, with sharp incisors in front, flat molars in back, and conical incisors and premolars in between.

As it happens, there are certain extinct creatures, to which have 22 been given the name "therapsids," which have their leg bones vertical and their teeth differentiated just as in the case of mammals.—And yet they are considered reptiles and not mammals. Why? Because there is another bony difference to be considered.

In living mammals, the lower jaw contains a single bone; in rep- 23 tiles, it is made up of a number of bones. The therapsid lower jaw is made up of seven bones and because of that those creatures are classified as reptiles. And yet in the therapsid lower jaw, the one bone making up the central portion of the lower jaw is by far the largest. The other six bones, three on each side, are crowded into the rear angle of the jaw.

There seems no question, then, that if the therapsids are reptiles 24 they are nevertheless well along the pathway towards mammals.

But how far along the pathway are they? For instance, did they 25 have hair? It might seem that it would be impossible to tell whether an extinct animal had hair or not just from the bones, but let's see—

Hair is an insulating device. It keeps body heat from being lost too 26 rapidly. Reptiles keep their body temperature at about that of the outside environment. They don't have to be concerned over loss of heat and hair would be of no use to them.

27   Mammals, however, maintain their internal temperature at nearly 100° F. regardless of the outside temperature; they are "warm-blooded." This gives them the great advantage of remaining agile and active in cold weather, when the chilled reptile is sluggish. But then the mammal must prevent heat loss by means of a hairy covering. (Birds, which also are warm-blooded, use feathers as an insulating device.)

28   With that in mind, let's consider the bones. In reptiles, the nostrils open into the mouth just behind the teeth. This means that reptiles can only breathe with their mouths empty. When they are biting or chewing, breathing must stop. This doesn't bother a reptile much, for it can suspend its need for oxygen for considerable periods.

29   Mammals, however, must use oxygen in their tissues constantly, in order to keep the chemical reactions going that serve to keep their body temperature high. The oxygen supply must not be cut off for more than very short intervals. Consequently mammals have developed a bony palate, a roof to the mouth. When they breathe, air is led above the mouth to the throat. This means they can continue breathing while they bite and chew. It is only when they are actually in the act of swallowing that the breath is cut off and this is only a matter of a couple of seconds at a time.

30   The later therapsid species had, as it happened, a palate. If they had a palate, it seems a fair deduction that they needed an uninterrupted supply of oxygen that makes it look as though they were warm-blooded. And if they were warm-blooded, then very likely they had hair, too.

31   The conclusion, drawn from the bones alone, would seem to be that some of the later therapsids had hair, even though, judging by their jawbones, they were still reptiles.

32   The thought of hairy reptiles is astonishing. But that is only because the accident of evolution seems to have wiped out the intermediate forms. The only therapsids alive seem to be those that have developed *all* the mammalian characteristics, so that we call them mammals. The only reptiles alive are those that developed *none* of the mammalian characteristics.

Those therapsids that developed some but not others seem to be extinct. ₃₃

33

Only the duckbill and the spiny anteater remain near the border line. They have developed the hair and the milk and the singleboned lower jaw and the four-chambered heart, but not the nipples or the ability to bring forth live young.

34

For all we know, some of the extinct therapsids, while still having their many-boned lower jaw (which is why we call them reptiles instead of mammals), may have developed even beyond the duckbill in other ways. Perhaps some late therapsids had nipples and brought forth living young. We can't tell from the bones alone.

35

If we had a complete record of the therapsids, flesh and blood, as well as teeth and bone, we might decide that the duckbill was on the therapsid side of the line and not on the mammalian side.—Or are there any other pieces of evidence that can be brought into play?

36

An American zoologist, Giles T. MacIntyre, of Queens College, has taken up the matter of the trigeminal nerve, which leads from the jaw muscles to the brain.

37

In all reptiles, without exception, the trigeminal nerve passes through the skull at a point that lies between two of the bones making up the skull. In all mammals that bring forth living young, without exception, the nerve actually passes *through* a particular skull bone.

38

Suppose we ignore all the matter of hair and milk and eggs, and just consider the trigeminal nerve. In the duckbill, does the nerve pass through a bone, or between two bones? It has seemed in the past that the nerve passed through a bone and that put the duckbill on the mammalian side of the dividing line.

39

Not so, says MacIntyre. The study of the trigeminal nerve was made in adult duckbills, where the skull bones are fused together and the boundaries are hard to make out. In young duckbills, the skull bones are more clearly separated and in them it can be seen, MacIntyre says, that the trigeminal nerve goes between two bones.

40

In that case, there is a new respect in which the duckbill falls on the reptilian side of the line and MacIntyre thinks it ought not to be considered a mammal, but as a surviving species of the otherwise long-extinct therapsid line.

41

42   And so, a hundred seventy years after zoologists began to puzzle out the queer mixture of characteristics that go to make up the duckbill platypus—there is still argument as to what to call it.

43   Is the duckbill platypus a mammal? A reptile? Or just a duckbill platypus?

XXXXXXXXXXXXXXXXXX **FOR DISCUSSION** XXXXXXXXXXXXXXXXXX

1. Taxonomists place individual specimens, such as the stuffed platypus that first arrived in England in 1800 from the strange land of Australia, into categories based on certain significant characteristics. As reported by Isaac Asimov, what are the chief distinguishing characteristics of mammals? Of reptiles?

2. Which mammalian features does the platypus lack? Which reptilian characteristics does it possess?

3. How does the EXAMPLE of the platypus show the limitations of the zoological CLASSIFICATION system? Of classification systems in general?

4. What new EVIDENCE does Asimov cite in favor of reclassifying the platypus? How convincing do you find this ARGUMENT?

XXXXXXXXXXXXX **STRATEGIES AND STRUCTURES** XXXXXXXXXXXXX

1. Why do you think Asimov begins his case for reclassifying the platypus by recounting the confused history of how the animal got its name? How does this history prepare readers for the rest of his essay?

2. Why does it matter what we *call* a platypus? For what ultimate PURPOSE is Asimov concerned with the creature's name and formal CLASSIFICATION?

3. What is Asimov's purpose in referring to extinct creatures, beginning in paragraph 18? What is the function of the therapsids in his line of reasoning (22)?

4. This essay for reclassification ends with three alternatives (43). Why three instead of just two?

5. The logic of paragraph 32 depends upon an unstated assumption about the order of evolution. Which does Asimov assume came first, reptiles or mammals? How does this assumption influence his entire ARGUMENT?

XXXXXXXXXXXXX **WORDS AND FIGURES OF SPEECH** XXXXXXXXXXXXX

1. Why does Asimov use the word "innocent" to DESCRIBE the zoologists who think the first stuffed platypus to reach England is a fake (4)? Whose perspective is Asimov representing here?

2. Why was the term "paradoxical" an appropriate part of the platypus's early scientific name (6)? How does it differ in meaning from *ambiguous* and *ambivalent*?

3. Asimov refers to the "egg-forming machinery" of the female platypus (9). How technically scientific is this term? What does his use of such terms suggest about the nature of the AUDIENCE for whom he is writing?

4. What is meant by "the pressures of natural selection" (12)?

XXXXXXXXXXXXXXXXXXXXX **FOR WRITING** XXXXXXXXXXXXXXXXXXXXXXX

1. In a paragraph or two, explain why a whale is CLASSIFIED as a mammal instead of a fish.

2. What's the scientific background for the notion that humans belong in the great-ape category? DNA studies indicate that the genes of gorillas differ from those of both humans and chimpanzees by about 2.3 percent. Humans and chimps, however, share 98.4 percent of their genes—a difference of only 1.6 percent. Science writer David Quammen addresses this EVIDENCE in "Beast in the Mirror: Science Uncovers Another Chimpanzee," a chapter in *The Boilerplate Rhino* (2001). Write an essay that classifies human beings within the animal kingdom, taking into account the facts presented in Quammen's book. If you cite Quammen's book, be sure to document those facts accordingly.

CHAPTER SIX

PROCESS ANALYSIS

XXXXXXXXXXXXXXXXXXXXXXXXXXXXXXXXXXXXXXXXXXXXXXXXXXXXXXX

The essays in this chapter are examples of PROCESS ANALYSIS,* writing that explains *how*. Process analysis breaks a process into the sequence of actions that leads to an end result. Basically, there are two kinds of process analysis: *directive* and *explanatory*. A directive process analysis explains how to make or do something—how to throw a boomerang, for instance. An explanatory process analysis explains how something works; it tells you what makes the boomerang come back.

Here is an example of the how-to-do-it kind:

> Hold the boomerang . . . with the V-point, called the elbow, pointing toward you, and with the flat side facing out. . . . Bring the boomerang back behind you and snap it forward as if you were throwing a baseball.
>
> howstuffworks.com

This kind of process analysis is often addressed to the second person (you) because the author is giving instructions directly to the reader. Sometimes the you is understood, as in a recipe: [you] combine the milk with the eggs; then add a pinch of salt and the juice of one lemon.

Here is an example of the how-it-works kind of process analysis. In this kind, the third-person pronoun (*he, she, it, they*) is usually used because the author is giving information to the reader *about* something.

> The uneven force caused by the difference in speed between the two wings applies a constant force at the top of the spinning

---

*Words printed in SMALL CAPITALS are defined in the Glossary.

Bring behind head, then snap forward

boomerang. . . . Like a leaning bicycle wheel, the boomerang is constantly turning to the left or right, so that it travels in a circle and comes back to its starting point.

howstuffworks.com

Sometimes a process is best explained by showing how it works, so you may want to add diagrams or drawings to the written text. The analysis on the previous page of how to throw a boomerang, for example, might benefit from a clearly labeled diagram like the one above.

Most processes that you analyze will be linear rather than cyclical. Even if the process is repeatable, your analysis will proceed chronologically step by step, stage by stage to an end result that is different from the starting point. Consider this explanatory analysis of how fresh oranges are turned into orange juice concentrate:

As the fruit starts to move along a concentrate plant's assembly line, it is first culled. . . . Moving up a conveyer belt, oranges are scrubbed with detergent before they roll on into juicing machines. There are several kinds of juicing machines, and they are something to see. One is called the Brown Seven Hundred. Seven hundred oranges a minute go into it and and are split and reamed on the same kind of rosettes that are in the centers of ordinary kitchen reamers. The rinds that come pelting out the bottom are integral halves, just like the rinds of oranges squeezed in a kitchen. Another machine is the Food Machinery Corporation's FMC In-line Extractor. It has a shining row of aluminum teeth. When an orange tumbles in, the upper jaw comes crunching down on it while at the same time the orange is penetrated from below by a perforated steel tube. As the jaws crush the outside, the juice goes through the perforations in the tube and down into the plumbing of the concentrate plant. All in a second, the juice has been removed and the rind has been crushed and shredded beyond recognition.

From either machine, the juice flows on into a thing called the finisher, where seeds, rag, and pulp are removed. The finisher has a big stainless-steel screw that steadily drives the juice through a fine-mesh screen. From the finisher, it flows on into holding tanks.

JOHN MCPHEE, *Oranges*

John McPhee divides the process of making orange juice concentrate from fresh fruit into five stages: (1) culling, (2) scrubbing, (3) extracting, (4) straining, (5) storing. When you plan an essay that analyzes a process, make a list of all the stages or phases in the process you are analyzing. Make sure that they are separate and distinct and that you haven't left any out. When you are satisfied that your list is complete, you are ready to decide upon the order in which you will present the steps.

The usual order of process analysis is chronological, beginning with the earliest stage of the process (the culling of the split and rotten oranges from the rest) and ending with the last, or with the finished product (concentrated orange juice in holding tanks). Notice that after they leave the conveyer belt, McPhee's oranges come to a fork in the road. They can go in different directions, depending upon what kind of juicing machine is being used. McPhee briefly follows the oranges into one kind of juicer and then comes back to the other. He has stopped time and forward motion for a moment. Now he picks them up again and proceeds down the line: "from either machine, the juice flows on into a thing called the finisher" where it is strained. From the straining stage, the orange concentrate goes into the fifth (and final) holding stage, where it is stored in large tanks.

Another lesson to take away here: if the order of the process you are analyzing is controlled by a piece of machinery or other mechanism, let it work for you. McPhee, in fact, lets several machines— conveyor belt, extractor, and finisher—help him organize his analysis.

Some stages in a process analysis may be more complicated than others. Suppose you are explaining to someone how to replace a light switch. You might break the process down into six stages: (1) select and purchase the new switch; (2) turn off the power at the breaker box; (3) remove the switch plate; (4) disconnect the old switch and install the new one; (5) replace the switch plate; (6) turn the power back on. Obviously, one of these stages—"disconnect the old switch and install the new one"—is more complicated than the others. When this happens, you can break down the more complicated stage into its constituent steps, as McPhee does with his analysis of the production of orange juice concentrate.

The most complicated stage in McPhee's process analysis is the third one, extracting. He breaks it into the following steps: (1) an orange enters the extractor; (2) it is crushed by the extractor's steel jaws; (3) at the same time, the orange is "penetrated from below by a perforated steel tube"; (4) the extracted juice flows on to the next stage of the process. All of this happens "in a second," says McPhee; but for purposes of analysis and explanation, the steps must be presented in sequence, using such TRANSITIONS as "when," "while at the same time," "all in a second," "from . . . to," "next," and "then."

McPhee's process analysis is explanatory; it tells how orange juice concentrate is made. When you are telling someone how to do something (a directive process analysis), the method of breaking the process into steps and stages is the same. Here's how our analysis of how to change a light switch might break down the most complicated step in the process, the one where the old switch is removed and replaced. The transitions and other words that signal the order and timing of the steps *within* this stage are printed in italics:

To remove the old switch, *first* unscrew the two terminal screws on the sides. *If* the wires are attached to the back of the switch, *instead* clip off the old wires as closely to the switch as possible. As necessary, strip the insulation from the ends of the wires *until* approximately half an inch is exposed. *Next*, unscrew the green grounding screw, *and* disconnect the bare wire attached to it. You are *now* ready to remove the old switch and replace it with the new one. *Either* insert the ends of the insulated wires into the holes on the back of the new switch, *or* bend the ends of the wires around the terminal screws *and* tighten the screws. *Reattach* the bare wire to the green terminal. *Finally*, secure the new switch by tightening the two long screws at top and bottom into the ears on the old switch box.

Explaining this stage in our analysis is further complicated because we have to stop the flow of information (with "if . . . instead"; "either . . . or . . . and") to go down a fork in the road—the wires can be attached either to the screws on the sides of the switch or to holes in the rear—before getting back on track. And we now have to signal a move on to the next stage: "Once the new switch is installed, replacing the switch plate is a snap."

Actually, this simple next-to-last stage (don't forget to turn the power back on) requires a *twist* of the little screw in the center of the switch plate, which can serve to remind us that the forward movement of a process analysis, step by step, from beginning to end, is much like the twisting and turning of the PLOT in a NARRATIVE. Like plot in narrative, a process is a sequence of events or actions. You are the NARRATOR, and you are telling the exciting story of how something is made or done or how it works. Also as with a narrative, you will want your process analysis to make a point so the reader knows why you're analyzing the process and what to expect.

You may simply conclude your story with the product or end result of the process you've been analyzing. But you may want to round out your account by summarizing the stages you have just gone through or by encouraging the reader to follow your directions—"Changing a light switch yourself is easy, and it can save money"—or by explaining why the process is important. The production of orange juice concentrate, for example, transformed Florida's citrus industry. In what is called "the old fresh-fruit days," 40 percent of the oranges grown in Florida were left to rot in the fields because they couldn't travel well. "Now," as McPhee notes, "with the exception of split and rotten fruit, all of Florida's orange crop is used." This is not exactly the end product of the process McPhee is analyzing, but it is an important consequence and one that makes technical advances in the citrus industry seem more worth reading about.

One other detail, though a minor one, in McPhee's analysis that you may find interesting: when all that fresh fruit was left to rot on the ground because it couldn't be shipped and local people couldn't use it all, the cows stepped in to help. Thus McPhee notes that in the days before orange juice concentrate, "Florida milk tasted like orangeade." Details like this may not make the process you are analyzing clearer or more accurate, but they may well make the reader more interested in the process itself.

A Brief Guide to Writing a Process Analysis

As you write a PROCESS ANALYSIS, you need to say what process you're analyzing and to identify some of its most important steps. These moves are fundamental to any process analysis. Will Shortz makes these basic moves of process analysis in his essay in this chapter:

> Solving a sudoku puzzle involves pure logic. No guesswork is needed—or even desirable. Getting started involves mastering just a few simple techniques.
>
> WILL SHORTZ, "How to Solve Sudoku"

Shortz identifies the process he's analyzing ("solving a sudoku puzzle") and indicates the important steps that make up the process (using "pure logic," avoiding "guesswork," "mastering just a few simple techniques").

The following guidelines will help you to make these basic moves as you draft a process analysis. They will also help you to choose a process to analyze, divide it into steps, and put those steps in order, using appropriate transitions and pronouns.

Coming Up with a Subject

Your first challenge is to find a process worth analyzing. You might start by considering processes you are already familiar with, such as running a marathon, training a puppy, or playing a video game. Or you might think about processes you are interested in and want to learn more about. Do you wonder how bees make honey, how to tune a guitar, how to change the oil in a car engine, or how the oil and gas in your car are produced and refined? Whatever process you choose, you will need to understand it fully yourself before you can explain it clearly to your readers.

Considering Your Purpose and Audience

When your PURPOSE is to tell readers how to do something, a basic set of instructions will usually do the job, as when you give someone the recipe for your Aunt Mary's famous pound cake. When, however, you want your AUDIENCE to understand, not duplicate, a complicated process—such as the chemistry that makes a cake rise—your analysis should be explanatory. So instead of giving instructions ("add the sugar to the butter"), you would go over the inner workings of the process in some detail, telling readers, for example, what happens when they add baking powder to the cake mixture.

The nature of your audience will also influence the information you include. How much do your intended readers already know about the process? Why might they want to know more, or less? If you are giving a set of instructions, will they require any special tools or equipment? What problems are they likely to encounter? Will they need to know where to find more information on your topic? Asking questions like these will help you select the appropriate steps and details.

Generating Ideas: Asking How Something Works

When you analyze a process, the essential question to ask yourself is *how*. How does a cake rise? How do I back out of the garage?

To get started, ask yourself a "how" question about your subject, research the answer (if necessary), and write down all the steps involved. For instance, "How do I back out of the garage?" might result in a list like this: put the car in reverse, step on the gas, turn the key in the ignition, look in the rearview mirror. Although this list includes all the essential steps for backing a car out of a garage, you wouldn't want your reader to follow them in this order. Once you have a complete list of steps, think about the best order in which to present them to your reader.

Also think about whether you should demonstrate the process—or a complex part of it—visually. If you decide to include one or more diagrams or drawings, make sure there are words to accompany each visual. Either DESCRIBE what the visual shows, or label the parts of a diagram (the parts of an engine, for instance).

Templates for Analyzing a Process

The following templates can help you to generate ideas for an essay that analyzes a process and then to start drafting. Don't take these as formulas where you just have to fill in the blanks. There are no easy formulas for good writing. But these templates can help you plot out some of the key moves of process analysis and thus may serve as good starting points.

> ➤ **In order to understand how process X works, we can divide it into the following steps: _____, _____, and _____.**
>
> ➤ **The various steps that make up X can be grouped into the following stages: _____, _____, and _____.**
>
> ➤ **The end result of X is _____.**
>
> ➤ **In order to repeat X, you must first _____; then _____ and _____; and finally _____.**
>
> ➤ **The tools and materials you will need to replicate X include _____, _____, and _____.**
>
> ➤ **The most important reasons for understanding/repeating X are _____, _____, and _____.**

For more techniques to help you generate ideas and start writing, see Chapter 1.

Putting the Steps in Order

When you write about a process, you must present its main steps in order. If the process is a linear one, such as backing out of a garage or driving to a particular address in Dallas, you simply start at the earliest point in time and move forward chronologically, step by step, to the end result. If the process is cyclical, such as what's happening in your car engine as you drive, you will have to pick a logical point in the process and then proceed through the rest of the cycle. If, however, the process you are analyzing does not naturally follow chronology, try arranging the steps from most important to least important, or the other way around.

Stating Your Point

A good process analysis should have a point to make, and that point should be clearly expressed in a THESIS STATEMENT. Make sure your thesis statement identifies the process, indicates its end result, and tells the reader why you're analyzing it. For example:

> You cannot understand how the Florida citrus industry works without understanding how fresh orange juice gets processed into "concentrate."
>
> JOHN McPHEE, *Oranges*

McPhee's thesis statement clearly tells the reader what process he's analyzing (making "concentrate" from fresh oranges), its end result (orange juice concentrate), and why he is analyzing it (to understand the Florida citrus industry).

Using Appropriate Transitions

As you move from one step to another, include clear TRANSITIONS, such as *next*, *from there*, *after five minutes*, *then*. Because the actions and events that make up a process are repeatable, you will frequently use such expressions as *usually*, *normally*, *in most cases*, *whenever*, Also, use transitions like *sometimes*, *rarely*, and *in one instance* to note any deviations from the normal order.

Using Appropriate Pronouns

In addition to appropriate transition words, be careful to use pronouns that fit the kind of analysis you are writing. In an explanatory process analysis, you will focus on the things (oranges) and activities (culling and scrubbing) that make up the process. Thus, you will usually write about the process in the third person (*he, she, it,* and *they*), as John McPhee does: "Moving up a conveyor belt, oranges are scrubbed with detergent before <u>they</u> roll on into the juicing machines." In a directive process analysis, by contrast, you are telling the reader directly how to do something. So you should typically use the second person (*you*): "When making orange juice, first <u>you</u> need to cut the oranges in half."

Concluding a Process Analysis

A process analysis is not complete until it explains how the process ends—and the significance of that result. For example, in concluding a process analysis about training a puppy, you might say not only what the result will be but why it is important or desirable: "A well-trained dog will behave when guests visit, won't destroy your carpeting and furniture, and will make less work for you in the long run." In the case of processing oranges into concentrate, John McPhee concludes his essay by telling readers not only that the process yielded a new, concentrated form of orange juice, but that it totally changed the Florida citrus industry and saved much of the crop from going to waste—or winding up as orange-flavored milk.

EVERYDAY PROCESS ANALYSIS
Roz Chast Recipes

In this *New Yorker* cartoon, Roz Chast offers several recipes for economic melts—or meltdowns. Designed to amuse, her cartoon makes fun of the U.S. Treasury Department's "recipe" for reviving the economy after the 2008 financial crisis, which featured a $700 billion bailout package—with all the trimmings. Costly ingredients aside, a simple set of instructions like these is one of the most common forms of how-to writing, or process analysis. No matter what process you're analyzing—from baking a cake to reversing the effects of global recession—follow this recipe: identify the end result of the process (and your reasons for analyzing it), specify the main ingredients or components in the process, break the process into steps, serve.

WILL SHORTZ

HOW TO SOLVE SUDOKU

Will Shortz (b. 1952) is the crossword puzzle editor for the *New York Times*. Shortz grew up on a horse farm in Indiana and attended Indiana University, where he earned a degree in "enigmatology" (the study of puzzles). In 1978, he founded the American Crossword Puzzle Tournament, followed by the World Puzzle Championship in 1992. A specialist in crossword puzzles, Shortz has also mastered the art of sudoku, a wordless puzzle that is wildly popular in Japan but that was actually invented, according to Shortz, by the American architect Howard Garnes. In "How to Solve Sudoku" (2005), the introduction to one of Shortz's many sudoku collections, he reveals the process of how you, too, can master this art.

XXXXXXXXXXXXXXXXXXXXXXXXXXXXXXXXXXXXXXXXXXXXXXXXXXXXXXX

A sudoku puzzle consists of a 9 × 9-square grid subdivided into   1
nine 3 × 3 boxes. Some of the squares contain numbers. The object is to fill in the remaining squares so that every row, every column, and every 3 × 3 box contains each of the numbers from 1 to 9 exactly once.

Solving a sudoku puzzle involves pure logic. No guesswork is   2
needed—or even desirable. Getting started involves mastering just a few simple techniques.

Take the example on the next page (in which we've labeled the   3
nine 3 × 3 boxes A to I as shown). Note that the boxes H and I already have 8's filled in, but box G does not. Can you determine where the 8 goes here?

The 8 can't appear in the top row of squares in box G, because an   4
8 already appears in the top row of I—and no number can be repeated in a row. Similarly, it can't appear in the middle row of G, because an 8 already appears in the middle row of H. So, by process of elimination,

5	8	6					1	2
			5	2	8	6		
2	4		8	1				3
			5		3		9	
			8	1	2	4		
4		5	6			7	3	8
	5		2	3			8	1
7					8			
3	6				5			

A	B	C
D	E	F
G	H	I

an 8 must appear in the bottom row of G. Since only one square in this row is empty—next to the 3 and 6—you have your first answer. Fill in an 8 to the right of the 6.

5   Next, look in the three left-hand boxes of the grid, A, D, and G. An 8 appears in both A and G (the latter being the one you just entered). In box A, the 8 appears in the middle column, while in G the 8 appears on the right. By elimination, in box D, an 8 must go in the leftmost column. But which square? The column here has two squares open.

6   The answer is forced by box E. Here an 8 appears in the middle row. This means an 8 cannot appear in the middle row of D. Therefore, it must appear in the top row of the leftmost column of D. You have your second answer.

7   In solving a sudoku, build on the answers you've filled in as far as possible—left, right, up, and down—before moving on.

For a different kind of logic, consider the sixth row of num-   8
bers—4, ?, 5, 6, ?, ?, 7, 3, 8. The missing numbers must be 1, 2, and
9, in some order. The sixth square can't be a 1, because box E already
has a 1. And it can't be a 2, because a 2 already appears in the sixth
column in box B. So the sixth square in the sixth row has to be a 9.
Fill this in.

Now you're left with just 1 and 2 for the empty squares of this   9
row. The fifth square can't be a 1, because box E already has a 1. So the
fifth square must be a 2. The second square, by elimination, has a 1.
Voilà! Your first complete row is filled in.

Box E now has only two empty squares, so this is a good spot to   10
consider next. Only the 4 and 7 remain to be filled in. The leftmost
square of the middle row can't be a 4, because a 4 already appears in
this row in box F. So it must be 7. The remaining square must be 4.
Your first complete box is done.

One more tip, and then you're on your own.   11

Consider 3's in the boxes A, B, and C. Only one 3 is filled in—   12
in the third row, in box C. In box A you don't have enough information to fill in a 3 yet. However, you know the 3 can't appear in A's
bottom row, because 3 appears in the bottom row of C. And it can't
appear in the top row, because that row is already done. Therefore, it
must appear in the middle row. Which square you don't know yet.
But now, by elimination, you do know that in box B a 3 must appear
in the top row. Specifically, it must appear in the fourth column,
because 3's already appear in the fifth and sixth columns of E and H.
Fill this in.

Following logic, using these and other techniques left for you   13
to discover, you can work your way around the grid, filling in the
rest of the missing numbers. The complete solution is shown
on the next page.

Remember, don't guess. Be careful not to repeat a number where   14
you shouldn't, because a wrong answer may force you to start over. And
don't give up. Soon you'll be a sudoku master!

5	8	6	3	7	4	9	1	2
1	3	7	9	5	2	8	6	4
2	4	9	8	1	6	5	7	3
8	7	2	5	4	3	1	9	6
6	9	3	7	8	1	2	4	5
4	1	5	6	2	9	7	3	8
9	5	4	2	3	7	6	8	1
7	2	1	4	6	8	3	5	9
3	6	8	1	9	5	4	2	7

XXXXXXXXXXXXXXXXXX **FOR DISCUSSION** XXXXXXXXXXXXXXXXXX

1. Solving a sudoku, according to Will Shortz, is a matter of "pure logic" (2). As Shortz ANALYZES THE PROCESS, what's so logical about it?

2. One of the rules of the game is "don't guess" (14). Why not? Judging from Shortz's analysis of the puzzle-solving process, what would happen if you *did* guess?

3. Why do you suppose anyone would want to solve a sudoku puzzle, a crossword puzzle, or any other kind of puzzle?

4. In your opinion, are guides or tips for how to solve puzzles or win games useful, or is it better to figure out puzzles and games "on your own" (11)?

XXXXXXXXXXXXX **STRATEGIES AND STRUCTURES** XXXXXXXXXXXXX

1. Shortz could have begun his analysis with any of the blank boxes in the puzzle he is solving. Why does he choose to begin with sections H and I? Is this a good starting place for his PROCESS ANALYSIS? Why or why not?

2. Shortz uses clear TRANSITIONS between the different moves he makes to solve a sample puzzle. Point out several, and explain how they help to organize his analysis.

3. What is the end result of each move or step in the process that Shortz is analyzing? What is the end result of the whole process? Where and how does Shortz state it most directly?

4. Shortz leaves some puzzle-solving techniques for the reader "to discover" (13). Is this a good strategy, or should he have explained how he derived all the numbers in the finished puzzle? Explain.

5. How important are the visuals in Shortz's text? What do they contribute to his process analysis? In particular, what is the PURPOSE of the smaller square labeled A–I?

6. Shortz uses a single extended EXAMPLE to illustrate his analysis. Is this a good strategy, or should he have referred to several other puzzles as well? Explain.

XXXXXXXXXXXX **Words and Figures of Speech** XXXXXXXXXXXX

1. *Sudoku* is short for the Japanese phrase "suji wa dokushin ni kagiru" ("only single numbers allowed"). The original name was "Number Place." Why do you think the Japanese name has stuck?

2. Sudoku puzzles are sometimes referred to as "wordless crossword puzzles." How and how well does this OXYMORON describe the game?

3. In what sense of the word do puzzles have "objects" (1)?

4. Why do you think Shortz ends his PROCESS ANALYSIS by encouraging the reader to become a sudoku "master" (13)? How does *mastering* a type of puzzle differ from solving one?

XXXXXXXXXXXXXXXXXXXX **For Writing** XXXXXXXXXXXXXXXXXXXXXX

1. Write a paragraph explaining the next step you would take in solving Shortz's sample puzzle and why that's the best move.

2. Choose a type of puzzle or a game you enjoy and write an essay that gives the step-by-step PROCESS of how readers can begin to solve or play it. Use a particular EXAMPLE of a puzzle you've solved or a game you've won to illustrate the process.

JON KATZ

How Boys Become Men

Jon Katz (b. 1947) is a mystery writer and media critic. A former executive producer for CBS *Morning News*, he has also written a number of books about dogs, including *Izzy and Lenore* (2008), as well as columns for *Rolling Stone*, *HotWired*, and slashdot.org, a website dedicated to "News for Nerds." For Katz, the Internet is different from other, more traditional media, such as books and newspapers, because it is interactive. Interactivity, however, is not a trait that most men come by naturally in their personal lives, says Katz. Why? Because "sensitivity" has been beaten out of them as boys. Katz analyzes this male maturation process in "How Boys Become Men," first published in 1993 in *Glamour*, a magazine for young women.

XXXXXXXXXXXXXXXXXXXXXXXXXXXXXXXXXXXXXXXXXXXXXXXXXXXXXXX

1   Two nine-year-old boys, neighbors and friends, were walking home from school. The one in the bright blue windbreaker was laughing and swinging a heavy-looking book bag toward the head of his friend, who kept ducking and stepping back. "What's the matter?" asked the kid with the bag, whooshing it over his head. "You chicken?"

2   His friend stopped, stood still and braced himself. The bag slammed into the side of his face, the thump audible all the way across the street where I stood watching. The impact knocked him to the ground, where he lay mildly stunned for a second. Then he struggled up, rubbing the side of his head. "See?" he said proudly. "I'm no chicken."

3   No. A chicken would probably have had the sense to get out of the way. This boy was already well on the road to becoming a *man*, having learned one of the central ethics of his gender: Experience pain rather than show fear.

Women tend to see men as a giant problem in need of solution.   4
They tell us that we're remote and uncommunicative, that we need to
demonstrate less machismo and more commitment, more humanity. But
if you don't understand something about boys, you can't understand
why men are the way we are, why we find it so difficult to make friends
or to acknowledge our fears and problems.

Boys live in a world with its own Code of Conduct, a set of ruth-   5
less, unspoken, and unyielding rules:

> Don't be a goody-goody.
>
> Never rat. If your parents ask about bruises, shrug.
>
> Never admit fear. Ride the roller coaster, join the fistfight, do
> what you have to do. Asking for help is for sissies.
>
> Empathy is for nerds. You can help your best buddy, under
> certain circumstances. Everyone else is on his own.
>
> Never discuss anything of substance with anybody. Grunt,
> shrug, dump on teachers, laugh at wimps, talk about comic
> books. Anything else is risky.

Boys are rewarded for throwing hard. Most other activities—reading,   6
befriending girls, or just thinking—are considered weird. And if there's
one thing boys don't want to be, it's weird.

More than anything else, boys are supposed to learn how to handle   7
themselves. I remember the bitter fifth-grade conflict I touched off by
elbowing aside a bigger boy named Barry and seizing the cafeteria's last
carton of chocolate milk. Teased for getting aced out by a wimp, he had
to reclaim his place in the pack. Our fistfight, at recess, ended with my
knees buckling and my lip bleeding while my friends, sympathetic but
out of range, watched resignedly.

When I got home, my mother took one look at my swollen face and   8
screamed. I wouldn't tell her anything, but when my father got home I
cracked and confessed, pleading with them to do nothing. Instead, they
called Barry's parents, who restricted his television for a week.

The following morning, Barry and six of his pals stepped out from   9
behind a stand of trees. "It's the rat," said Barry.

10   I bled a little more. *Rat* was scrawled in crayon across my desk.

11   They were waiting for me after school for a number of afternoons to follow. I tried varying my routes and avoiding bushes and hedges. It usually didn't work.

12   I was as ashamed for telling as I was frightened. "You did ask for it," said my best friend. Frontier Justice has nothing on Boy Justice.

13   In panic, I appealed to a cousin who was several years older. He followed me home from school, and when Barry's gang surrounded me, he came barreling toward us. "Stay away from my cousin," he shouted, "or I'll kill you."

14   After they were gone, however, my cousin could barely stop laughing. "You were afraid of *them?*" he howled. "They barely came up to my waist."

15   Men remember receiving little mercy as boys; maybe that's why it's sometimes difficult for them to show any.

16   "I know lots of men who had happy childhoods, but none who have happy memories of the way other boys treated them," says a friend. "It's a macho marathon from third grade up, when you start butting each other in the stomach."

17   "The thing is," adds another friend, "you learn early on to hide what you feel. It's never safe to say, 'I'm scared.' My girlfriend asks me why I don't talk more about what I'm feeling. I've gotten better at it, but it will *never* come naturally."

18   You don't need to be a shrink to see how the lessons boys learn affect their behavior as men. Men are being asked, more and more, to show sensitivity, but they dread the very word. They struggle to build their increasingly uncertain work lives but will deny they're in trouble. They want love, affection, and support but don't know how to ask for them. They hide their weaknesses and fears from all, even those they care for. They've learned to be wary of intervening when they see others in trouble. They often still balk at being stigmatized as weird.

19   Some men get shocked into sensitivity—when they lose their jobs, their wives, or their lovers. Others learn it through a strong marriage, or through their own children.

20   It may be a long while, however, before male culture evolves to the point that boys can learn more from one another than how to hit curve balls. Last month, walking my dog past the playground near my house, I saw three boys encircling a fourth, laughing and pushing him. He was

skinny and rumpled, and he looked frightened. One boy knelt behind him while another pushed him from the front, a trick familiar to any former boy. He fell backward.

When the others ran off, he brushed the dirt off his elbows and walked toward the swings. His eyes were moist and he was struggling for control.   21

"Hi," I said through the chain-link fence. "How ya doing?"   22

"Fine," he said quickly, kicking his legs out and beginning his swing.   23

XXXXXXXXXXXXXXXXXX **FOR DISCUSSION** XXXXXXXXXXXXXXXXXXXX

1. In order to explain how boys become men, Jon Katz must first explain how boys become boys. By what specific "rules" does this process occur, according to him (5)?

2. Is Katz right, do you think, in his PROCESS ANALYSIS of how boys are brought up? Why or why not?

3. The end result of how they learn to behave as boys, says Katz, is that men find it difficult "to make friends or to acknowledge our fears and problems" (4). They lack "sensitivity" (19). Do you agree? In your experience, is Katz's analysis accurate or inaccurate? Explain.

4. According to Katz, women are puzzled by "male culture" (20). How, in his view, do women regard men? Do you agree or disagree with this analysis? Why?

5. What evidence, if any, can you find in Katz's essay to indicate that the author has learned as an adult male to behave in ways he was not taught as a boy? By what processes, according to Katz, do men sometimes learn such new kinds of behavior?

XXXXXXXXXXXXX **STRATEGIES AND STRUCTURES** XXXXXXXXXXXXX

1. Katz tells the story in paragraphs 1 and 2 of a boy who prefers to get knocked down rather than be called a "chicken." Why do you think he begins with this incident? What stage or aspect of the boy training process is he illustrating?

2. The longest of the ANECDOTES that Katz tells to show how boys learn to behave is the one about himself. Where does it begin and end? By what process or processes is he being taught here?

3. What is the role of the older cousin in the NARRATIVE Katz tells about himself as a boy? How does the cousin's response in paragraph 14 illustrate the process Katz is analyzing?

4. Where else in his essay does Katz tell a brief story to illustrate what he is saying about how boys are trained? How do these stories support his main point? What would the essay be like without any of the stories?

5. "If you don't understand something about boys, you can't understand why men are the way we are . . . " (4). To whom is Katz speaking here? What PURPOSES might he have for explaining the male maturation process to this particular AUDIENCE?

6. Besides ANALYZING THE PROCESSES by which boys learn to behave according to a rigid "Code of Conduct," Katz's essay also analyzes the lasting EFFECTS caused by this early training (5). What are some of these effects?

XXXXXXXXXXXX **WORDS AND FIGURES OF SPEECH** XXXXXXXXXXXX

1. How does your dictionary define "machismo" (4)? What language(s) does it derive from?

2. To feel *sympathy* for someone means to have feelings and emotions similar to theirs. What does "empathy" mean (5)?

3. How does Katz's use of the various meanings of the words "chicken" and "rat" help him to make his point about how boys become men (1–3, 5, 9–10)?

4. Verbal IRONY is the use of one word or phrase to imply another with a quite different meaning. What's ironic about the boy's reply to Katz's question in paragraph 23?

XXXXXXXXXXXXXXXXXXXX **FOR WRITING** XXXXXXXXXXXXXXXXXXXXXX

1. Write a brief Code of Conduct like the one in paragraph 5 that lays out the unspoken rules of the "culture," male or female, in which you grew up.

2. Write an essay that ANALYZES THE PROCESS of how boys become men, as *you* see it. Or, alternatively, write an analysis of the process(es) by which *girls* are typically socialized to become women in America or somewhere else. Draw on your own personal experience, or what you know from others, or both. Feel free to use ANECDOTES and other elements of NARRATIVE as appropriate to illustrate your analysis.

ALLEGRA GOODMAN

So, You Want to Be a Writer? Here's How.

Allegra Goodman (b. 1967) is a novelist, short story writer, and mother of four. After growing up in Honolulu, she studied at Harvard, then earned a Ph.D. in English from Stanford University. Her most recent novels include *Intuition* (2006) and *The Other Side of the Island* (2008). "If there's one thing I've learned over the years," says Goodman, who is fascinated by the writing process, "it's the value of revision. I write draft after draft, rereading, rethinking, rephrasing every step of the way." In the following essay, published in the *Boston Globe* in 2008, Goodman gives advice on the process of becoming a writer.

XXXXXXXXXXXXXXXXXXXXXXXXXXXXXXXXXXXXXXXXXXXXXXXXXXXXXXXXXXXX

When people hear that I'm a novelist, I get one comment more than any other. "I'm a physician (or a third-grade teacher, or a venture capitalist) but what I really want to do is write." A mother of three muses: "I've always loved writing since I was a little girl." A physicist declares, "I've got a great idea for a mystery-thriller-philosophical-love story—if I only had the time." I nod, resisting the temptation to reply: "And I have a great idea for a unified field theory—if I just had a moment to work it out on paper."   1

Book sales are down, but creative writing enrollments are booming. The longing to write knows no bounds. A lactation consultant[1] told me, "I have a story inside of me. I mean, I know everybody has a story, but I really have a story."   2

Forthwith, some advice for those of you who have always wanted to write, those with best-selling ideas, and those who really have a story.   3

---

1. Someone who advises mothers that choose to nurse their infants.

4   To begin, don't write about yourself. I'm not saying you're uninteresting. I realize that your life has been so crazy no one could make
this stuff up. But if you want to be a writer, start by writing about other
people. Observe their faces, and the way they wave their hands around.
Listen to the way they talk. Replay conversations in your mind—not
just the words, but the silences as well. Imagine the lives of others. If
you want to be a writer, you need to get over yourself. This is not just
an artistic choice; it's a moral choice. A writer attempts to understand
others from the inside.

5   Find a peaceful place to work. Peace does not necessarily entail an
artists' colony or an island off the coast of Maine. You might find peace
in your basement, or at a cafe in Davis Square,[2] or amid old ladies
rustling magazines at the public library. Peace is not the same as quiet.
Peace means you avoid checking your e-mail every ten seconds. Peace
means you are willing to work offline, screen calls, and forget your to-do
list for an hour. If this is difficult, turn off your Web browser, or try
writing without a computer altogether. Treat yourself to pen and paper
and make a mess, crossing out sentences, crumpling pages, inserting
paragraphs in margins. Remember spiral-bound notebooks, and thank-
you notes with stamps? Handwriting is arcane in all the best ways. Writing in ink doesn't feel like work; it feels like secret diaries and treasure
maps and art.

6   Read widely, and dissect books in your mind. What, exactly, makes
David Sedaris[3] funny? How does George Orwell[4] fill us with dread? If
you want to be a novelist, read novels new and old, satirical, experimen-
tal, Victorian, American. Read nonfiction as well. Consider how biogra-
phers select details to illuminate a life in time. If you want to write
nonfiction, study histories and essays, but also read novels and think
about narrative, and the novelist's artful release of information. Don't
forget poetry. Why? Because it's good to go where words are wor-

---

2. Central intersection in Somerville, Massachusetts, a city north of Boston.

3. Best-selling American author (b. 1956), known for his witty autobiographical writing.

4. British novelist and essayist (1903–1950), whose dystopian novel *1984* is a foreboding
story of a repressive totalitarian government.

shipped, and essential to remember that you are not a poet. Lyric poets linger on a mood or fragmentary phrase; prose writers must move along to tell their story, and catch their train.

And this is true for everyone, but especially for women: If you   7
don't value your own time, other people won't either. Trust me, you can't write a novel in stolen minutes outside your daughter's tap class. Virginia Woolf[5] declared that a woman needs a room of her own. Well, the room won't help, if you don't shut the door. Post a note. "Book in progress, please do not disturb unless you're bleeding." Or these lines from Samuel Taylor Coleridge,[6] which I have adapted for writing mothers: " . . . Beware! Beware! / Her flashing eyes, her floating hair! Weave a circle round her thrice, / And close your eyes with holy dread, / For she on honey-dew hath fed, / and drunk the milk of Paradise."

---

5. British novelist and essayist (1882–1941). In her book *A Room of One's Own* (1929), Woolf noted that "a woman must have money and a room of her own if she is to write fiction."

6. British Romantic poet and critic (1772–1834). Goodman adapts lines from his poem "Kubla Khan" (1816), which Coleridge claimed he was unable to complete after being interrupted during its composition.

⟩⟩⟩⟩⟩⟩⟩⟩⟩⟩⟩⟩ FOR DISCUSSION ⟨⟨⟨⟨⟨⟨⟨⟨⟨⟨⟨⟨

1. Why, according to Allegra Goodman, should aspiring writers write about other people instead of themselves? Do you think this is sensible advice? Why or why not?

2. What PROCESS is Goodman ANALYZING exactly—how to write or how to become a writer? Is her analysis explanatory or directive? Explain.

3. Why does Goodman recommend writing by hand in ink?

4. Why does Goodman think all writers should study poetry? Is she right? Why or why not?

5. What special advice does Goodman have for women writers? Why, in her view, do they need such advice even more than men do?

XXXXXXXXXXXXXX **STRATEGIES AND STRUCTURES** XXXXXXXXXXXXX

1. What is the end result of the PROCESS that Goodman is ANALYZING? Where and how does she first introduce it?

2. In the beginning of her essay, Goodman tells about all the people she has met who want to be writers. Is this an effective way to begin? Why or why not?

3. Goodman tells us early on who she has in mind as her main AUDIENCE for the advice she gives. Who is it? In what ways is her essay directed toward this audience? Explain.

4. Goodman divides the process that she is analyzing into three basic stages. What are they? Does she use chronology to organize them? If not, how are they organized?

5. What steps is the reading stage of the process further broken into? What about the other stages? Why does Goodman break them down in this way?

6. Why does Goodman end her analysis with the words of another writer? Is this an effective strategy? Why or why not?

7. In paragraph 6, Goodman COMPARES the writer of prose to the writer of poetry. Which kind of writer—or aspiring writer—is her advice aimed at? How does she DEFINE the kind of writer she has in mind?

XXXXXXXXXXXXX **WORDS AND FIGURES OF SPEECH** XXXXXXXXXXXX

1. Why is writing about other people rather than oneself a "moral" choice, according to Goodman (4)? What's moral about it?

2. The writer, says Goodman, needs "a peaceful place to work" (5). How does she DEFINE "peaceful"?

3. Why does Goodman use the word "arcane" instead of *old-fashioned* or *outmoded* to DESCRIBE handwriting (5)?

4. What does Goodman mean by "artful" when she uses it to describe how the novelist releases information in a NARRATIVE (6)?

5. Explain the ALLUSION to Virginia Woolf in the last paragraph of Goodman's essay. What PURPOSE does it serve in her analysis?

XXXXXXXXXXXXXXXXXX **FOR WRITING** XXXXXXXXXXXXXXXXXXX

1. In a paragraph or two, ANALYZE THE PROCESS you follow for managing your time when you write.

2. Write an essay analyzing the process you have gone through so far in learning how to be a writer. Be sure to say how much farther you have to go in order to reach your goal and what advice you have for other writers.

ALEXANDER PETRUNKEVITCH

The Spider and the Wasp

Alexander Petrunkevitch (1875–1964), a native of Russia who came to the United States in his late twenties, was a world-renowned expert on spiders. Beginning in 1911 with an index to the spiders of Central and South America, he studied and wrote about arachnids for more than fifty years. In "The Spider and the Wasp," first published in *Scientific American* in 1952, Petrunkevitch analyzes the process by which a female digger wasp converts a living tarantula into food for her young. The process, he says, is "a classic example of what looks like intelligence pitted against instinct."

XXXXXXXXXXXXXXXXXXXXXXXXXXXXXXXXXXXXXXXXXXXXXXXXXXXXXXXXXXXXX

1 To hold its own in the struggle for existence, every species of animal must have a regular source of food, and if it happens to live on other animals, its survival may be very delicately balanced. The hunter cannot exist without the hunted; if the latter should perish from the earth, the former would, too. When the hunted also prey on some of the hunters, the matter may become complicated.

2 This is nowhere better illustrated than in the insect world. Think of the complexity of a situation such as the following: There is a certain wasp, *Pimpla inquisitor*, whose larvae feed on the larvae of the tussock moth. *Pimpla* larvae in turn serve as food for the larvae of a second wasp, and the latter in their turn nourish still a third wasp. What subtle balance between fertility and mortality must exist in the case of each of these four species to prevent the extinction of all of them! An excess of mortality over fertility in a single member of the group would ultimately wipe out all four.

3 This is not a unique case. The two great orders of insects, Hymenoptera and Diptera, are full of such examples of interrelationship.

And the spiders (which are not insects but members of a separate order of arthropods) also are killers and victims of insects.

The picture is complicated by the fact that those species which are 4 carnivorous in the larval stage have to be provided with animal food by a vegetarian mother. The survival of the young depends on the mother's correct choice of a food which she does not eat herself.

In the feeding and safeguarding of their progeny the insects and 5 spiders exhibit some interesting analogies to reasoning and some crass examples of blind instinct. The case I propose to describe here is that of the tarantula spiders and their arch-enemy, the digger wasps of the genus *Pepsis*. It is a classic example of what looks like intelligence pitted against instinct—a strange situation in which the victim, though fully able to defend itself, submits unwittingly to its destruction.

Most tarantulas live in the Tropics, but several species occur in the tem- 6 perate zone and a few are common in the southern U.S. Some varieties are large and have powerful fangs with which they can inflict a deep wound. These formidable looking spiders do not, however, attack man; you can hold one in your hand, if you are gentle, without being bitten. Their bite is dangerous only to insects and small mammals such as mice; for a man it is no worse than a hornet's sting.

Tarantulas customarily live in deep cylindrical burrows, from 7 which they emerge at dusk and into which they retire at dawn. Mature males wander about after dark in search of females and occasionally stray into houses. After mating, the male dies in a few weeks, but a female lives much longer and can mate several years in succession. In a Paris museum is a tropical specimen which is said to have been living in captivity for 25 years.

A fertilized female tarantula lays from 200 to 400 eggs at a time; 8 thus it is possible for a single tarantula to produce several thousand young. She takes no care of them beyond weaving a cocoon of silk to enclose the eggs. After they hatch, the young walk away, find convenient places in which to dig their burrows and spend the rest of their lives in solitude. Tarantulas feed mostly on insects and millepedes. Once their appetite is appeased, they digest the food for several days before eating again. Their sight is poor, being limited to sensing a change in the intensity of light and to the perception of moving objects. They apparently have little or no sense of hearing, for a hungry tarantula will pay no attention to a loudly chirping cricket placed in its cage unless the insect happens to touch one of its legs.

9   But all spiders, and especially hairy ones, have an extremely delicate sense of touch. Laboratory experiments prove that tarantulas can distinguish three types of touch: pressure against the body wall, stroking of the body hair and riffling of certain very fine hairs on the legs called trichobothria. Pressure against the body, by a finger or the end of a pencil, causes the tarantula to move off slowly for a short distance. The touch excites no defensive response unless the approach is from above where the spider can see the motion, in which case it rises on its hind legs, lifts its front legs, opens its fangs and holds this threatening posture as long as the object continues to move. When the motion stops, the spider drops back to the ground, remains quiet for a few seconds and then moves slowly away.

10   The entire body of a tarantula, especially its legs, is thickly clothed with hair. Some of it is short and woolly, some long and stiff. Touching this body hair produces one of two distinct reactions. When the spider is hungry, it responds with an immediate and swift attack. At the touch of a cricket's antennae the tarantula seizes the insect so swiftly that a motion picture taken at the rate of 64 frames per second shows only the result and not the process of capture. But when the spider is not hungry, the stimulation of its hairs merely causes it to shake the touched limb. An insect can walk under its hairy belly unharmed.

11   The trichobothria, very fine hairs growing from disk-like membranes on the legs, were once thought to be the spider's hearing organs, but we now know that they have nothing to do with sound. They are sensitive only to air movement. A light breeze makes them vibrate slowly without disturbing the common hair. When one blows gently on the trichobothria, the tarantula reacts with a quick jerk of its four front legs. If the front and hind legs are stimulated at the same time, the spider makes a sudden jump. This reaction is quite independent of the state of its appetite.

These three tactile responses—to pressure on the body wall, to moving of the common hair and to flexing of the trichobothria—are so different from one another that there is no possibility of confusing them. They serve the tarantula adequately for most of its needs and enable it to avoid most annoyances and dangers. But they fail the spider completely when it meets its deadly enemy, the digger wasp *Pepsis*.

These solitary wasps are beautiful and formidable creatures. Most species are either a deep shiny blue all over, or deep blue with rusty wings. The largest have a wing span of about four inches. They live on nectar. When excited, they give off a pungent odor—a warning that they are ready to attack. The sting is much worse than that of a bee or common wasp, and the pain and swelling last longer. In the adult stage the wasp lives only a few months. The female produces but a few eggs, one at a time at intervals of two or three days. For each egg the mother must provide one adult tarantula, alive but paralyzed. The tarantula must be of the correct species to nourish the larva. The mother wasp attaches the egg to the paralyzed spider's abdomen. Upon hatching from the egg, the larva is many hundreds of times smaller than its living but helpless victim. It eats no other food and drinks no water. By the time it has finished its single gargantuan meal and become ready for wasphood, nothing remains of the tarantula but its indigestible chitinous skeleton.

The mother wasp goes tarantula-hunting when the egg in her ovary is almost ready to be laid. Flying low over the ground late on a sunny afternoon, the wasp looks for its victim or for the mouth of a tarantula burrow, a round hole edged by a bit of silk. The sex of the spider makes no difference, but the mother is highly discriminating as to species. Each species of *Pepsis* requires a certain species of tarantula, and the wasp will not attack the wrong species. In a cage with a tarantula which is not its normal prey the wasp avoids the spider, and is usually killed by it in the night.

Yet when a wasp finds the correct species, it is the other way about. To identify the species the wasp apparently must explore the spider with her antennae. The tarantula shows an amazing tolerance to this exploration. The wasp crawls under it and walks over it without evoking any hostile response. The molestation is so great and so persistent that the tarantula often rises on all eight legs, as if it were on stilts. It may stand this way for several minutes. Meanwhile the wasp, having satisfied itself that the victim is of the right species, moves off a few inches to dig the spider's grave. Working vigorously with legs and jaws, it excavates a hole 8 to 10 inches deep with a diameter slightly larger than the spider's girth. Now and again the wasp pops out of the hole to make sure that the spider is still there.

16   When the grave is finished, the wasp returns to the tarantula to complete her ghastly enterprise. First she feels it all over once more with her antennae. Then her behavior becomes more aggressive. She bends her abdomen, protruding her sting, and searches for the soft membrane at the point where the spider's leg joins its body—the only spot where she can penetrate the horny skeleton. From time to time, as the exasperated spider slowly shifts ground, the wasp turns on her back and slides along with the aid of her wings, trying to get under the tarantula for a shot at the vital spot. During all this maneuvering, which can last for several minutes, the tarantula makes no move to save itself. Finally the wasp corners it against some obstruction and grasps one of its legs in her powerful jaws. Now at last the harassed spider tries a desperate but vain defense. The two contestants roll over and over on the ground. It is a terrifying sight and the outcome is always the same. The wasp finally manages to thrust her sting into the soft spot and holds it there for a few seconds while she pumps in the poison. Almost immediately the tarantula falls paralyzed on its back. Its legs stop twitching; its heart stops beating. Yet it is not dead, as is shown by the fact that if taken from the wasp it can be restored to some sensitivity by being kept in a moist chamber for several months.

17   After paralyzing the tarantula, the wasp cleans herself by dragging her body along the ground and rubbing her feet, sucks the drop of blood oozing from the wound in the spider's abdomen, then grabs a leg of the flabby, helpless animal in her jaws and drags it down to the bottom of the grave. She stays there for many minutes, sometimes for several hours, and what she does all that time in the dark we do not know. Eventually she lays her egg and attaches it to the side of the spider's abdomen with a sticky secretion. Then she emerges, fills the grave with soil carried bit by bit in her jaws, and finally tramples the ground all around to hide any trace of the grave from prowlers. Then she flies away, leaving her descendant safely started in life.

In all this the behavior of the wasp evidently is qualitatively different 18
from that of the spider. The wasp acts like an intelligent animal. This
is not to say that instinct plays no part or that she reasons as man
does. But her actions are to the point; they are not automatic and can
be modified to fit the situation. We do not know for certain how she
identifies the tarantula—probably it is by some olfactory or chemo-
tactile sense—but she does it purposefully and does not blindly tackle
a wrong species.

On the other hand, the tarantula's behavior shows only confusion. 19
Evidently the wasp's pawing gives it no pleasure, for it tries to move
away. That the wasp is not simulating sexual stimulation is certain,
because male and female tarantulas react in the same way to its
advances. That the spider is not anesthetized by some odorless secretion is easily shown by blowing lightly at the tarantula and making it
jump suddenly. What, then, makes the tarantula behave as stupidly as
it does?

No clear, simple answer is available. Possibly the stimulation by 20
the wasp's antennae is masked by a heavier pressure on the spider's
body, so that it reacts as when prodded by a pencil. But the explanation
may be much more complex. Initiative in attack is not in the nature of
tarantulas; most species fight only when cornered so that escape is
impossible. Their inherited patterns of behavior apparently prompt them
to avoid problems rather than attack them. For example, spiders always
weave their webs in three dimensions, and when a spider finds that there
is insufficient space to attach certain threads in the third dimension, it
leaves the place and seeks another, instead of finishing the web in a single plane. This urge to escape seems to arise under all circumstances, in
all phases of life and to take the place of reasoning. For a spider to
change the pattern of its web is as impossible as for an inexperienced
man to build a bridge across a chasm obstructing his way.

In a way the instinctive urge to escape is not only easier but more 21
efficient than reasoning. The tarantula does exactly what is most efficient
in all cases except in an encounter with a ruthless and determined
attacker dependent for the existence of her own species on killing as
many tarantulas as she can lay eggs. Perhaps in this case the spider fol-

lows its usual pattern of trying to escape, instead of seizing and killing the wasp, because it is not aware of its danger. In any case, the survival of the tarantula species as a whole is protected by the fact that the spider is much more fertile than the wasp.

XXXXXXXXXXXXXXXXXXXX **For Discussion** XXXXXXXXXXXXXXXXXXXX

1. The first half of paragraph 8 of "The Spider and the Wasp" is a miniature PROCESS ANALYSIS. What process does it analyze?

2. By what "process of capture" does the tarantula get its food in paragraph 10? Alexander Petrunkevitch observes "the result" of the process here. Why doesn't he also analyze the process itself into steps?

3. Petrunkevitch begins his main process analysis with its end result and then returns to the wasp's hunt for her prey. That end result is DESCRIBED in paragraph 13. What is it?

4. Petrunkevitch describes the process by which the wasp converts the spider into food as a case of "intelligence pitted against instinct" (5). What does the spider do (or not do) that seems merely instinctive? What in the wasp's behavior looks like intelligence at work?

5. If a digger wasp's favorite kind of tarantula always loses the deadly struggle between them, why don't tarantulas die out as a species?

6. What might happen to the digger wasp as a species if it were a more prolific breeder? If the tarantula were less prolific? What delicate natural balance do spider and wasp together illustrate?

XXXXXXXXXXXXXX **Strategies and Structures** XXXXXXXXXXXXXX

1. What is Petrunkevitch's main point in ANALYZING THE PROCESS of how a wasp conquers a spider? What's his reason for analyzing this process, and where in his essay does he clearly state his THESIS?

2. Point out the six stages—from hunting to burying—into which Petrunkevitch analyzes the process by which the wasp conquers the spider.

3. How does Petrunkevitch's account of the other wasp larvae in paragraph 2 prepare us for the case of the spider and the digger wasp?

4. Petrunkevitch refers to the wasp as the spider's "arch-enemy" (5). How else does he give their struggle human characteristics and a human scale? Give several EXAMPLES from the text.

5. Petrunkevitch analyzes the process of how a wasp conquers a spider in chronological order in paragraphs 14 through 17. What TRANSITIONS does he use to organize and connect the various steps?

6. Petrunkevitch's process analysis incorporates elements of the COMPARISON AND CONTRAST essays discussed in Chapter 7. Which does he stress: the differences between spiders and wasps, or their similarities? Point to specific passages to support your answer.

XXXXXXXXXXXX **WORDS AND FIGURES OF SPEECH** XXXXXXXXXXXX

1. "Gargantuan" means "gigantic" (13). Who is Gargantua?

2. In addition to scientific terms ("Hymenoptera," "Diptera," "trichobothria"), Petrunkevitch uses such nontechnical terms as "wasphood" and "prowlers" (3, 9, 11, 13, 17). Point out additional EXAMPLES of both kinds of language. What does Petrunkevitch's "mixed" vocabulary tell you about his AUDIENCE for this essay?

3. Choose four of the following words with which you are least familiar, and look up their exact meanings in your dictionary: "subtle" (2), "carnivorous" (4), "progeny" (5), "formidable" (6, 13), "appeased" (8), "tactile" (12), "pungent" (13), "chitinous" (13), "olfactory" (18), "simulating" (19), "anesthetized" (19), "chasm" (20).

XXXXXXXXXXXXXXXXXXXX **FOR WRITING** XXXXXXXXXXXXXXXXXXXX

1. Make a list of the steps you went through to master some complex activity, perhaps one in which instinct eventually took over from conscious intelligence. EXAMPLES might be swimming, sailing, driving a car, riding a bike, or playing a musical instrument.

2. ANALYZE THE PROCESS by which an insect or animal or bird you have observed meets its basic needs. Examples might be getting food; building a nest or burrow; or producing, looking after, or training its young. Alternatively, if you have trained an animal to do something that goes beyond mere instinct, analyze the training process that you (and the animal) went through.

PHILIP WEISS

How to Get Out of a
Locked Trunk

Philip Weiss is an investigative journalist and former columnist for the
New York Observer. He has also been a contributor to the Jewish World
Review, Esquire, and Harper's, in which "How to Get Out of a Locked
Trunk" was first published (1992). Weiss is the author of the political
novel Cock-A-Doodle-Doo (1995) and the investigative work American
Taboo: A Murder in the Peace Corps (2004). About to be married when
he wrote this essay, Weiss obsessively analyzes his way out of the trunks
of locked cars, a strange fixation that suggests his bachelor self may be
carrying some extra baggage. The essay also analyzes how Weiss got out
of his condition.

XXXXXXXXXXXXXXXXXXXXXXXXXXXXXXXXXXXXXXXXXXXXXXXXXXXXXXXXXXX

1   On a hot Sunday last summer my friend Tony and I drove my rental
car, a '91 Buick, from St. Paul to the small town of Waconia, Minnesota, forty miles southwest. We each had a project. Waconia is Tony's
boyhood home, and his sister had recently given him a panoramic postcard
of Lake Waconia as seen from a high point in the town early in the century.
He wanted to duplicate the photograph's vantage point, then hang the two
pictures together in his house in Frogtown. I was hoping to see Tony's
father, Emmett, a retired mechanic, in order to settle a question that had
been nagging me: Is it possible to get out of a locked car trunk?

2   We tried to call ahead to Emmett twice, but he wasn't home. Tony
thought he was probably golfing but that there was a good chance he'd
be back by the time we got there. So we set out.

3   I parked the Buick, which was a silver sedan with a red interior, by
the graveyard near where Tony thought the picture had been taken. He
took his picture and I wandered among the headstones, reading the epi-

taphs. One of them was chillingly anti-individualist. It said, "Not to do my will, but thine."

Trunk lockings had been on my mind for a few weeks. It seemed   4
to me that the fear of being locked in a car trunk had a particular hold on the American imagination. Trunk lockings occur in many movies and books—from *Goodfellas* to *Thelma and Louise* to *Humboldt's Gift*.[1] And while the highbrow national newspapers generally shy away from trunk lockings, the attention they receive in local papers suggests a widespread anxiety surrounding the subject. In an afternoon at the New York Public Library I found numerous stories about trunk lockings. A Los Angeles man is discovered, bloodshot, banging the trunk of his white Eldorado following a night and a day trapped inside; he says his captors went on joyrides and picked up women. A forty-eight-year-old Houston doctor is forced into her trunk at a bank ATM and then the car is abandoned, parked near the Astrodome.[2] A New Orleans woman tells police she gave birth in a trunk while being abducted to Texas. Tests undermine her story, the police drop the investigation. But so what if it's a fantasy? That only shows the idea's hold on us.

Every culture comes up with tests of a person's ability to get out of   5
a sticky situation. The English plant mazes. Tropical resorts market those straw finger-grabbers that tighten their grip the harder you pull on them, and Viennese intellectuals gave us the concept of childhood sexuality—figure it out, or remain neurotic for life.

At least you could puzzle your way out of those predicaments.   6
When they slam the trunk, though, you're helpless unless someone finds you. You would think that such a common worry should have a ready fix, and that the secret of getting out of a locked trunk is something we should all know about.

I phoned experts but they were very discouraging.   7

---

1. *Humboldt's Gift* (1975), a novel by Saul Bellow about a spiritually empty writer whose life is reawakened by a mob member; *Goodfellas* (1990), a gangster movie; *Thelma and Louise* (1991), a road movie about two women trying to escape oppressive marriages.

2. A large sports arena in Houston, Texas.

8   "You cannot get out. If you got a pair of pliers and bat's eyes, yes. But you have to have a lot of knowledge of the lock," said James Foote at Automotive Locksmiths in New York City.

9   Jim Frens, whom I reached at the technical section of *Car and Driver*[3] in Detroit, told me the magazine had not dealt with this question. But he echoed the opinion of experts elsewhere when he said that the best hope for escape would be to try and kick out the panel between the trunk and the backseat. That angle didn't seem worth pursuing. What if your enemies were in the car, crumpling beer cans and laughing at your fate? It didn't make sense to join them.

10   The people who deal with rules on auto design were uncomfortable with my scenarios. Debra Barclay of the Center for Auto Safety, an organization founded by Ralph Nader,[4] had certainly heard of cases, but she was not aware of any regulations on the matter. "Now, if there was a defect involved—" she said, her voice trailing off, implying that trunk locking was all phobia. This must be one of the few issues on which she and the auto industry agree. Ann Carlson of the Motor Vehicle Manufacturers Association became alarmed at the thought that I was going to play up a non-problem: "In reality this very rarely happens. As you say, in the movies it's a wonderful plot device," she said. "But in reality apparently this is not that frequent an occurrence. So they have not designed that feature into vehicles in a specific way."

11   When we got to Emmett's one-story house it was full of people. Tony's sister, Carol, was on the floor with her two small children. Her husband, Charlie, had one eye on the golf tournament on TV, and Emmett was at the kitchen counter, trimming fat from meat for lunch. I have known Emmett for fifteen years. He looked better than ever. In his retirement he had sharply changed his diet and lost a lot of weight. He had on shorts. His legs were tanned and muscular. As always, his manner was humorous, if opaque.

---

3. A monthly magazine for car enthusiasts.

4. American attorney and political activist (b. 1934) who was an early advocate of automobile safety.

Tony told his family my news: I was getting married in three   12
weeks. Charlie wanted to know where my fiancée was. Back East, getting
everything ready. A big-time hatter was fitting her for a new hat.

Emmett sat on the couch, watching me. "Do you want my advice?"   13
"Sure."   14

He just grinned. A gold tooth glinted. Carol and Charlie pressed   15
him to yield his wisdom.

Finally he said, "Once you get to be thirty, you make your own   16
mistakes."

He got out several cans of beer, and then I brought up what was on   17
my mind.

Emmett nodded and took off his glasses, then cleaned them and   18
put them back on.

We went out to his car, a Mercury Grand Marquis, and Emmett   19
opened the trunk. His golf clubs were sitting on top of the spare tire in
a green golf bag. Next to them was a toolbox and what he called his
"burglar tools," a set of elbowed rods with red plastic handles he used to
open door locks when people locked their keys inside.

Tony and Charlie stood watching. Charlie is a banker in Min-   20
neapolis. He enjoys gizmos and is extremely practical. I would describe
him as unflappable. That's a word I always wanted to apply to myself,
but my fiancée had recently informed me that I am high-strung. Though
that surprised me, I didn't quarrel with her.

For a while we studied the latch assembly. The lock closed in much   21
the same way that a lobster might clamp on to a pencil. The claw portion, the jaws of the lock, was mounted inside the trunk lid. When you
shut the lid, the jaws locked on to the bend of a U-shaped piece of metal
mounted on the body of the car. Emmett said my best bet would be to
unscrew the bolts. That way the U-shaped piece would come loose and
the lock's jaws would swing up with it still in their grasp.

"But you'd need a wrench," he said.   22

It was already getting too technical. Emmett had an air of endless   23
patience, but I felt defeated. I could only imagine bloodied fingers,
cracked teeth. I had hoped for a simple trick.

Charlie stepped forward. He reached out and squeezed the lock's   24
jaws. They clicked shut in the air, bound together by heavy springs.

Charlie now prodded the upper part of the left-hand jaw, the thicker part. With a rough flick of his thumb, he was able to force the jaws to snap open. Great.

25   Unfortunately, the jaws were mounted behind a steel plate the size of your palm in such a way that while they were accessible to us, standing outside the car, had we been inside the trunk the plate would be in our way, blocking the jaws.

26   This time Emmett saw the way out. He fingered a hole in the plate. It was no bigger than the tip of your little finger. But the hole was close enough to the latch itself that it might be possible to angle something through the hole from inside the trunk and nudge the jaws apart. We tried with one of my keys. The lock jumped open.

27   It was time for a full-dress test. Emmett swung the clubs out of the trunk, and I set my can of Schmidt's on the rear bumper and climbed in. Everyone gathered around, and Emmett lowered the trunk on me, then pressed it shut with his meaty hands. Total darkness. I couldn't hear the people outside. I thought I was going to panic. But the big trunk felt comfortable. I was pressed against a sort of black carpet that softened the angles against my back.

28   I could almost stretch out in the trunk, and it seemed to me I could make them sweat if I took my time. Even Emmett, that sphinx, would give way to curiosity. Once I was out he'd ask how it had been and I'd just grin. There were some things you could only learn by doing.

29   It took a while to find the hole. I slipped the key in and angled it to one side. The trunk gasped open.

30   Emmett motioned the others away, then levered me out with his big right forearm. Though I'd only been inside for a minute, I was disoriented—as much as anything because someone had moved my beer while I was gone, setting it down on the cement floor of the garage. It was just a little thing, but I could not be entirely sure I had gotten my own beer back.

31   Charlie was now raring to try other cars. We examined the latch on his Toyota, which was entirely shielded to the trunk occupant (i.e., no hole in the plate), and on the neighbor's Honda (ditto). But a 1991 Dodge Dynasty was doable. The trunk was tight, but its lock had a feature one of the mechanics I'd phoned described as a "tailpiece": a finger-

like extension of the lock mechanism itself that stuck out a half inch into the trunk cavity; simply by twisting the tailpiece I could free the lock. I was even faster on a 1984 Subaru that had a little lever device on the latch.

We went out to my rental on Oak Street. The Skylark was in direct [32] sun and the trunk was hot to the touch, but when we got it open we could see that its latch plate had a perfect hole, a square in which the edge of the lock's jaw appeared like a face in a window.

The trunk was shallow and hot. Emmett had to push my knees [33] down before he could close the lid. This one was a little suffocating. I imagined being trapped for hours, and even before he had got it closed I regretted the decision with a slightly nauseous feeling. I thought of Edgar Allan Poe's live burials,[5] and then about something my fiancée had said more than a year and a half before. I had been on her case to get married. She was divorced, and at every opportunity I would reissue my proposal—even during a commercial. She'd interrupted one of these chirps to tell me, in a cold, throaty voice, that she had no intention of ever going through another divorce: "This time, it's death out." I'd carried those words around like a lump of wet clay.

As it happened, the Skylark trunk was the easiest of all. The hole [34] was right where it was supposed to be. The trunk popped open, and I felt great satisfaction that we'd been able to figure out a rule that seemed to apply about 60 percent of the time. If we publicized our success, it might get the attention it deserved. All trunks would be fitted with such a hole. Kids would learn about it in school. The grip of the fear would relax. Before long a successful trunk-locking scene would date a movie like a fedora[6] dates one today.

When I got back East I was caught up in wedding preparations. I live in [35] New York, and the wedding was to take place in Philadelphia. We set up camp there with five days to go. A friend had lent my fiancée her BMW,

5. American author (1809–1849) known for his eerie short stories and poems; his story "The Premature Burial" recounts the terror of a man buried alive.

6. Brimmed men's hat popular from the 1920s through the 1950s, often worn by gangsters and detectives in movies from that era.

and we drove it south with all our things. I unloaded the car in my parents' driveway. The last thing I pulled out of the trunk was my fiancée's hat in its heavy cardboard shipping box. She'd warned me I was not allowed to look. The lid was free but I didn't open it. I was willing to be surprised.

36   When the trunk was empty it occurred to me I might hop in and give it a try. First I looked over the mechanism. The jaws of the BMW's lock were shielded, but there seemed to be some kind of cable coming off it that you might be able to manipulate so as to cause the lock to open. The same cable that allowed the driver to open the trunk remotely . . .

37   I fingered it for a moment or two but decided I didn't need to test out the theory.

XXXXXXXXXXXXXXXXXXXXX **FOR DISCUSSION** XXXXXXXXXXXXXXXXXXXXX

1. So, according to Philip Weiss, how *do* you get out of a locked trunk? How, according to his fiancée, do you get out of a marriage? What is the implication of Weiss's addressing these two problems in the same essay?

2. Of the cars he tests, which one alarms Weiss most yet turns out to be the easiest to get out of? Why is he so alarmed, do you think? Why is he so anxious to find a "simple trick" that will fit all instances (23)?

3. Why does Weiss say, "There were some things you could only learn by doing" (28)? What might some of them be?

4. Why do you think Weiss refrains from taking a peek at his fiancée's new hat, since the lid is "free" and the box would be so easy to open (35)? Incidentally, how does Weiss know that the lid is free?

XXXXXXXXXXXXX **STRATEGIES AND STRUCTURES** XXXXXXXXXXXXX

1. What is Weiss's PURPOSE in ANALYZING THE PROCESS of getting out of a locked trunk? What AUDIENCE does Weiss think will be interested in his analysis? Why?

2. Weiss's essay is divided into three parts—paragraphs 1 through 10, 11 through 34, and 35 through 37. In which section does Weiss most fully analyze the process of getting out of a locked car trunk? Is his analysis explanatory or directive? Explain.

3. Why do you think the last section of Weiss's essay is the shortest? How—and how effectively—does it bring the essay to a satisfying conclusion?

4. What is Weiss's purpose in citing several "experts" in paragraphs 7 through 10? What is Emmett's role in the big experiment?

5. "It's a wonderful plot device," Weiss quotes one expert as saying about being locked in a car trunk (10). Is she right? Where in his essay is Weiss telling a story, and where is he analyzing a process? Give specific EXAMPLES from the text.

6. Like NARRATIVES, which often report events chronologically, process analyses are often organized in the chronological order of the steps or stages of the process that is being analyzed. Where does Weiss use chronology either to tell a story or to analyze a process? Give specific examples from the text.

XXXXXXXXXXXX **WORDS AND FIGURES OF SPEECH** XXXXXXXXXXXX

1. The lock on the trunk of Emmett's Mercury Grand Marquis, says Weiss, "closed in much the same way that a lobster might clamp on to a pencil" (21). How effective do you find this SIMILE for explaining how this particular trunk locks? Where else does Weiss use FIGURES OF SPEECH as a tool of PROCESS ANALYSIS?

2. A phobia is an irrational fear (10). Point out specific EXAMPLES in his essay where Weiss (or his persona) might be said to exhibit phobic behavior. What's he afraid of?

3. To whom is Weiss referring when he mentions "Viennese intellectuals" (5)? Why is he ALLUDING to them? Why does he allude to Poe in paragraph 33?

4. "Not to do my will, but thine" (3). What are the implications of this inscription, which Weiss reads on a tombstone at the beginning of his essay?

5. "Case," "reissue," "chirp," and "death out" (33): why does Weiss use these words in the ANECDOTE about his proposals? What about "willing" (35)?

XXXXXXXXXXXXXXXXXX **FOR WRITING** XXXXXXXXXXXXXXXXXXXXXXX

1. Has anyone you know ever exhibited phobic behavior? Explain how the phobia manifested itself and what specific steps the victim took to deal with it.

2. "Every culture," writes Weiss, "comes up with tests of a person's ability to get out of a sticky situation" (5). Have you ever been in such a situation? How did you get out of it? Write an essay ANALYZING THE PROCESS.

CHAPTER SEVEN

COMPARISON AND CONTRAST

XXXXXXXXXXXXXXXXXXXXXXXXXXXXXXXXXXXXXXXXXXXXXXXXXXXXX

If you are thinking of buying a new car, you will want to do some COMPARISON* shopping. You might compare the Mazda Miata to the Mitsubishi Spyder, for example: both are sporty convertibles with similar features in about the same price range. If you're in the market for a convertible, you would be wasting your time getting a quote on a van or pickup. That would be comparing apples to oranges, and true comparisons can be made only among like kinds. Your final decision, however, will be based more on differences (in acceleration, fuel economy, trunk space) than on the similarities. Your comparison, that is, will also entail CONTRAST. (Strictly speaking, a *comparison* looks at both the similarities and the differences between two subjects, whereas a *contrast* looks mainly at the differences.)

Drawing comparisons in writing is a lot like comparison shopping. It points out similarities in different subjects and differences in similar ones. Consider the following comparison between two items we might normally think of as identical:

> The common yo-yo is crudely made, with a thick shank between two widely spaced wooden disks. The string is knotted or stapled to the shank. With such an instrument nothing can be done except the simple up-down movement. My yo-yo, on the other hand, was a perfectly balanced construction of hard wood, slightly weighted, flat, with only a sixteenth of an inch

*Words printed in SMALL CAPITALS are defined in the Glossary.

246

between the halves. The string was not attached to the shank, but looped over it in such a way as to allow the wooden part to spin freely on its own axis. The gyroscopic effect thus created kept the yo-yo stable in all attitudes.

FRANK CONROY, *Stop-Time*

Why is Frank Conroy comparing yo-yos here? He is not going to buy one, nor is he telling the reader what kind to buy. Conroy is a man with a message: all yo-yos are not created equal. They may look alike and they may all go up and down on a string, but he points out meaningful (if you are interested in yo-yos) differences between them. There are good yo-yos, Conroy is saying, and bad yo-yos.

Once Conroy has brought together like kinds (apples to apples, yo-yos to yo-yos) and established in his own mind a basis for comparing them (the "common" kind versus "my" kind), he can proceed in one of two ways. He can dispense his information in "chunks" or in "slices" (as when selling bologna). These basic methods of organizing a comparison or contrast are sometimes called the subject-by-subject and the point-by-point methods. The subject-by-subject method treats several aspects of one subject, then discusses the same aspects of the other. So the author provides chunks of information all about one subject before moving on to the other subject. Point-by-point organization shifts back and forth between each subject, treating each point of similarity and difference before going on to the next one.

In his comparison, Conroy uses the subject-by-subject method. He first gives several traits of the inferior, "common" yo-yo ("crudely made," string fixed to the shank, only goes up and down); then he gives contrasting traits of his superior yo-yo ("perfectly balanced," string loops over the shank, "spins freely on its own axis"). Now let's look at an example of a comparison that uses the point-by-point method to compare two great basketball players, Wilt ("the Stilt") Chamberlain and Bill Russell:

Russell has been above all a team player—a man of discipline, self-denial and killer instinct; in short, a *winner*, in the best American Calvinist tradition. Whereas Russell has been able somehow to squeeze out his last ounce of ability, Chamberlain's performances have been marked by a seeming nonchalance—as if, recognizing his Gigantistic fate, he were more concerned with personal style than with winning. "I never want to set records. The only thing I strive for is perfection," Chamberlain has said.

JAMEY LARNER, "David vs. Goliath"

Paragraph by paragraph, Jamey Larner goes on like this, alternating "slices" of information about each player: Chamberlain's free throws were always uncertain; Russell's were always accurate in the clutch. Chamberlain was efficient; Russell was more so. Chamberlain was fast; Russell was faster. Chamberlain was Goliath at 7-feet-3-inches tall; Russell was David at 6-feet-9. The fans expected Chamberlain to lose; they expected Russell to win.

Point by point, Larner goes back and forth between his two subjects, making one meaningful (to basketball fans) distinction after another. But why, finally, is he bringing these two players together? What's his reason for comparing them at all? Larner has a point to make, just as Conroy does when he compares two yo-yos and just as you should when you compare something in your writing. The author compares these two to ARGUE that although the giant Chamberlain was "typecast" by the fans to lose to Russell the giant-killer, Wilt "the Stilt," defying all expectations, was the one who (arguably) became the greatest basketball player ever. (This decision was made without consulting Michael Jordan or LeBron James.)

Whether you use chunks or slices, you can take a number of other hints from Conroy and Larner. First, choose subjects that belong to the same general class or category: two toys, two athletes, two religions, two mammals. You might point out many differences between a mattress and motorcycle, but any distinctions you make between them are not likely to be meaningful because there is little logical basis for comparing them.

Even more important, you need to have a good reason for bringing your subjects together in the first place—and a main point to make about them. Then, whether you proceed subject by subject or point by point, stick to two and only two subjects at a time.

And, finally, don't feel that you must always give equal weight to similarities and differences. You might want to pay more attention to the similarities if you wish to convince your parents that a two-seater convertible actually has a lot in common with the big, safe SUV they want you to consider—they both have wheels, brakes, and an engine, for example. But you might want to emphasize the differences between your two subjects if the similarities are readily apparent, as between two yoyos and two basketball stars.

A Brief Guide to Writing a Comparison and Contrast Essay

As you begin to write a comparison, you need to identify your subjects, state the basis on which you're comparing them, and indicate whether you plan to emphasize their similarities or their differences. Michael Powell makes these basic moves of comparison as he begins his essay in this chapter:

> Two Methodist churches have stood on the same block on Capitol Hill for a century, one congregation black and the other white. . . . Again and again these congregations have tried to bridge centuries of misunderstanding, only to falter and drift back.
>
> MICHAEL POWELL, "Two Churches, Black and White"

Powell identifies his subjects (two churches), states the basis on which he is comparing them (Methodist, on the same block for a century), and indicates that he is planning to emphasize their differences (black and white, "centuries of misunderstanding"). Here is one more example from this chapter:

> They were two strong men, these oddly different generals, and they represented the strengths of two conflicting currents that, through them, had come into final collision.
>
> BRUCE CATTON, "Grant and Lee: A Study in Contrasts"

The following guidelines will help you to make these basic moves as you draft a comparison. They will also help you to come up with two subjects to compare, present their similarities and differences in an organized way, and state your point in comparing them.

Coming Up with Your Subjects

The first thing you need to do when composing a comparison essay is to choose two subjects that are alike as well as different. Make sure that your subjects have enough in common to provide a solid basis of comparison. A cruise ship and a jet, for instance, are very different machines; but both are modes of transportation, and that shared characteristic can become the basis for comparing them.

When you look for two subjects that have shared characteristics, don't stretch your comparison too far. The Duchess in Lewis Carroll's *Alice in Wonderland* compares mustard to flamingos because they "both bite." In the real world, however, don't bring two subjects together when the differences between them are far more significant than the similarities. Better to compare mustard and ketchup or flamingos and roseate spoonbills.

Considering Your Purpose and Audience

Suppose that you are comparing cell phones because the screen cracked on your old one and you need to replace it. In this case, your PURPOSE is to evaluate them and decide which cell phone fits your needs best. However, if you were writing the comparison for *Consumer Reports*, you would be comparing and contrasting cell phones in order to inform readers about them.

With comparisons, one size does not fit all. Whether you're writing a comparison to inform, to evaluate, or for some other purpose, always keep the specific needs of your AUDIENCE in mind. How much do your readers already know about your topic? Why should they want or need to know more? What distinctions can you make that they haven't already thought of?

Generating Ideas: Asking How Two Things Are Alike or Different

Once you have a clear basis for comparing two subjects—flamingos and roseate spoonbills are both large pink birds; mustard and ketchup are both condiments; cruise ships and jets are both modes of transportation—look for specific points of comparison between them. Ask yourself: How, specifically, are my two subjects alike? How do they differ?

As you answer these questions, make a point-by-point list of the similarities and differences between your subjects. When you draw up your list, make sure you look at the same elements in both subjects. For example, if you are comparing two cell phone models, you might list such elements as the price, size, and accessories available for each one. Preparing such a list will help you to determine whether your two subjects are actually worth comparing—and will also help you to get the similarities and differences straight in your own mind before attempting to explain them to your audience.

Templates for Comparing

The following templates can help you to generate ideas for a comparison and then to start drafting. Don't take these as formulas where you just have to fill in the blanks. There are no easy formulas for good writing. But these templates can help you plot out some of the key moves of comparison and contrast and thus may serve as good starting points.

> ➤ **X and Y can be compared on the grounds that both are** _____.

> ➤ **Like X, Y is also** _____, _____, **and** _____.

> ➤ **Although X and Y are both** _____, **the differences between them far outweigh the similarities. For example, X is** _____, _____, **and** _____, **while Y is** _____, _____, **and** _____.

> ➤ **Unlike X, Y is** _____.

> ➤ **Despite their obvious differences, X and Y are basically alike in that** _____.

> ➤ **At first glance, X and Y seem** _____; **however, a closer look reveals** _____.

> ➤ **In comparing X and Y, we can clearly see that** _____.

For more techniques to help you generate ideas and start writing, see Chapter 1.

Organizing a Comparison

As we discussed earlier, there are fundamentally two ways to organize a comparison: point by point or subject by subject. With a point-by-point organization (like Larner's comparison of Wilt Chamberlain and Bill Russell), you discuss each point of comparison (or contrast) between your two subjects before going on to the next point. With the subject-by-subject method, you discuss each subject individually, making a number of points about one subject and then covering more or less the same points about the other subject. This is the organization Conroy follows in his comparison of yo-yos.

Which method of organization should you use? You will probably find that the point-by-point method works best for beginning and ending an essay, while the subject-by-subject method serves you well for longer stretches in the main body.

One reason for using the subject-by-subject method to organize most of your essay is that the point-by-point method, when relentlessly applied, can make the reader a little seasick as you jump back and forth from your first subject to your second. With the subject-by-subject method, you do not have to give equal weight to both subjects. The subject-by-subject method is, thus, indispensable for treating a subject in depth, whereas the point-by-point method is an efficient way to establish a basis of comparison at the beginning, to remind readers along the way why two subjects are being compared, and to sum up your essay at the end.

Stating Your Point

Your main point in drawing a comparison will determine whether you emphasize similarities or differences. For instance, if your thesis is that there are certain fundamental qualities that all successful coaches share—and you're comparing the best coaches from your own high school days to make this point—you will focus on the similarities among them. However, if you're comparing blind dates to make the point that it's difficult to be prepared for a blind date because no two are alike, you would focus on the differences among the blind dates you've had.

Whatever the main point of your comparison might be, state it clearly right away in an explicit THESIS STATEMENT: "Blind dates are inherently unpredictable; since no two are alike, the best way to go into one is with no expectations at all." Be sure to indicate to readers which you are going to emphasize—the similarities or differences between your subjects. Then, in the body of your essay, use specific points of comparison to show those similarities or differences and to prove your main point.

Providing Sufficient Points of Comparison

No matter how you organize a comparison essay, you will have to provide a sufficient number of points of comparison between your subjects to demonstrate that they are truly comparable and to justify your reasons for comparing them. How many points of comparison are enough to do the job?

Sufficiency isn't strictly a matter of numbers. It depends, in part, on just how inclined your audience is to accept (or reject) the main point your comparison is intended to make. If you are comparing subjects that your readers are not familiar with, you may have to give more examples of similarities or differences than you would if your readers already know a lot about your subjects. For instance, if you're comparing the racing styles of cyclists Greg LeMond and Lance Armstrong, readers who think the Tour de France is a vacation package are going to require more (and more basic) points of comparison than avid cycling fans will.

To determine how many points of comparison you need to make, consider your intended readers, and choose the points of comparison you think they will find most useful, interesting, or otherwise convincing. Then give a sufficient number to get your larger point across, but not so many that you run the comparison into the ground.

EVERYDAY COMPARISON
A Coffee Mug

"Poetry was what we did at Kenyon, the way at Ohio State they played football."
—E. L. Doctorow

This coffee mug, purchased in the campus bookstore of Kenyon College in Gambier, Ohio, quotes the novelist E. L. Doctorow, who graduated from—Kenyon. When you draw a comparison like Doctorow's, you need to choose two subjects (Kenyon and Ohio State) that are in the same general category (schools in Ohio) but that are different enough in their particular details (poetry, football) to make the comparison interesting. Which details you choose to emphasize, however, will depend on your purpose in drawing the comparison. The purpose of the Kenyon coffee mug is to promote the liberal arts: "We grapple with metaphors," as one Kenyon administrator put it; "they clench in the mud." Down the road at Ohio State, however, a competing coffee mug might emphasize the range of academic programs offered by a large state university: "The way they do poetry at Kenyon, we do football at Ohio State—and medieval literature, metallurgy, aviation, law, business, and medicine."

JEFF JACOBY

Watching Oprah
from Behind the Veil

Jeff Jacoby (b. 1959) is a columnist for the *Boston Globe*. Before turning to journalism, Jacoby practiced law, worked on a political campaign, assisted the president of Boston University, and hosted a television show, *Talk of New England*. In 2004 he received the Thomas Paine Award, presented to journalists dedicated "to the preservation and championing of individual liberty." First published in the *Globe* in 2008, "Watching Oprah from Behind the Veil" compares the life and circumstances of an American icon with those of the Arab women who have made her show the most popular English-language program in Saudi Arabia.

XXXXXXXXXXXXXXXXXXXXXXXXXXXXXXXXXXXXXXXXXXXXXXXXXXXXXXXXXXXXX

She has been called the most influential woman of our time. They are   1
among the most disempowered women on earth.

She is a self-made billionaire, with worldwide interests that range   2
from television to publishing to education. They are forbidden to get a
job without the permission of a male "guardian," and the overwhelming
majority of them are unemployed.

She has a face that is recognized the world over. They cannot leave   3
home without covering their face and obscuring their figure in a cloak.

She is famous for her message of confidence, self-improvement,   4
and spiritual uplift. They are denied the right to make the simplest decisions, treated by law like children who cannot be trusted with authority
over their own well-being.

She, of course, is Oprah Winfrey. They are the multitude of Saudi   5
Arabian women whose devotion to her has made *The Oprah Winfrey
Show*—broadcast twice daily on a Dubai-based satellite channel—the
highest-rated English-language program in the kingdom.

6   A recent *New York Times* story—"Veiled Saudi Women Are Discovering an Unlikely Role Model in Oprah Winfrey"—explored the appeal of America's iconic talk-show host for the marginalized women of the Arabian peninsula.

7   "In a country where the sexes are rigorously separated, where topics like sex and race are rarely discussed openly, and where a strict code of public morality is enforced by religious police," the *Times* noted, "Ms. Winfrey provides many young Saudi women with new ways of thinking about the way local taboos affect their lives. . . . Some women here say Ms. Winfrey's assurances to her viewers—that no matter how restricted or even abusive their circumstances may be, they can take control in small ways and create lives of value—help them find meaning in their cramped, veiled existence."

8   And so they avidly analyze Oprah's clothes and hairstyles, and circulate "dog-eared copies" of her magazine, *O*, and write letters telling her of their dreams and disappointments. Many undoubtedly dream of doing what she did—freeing themselves from the shackling circumstances into which they were born and rising as high as their talents can take them.

9   But the television star never faced the obstacles that confront her Saudi fans.

10   That is not to minimize the daunting odds Oprah overcame. She was born to an unwed teenage housemaid in pre–civil rights Mississippi, and spent her first years in such poverty that at times she wore dresses made from potato sacks. She was sexually molested as a child, and ran away from home as a young teen. It was a squalid beginning, one that would have defeated many people not blessed with Oprah's intelligence and drive and native gifts.

11   But whatever else may be said of Oprah's life, it was never crippled by Wahhabism, the fundamentalist strain of Islam that dominates Saudi Arabia and immiserates Saudi women in ruthless gender apartheid. Strict sex segregation is the law of the land. Women are forbidden to drive, to vote, to freely marry or divorce, to appear in public without a husband or other male guardian, or to attend university without their father's permission. They can be jailed—or worse—for riding in a car with a man to whom they are unrelated. Their testimony in court carries less weight than a man's. They cannot even file a criminal complaint

without a male guardian's permission—not even in cases of domestic abuse, when it is their "guardian" who has attacked them.

Could Oprah herself have surmounted such pervasive repression? 12

Some Saudi women manage to find jobs, but Wahhabist opposition 13
is fierce. In 2006, Youssef Ibrahim reported in the *New York Sun* on Nabil Ramadan, the owner of a fast-food restaurant in Ranoosh who hired two women to take telephone orders. Within twenty-four hours, the religious police had him arrested and shut down the restaurant for "promoting lewdness." Ramadan was sentenced by a religious court to ninety lashes on his back and buttocks.

Is it any wonder that women trapped in a culture that treats them 14
so wretchedly idolize someone like Oprah, who epitomizes so much that is absent from their lives? A nation that degrades its women degrades itself, and Oprah's message is an antidote to degradation. Why do they love her? Because all the lies of the Wahhabists cannot stifle the truth she embodies: The blessings of liberty were made for women, too.

XXXXXXXXXXXXXXXXXX FOR DISCUSSION XXXXXXXXXXXXXXXXXXX

1. According to Jeff Jacoby, why do Oprah Winfrey and her show appeal to so many women in Saudi Arabia?

2. What particular lesson about living in "restricted or even abusive" circumstances does Oprah have to teach these women (7)?

3. What obstacles to Saudi women face that Oprah did not, even though she grew up poor in "pre–civil rights Mississippi" (10)?

4. What is the root cause, according to Jacoby, of the "ruthless gender apartheid" that many Saudi women must contend with (11)?

XXXXXXXXXXXXX STRATEGIES AND STRUCTURES XXXXXXXXXXXXX

1. Do you think Jacoby's intended AUDIENCE for this COMPARISON essay is mostly female, mostly male, or both? Why do you think so?

2. On what basis is Jacoby comparing some of "the most disempowered women on earth" to the "influential" Oprah Winfrey (1)? What common ground do they share?

3. Why does Jacoby wait until the fifth paragraph to name his subjects? What is the effect of referring to them at first as "she" and "they"? What does this contribute to his comparison?

4. Does Jacoby rely more on the point-by-point or subject-by-subject method for organizing his comparison? Is this method of organization effective for this essay? Explain.

5. What is the main point of Jacoby's comparison? Where does he state it most directly?

6. What are some of Jacoby's most effective points of comparison? Does he give a sufficient number of them to support his point? Explain.

7. Jacoby includes a brief NARRATIVE about Oprah's life in paragraph 10. What PURPOSE does this story serve in his comparison? Where else does Jacoby incorporate narrative in his essay?

XXXXXXXXXXXX **WORDS AND FIGURES OF SPEECH** XXXXXXXXXXXX

1. Though many Arab women wear veils, Jacoby is not simply referring to their attire in his title. Explain the METAPHORIC implications of the phrase "from behind the veil."

2. Why does Jacoby put the word *guardian* in quotation marks (2)?

3. "Immiserates," meaning makes miserable, probably does not appear in your dictionary (11). Why not? Should Jacoby have used a more common word? Explain.

4. "Apartheid" is a South African term that refers to a systematic policy of discrimination based on race (11). How valid do you find Jacoby's use of this term in the context of gender? Explain.

XXXXXXXXXXXXXXXXXXX **FOR WRITING** XXXXXXXXXXXXXXXXXXXXX

1. Compile a list of the points of COMPARISON you would make if you were comparing Oprah Winfrey to those who watch her show and read her magazine in the United States.

2. Write an essay comparing the characteristics and values of an influential (or notorious) public figure with those of a particular group of his or her most avid admirers (or detractors).

BRUCE CATTON

GRANT AND LEE:
A STUDY IN CONTRASTS

Bruce Catton (1899–1979) was a noted historian of the Civil War, winner of both the Pulitzer Prize and the National Book Award for *A Stillness at Appomattox* (1953). Among Catton's many other Civil War books are *This Hallowed Ground* (1956), *The Army of the Potomac* (1962), *Terrible Swift Sword* (1963), and *Grant Takes Command* (1969). It was not, said Catton, "the strategy or political meanings" of the Civil War that most fascinated him, but the "almost incomprehensible emotional experience which this war brought to our country." First published in the essay collection *The American Story* (1955), "Grant and Lee: A Study in Contrasts" looks at two great Americans—one "the modern man emerging," the other from "the age of chivalry."

XXXXXXXXXXXXXXXXXXXXXXXXXXXXXXXXXXXXXXXXXXXXXXXXXXXXX

When Ulysses S. Grant and Robert E. Lee met in the parlor of a modest house at Appomattox Court House, Virginia, on April 9, 1865, to work out the terms for the surrender of Lee's Army of Northern Virginia, a great chapter in American life came to a close, and a great new chapter began.

These men were bringing the Civil War[1] to its virtual finish. To be sure, other armies had yet to surrender, and for a few days the fugitive Confederate government would struggle desperately and vainly, trying to find some way to go on living now that its chief support was gone. But

1. American war (1861–65) fought between "the Union" (Northern states that stayed loyal to the federal government under President Abraham Lincoln) and "the Confederacy" (eleven slave-holding Southern states [and their sympathizers] that formed a separate government under Jefferson Davis).

in effect it was all over when Grant and Lee signed the papers. And the little room where they wrote out the terms was the scene of one of the poignant, dramatic contrasts in American history.

3   They were two strong men, these oddly different generals, and they represented the strengths of two conflicting currents that, through them, had come into final collision.

4   Back of Robert E. Lee was the notion that the old aristocratic concept might somehow survive and be dominant in American life.

5   Lee was tidewater Virginia,[2] and in his background were family, culture, and tradition . . . the age of chivalry transplanted to a New World which was making its own legends and its own myths. He embodied a way of life that had come down through the age of knighthood and the English country squire. America was a land that was beginning all over again, dedicated to nothing much more complicated than the rather hazy belief that all men had equal rights and should have an equal chance in the world. In such a land Lee stood for the feeling that it was somehow of advantage to human society to have a pronounced inequality in the social structure. There should be a leisure class, backed by ownership of land; in turn, society itself should be keyed to the land as the chief source of wealth and influence. It would bring forth (according to this ideal) a class of men with a strong sense of obligation to the community; men who lived not to gain advantage for themselves, but to meet the solemn obligations which had been laid on them by the very fact that they were privileged. From them the country would get its leadership; to them it could look for the higher values—of thought, of conduct, of personal deportment—to give it strength and virtue.

6   Lee embodied the noblest elements of this aristocratic ideal. Through him, the landed nobility justified itself. For four years, the Southern states had fought a desperate war to uphold the ideals for which Lee stood. In the end, it almost seemed as if the Confederacy fought for Lee; as if he himself was the Confederacy . . . the best thing

---

2. Coastal region of eastern Virginia. Jamestown, the first British colony in North America, was settled in this region in 1607.

that the way of life for which the Confederacy stood could ever have to offer. He had passed into legend before Appomattox. Thousands of tired, underfed, poorly clothed Confederate soldiers, long since past the simple enthusiasm of the early days of the struggle, somehow considered Lee the symbol of everything for which they had been willing to die. But they could not quite put this feeling into words. If the Lost Cause, sanctified by so much heroism and so many deaths, had a living justification, its justification was General Lee.

Grant, the son of a tanner on the Western frontier, was everything   7
Lee was not. He had come up the hard way and embodied nothing in particular except the eternal toughness and sinewy fiber of the men who grew up beyond the mountains. He was one of a body of men who owed reverence and obeisance to no one, who were self-reliant to a fault, who cared hardly anything for the past but who had a sharp eye for the future.

These frontier men were the precise opposites of the tidewater aris-   8
tocrats. Back of them, in the great surge that had taken people over the Alleghenies[3] and into the opening Western country, there was a deep, implicit dissatisfaction with a past that had settled into grooves. They stood for democracy, not from any reasoned conclusion about the proper ordering of human society, but simply because they had grown up in the middle of democracy and knew how it worked. Their society might have privileges, but they would be privileges each man had won for himself. Forms and patterns meant nothing. No man was born to anything, except perhaps to a chance to show how far he could rise. Life was competition.

Yet along with this feeling had come a deep sense of belonging to a   9
national community. The Westerner who developed a farm, opened a shop, or set up in business as a trader, could hope to prosper only as his own community prospered—and his community ran from the Atlantic to the Pacific and from Canada down to Mexico. If the land was settled, with towns and highways and accessible markets, he could better himself. He saw his fate in terms of the nation's own destiny. As its horizons

---

3. Mountain range that runs from north-central Pennsylvania to southwestern Virginia.

expanded, so did his. He had, in other words, an acute dollars-and-cents stake in the continued growth and development of his country.

10   And that, perhaps, is where the contrast between Grant and Lee becomes most striking. The Virginia aristocrat, inevitably, saw himself in relation to his own region. He lived in a static society which could endure almost anything except change. Instinctively, his first loyalty would go to the locality in which that society existed. He would fight to the limit of endurance to defend it, because in defending it he was defending everything that gave his own life its deepest meaning.

11   The Westerner, on the other hand, would fight with an equal tenacity for the broader concept of society. He fought so because everything he lived by was tied to growth, expansion, and a constantly widening horizon. What he lived by would survive or fall with the nation itself. He could not possibly stand by unmoved in the face of an attempt to destroy the Union. He would combat it with everything he had, because he could only see it as an effort to cut the ground out from under his feet.

12   So Grant and Lee were in complete contrast, representing two diametrically opposed elements in American life. Grant was the modern man emerging; beyond him, ready to come on the stage, was the great age of steel and machinery, of crowded cities and a restless burgeoning vitality. Lee might have ridden down from the old age of chivalry, lance in hand, silken banner fluttering over his head. Each man was the perfect champion of his cause, drawing both his strengths and his weaknesses from the people he led.

13   Yet it was not all contrast, after all. Different as they were—in background, in personality, in underlying aspiration—these two great soldiers had much in common. Under everything else, they were marvelous fighters. Furthermore, their fighting qualities were really very much alike.

14   Each man had, to begin with, the great virtue of utter tenacity and fidelity. Grant fought his way down the Mississippi Valley in spite of acute personal discouragement and profound military handicaps. Lee hung on in the trenches at Petersburg after hope itself had died. In each man there was an indomitable quality . . . the born fighter's refusal to give up as long as he can still remain on his feet and lift his two fists.

Union general Ulysses S. Grant, 1864. Photograph by Mathew Brady.

Confederate general Robert E. Lee, 1860.

Daring and resourcefulness they had, too; the ability to think faster   15
and move faster than the enemy. These were the qualities which gave
Lee the dazzling campaigns of Second Manassas and Chancellorsville
and won Vicksburg for Grant.

Lastly, and perhaps greatest of all, there was the ability, at the end,   16
to turn quickly from war to peace once the fighting was over. Out of the
way these two men behaved at Appomattox came the possibility of a
peace of reconciliation. It was a possibility not wholly realized, in the
years to come, but which did, in the end, help the two sections to
become one nation again . . . after a war whose bitterness might have
seemed to make such a reunion wholly impossible. No part of either
man's life became him more than the part he played in this brief meeting in the McLean house at Appomattox. Their behavior there put all
succeeding generations of Americans in their debt. Two great Americans, Grant and Lee—very different, yet under everything very much
alike. Their encounter at Appomattox was one of the great moments of
American history.

XXXXXXXXXXXXXXXXXX **FOR DISCUSSION** XXXXXXXXXXXXXXXXXX

1. Bruce Catton writes that Generals Lee and Grant represented two conflicting
currents of American culture. What were these currents? What CONTRASTING
qualities and ideals does Catton associate with each man?

2. What qualities, according to Catton, did Grant and Lee have in common?
What did these shared qualities enable each man to accomplish?

3. With Lee's surrender, says Catton, "a great new chapter of American history
began" (1). What characteristics of the new era does Catton anticipate in his
DESCRIPTION of Grant?

4. Catton does not describe, in any detail, how Grant and Lee behaved as they
worked out the terms of peace at Appomattox. What does he imply about the
conduct of the two men in general?

XXXXXXXXXXXX **STRATEGIES AND STRUCTURES** XXXXXXXXXXXX

1. Beginning with paragraph 3, Catton gets down to the particulars of his CON-TRAST between the two generals. How does Catton organize his contrast—point by point or subject by subject? In what paragraphs does he turn to the similarities between the two men and how are they organized?

2. Which sentence in the final paragraph brings together both the differences and the similarities outlined in the preceding paragraphs? How does this paragraph recall the opening paragraphs of the essay? Why might Catton end with an echo of his beginning?

3. Catton does not really give specific reasons for the Confederacy's defeat. What general explanation does he hint at, however, when he associates Lee with a "static society" and Grant with a society of "restless burgeoning vitality" (10, 12)? What is Catton's PURPOSE in drawing this extensive COMPARISON?

4. In comparing and contrasting the two generals in this essay, Catton also DESCRIBES two regional types. What are some of the specific personal characteristics Catton ascribes to Grant and Lee that, at the same time, make them representative figures?

XXXXXXXXXXXX **WORDS AND FIGURES OF SPEECH** XXXXXXXXXXXX

1. Catton DESCRIBES the parlor where Grant and Lee met as the "scene" of a "dramatic" CONTRAST, and he says that a new era was "ready to come on stage" (2). What view of history is suggested by these METAPHORS?

2. What does Catton mean by "the Lost Cause" in paragraph 6?

3. What is the precise meaning of "obeisance" (7)? Why might Catton choose this term instead of the more common *obedience* when describing General Grant?

4. Look up any of the following words with which you are not on easy terms: "fugitive" (2), "poignant" (2), "chivalry" (5), "sinewy" (7), "implicit" (8), "tenacity" (11), "diametrically" (12), "acute" (14), "profound" (14), "indomitable" (14). What words would you substitute to help make the TONE of the essay less formal?

XXXXXXXXXXXXXXXXXXXX **FOR WRITING** XXXXXXXXXXXXXXXXXXXX

1. Photographs of Grant and Lee are included with this essay. Consider what each photograph contributes to your understanding of the men and their roles in history. Write several paragraphs COMPARING AND CONTRASTING the two photographs and what they reveal about each man.

2. Write an essay comparing and contrasting a pair of important historical or public figures with whom you are familiar—Thomas Jefferson and Alexander Hamilton or Hillary Clinton and Michelle Obama, for example.

MICHAEL POWELL

TWO CHURCHES, BLACK AND WHITE

Michael Powell (b. 1958) is a staff writer for the *New York Times*. Before joining the *Times* in 2007, he reported on politics, science, and culture for *New York Newsday*, the *New York Observer*, and the *Washington Post*. In "Two Churches, Black and White," which appeared in the *Times* on January 19, 2009, Powell compares and contrasts two Methodist churches in Washington, D.C., on the eve of Barack Obama's inauguration. Once a single church, the two split apart in 1829 when "the white members of Ebenezer Methodist Church cast out their black brethren." After a detailed comparison of the institutions that resulted from this split, Powell wonders "whether these fractured congregations might yet make each other whole."

XXXXXXXXXXXXXXXXXXXXXXXXXXXXXXXXXXXXXXXXXXXXXXXXXXXXXXXXXXX

1   Two Methodist churches have stood on the same block on Capitol Hill[1] for a century, one congregation black and the other white, and in between lies the sorry detritus of a nation's racial history.

2   Again and again these congregations have tried to bridge centuries of misunderstanding, only to falter and drift back. This week they will try again, throwing open their doors together to tend to those celebrating the inauguration of the first black president.

3   "We did not choose but it was chosen for us that we would come together at this moment," said the Rev. Alisa Lasater, the pastor of Capitol Hill United Methodist Church. "If we want to be the heart of our community, we need to learn to see into each others' heart."

---

1. The area east of the U.S. Capitol building in Washington, D.C. The U.S. Congress is also commonly referred to as "Capitol Hill."

In the voice of these churchgoers can be heard the story of race in   4
the nation's capital and perhaps in the country itself. There are slights
and misunderstandings and reconciliations, with miles traveled and more
to go. President-elect Barack Obama spoke to such divisions recently in
an interview with ABC News, saying he wanted to find that rare church
that spanned Washington's separate worlds, not least of race.

"You've got one part of Washington, which is a company town, all   5
about government, and is generally pretty prosperous," Mr. Obama
said. "And then you've got another half of D.C. that is going through
enormous challenges. I want to see if we can bring those two Washington, D.C.'s together."

Mr. Obama's inauguration might offer the nation a new turn, and   6
from that the congregations draw hope. But race's complications are
many, and as these members are reminded daily, they often find themselves speaking from starkly different wells of understanding. The inaugural suggests a nation that, even in unity, experiences history from
separate racial vantage points. Once, these two churches were one. In
1829, the white members of Ebenezer Methodist Church cast out their
black brethren: You tap your feet too insistently, they said, and sing too
loudly. So the blacks walked around the corner and founded Little
Ebenezer Church.

Each Ebenezer thrived. Middle-class whites drawn by a prosperous   7
capital crowded into their church, and 1,200 blacks filled the other, the
balconies creaking beneath the weight of worshipers. The white
Ebenezer—known today as Capitol Hill United Methodist—now has
about 150 members, mostly liberal young people who work on the Hill.
At Ebenezer, about 60 elderly blacks attend services; its funerals greatly
outnumber weddings.

Push for Reconciliation

A few years back, the bishop of the Baltimore-Washington Conference   8
of the United Methodist Church ordered these churches, sundered by
the sin of racism, to reconcile. Congregants broached tender questions of
race, and this weekend they joined as a youth group from Maryland

spread its sleeping bags at Ebenezer while Capitol Hill volunteers fed and cared for them.

9   "Our bishop called upon us to offer radical hospitality, and we want to reflect both our history and the change," said the Rev. John M. Blanchard Jr., 65, the pastor at Ebenezer. "There is a providential nature to the fact that it is Obama."

10   The churches—Capitol Hill United was rebuilt on its original site in 1964, and Ebenezer is a cavernous late-nineteenth-century church with luminous stained-glass windows—sit on a well-heeled block on Capitol Hill, a place of brick row houses with wrought-iron fences.

11   It is a liberal bastion; several homeowners are civil rights veterans, and their eyes welled with tears as they watched on election night.

12   Divisions persist. Race in America offers no fairy tales. "Our congregations have existed almost back to back on the same block for well over a century, and we still struggle to talk," said Dottie Yunger, a divinity student who has worked with the congregations. "Reverend Martin Luther King[2] was right: the most segregated hour is 11 on Sunday, especially on Capitol Hill."

Different Resonance

13   On the morning after election night, Ms. Lasater ran into a bleary-eyed Mr. Blanchard on Southeast Fourth Street. "It's a very good day," she said by way of greeting. He grinned and replied, "It is such a good day."

14   At Capitol Hill United, many labored long hours for Mr. Obama and most voted for him, and their relief was great. The age of Bush was nearly gone. The environment, the Iraq war, civil liberties: so much would be different.

15   "I was very moved that my child would come into the world and know only a black president," said Abbey Levenshus, a member of Capitol Hill United who is pregnant. "But there's no doubt we experienced it very differently from Ebenezer."

---

2. African American minister and civil rights leader (1929–1968). He was awarded the Nobel Peace Prize in 1964.

At Ebenezer, age tempered the temptation to volunteer. But Mr. 16
Obama's victory plumbed their emotional depths. The congregation
came of age in a Washington legally segregated by race. Lucy K. Brown,
90, recalls walking twenty blocks to a black public school rather than
across the street to the white one; Jack Green, 75, recalls the police chasing him out of whites-only swimming pools.

Mr. Green, a dapper retired police officer, stood guard along 17
Dwight D. Eisenhower's[3] inaugural parade route in 1953 and listened as
the white District of Columbia police band played "Dixie," about a
freed slave longing for the plantation.

Did he believe he would ever see a black president? Like everyone 18
in his congregation who was asked this question, he wagged his head.

"Never," he said. "I still will not until I see him put his hand on 19
that Bible. Then I will believe."

To wander into Ebenezer on a Sunday is to find family gone gray. 20
As a child, Mr. Green took Bible instruction from Mrs. Brown, who
remains petite in a purple dress with auburn locks swept up in a bun.
White-haired members sit in pews that have borne family nameplates
for more than a hundred years. On one day in 1913, Ebenezer raised
$6,000 and paid off the mortgage; a photo shows smiling churchgoers
burning their deed.

By the time the Rev. Dr. Martin King Jr. led the March on Wash- 21
ington,[4] so many whites had fled Capitol Hill that the blocks around
Ebenezer became more brown than not. That river reversed course fifteen years ago as real estate prices surged. For years, racially restrictive
lending practices made it difficult for blacks to buy homes on Capitol
Hill; now rising rents are forcing them out. (Washington's black population has dipped to 57 percent from 70 percent in 1970.)

Mr. Blanchard worries that the end for his church beckons. "We 22
are in danger of becoming a museum," he said.

---

3. World War II Army commander (1890–1969) and U.S. president who served two
terms in office.

4. Civil rights demonstration in 1963 in which a quarter of a million people marched to
the capital, peacefully protesting for jobs and freedom.

23   Capitol Hill United charted an inverse arc. As Ebenezer surged, Capitol Hill's white members—FBI agents, mint workers, police officers—moved to the suburbs. Now its congregation is growing. One young dynamic woman has followed another as minister, having an effect not unlike defibrillators clamped to the church's heart.

24   The congregation regards talk of partisan politics as plague. "We try not to ask who you work for," Ms. Levenshus said. "Although one member said it was much easier to come out as a gay man than as a Republican."

25   In 2005, after years of prayer and passionate debate, it became a "reconciling congregation," which is to say it openly welcomes gay men and lesbians and favors gay ordination. A few older members walked out.

26   The congregants heeded the call to reconcile with their black neighbors. "I'll say this for both congregations," Ms. Lasater said. "It took courage to ask why there are two Methodist churches, one black and one white, on the same block in 2008."

Painful Talk

27   So many slights accumulated. In the early 1960s, the Capitol Hill United pastor invited his Ebenezer counterpart, who held a doctorate of divinity, to deliver a guest sermon. On Saturday night, the pastor rescinded his offer.

28   "As a 10-year-old, I thought it was horrible," said Joan Askew, an Ebenezer member and the daughter of that black pastor. "But as I saw what racism was about, well, I see it now as a time and place."

29   A year ago, twenty-five whites from Capitol Hill United showed up to meet with seven Ebenezer blacks. Well-intentioned talk became a web. The whites are can-do, let's-move-the-agenda-forward. Ebenezer members listened.

30   "We struggle with cultural communication," Mr. Blanchard said. "They are younger, and they are so eager to make up for history that they talk a lot. I remind them that just because I don't say anything doesn't mean I agree with you."

Ebenezer congregants sound less worried about apologies for ancient slights. Their fear is that the bishop will merge the congregations and sell their church (the bishop has never mentioned merging). And the gay policy disquieted some. A shared prayer service grew tense with an Ebenezer member bowed her head and said that homosexuality ran counter to God's will. Capitol Hill members stood and prayed that God might open her eyes.

31

"The lifestyles of some of their young people are very different," Mrs. Brown said. "But they have choirs and reach out to the less fortunate. We learn."

32

Mr. Blanchard challenged his elderly congregation to cast eyes outward. "Why don't we have homeless men sleeping on our porch as does Capitol Hill?" he said. "Why are they so good at welcoming the stranger into their midst? I'd love to have some of their vitality."

33

Where this ends is not clear; the churches cherish their separate identities. The question still unanswered in light of the inauguration of a president half-black and half-white is whether these fractured congregations might yet make each other whole.

34

"Reconciliation is jagged and messy, but racism is a sin against the body of Christ," Ms. Lasater said. "We are broken when we are separate."

35

✕✕✕✕✕✕✕✕✕✕✕✕✕✕✕✕✕✕ FOR DISCUSSION ✕✕✕✕✕✕✕✕✕✕✕✕✕✕✕✕✕✕

1. Why have there been two separate Methodist churches "almost back to back on the same block" in Washington D.C. for over a hundred years (12)?

2. What are some of the main differences between the two churches as Michael Powell COMPARES them? What are some of their main similarities?

3. Why does the pastor of Ebenezer Methodist think his church is "in danger of becoming a museum" (22)?

4. What led the two churches to attempt to reconcile their differences? According to Powell, what challenges do they face in this process?

5. According to Powell, are the two churches likely to merge? Why or why not?

1. Why and how does Powell use the election of Barack Obama as the occasion for COMPARING Capitol Hill and Ebenezer Methodist churches? Is this an effective strategy? Why or why not?

2. What is Powell's PURPOSE in comparing the two churches? To ARGUE that they should merge? To show how one church is superior to the other? Some other purpose? Explain.

3. Where does Powell state the main point of his comparison most directly? What is it?

4. In the last paragraphs of his comparison, does Powell focus more on the differences or the similarities between his two subjects? Why this emphasis? Explain.

5. In addition to comparing the two churches, Powell also analyzes why they split apart. What are some of the main CAUSES of the split? How convincing do you find his analysis? Explain.

1. Where and why does Powell use language that has a religious or biblical TONE? Point out several examples.

2. In the Bible, the prophet Samuel placed a stone between two towns and called it an "Ebenezer," meaning a stone indicating help from God (1 Samuel 7:12–14). Why would a church name itself after such a marker?

3. What are the implications of referring to the block on which the two churches are located as a "liberal bastion" (11)?

4. Why does Powell compare the effect of the recent pastors of Capitol Hill United Methodist to that of "defibrillators clamped to the church's heart" (23)? What does this SIMILE suggest about the state of the church before these pastors arrived?

5. Why does Powell refer to "fairy tales" in paragraph 12?

XXXXXXXXXXXXXXXXXXXX **FOR WRITING** XXXXXXXXXXXXXXXXXXXXX

1. Re-read Powell's essay and make a list indicating whether the subject of each paragraph is C (for Capitol Hill), E (for Ebenezer), or C/E (for both). Decide how effective you find Powell's method of organization; then use your tally to write a paragraph about how (or how not) to organize a COMPARISON.

2. Write an essay comparing two churches, two schools, or two other institutions that are similar to each other. To help support your points of comparison, use brief direct quotations from representative figures of both institutions.

GARY SOTO

LIKE MEXICANS

Gary Soto (b. 1952), who grew up in Fresno, California, teaches Chicano studies and English literature at the University of California at Riverside. He is the author of eleven books of poetry, numerous stories for children and young adults, and three novels: *Nickel and Dime* (2000), *Poetry Lover* (2001), and *Amnesia in a Republican Country* (2003). Soto's memoir, *Living up the Street* (1985), won an American Book Award. In "Like Mexicans," from *Small Faces* (1986), another collection of reminiscences about growing up in the barrio, Soto compares his future wife's Japanese American family with his own Mexican American one.

XXXXXXXXXXXXXXXXXXXXXXXXXXXXXXXXXXXXXXXXXXXXXXXXXXXXX

1   My grandmother gave me bad advice and good advice when I was in my early teens. For the bad advice, she said that I should become a barber because they made good money and listened to the radio all day. "Honey, they don't work como burros," she would say every time I visited her. She made the sound of donkeys braying. "Like that, honey!" For the good advice, she said that I should marry a Mexican girl. "No Okies, hijo"—she would say—"Look, my son. He marry one and they fight every day about I don't know what and I don't know what." For her, everyone who wasn't Mexican, black, or Asian were Okies. The French were Okies, the Italians in suits were Okies. When I asked about Jews, whom I had read about, she asked for a picture. I rode home on my bicycle and returned with a calendar depicting the important races of the world. "Pues si, son Okies tambien!"[1] she said, nodding her head. She waved the calendar away and we went to the living room where she lectured me on the virtues of the

1. Well yes, they're Okies too.

Mexican girl: first, she could cook and, second, she acted like a woman, not a man, in her husband's home. She said she would tell me about a third when I got a little older.

I asked my mother about it—becoming a barber and marrying 2 Mexican. She was in the kitchen. Steam curled from a pot of boiling beans, the radio was on, looking as squat as a loaf of bread. "Well, if you want to be a barber—they say they make good money." She slapped a round steak with a knife, her glasses slipping down with each strike. She stopped and looked up. "If you find a good Mexican girl, marry her of course." She returned to slapping the meat and I went to the backyard where my brother and David King were sitting on the lawn feeling the inside of their cheeks.

"This is what girls feel like," my brother said, rubbing the inside of 3 his cheek. David put three fingers inside his mouth and scratched. I ignored them and climbed the back fence to see my best friend, Scott, a second-generation Okie. I called him and his mother pointed to the side of the house where his bedroom was, a small aluminum trailer, the kind you gawk at when they're flipped over on the freeway, wheels spinning in the air. I went around to find Scott pitching horseshoes.

I picked up a set of rusty ones and joined him. While we played, 4 we talked about school and friends and record albums. The horseshoes scuffed up dirt, sometimes ringing the iron that threw out a meager shadow like a sundial. After three argued-over games, we pulled two oranges apiece from his tree and started down the alley still talking school and friends and record albums. We pulled more oranges from the alley and talked about who we would marry. "No offense, Scott," I said with an orange slice in my mouth, "but I would never marry an Okie." We walked in step, almost touching, with a sled of shadows dragging behind us. "No offense, Gary," Scott said, "but I would *never* marry a Mexican." I looked at him: a fang of orange slice showed from his munching mouth. I didn't think anything of it. He had his girl and I had mine. But our seventh-grade vision was the same: to marry, get jobs, buy cars and maybe a house if we had money left over.

We talked about our future lives until, to our surprise, we were on 5 the downtown mall, two miles from home. We bought a bag of popcorn at Penneys and sat on a bench near the fountain watching Mexican and Okie girls pass. "That one's mine," I pointed with my chin when a girl with eyebrows arched into black rainbows ambled by. "She's cute," Scott said about a girl with yellow hair and a mouthful of gum. We dreamed aloud, our chins busy pointing out girls. We agreed that we couldn't wait to become men and lift them onto our laps.

6   But the woman I married was not Mexican but Japanese. It was a surprise to me. For years, I went about wide-eyed in my search for the brown girl in a white dress at a dance. I searched the playground at the baseball diamond. When the girls raced for grounders, their hair bounced like something that couldn't be caught. When they sat together in the lunchroom, heads pressed together, I knew they were talking about us Mexican guys. I saw them and dreamed them. I threw my face into my pillow, making up sentences that were good as in the movies.

7   But when I was twenty, I fell in love with this other girl who worried my mother, who had my grandmother asking once again to see the calendar of the Important Races of the World. I told her I had thrown it away years before. I took a much-glanced-at snapshot from my wallet. We looked at it together, in silence. Then grandma reclined in her chair, lit a cigarette, and said, "Es pretty." She blew and asked with all her worry pushed up to her forehead: "Chinese?"

8   I was in love and there was no looking back. She was the one. I told my mother who was slapping hamburger into patties. "Well, sure if you want to marry her," she said. But the more I talked, the more concerned she became. Later I began to worry. Was it all a mistake? "Marry a Mexican girl," I heard my mother say in my mind. I heard it at breakfast. I heard it over math problems, between Western Civilization and cultural geography. But then one afternoon while I was hitchhiking home from school, it struck me like a baseball in the back: my mother wanted me to marry someone of my own social class—a poor girl. I considered my fiancée, Carolyn, and she didn't look poor, though I knew she came from a family of farm workers and pull-yourself-up-by-your-bootstraps ranchers. I asked my brother, who was marrying Mexican poor that fall, if I should marry a poor girl. He screamed "Yeah" above his terrible guitar playing in his bedroom. I considered my sister who had married Mexican. Cousins were dating Mexican. Uncles were

remarrying poor women. I asked Scott, who was still my best friend, and he said, "She's too good for you, so you better not."

I worried about it until Carolyn took me home to meet her parents. We drove in her Plymouth until the houses gave way to farms and ranches and finally her house fifty feet from the highway. When we pulled into the drive, I panicked and begged Carolyn to make a U-turn and go back so we could talk about it over a soda. She pinched my cheek, calling me a "silly boy." I felt better, though, when I got out of the car and saw the house: the chipped paint, a cracked window, boards for a walk to the back door. There were rusting cars near the barn. A tractor with a net of spiderwebs under a mulberry. A field. A bale of barbed wire like children's scribbling leaning against an empty chicken coop. Carolyn took my hand and pulled me to my future mother-in-law who was coming out to greet us. 9

We had lunch: sandwiches, potato chips, and iced tea. Carolyn and her mother talked mostly about neighbors and the congregation at the Japanese Methodist Church in West Fresno. Her father, who was in khaki work clothes, excused himself with a wave that was almost a salute and went outside. I heard a truck start, a dog bark, and then the truck rattle away. 10

Carolyn's mother offered another sandwich, but I declined with a shake of my head and a smile. I looked around when I could, when I was not saying over and over that I was a college student, hinting that I could take care of her daughter. I shifted my chair. I saw newspapers piled in corners, dusty cereal boxes and vinegar bottles in corners. The wallpaper was bubbled from rain that had come in from a bad roof. Dust. Dust lay on lamp shades and window sills. These people are just like Mexicans, I thought. Poor people. 11

Carolyn's mother asked me through Carolyn if I would like a *sushi*. A plate of black and white things were held in front of me. I took one, wide-eyed, and turned it over like a foreign coin. I was biting into one when I saw a kitten crawl up the window screen over the sink. I chewed and the kitten opened its mouth of terror as she crawled higher, wanting in to paw the leftovers from our plates. I looked at Carolyn who said that the cat was just showing off. I looked up in time to see it fall. It crawled up, then fell again. 12

13   We talked for an hour and had apple pie and coffee, slowly. Finally, we got up with Carolyn taking my hand. Slightly embarrassed, I tried to pull away but her grip held me. I let her have her way as she led me down the hallway with her mother right behind me. When I opened the door, I was startled by a kitten clinging to the screen door, its mouth screaming "cat food, dog biscuits, *sushi*. . . . " I opened the door and the kitten, still holding on, whined in the language of hungry animals. When I got into Carolyn's car, I looked back: the cat was still clinging. I asked Carolyn if it were possibly hungry, but she said the cat was being silly. She started the car, waved to her mother, and bounced us over the rain-pocked drive, patting my thigh for being her lover baby. Carolyn waved again. I looked back, waving, then gawking at a window screen where there were now three kittens clawing and screaming to get in. Like Mexicans, I thought. I remembered the Molinas and how the cats clung to their screens—cats they shot down with squirt guns. On the highway, I felt happy, pleased by it all. I patted Carolyn's thigh. Her people were like Mexicans, only different.

XXXXXXXXXXXXXXXXXX **For Discussion** XXXXXXXXXXXXXXXXXX

1. After COMPARING his future wife's family to his own, Gary Soto concludes that they are much alike, "only different" (13). How and how well does this conclusion summarize the main point of Soto's comparison? Explain.

2. How does Soto's grandmother DEFINE an "Okie" (1)? Why doesn't she want him to marry one?

3. Why does Soto say that his grandmother gave him bad advice and good advice (1)? Which is which, and why?

4. "It was a surprise to me," says Soto about marrying a girl of Japanese descent (6). Why didn't he marry a Mexican girl, as his grandmother advised?

5. What does Soto imply about ethnic and racial stereotypes when he refers to the calendar showing the "Important Races of the World" (1, 7)? Why does his grandmother ask for the calendar again?

XXXXXXXXXXXXXX **Strategies and Structures** XXXXXXXXXXXXXX

1. Before COMPARING them with Japanese Americans, Soto explains what Mexican Americans are "like." What are some of the specifics by which he characterizes himself and his family? What is his PURPOSE for citing these particular traits?

2. We meet Carolyn's family in paragraph 10. How has Soto already prepared us to expect more similarities than differences between the two families? Cite details by which Soto explains what Carolyn's people are "like."

3. Why does Soto refer so often to the kittens of Carolyn's family's house? What role do they play in his comparison?

4. Besides giving advice, Soto's grandmother, like all the other adult women in "Like Mexicans," is engaged in what activity? Why do you think Soto focuses on this?

5. Soto's comparison of two American families has many elements of NARRATIVE. Who is the NARRATOR: a young man growing up in a Mexican American neighborhood, an older man looking back at him, or both? Explain.

XXXXXXXXXXXX **WORDS AND FIGURES OF SPEECH** XXXXXXXXXXXX

1. What is the effect of Soto's DESCRIPTION of the orange slice in Scott's mouth as a "fang" (4)? Why do you think he says, "I didn't think anything of it" (4)?

2. What does Soto mean by the term "social class" in paragraph 8?

3. Why do you think Soto COMPARES *sushi* to a foreign coin (12)? Give examples of other SIMILES like this one in his essay.

4. What is the derivation of Soto's grandmother's favorite ethnic slur, "Okies"?

5. When Soto mentions Jews to his grandmother, she calls for the calendar of the races. Is "Jews" a racial or an ethnic category? What's the difference? How about "Hispanic" or "Japanese American"?

XXXXXXXXXXXXXXXXX **FOR WRITING** XXXXXXXXXXXXXXXXXXXXX

1. Write a paragraph COMPARING and CONTRASTING your family with that of a close friend, spouse, or partner. Choose one specific point of comparison—how or what they eat, how they interact within their family, how they celebrate special occasions, and so forth.

2. Whether or not you grew up in a racially or ethnically diverse neighborhood, you may recall friends and acquaintances who differed from each other in social, economic, physical, religious, or other ways. Write an essay comparing and contrasting several of these friends.

DEBORAH TANNEN

GENDER IN THE CLASSROOM

Deborah Tannen (b. 1945) is a linguist at Georgetown University. She specializes, she says, in "the language of everyday conversation." "Gender in the Classroom," which originally appeared in the *Chronicle of Higher Education*, grew out of her research for *You Just Don't Understand* (1990), a book about the various conversational styles of men and women. In the United States, says Tannen, the sexes bond differently. Women do it by talking with each other about their troubles; men do it by exchanging "playful insults." In this essay, Tannen compares and contrasts the various behaviors that result from gender-related styles of talking and then explains how she changes her teaching methods to accommodate these behaviors.

XXXXXXXXXXXXXXXXXXXXXXXXXXXXXXXXXXXXXXXXXXXXXXXXXXXXXXXX

1   When I researched and wrote my latest book, *You Just Don't Understand: Women and Men in Conversation*, the furthest thing from my mind was reevaluating my teaching strategies. But that has been one of the direct benefits of having written the book.

2   The primary focus of my linguistic research always has been the language of everyday conversation. One facet of this is conversational style: how different regional, ethnic, and class backgrounds, as well as age and gender, result in different ways of using language to communicate. *You Just Don't Understand* is about the conversational styles of women and men. As I gained more insight into typically male and female ways of using language, I began to suspect some of the causes of the troubling facts that women who go to single-sex schools do better in later life, and that when young women sit next to young men in classrooms, the males talk more. This is not to say that all men talk in class, nor that no women do. It is simply that a greater percentage of discussion time is taken by men's voices.

The research of sociologists and anthropologists such as Janet 3
Lever, Marjorie Harness Goodwin, and Donna Eder has shown that
girls and boys learn to use language differently in their sex-separate peer
groups. Typically, a girl has a best friend with whom she sits and talks,
frequently telling secrets. It's the telling of secrets, the fact and the way
that they talk to each other, that makes them best friends. For boys,
activities are central: Their best friends are the ones they do things with.
Boys also tend to play in larger groups that are hierarchical. High-status
boys give orders and push low-status boys around. So boys are expected
to use language to seize center stage: by exhibiting their skill, displaying
their knowledge, and challenging and resisting challenges.

These patterns have stunning implications for classroom interac- 4
tion. Most faculty members assume that participating in class discussion
is a necessary part of successful performance. Yet speaking in a classroom is more congenial to boys' language experience than to girls', since
it entails putting oneself forward in front of a large group of people,
many of whom are strangers and at least one of whom is sure to judge
speakers' knowledge and intelligence by their verbal display.

Another aspect of many classrooms that makes them more hos- 5
pitable to most men than to most women is the use of debate-like for-
mats as a learning tool. Our educational system, as Walter Ong[1] argues
persuasively in his book *Fighting for Life* (Cornell University Press,
1981), is fundamentally male in that the pursuit of knowledge is
believed to be achieved by ritual opposition: public display followed by
argument and challenge. Father Ong demonstrates that ritual opposition—what he calls "adversativeness" or "agonism"—is fundamental to
the way most males approach almost any activity. (Consider, for example, the little boy who shows he likes a little girl by pulling her braids
and shoving her.) But ritual opposition is antithetical to the way most
females learn and like to interact. It is not that females don't fight, but
that they don't fight for fun. They don't *ritualize* opposition.

---

1. Cultural historian, philosopher, and Jesuit priest (1912–2003); a long-time faculty
member at St. Louis University.

6   Anthropologists working in widely disparate parts of the world have found contrasting verbal rituals for women and men. Women in completely unrelated cultures (for example, Greece and Bali) engage in ritual laments: spontaneously produced rhyming couplets that express their pain, for example, over the loss of loved ones. Men do not take part in laments. They have their own, very different verbal ritual: a contest, a war of words in which they vie with each other to devise clever insults.

7   When discussing these phenomena with a colleague, I commented that I see these two styles in American conversation: Many women bond by talking about troubles, and many men bond by exchanging playful insults and put-downs, and other sorts of verbal sparring. He exclaimed: "I never thought of this, but that's the way I teach: I have students read an article, and then I invite them to tear it apart. After we've torn it to shreds, we talk about how to build a better model."

8   This contrasts sharply with the way I teach: I open the discussion of readings by asking, "What did you find useful in this? What can we use in our own theory building and our own methods?" I note what I see as weaknesses in the author's approach, but I also point out that the writer's discipline and purposes might be different from ours. Finally, I offer personal anecdotes illustrating the phenomena under discussion and praise students' anecdotes as well as their critical acumen.

9   These different teaching styles must make our classrooms wildly different places and hospitable to different students. Male students are more likely to be comfortable attacking the readings and might find the inclusion of personal anecdotes irrelevant and "soft." Women are more likely to resist discussion they perceive as hostile, and, indeed, it is women in my classes who are most likely to offer personal anecdotes.

10   A colleague who read my book commented that he had always taken for granted that the best way to deal with students' comments is to challenge them: this, he felt it was self-evident, sharpens their minds and helps them develop debating skills. But he had noticed that women were relatively silent in his classes, so he decided to try beginning discussion with relatively open-ended questions and letting comments go unchallenged. He found, to his amazement and satisfaction, that more women began to speak up.

Though some of the women in his class clearly liked this better, perhaps some of the men liked it less. One young man in my class wrote in a questionnaire about a history professor who gave students questions to think about and called on people to answer them: "He would then play devil's advocate . . . i.e., he debated us. . . . That class *really* sharpened me intellectually. . . . We as students do need to know how to defend ourselves." This young man valued the experience of being attacked and challenged publicly. Many, if not most, women would shrink from such a "challenge," experiencing it as a public humiliation. 11

A professor at Hamilton College told me of a young man who was upset because he felt his class presentation had been a failure. The professor was puzzled because he had observed that class members had listened attentively and agreed with the student's observations. It turned out that it was this very agreement that the student interpreted as failure: Since no one had engaged his ideas by arguing with him, he felt they had found them unworthy of attention. 12

So one reason men speak in class more than women is that many of them find the "public" classroom setting more conducive to speaking, whereas most women are more comfortable speaking in private to a small group of people they know well. A second reason is that men are more likely to be comfortable with the debate-like form that discussion may take. Yet another reason is the different attitudes toward speaking in class that typify women and men. 13

Students who speak frequently in class, many of whom are men, assume that it is their job to think of contributions and try to get the floor to express them. But many women monitor their participation not only to get the floor but to avoid getting it. Women students in my class tell me that if they have spoken up once or twice, they hold back for the rest of the class because they don't want to dominate. If they have spoken a lot one week, they will remain silent the next. These different ethics of participation are, of course, unstated, so those who speak freely assume that those who remain silent have nothing to say, and those who are reining themselves in assume that the big talkers are selfish and hoggish. 14

When I looked around my classes, I could see these differing ethics and habits at work. For example, my graduate class in analyzing conver- 15 sation had twenty students, eleven women and nine men. Of the men, four were foreign students: two Japanese, one Chinese, and one Syrian. With the exception of the three Asian men, all the men spoke in class at least occasionally. The biggest talker in the class was a woman, but there were also five women who never spoke at all, only one of whom was Japanese. I decided to try something different.

16   I broke the class into small groups to discuss the issues raised in the readings and to analyze their own conversational transcripts. I devised three ways of dividing the students into groups: one by the degree program they were in, one by gender, and one by conversational style, as closely as I could guess it. This meant that when the class was grouped according to conversational style, I put Asian students together, fast talkers together, and quiet students together. The class split into groups six times during the semester, so they met in each grouping twice. I told students to regard the groups as examples of interactional data and to note the different ways in which they participated in the different groups. Toward the end of the term, I gave them a questionnaire asking about their class and group participation.

17   I could see plainly from my observation of the groups at work that women who never opened their mouths in class were talking away in the small groups. In fact, the Japanese woman commented that she found it particularly hard to contribute to the all-woman group she was in because "I was overwhelmed by how talkative the female students were in the female-only group." This is particularly revealing because it highlights that the same person who can be "oppressed" into silence in one context can become the talkative "oppressor" in another. No one's conversational style is absolute; everyone's style changes in response to the context and others' styles.

18   Some of the students (seven) said they preferred the same-gender groups; others preferred the same-style groups. In answer to the question "Would you have liked to speak in class more than you did?" six of the seven who said yes were women; the one man was Japanese. Most startlingly, this response did not come only from quiet women; it came from women who had indicated they had spoken in class never, rarely, sometimes and often. Of the eleven students who said the amount they had spoken was fine, seven were men. Of the four women who checked,

"fine," two added qualifications indicating it wasn't completely fine: One wrote in "maybe more," and one wrote, "I have an urge to participate often but feel I should have something more interesting/relevant/ wonderful/intelligent to say!"

I counted my experiment a success. Everyone in the class found the small groups interesting, and no one indicated he or she would have preferred that the class not break into groups. Perhaps most instructive, however, was the fact that the experience of breaking into groups, and of talking about participation in class, raised everyone's awareness about classroom participation. After we had talked about it, some of the quietest women in the class made a few voluntary contributions, though sometimes I had to insure their participation by interrupting the students who were exuberantly speaking out.

19

Americans are often proud that they discount the significance of cultural differences: "We're all individuals," many people boast. Ignoring such issues as gender and ethnicity becomes a source of pride: "I treat everyone the same." But treating people the same is not equal treatment if they are not the same.

20

The classroom is a different environment for those who feel comfortable putting themselves forward in a group than it is for those who find the prospect of doing so chastening, or even terrifying. When a professor asks, "Are there any questions?," students who can formulate statements the fastest have the greatest opportunity to respond. Those who need significant time to do so have not really been given a chance at all, since by the time they are ready to speak, someone else has taken the floor.

21

In a class where some students speak out without raising hands, those who feel they must raise their hands and wait to be recognized do not have equal opportunity to speak. Telling them to feel free to jump in will not make them feel free; one's sense of timing, of one's rights and obligations in a classroom, are automatic, learned over years of interaction. They may be changed over time, with motivation and effort, but they cannot be changed on the spot. And everyone assumes his or her own way is best. When I asked my students how the class could be changed to make it easier for them to speak more, the most talkative woman said she would prefer it if no one had to raise hands, and a for-

22

eign student said he wished people would raise their hands and wait to be recognized.

23   My experience in this class has convinced me that small-group interaction should be part of any class that is not a small seminar. I also am convinced that having the students become observers of their own interaction is a crucial part of their education. Talking about ways of talking in class makes students aware that their ways of talking affect other students, that the motivations they impute to others may not truly reflect others' motives, and that the behaviors they assume to be self-evidently right are not universal norms.

24   The goal of complete equal opportunity in class may not be attainable, but realizing that one monolithic classroom-participation structure is not equal opportunity is itself a powerful motivation to find more diverse methods to serve diverse students—and every classroom is diverse.

XXXXXXXXXXXXXXXXXXX **For Discussion** XXXXXXXXXXXXXXXXXXXX

1. According to Deborah Tannen, speaking up in class is typically more "congenial" to whom, women or men (4)? What accounts for this difference, according to her COMPARISON of "the language experience" (4)?

2. Men, says Tannen, "ritualize opposition"; women don't (5). Why not? What is the difference, according to the authorities she cites, between how men fight and how women fight? Do you agree?

3. One of Tannen's colleagues teaches by asking students to read an article and then "tear it apart" (7). How does Tannen say this compares with the way she teaches?

4. Tannen CONTRASTS the "ethics of [class] participation" by men with those of women (14). What differences does she find? What are the consequences of their being "unstated" (14)?

5. Tannen, in paragraph 18, presents the results of her questionnaire about class and group participation. What are some of those results? What do you think of her findings?

6. Tannen says that her research in the conversation of men and women caused her to change her classroom teaching strategies. What are some of the changes she made? How compelling do you find her reasons for making them?

XXXXXXXXXXXXX **STRATEGIES AND STRUCTURES** XXXXXXXXXXXXX

1. Tannen's title announces that she is COMPARING men and women, and that the basis on which she compares them is their classroom behavior. Where does she first indicate what particular aspects of this behavior she will focus on? What are some of them?

2. This essay was originally published in the *Chronicle of Higher Education*, a periodical read by teachers and other educators. In what ways does Tannen tailor her essay to suit this AUDIENCE? How might this essay be different if she had written it for an audience of first-year college students?

3. In paragraph 13, Tannen sums up two of the points of comparison that she has previously made. What are they, and why do you think she summarizes them here? What new point of comparison does she then introduce, and how does she develop it in the next paragraph(s)?

4. "No one's conversational style is absolute," says Tannen; "everyone's style changes in response to the context and others' styles" (17). How does the EXAMPLE of the Japanese woman in her class illustrate the principle that people have different styles of conversation in different situations?

5. Besides COMPARING AND CONTRASTING the behavior of men and women, Tannen is advancing an ARGUMENT about equal opportunity in the classroom (24). What is the main point of her argument? How and how well does she support her main point?

6. "I broke the class into small groups," says Tannen in paragraph 16. Where else in her essay do you find Tannen telling a brief, illustrative story or ANECDOTE about what she did or said? How do the NARRATIVE elements in her essay support the comparison she is making in it?

XXXXXXXXXXXXX **WORDS AND FIGURES OF SPEECH** XXXXXXXXXXXXX

1. Roughly speaking, one's "sex" is biological while one's "gender" is not, or not entirely. Why do you think Tannen uses the second term in her essay rather than the first one?

2. "Behavior" is usually a collective noun, as in the sentence "Their behavior last night was atrocious." Why do you suppose social scientists like Tannen often use the plural form, "behaviors," in their writing (23)? What is the significance of this difference in terminology?

3. Like that of other social scientists, Tannen's writing style is peppered with compound nouns and nouns used as adjectives—for example, "single-sex schools" and "sex-separate peer groups" (2, 3). Point out other expressions like these throughout her essay.

4. What is the meaning of the word "hierarchical" (3), and why does Tannen use it to refer to boys?

5. What is the difference between "ritual opposition" as Tannen uses the term and just plain opposition (5)? What other behaviors does Tannen cite that might be considered rituals?

XXXXXXXXXXXXXXXXXXXX **FOR WRITING** XXXXXXXXXXXXXXXXXXXXXX

1. How do Tannen's observations on gender in the classroom compare with your own? Write a paragraph COMPARING AND CONTRASTING some aspect of the classroom behaviors of the two genders.

2. Commenting on the differences in the ways girls and boys use language to make friends, Tannen writes: "Typically, a girl has a best friend with whom she sits and talks, frequently telling secrets" (3). Talking together makes them best friends. Boys, she says, make friends through "activities" (3). Consequently, they "use language to seize center stage," to take control (3). How do Tannen's observations square with your experience of making friends while growing up? Write an essay in which you compare and contrast how you made same-sex friends with the way, as you recall, the "opposite" gender did so. Give specific EXAMPLES and include ANECDOTES when possible.

DAVID SEDARIS

REMEMBERING MY CHILDHOOD ON THE CONTINENT OF AFRICA

David Sedaris (b. 1956) is a satirist and playwright who contributes to *Esquire* and other magazines, and whose voice can be heard regularly on NPR's *This American Life*. Named humorist of the year in 2001 by *Time* magazine, he is the author of several essay collections, including *Me Talk Pretty One Day* (2000), from which this selection is taken, and *When You Are Engulfed in Flames* (2008). Although Sedaris once worked as a Christmas elf for Macy's department store, he did not grow up in the exotic settings he remembers here. In this essay, Sedaris steals memories from his partner Hugh, the son of a career diplomat, who actually grew up in Africa. Point by point, Sedaris compares his childhood with Hugh's. "Certain events are parallel," he says: for example, they both saw the same movie about a talking Volkswagen. But by comparison with Hugh's early years in the Congo and Ethiopia, Sedaris's own childhood in North Carolina was "unspeakably dull."

XXXXXXXXXXXXXXXXXXXXXXXXXXXXXXXXXXXXXXXXXXXXXXXXXXXXXXXXXX

W hen Hugh was in the fifth grade, his class took a field trip to an Ethiopian slaughterhouse. He was living in Addis Ababa at the time, and the slaughterhouse was chosen because, he says, "it was convenient." 1

This was a school system in which the matter of proximity outweighed such petty concerns as what may or may not be appropriate for a busload of eleven-year-olds. "What?" I asked. "Were there no autopsies scheduled at the local morgue? Was the federal prison just a bit too far out of the way?" 2

Hugh defends his former school, saying, "Well, isn't that the whole point of a field trip? To see something new?" 3

4   "Technically yes, but . . . "

5   "All right then," he says. "So we saw some new things."

6   One of his field trips was literally a trip to a field where the class watched a wrinkled man fill his mouth with rotten goat meat and feed it to a pack of waiting hyenas. On another occasion they were taken to examine the bloodied bedroom curtains hanging in the palace of the former dictator. There were tamer trips, to textile factories and sugar refineries, but my favorite is always the slaughterhouse. It wasn't a big company, just a small rural enterprise run by a couple of brothers operating out of a low-ceilinged concrete building. Following a brief lecture on the importance of proper sanitation, a small white piglet was herded into the room, its dainty hooves clicking against the concrete floor. The class gathered in a circle to get a better look at the animal, who seemed delighted with the attention he was getting. He turned from face to face and was looking up at Hugh when one of the brothers drew a pistol from his back pocket, held it against the animal's temple, and shot the piglet, execution-style. Blood spattered, frightened children wept, and the man with the gun offered the teacher and bus driver some meat from a freshly slaughtered goat.

7   When I'm told such stories, it's all I can do to hold back my feelings of jealousy. An Ethiopian slaughterhouse. Some people have all the luck. When I was in elementary school, the best we ever got was a trip to Old Salem or Colonial Williamsburg, one of those preserved brick villages where time supposedly stands still and someone earns his living as a town crier. There was always a blacksmith, a group of wandering patriots, and a collection of bonneted women hawking corn bread or gingersnaps made "the ol'-fashioned way." Every now and then you might come across a doer of bad deeds serving time in the stocks, but that was generally as exciting as it got.

8   Certain events are parallel, but compared with Hugh's, my childhood was unspeakably dull. When I was seven years old, my family moved to North Carolina. When he was seven years old, Hugh's family moved to the Congo. We had a collie and a house cat. They had a monkey and two horses named Charlie Brown and Satan. I threw stones at stop signs. Hugh threw stones at crocodiles. The verbs are the same, but he definitely wins the prize when it comes to nouns and objects. An

eventful day for my mother might have involved a trip to the dry cleaner or a conversation with the potato-chip deliveryman. Asked one ordinary Congo afternoon what she'd done with her day, Hugh's mother answered that she and a fellow member of the Ladies' Club had visited a leper colony on the outskirts of Kinshasa. No reason was given for the expedition, though chances are she was staking it out for a future field trip.

Due to his upbringing, Hugh sits through inane movies never realizing that they're often based on inane television shows. There were no poker-faced sitcom martians in his part of Africa, no oil-rich hillbillies or aproned brides trying to wean themselves from the practice of witchcraft.[1] From time to time a movie would arrive packed in a dented canister, the film scratched and faded from its slow trip around the world. The theater consisted of a few dozen folding chairs arranged before a bedsheet or the blank wall of a vacant hangar out near the airstrip. Occasionally a man would sell warm soft drinks out of a cardboard box, but that was it in terms of concessions. 9

When I was young, I went to the theater at the nearby shopping center and watched a movie about a talking Volkswagen.[2] I believe the little car had a taste for mischief but I can't be certain, as both the movie and the afternoon proved unremarkable and have faded from my memory. Hugh saw the same movie a few years after it was released. His family had left the Congo by this time and were living in Ethiopia. Like me, Hugh saw the movie by himself on a weekend afternoon. Unlike me, he left the theater two hours later, to find a dead man hanging from a telephone pole at the far end of the unpaved parking lot. None of the people who'd seen the movie seemed to care about the dead man. They stared at him for a moment or two and then headed home, saying they'd never seen anything as crazy as that talking Volkswagen. His father was late picking him up, so Hugh just stood there for an hour, watching the 10

---

1. References to *My Favorite Martian, The Beverly Hillbillies,* and *Bewitched,* American TV shows popular in the 1960s.

2. Probably Herbie, a Volkswagen Beetle, the main character in a series of Disney films, beginning with *The Love Bug* (1969).

dead man dangle and turn in the breeze. The death was not reported in the newspaper, and when Hugh related the story to his friends, they said, "You saw the movie about the talking car?"

11   I could have done without the flies and the primitive theaters, but I wouldn't have minded growing up with a houseful of servants. In North Carolina it wasn't unusual to have a once-a-week maid, but Hugh's family had houseboys, a word that never fails to charge my imagination. They had cooks and drivers, and guards who occupied a gatehouse, armed with machetes. Seeing as I had regularly petitioned my parents for an electric fence, the business with the guards strikes me as the last word in quiet sophistication. Having protection suggests that you are important. Having that protection paid for by the government is even better, as it suggests your safety is of interest to someone other than yourself.

12   Hugh's father was a career officer with the U.S. State Department, and every morning a black sedan carried him off to the embassy. I'm told it's not as glamorous as it sounds, but in terms of fun for the entire family, I'm fairly confident that it beats the sack race at the annual IBM picnic. By the age of three, Hugh was already carrying a diplomatic passport. The rules that applied to others did not apply to him. No tickets, no arrests, no luggage search: he was officially licensed to act like a brat. Being an American, it was expected of him, and who was he to deny the world an occasional tantrum?

13   They weren't rich, but what Hugh's family lacked financially they more than made up for with the sort of exoticism that works wonders at cocktail parties, leading always to the remark "That sounds fascinating." It's a compliment one rarely receives when describing an adolescence spent drinking Icees at the North Hills Mall. No fifteen-foot python ever wandered onto my school's basketball court. I begged, I prayed nightly, but it just never happened. Neither did I get to witness a military coup in which forces sympathetic to the colonel arrived late at night to assassinate my next-door neighbor. Hugh had been at the Addis Ababa teen club when the electricity was cut off and soldiers arrived to evacuate the building. He and his friends had to hide in the back of a jeep and cover themselves with blankets during the ride home. It's something that sticks in his mind for one reason or another.

Among my personal highlights is the memory of having my picture 14 taken with Uncle Paul, the legally blind host of a Raleigh children's television show. Among Hugh's is the memory of having his picture taken with Buzz Aldrin on the last leg of the astronaut's world tour. The man who had walked on the moon placed his hand on Hugh's shoulder and offered to sign his autograph book. The man who led Wake County schoolchildren in afternoon song turned at the sound of my voice and asked, "So what's your name, princess?"

When I was fourteen years old, I was sent to spend ten days with 15 my maternal grandmother in western New York State. She was a small and private woman named Billie, and though she never came right out and asked, I had the distinct impression she had no idea who I was. It was the way she looked at me, squinting through her glasses while chewing on her lower lip. That, coupled with the fact that she never once called me by name. "Oh," she'd say, "are you still here?" She was just beginning her long struggle with Alzheimer's disease, and each time I entered the room, I felt the need to reintroduce myself and set her at ease. "Hi, it's me. Sharon's boy, David. I was just in the kitchen admiring your collection of ceramic toads." Aside from a few trips to summer camp, this was the longest I'd ever been away from home, and I like to think I was toughened by the experience.

About the same time I was frightening my grandmother, Hugh and 16 his family were packing their belongings for a move to Somalia. There were no English-speaking schools in Mogadishu, so, after a few months spent lying around the family compound with his pet monkey, Hugh was sent back to Ethiopia to live with a beer enthusiast his father had met at a cocktail party. Mr. Hoyt installed security systems in foreign embassies. He and his family gave Hugh a room. They invited him to join them at the table, but that was as far as they extended themselves. No one ever asked him when his birthday was, so when the day came, he kept it to himself. There was no telephone service between Ethiopia and Somalia, and letters to his parents were sent to Washington and then forwarded on to Mogadishu, meaning that his news was more than a month old by the time they got it. I suppose it wasn't much different than living as a foreign-exchange student. Young people do it all the time, but to me it sounds awful. The Hoyts had two sons about Hugh's age who were always saying things like "Hey that's *our* sofa you're sitting on" and "Hands off that ornamental stein. It doesn't belong to you."

17   He'd been living with these people for a year when he overheard Mr. Hoyt tell a friend that he and his family would soon be moving to Munich, Germany, the beer capital of the world.

18   "And that worried me," Hugh said, "because it meant I'd have to find some other place to live."

19   Where I come from, finding shelter is a problem the average teenager might confidently leave to his parents. It was just something that came with having a mom and a dad. Worried that he might be sent to live with his grandparents in Kentucky, Hugh turned to the school's guidance counselor, who knew of a family whose son had recently left for college. And so he spent another year living with strangers and not mentioning his birthday. While I wouldn't have wanted to do it myself, I can't help but envy the sense of fortitude he gained from the experience. After graduating from college, he moved to France knowing only the phrase "Do you speak French?"—a question guaranteed to get you nowhere unless you also speak the language.

20   While living in Africa, Hugh and his family took frequent vacations, often in the company of their monkey. The Nairobi Hilton, some suite of high-ceilinged rooms in Cairo or Khartoum: these are the places his people recall when gathered at a common table. "Was that the summer we spent in Beirut or, no, I'm thinking of the time we sailed from Cyprus and took the *Orient Express*[3] to Istanbul."

21   Theirs was the life I dreamt about during my vacations in eastern North Carolina. Hugh's family was hobnobbing with chiefs and sultans while I ate hush puppies at the Sanitary Fish Market in Morehead City, a beach towel wrapped like a hijab[4] around my head. Someone unknown to me was very likely standing in a muddy ditch and dreaming of an evening spent sitting in a clean family restaurant, drinking iced tea and

---

3. Luxury railroad train providing service across Europe to Turkey.

4. A veil worn by Muslim women. Hush puppies are balls of deep-fried cornmeal bread, a popular food in the American South.

working his way through an extra-large seaman's platter, but that did not concern me, as it meant I should have been happy with what I had. Rather than surrender to my bitterness, I have learned to take satisfaction in the life that Hugh has led. His stories have, over time, become my own. I say this with no trace of a kumbaya. There is no spiritual symbiosis; I'm just a petty thief who lifts his memories the same way I'll take a handful of change left on his dresser. When my own experiences fall short of the mark, I just go out and spend some of his. It is with pleasure that I sometimes recall the dead man's purpled face or the report of the handgun ringing in my ears as I studied the blood pooling beneath the dead white piglet. On the way back from the slaughter-house, we stopped for Cokes in the village of Mojo, where the gas-station owner had arranged a few tables and chairs beneath a dying canopy of vines. It was late afternoon by the time we returned to school, where a second bus carried me to the foot of Coffeeboard Road. Once there, I walked through a grove of eucalyptus trees and alongside a bald pasture of starving cattle, past the guard napping in his gatehouse, and into the waiting arms of my monkey.

XXXXXXXXXXXXXXXXXXXX **FOR DISCUSSION** XXXXXXXXXXXXXXXXXXXX

1. When he was in elementary school, David Sedaris went on field trips to places like Old Salem and Colonial Williamsburg (7). How do these experiences COMPARE with the typical field trips that his partner Hugh took as a child? What is his point in comparing the two experiences?

2. When they were growing up, both Sedaris and Hugh saw the same "unremarkable" movie about a talking Volkswagen (10). How was Hugh's experience different from Sedaris's?

3. Sedaris says that he has learned "to take satisfaction" in Hugh's experience rather than "surrender to my bitterness" (21). What does he claim to be "bitter" about? How seriously are we supposed to take this assertion?

4. After comparing and CONTRASTING their adventures for several pages, how does Sedaris finally "take" satisfaction from the life of his partner?

5. On the whole, whose childhood would you prefer to remember having lived, Sedaris's or his friend Hugh's? Why?

XXXXXXXXXXXXXXX **STRATEGIES AND STRUCTURES** XXXXXXXXXXXXXXX

1. In COMPARING his childhood with Hugh's, Sedaris obviously stresses the CONTRASTS. What similarities does he nonetheless mention?

2. In paragraph 8, Sedaris constructs a point-by-point mini-essay in comparison and contrast. How does the order of his sentences and their grammatical structure help to heighten the contrasts he draws between "parallel" events in his life and Hugh's?

3. Parallel lines run along together but never intersect. Point out examples in this essay where Sedaris shows events in the two boys' lives as parallel but contrasting.

4. What do Sedaris's references to television shows, movies, and other cultural phenomena suggest about his intended AUDIENCE? Does Sedaris assume that most of his audience had a childhood closer to Hugh's or to his own? Explain.

5. What specific details does Sedaris use to give the impression in his final paragraph that he has "stolen" (or stolen into) Hugh's memories?

6. Even though Sedaris's essay is organized as a comparison of events in his childhood and that of his partner, it has many elements of personal NARRATIVE. What are some of them? Cite specific examples from the text. (Imagine this essay *without* any narrative. How would it be different?)

XXXXXXXXXXXXXX **WORDS AND FIGURES OF SPEECH** XXXXXXXXXXXXXX

1. What does Sedaris mean when he says that his life and Hugh's shared the same verbs but different nouns and objects (8)?

2. Explain the IRONY in the following sentence: "Among my personal highlights is the memory of having my picture taken with Uncle Paul, the legally blind host of a Raleigh children's television show" (14).

3. A "hijab" is a sort of veil (21). Why does Sedaris use this term in the context of the Sanitary Fish Market in Morehead City?

4. Sedaris uses the African word "kumbaya" in paragraph 21. How does he DEFINE it?

5. On what basis is Sedaris drawing an ANALOGY between himself and a "petty thief" in paragraph 21?

XXXXXXXXXXXXXXXXXXX **FOR WRITING** XXXXXXXXXXXXXXXXXXXX

1. Have you and a friend or a family member ever had entirely different recollections of the same event? Ask that person to write out (or record) his or her recollection, and you do the same—separately. Then, in a paragraph or two, make a point-by-point COMPARISON of the two versions.

2. Write an essay comparing and CONTRASTING your childhood with that of someone whose childhood you know (or imagine) to be very different from your own. Your counterpart can be someone you know personally or whom you only know about.

CHAPTER EIGHT

DEFINITION

XXXXXXXXXXXXXXXXXXXXXXXXXXXXXXXXXXXXXXXXXXXXXXXXXXXXXXXXX

When you DEFINE* something, you tell what it is—and what it is not. The most basic definitions take the form of simple declarative sentences, often with the word *is*, as in the following famous definitions:

> Happiness is a warm puppy.
> CHARLES M. SCHULZ

> Man is a biped without feathers.
> PLATO

> Hope is the thing with feathers.
> EMILY DICKINSON

> Golf is a good walk spoiled.
> MARK TWAIN

All of these model definitions, you'll notice, work in the same way. They place the thing to be defined (happiness, man, hope, golf) into a general class (puppy, biped, thing, walk) and then add characteristics (warm, without feathers, with feathers, spoiled) that distinguish it from others in the same class.

This is the kind of defining—by general class and characteristics—that dictionaries do. *The American Heritage Dictionary*, for example, defines the word *scepter* as "a staff held by a sovereign . . . as an emblem of authority." Here the general class is "staff," and the characteristics

---

*Words printed in SMALL CAPITALS are defined in the Glossary.

 300

that differentiate it from other staffs—such as those carried by shepherds—are "held by a sovereign" and "as an emblem of authority."

The problem with a basic dictionary definition like this is that it often doesn't tell us everything we need to know. You might begin an essay with one, but you are not going to get very far with a topic unless you *extend* your definition. One way to give an *extended definition* is to name other similar items in the same category as the item you are defining.

Take the term *folklore*, for example. A standard definition of *folklore* is "the study of traditional materials." This basic definition is not likely to enlighten anyone who is not already familiar with what those "materials" are, however. So one folklorist defines his field by listing a host of similar items that all belong to it:

> Folklore includes myths, legends, folktales, jokes, proverbs, riddles, chants, charms, blessings, curses, oaths, insults, retorts, taunts, teases, toasts, tongue-twisters, and greeting and leave-taking formulas (e.g., See you later, alligator). It also includes folk costumes, folk dance, folk drama (and mime), folk art, folk belief (or superstition), folk medicine, folk instrumental music (e.g., fiddle tunes), folksongs (e.g., lullabies, ballads), folk speech (e.g., to paint the town red), and names (e.g., nicknames and place names).
>
> ALAN DUNDES, *The Study of Folklore*

Dundes's extended definition does not stop here; it goes on to include "latrinalia (writings on the walls of public bathrooms)," "envelope sealers (e.g., SWAK—Sealed With A Kiss)," "comments made after body emissions (e.g., after burps or sneezes)," and many others items that populate the field he is defining.

Another way to extend a basic definition is to specify additional characteristics of the item or idea you are defining. *Hydroponic tomatoes*, for example, are tomatoes grown mostly in water. Food expert Raymond Sokolov further defines this kind of tomato as one that is "mass-produced, artificially ripened, mechanically picked, and long-hauled." "It has no taste," he says, "and it won't go splat" (all additional negative characteristics). *Organic tomatoes*, by contrast, says Sokolov, are to be defined as tomatoes that are "squishable, blotchy, tart, and sometimes green-dappled."

To extend your definition further, you might give SYNONYMS for the word or concept you're defining, or trace its ETYMOLOGY, or word history. *Tomatoes*, for example, are commonly defined as "vegetables," but an extended definition might point out that they are actually synonymous with "berries" or "fleshy fruits" and that they derive their name from the Nahuatl word *tomatl*. How do I know this last obscure fact? Because my dictionary, like yours, includes etymologies along with many basic definitions. Etymologies trace the origins of a word and sometimes can help organize an entire essay.

For example, here is the beginning of an essay by biologist Stephen Jay Gould on the concept of evolution:

> The exegesis [interpretation] of evolution as a concept has occupied the lifetimes of a thousand scientists. In this essay, I present something almost laughably narrow in comparison—an exegesis of the word itself. I shall trace how organic change came to be called *evolution*. The tale is complex and fascinating as a pure antiquarian exercise in etymological detection. But more is at stake, for a past usage of this word has contributed to the most common, current misunderstanding among laymen of what scientists mean by evolution.
>
> STEPHEN JAY GOULD, *Ever Since Darwin*

The misunderstanding to which this paragraph refers is the idea that *evolution* means "progress." Gould's main point, however, is that for scientists, *evolution* simply signifies change, adaptation—with no implication of improvement.

Gould is writing to correct what he perceives as a grave error. There is more at stake for him here than just defining a word or idea—as there should be for you when you write an essay that defines something. Good definitions have good reasons for introducing and defining their key terms. When Tanya Barrientos, for example, defines herself as a *Latina* in one of the essays in this chapter, she is making a point about ethnic identity.

There is no set formula for writing good definitions, but there are some questions to keep in mind when you are working on one: What is the essential nature or main use of the thing you are defining? What are its distinguishing characteristics? How is it different from other things like it? And, perhaps most important, why do your readers need to know about it, and what point do you want to make?

A BRIEF GUIDE TO WRITING A DEFINITION ESSAY

As you write a definition, you need to identify your subject, assign it to a general class, and specify particular characteristics that distinguish it from others in that same class. Sean B. Carroll makes these fundamental moves in his essay in this chapter:

> The comparison of developmental genes between species became a new discipline at the interface of embryology and evolutionary biology—evolutionary development biology, or "Evo Devo" for short.
>
> SEAN B. CARROLL, "The Evo Devo Revolution"

Carroll identifies the term he is defining ("Evo Devo"), assigns it to a general class (new scientific disciplines), and specifies particular characteristics (it compares genes between species, it's "at the interface of embryology and evolutionary biology") that distinguish it from others in that class.

Basic definitions like this can be useful in almost any kind of essay. To define a concept in depth, however, you will need an *extended definition:* all the parts of a basic definition plus other important characteristics of the term.

The following guidelines will help you to make these basic moves of definition as you draft an essay—and to extend your definition by adding other distinguishing characteristics, giving synonyms, and tracing the etymology of key terms.

Coming Up with a Subject

When you compose a definition essay, your first challenge is to find a subject worth defining. That subject may be complex, like global warming, or modernism, or capitalism. Or you may devote an entire essay to a definition because you are arguing that a word or concept means something that others might not have thought of, or might disagree with, as Stephen Jay Gould does with his definition of *evolution*. As you consider possible subjects, it is often useful to jot down terms that are open to debate or controversy. For example: What constitutes *racism* or *sexual harassment*? What characterizes *friendship*? What is *intelligent design*? Whatever term you choose, you will need to discover its essential characteristics (such as the trust and loyalty involved in friendship) and make a specific point about it.

Considering Your Purpose and Audience

When you define something, you usually have a reason for doing so: You may be conveying useful information, demonstrating that you understand the term's meaning, arguing for a particular definition, or just entertaining the reader. Keep your PURPOSE in mind as you construct your definition, and adapt the TONE of your essay accordingly—objective when you want to inform, persuasive when you are arguing, humorous when you want the reader to smile.

Also consider why your AUDIENCE might want (or be reluctant) to know more about your term and what it means. How might the reader already define the term? What information can you supply to make it easier for the reader to understand your definition, or be more receptive to it? For example, a definition of *acid* in a lab manual for chemistry students would be considerably different from a definition of *acid* for a general audience. Whatever term you are defining, be sure to focus on those aspects of it that your audience is most likely to find interesting and useful.

Generating Ideas: Asking What Something Is—and Is Not

In order to define a term or concept, you need to know what its distinguishing characteristics are—what makes it different from other things in the same general class. For instance, suppose you wanted to define what a bodybuilder is. It might occur to you to say that bodybuilders are athletes who need to keep their body fat under control and to build up muscle strength. But these characteristics also apply to runners and swimmers. Among these three types of athletes, however, only body-builders train primarily for muscle definition and bulk. In other words, training for muscle definition and bulk is a characteristic that distinguishes bodybuilders from other athletes. Runners and swimmers need strong muscles, too, but what distinguishes them is their speed on the track or in the pool, characteristics that do *not* apply to bodybuilders. As you list the essential characteristics for your term, remember that definitions set up boundaries. They say, in effect: "This is the territory occupied by my concept, and everything outside these boundaries is something else."

Once you have identified the distinguishing characteristics for your term or concept, you can construct a basic definition of it—and then extend it from there. So a good basic definition of a bodybuilder might be "an athlete who trains primarily for muscle definition and bulk."

Templates for Defining

The following templates can help you to generate ideas for a definition and then to start drafting. Don't take these as formulas where you just have to fill in the blanks. There are no easy formulas for good writing. But these templates can help you plot out some of the key moves of definition and thus may serve as good starting points.

> ‣ In general, X can be defined as a kind of _____.
>
> ‣ What specifically distinguishes X from others in this class is _____.
>
> ‣ Other important distinguishing characteristics of X are _____, _____, and _____.
>
> ‣ X is often used to mean _____, but a better synonym would be _____ or _____.

> ‣ One way to define X is as the opposite of _____, the distinguishing characteristics of which are _____, _____, and _____.
>
> ‣ If we define X as _____, we can then define Y as _____.
>
> ‣ By defining X in this way, we can see that _____.

For more techniques to help you generate ideas and start writing, see Chapter 1.

Stating Your Point

In any definition essay, you need to explain the point your definition is intended to make. A THESIS STATEMENT—usually made in the introduction and perhaps reiterated with variations at the end—is a good way to do this. Here is a thesis statement for an essay defining a farmer, written by Craig Schafer, an Ohio State student who grew up on a farm in the Midwest: "By definition, a farmer is someone who tills the soil for a living, but I define a true farmer according to his or her attitudes toward the land." This is a good thesis statement because it defines the subject in an interesting way that may draw the reader in to the rest of the essay.

Adding Other Distinguishing Characteristics

Of all the ways you can extend a basic definition, perhaps the most effective is simply to specify additional characteristics that set your subject apart. To support his definition of a farmer as a person with certain attitudes toward the land, Schafer goes on to specify what those attitudes are, devoting a paragraph to each: A farmer is a born optimist, planting his crops "with no assurances that nature will cooperate." A farmer is devoted to the soil, sifting it through his fingers and "sniffing the fresh clean aroma of a newly plowed field." A farmer is self-denying, with a barn that is often "more modern than his house." And so on. As you compose a definition essay, make sure you provide enough characteristics to identify your subject thoroughly and completely.

Using Synonyms and Etymologies

Another way to extend a definition is by offering SYNONYMS. For example, if you were defining *zine* for readers who are unfamiliar with the
term, you might say that it is short for *magazine*. You could then explain
which characteristics of magazines apply to zines and which ones don't.
Both zines and magazines, you might point out, include printed articles
and artwork; but zines, unlike magazines, are typically self-published,
are photocopied and bound by hand, have very small circulations and
are rarely sold at newsstands, and include both original work and work
appropriated from other sources.

Often you can extend the definition of a term by tracing its history,
or ETYMOLOGY. This is what one engineer did when he asked: "Who are
we who have been calling ourselves engineers since the early nineteenth
century?" Here's part of his answer:

> The word *engineering* probably derives from the Latin word *inge-
> niatorum*. In 1325 a contriver of siege towers was called by the
> Norman word *engynours*. By 1420 the English were calling a
> trickster a *yngynore*. By 1592 we find the word *enginer* being
> given to a designer of phrases—a wordsmith.
>
> JOHN H. LIENHARD, "The Polytechnic Legacy"

Knowing the history of a word and its earlier variations can often help
you with a current definition. You can find the etymology of a word in
most dictionaries.

EVERYDAY DEFINITION
A Sign on a Balcony

A balcony, by definition, is a platform projecting from a wall of a build-ing at least one story off the ground. The authors of this cautionary sign—and their insurance company—wish to impress this key distinction upon the reader. When you define something, you say what class it belongs to (platforms) and what basic characteristics (at least one story above the ground) distinguish it from others in that class. You can then extend your definition to cover more ground by citing other distinguish-ing features of your subject. A balcony, for example, is usually sur-rounded by a railing, balustrade, or parapet—which is fortunate, because anyone who forgets that the balcony is not on ground level might also forget to read the sign.

DAVE BARRY

GUYS VS. MEN

Dave Barry (b. 1947) is a widely published humorist and former columnist for the *Miami Herald*, where he won a Pulitzer Prize for commentary in 1988. He is the author of many humor books, including *Dave Barry's Complete Guide to Guys* (1995), the introduction of which is included here. Despite its title, "Guys vs. Men" is not a comparative study of these two basic types of males. Men and manhood have been written about far too much already, says Barry. But guys and guyhood are neglected topics, and even though he "can't define exactly what it means to be a guy," Barry's essay lays out "certain guy characteristics" that distinguish his quarry from other warm-blooded animals in the field.

XXXXXXXXXXXXXXXXXXXXXXXXXXXXXXXXXXXXXXXXXXXXXXXXXXXXXXXXX

This is a book about guys. It's *not* a book about men. There are   1
already way too many books about men, and most of them are *way*
too serious.

Men itself is a serious word, not to mention *manhood* and *manly*.   2
Such words make being male sound like a very important activity, as
opposed to what it primarily consists of, namely, possessing a set of
minor and frequently unreliable organs.

But men tend to attach great significance to Manhood. This results   3
in certain characteristically masculine, by which I mean stupid, behavioral patterns that can produce unfortunate results such as violent crime,
war, spitting, and ice hockey. These things have given males a bad
name.[1] And the "Men's Movement," which is supposed to bring out the
more positive aspects of Manliness, seems to be densely populated with
loons and goobers.

1. Specifically, "asshole" [Barry's note].

4   So I'm saying that there's another way to look at males: not as aggressive macho dominators; not as sensitive, liberated, hugging drummers; but as *guys*.

5   And what, exactly, do I mean by "guys"? I don't know. I haven't thought that much about it. One of the major characteristics of guyhood is that we guys don't spend a lot of time pondering our deep innermost feelings. There is a serious question in my mind about whether guys actually *have* deep innermost feelings, unless you count, for example, loyalty to the Detroit Tigers,[2] or fear of bridal showers.

6   But although I can't define exactly what it means to be a guy, I can describe certain guy characteristics, such as:

Guys Like Neat Stuff

7   By "neat," I mean "mechanical and unnecessarily complex." I'll give you an example. Right now I'm typing these words on an *extremely* powerful computer. It's the latest in a line of maybe ten computers I've owned, each one more powerful than the last. My computer is chock full of RAM and ROM and bytes and megahertzes and various other items that enable a computer to kick data-processing butt. It is probably capable of supervising the entire U.S. air-defense apparatus while simultaneously processing the tax return of every resident of Ohio. I use it mainly to write a newspaper column. This is an activity wherein I sit and stare at the screen for maybe ten minutes, then, using only my forefingers, slowly type something like:

8   *Henry Kissinger[3] looks like a big wart.*

9   I stare at this for another ten minutes, have an inspiration, then amplify the original thought as follows:

10   *Henry Kissinger looks like a big fat wart.*

2. Major league baseball team that last won the World Series in 1984.

3. Henry Kissinger (b. 1923), U.S. Secretary of State 1973–77.

Then I stare at that for another ten minutes pondering whether I 11
should try to work in the concept of "hairy."

This is absurdly simple work for my computer. It sits there, hum- 12
ming impatiently, bored to death, passing the time between keystrokes
via brain-teaser activities such as developing a Unified Field Theory of
the universe and translating the complete works of Shakespeare
into rap.[4]

In other words, this computer is absurdly overqualified to work for 13
me, and yet soon, I guarantee, I will buy an *even more powerful* one. I
won't be able to stop myself, I'm a guy.

Probably the ultimate example of the fundamental guy drive to 14
have neat stuff is the Space Shuttle. Granted, the guys in charge of this
program *claim* it has a Higher Scientific Purpose, namely to see how
humans function in space. But of course we have known for years how
humans function in space: They float around and say things like: "Looks
real good, Houston!"

No, the real reason for the existence of the Space Shuttle is that it 15
is one humongous and spectacularly gizmo-intensive item of hardware.
Guys can tinker with it practically forever, and occasionally even get it
to work, and use it to place *other* complex mechanical items into orbit,
where they almost immediately break, which provides a great excuse to
send the Space Shuttle up *again*. It's Guy Heaven.

Other results of the guy need to have stuff are Star Wars, the recre- 16
ational boating industry, monorails, nuclear weapons, and wristwatches
that indicate the phase of the moon. I am not saying that women haven't
been involved in the development or use of this stuff. I'm saying that,
without guys, this stuff probably would not exist; just as, without
women, virtually every piece of furniture in the world would still be in
its original position. Guys do not have a basic need to rearrange furniture. Whereas a woman who could cheerfully use the same computer for
fifty-three years will rearrange her furniture on almost a weekly basis,
sometimes in the dead of night. She'll be sound asleep in bed, and suddenly, at 2 A.M., she'll be awakened by the urgent thought: *The blue-*

4. To be or not? I got to *know*.
  Might kill myself by the end of the *show* [Barry's note].

green sofa needs to go perpendicular to the wall instead of parallel, and it needs to go there RIGHT NOW. So she'll get up and move it, which of course necessitates moving other furniture, and soon she has rearranged her entire living room, shifting great big heavy pieces that ordinarily would require several burly men to lift, because there are few forces in Nature more powerful than a woman who needs to rearrange furniture. Every so often a guy will wake up to discover that, because of his wife's overnight efforts, he now lives in an entirely different house.

17   (I realize that I'm making gender-based generalizations here, but my feeling is that if God did not want us to make gender-based generalizations, She would not have given us genders.)

Guys Like a Really Pointless Challenge

18   Not long ago I was sitting in my office at the *Miami Herald*'s Sunday magazine, *Tropic*, reading my fan mail[5] when I heard several of my guy coworkers in the hallway talking about how fast they could run the forty-yard dash. These are guys in their thirties and forties who work in journalism, where the most demanding physical requirement is the ability to digest vending-machine food. In other words, these guys have absolutely no need to run the forty-yard dash.

19   But one of them, Mike Wilson, was writing a story about a star high-school football player who could run it in 4.38 seconds. Now if Mike had written a story about, say, a star high-school poet, none of my guy coworkers would have suddenly decided to find out how well they could write sonnets. But when Mike turned in his story, they became *deeply* concerned about how fast they could run the forty-yard dash. They were so concerned that the magazine editor, Tom Shroder, decided that they should get a stopwatch and go out to a nearby park and find out. Which they did, a bunch of guys taking off their shoes and running around barefoot in a public park on company time.

20   This is what I heard them talking about, out in the hall. I heard Tom, who was thirty-eight years old, saying that his time in the forty

---

5. Typical fan letter: "Who cuts your hair? Beavers?" [Barry's note].

had been 5.75 seconds. And I thought to myself: This is ridiculous. These are middle-aged guys, supposedly adults, and they're out there *bragging* about their performance in this stupid juvenile footrace. Finally I couldn't stand it anymore.

"Hey!" I shouted. "*I* could beat 5.75 seconds." 21

So we went out to the park and measured off forty yards, and the 22 guys told me that I had three chances to make my best time. On the first try my time was 5.78 seconds, just three-hundredths of a second slower than Tom's, even though, at forty-five, I was seven years older than he. So I just *knew* I'd beat him on the second attempt if I ran really, really hard, which I did for a solid ten yards, at which point my left hamstring muscle, which had not yet shifted into Spring Mode from Mail-Reading Mode, went, and I quote, "pop."

I had to be helped off the field. I was in considerable pain, and I 23 was obviously not going to be able to walk right for weeks. The other guys were very sympathetic, especially Tom, who took the time to call me at home, where I was sitting with an ice pack on my leg and twenty-three Advil in my bloodstream, so he could express his concern.

"Just remember," he said, *"you didn't beat my time."* 24

There are countless other examples of guys rising to meet pointless 25 challenges. Virtually all sports fall into this category, as well as a large part of U.S. foreign policy ("I'll bet you can't capture Manuel Noriega!"[6] "Oh YEAH??")

Guys Do Not Have a Rigid and Well-Defined Moral Code

This is not the same as saying that guys are bad. Guys *are* capable of 26 doing bad things, but this generally happens when they try to be Men and start becoming manly and aggressive and stupid. When they're being just plain guys, they aren't so much actively *evil* as they are *lost*. Because guys have never really grasped the Basic Human Moral Code, which I believe was invented by women millions of years ago when all the guys were out engaging in some other activity, such as seeing who

6. Manuel Noriega (b. 1934), Panamanian dictator removed from power by armed U.S. intervention in 1989.

could burp the loudest. When they came back, there were certain rules that they were expected to follow unless they wanted to get into Big Trouble, and they have been trying to follow these rules ever since, with extremely irregular results. Because guys have never *internalized* these rules. Guys are similar to my small auxiliary backup dog, Zippy, a guy dog[7] who has been told numerous times that he is *not* supposed to (1) get into the kitchen garbage or (2) poop on the floor. He knows that these are the rules, but he has never really understood *why*, and sometimes he gets to thinking: Sure, I am *ordinarily* not supposed to get into the garbage, but obviously this rule is not meant to apply when there are certain extenuating[8] circumstances, such as (1) somebody just threw away some perfectly good seven-week-old Kung Pao Chicken, and (2) I am home alone.

27   And so when the humans come home, the kitchen floor has been transformed into Garbage-Fest USA, and Zippy, who usually comes rushing up, is off in a corner disguised in a wig and sunglasses, hoping to get into the Federal Bad Dog Relocation Program before the humans discover the scene of the crime.

28   When I yell at him, he frequently becomes so upset that he poops on the floor.

29   Morally, most guys are just like Zippy, only taller and usually less hairy. Guys are *aware* of the rules of moral behavior, but they have trouble keeping these rules in the forefronts of their minds at certain times, especially the present. This is especially true in the area of faithfulness to one's mate. I realize, of course, that there are countless examples of guys being faithful to their mates until they die, usually as a result of being eaten by their mates immediately following copulation. Guys outside of the spider community, however, do not have a terrific record of faithfulness.

30   I'm not saying guys are scum. I'm saying that many guys who consider themselves to be committed to their marriages will stray if they are confronted with overwhelming temptation, defined as "virtually any temptation."

---

7. I also have a female dog, Earnest, who *never* breaks the rules [Barry's note].

8. I am taking some liberties here with Zippy's vocabulary. More likely, in his mind, he uses the term *mitigating* [Barry's note].

Okay, so maybe I *am* saying guys are scum. But they're not *mean-spirited* scum. And few of them—even when they are out of town on business trips, far from their wives, and have a clear-cut opportunity—will poop on the floor.   31

XXXXXXXXXXXXXXXXXX FOR DISCUSSION XXXXXXXXXXXXXXXXXX

1. Dave Barry starts to DEFINE what he means by "guys" and then says, "I don't know. I haven't thought that much about it" (5). He's being funny, right? Does his extended definition of guys lead you to believe that he has thought intelligently about what guys are? How so?

2. Males, says Barry, can be divided into two basic classes. What are the distinguishing characteristics of each?

3. To write his humor column, Barry doesn't ever need to buy a new, more powerful computer. But he says in paragraph 13 that he will do it anyway. What principle of guy behavior is he illustrating here?

4. In paragraph 16, Barry develops his definition of guys as neat-stuff-buying animals by CONTRASTING them with women. How does he define women in this paragraph? Do you think his definition is accurate? If not, how would you revise what he says?

5. Do you agree or disagree with Barry that "virtually all" sports fall into the "pointless challenge" category (25)? What about U.S. foreign policy?

6. Guys, says Barry, "are similar" to his dog Zippy (26). This is a definition by ANALOGY. What specific characteristics, according to Barry, do guys and Zippy have in common? Do you think the COMPARISON is just? In what one way does even Barry admit that unleashed guys are generally superior to dogs?

XXXXXXXXXXXXX STRATEGIES AND STRUCTURES XXXXXXXXXXXXX

1. Beginning in paragraph 6, Barry DEFINES guys by citing three of their distinguishing "guy characteristics." What are they? How does Barry use these characteristics to organize his entire essay?

2. The basic logic behind defining something is to put it into a set of ever-narrower categories or classes. In Barry's definition, guys belong to the class of males who like challenges. But this is still a very broad class, so Barry narrows it down further by adding the qualifier "pointless." Following this logic, why can't the high-school poet in paragraph 19 be defined as a guy? Point out other examples of this logic of elimination in Barry's essay, such as his definition of guys as "scum" in paragraph 31.

3. Why do you think Barry is so careful to specify the gender of God in paragraph 17? What AUDIENCE does he have in mind here?

4. From reading Barry's title, you might expect "Guys vs. Men" to be primarily a COMPARISON AND CONTRAST essay. Where and *why* does Barry switch from drawing a comparison between the two kinds of males to defining one kind to the exclusion of the other?

5. Barry's humor often comes from his use of specific EXAMPLES, as in "violent crime, war, spitting, and ice hockey" (3). Point out where his scrupulous examples help define specific terms. What would this essay be like *without* all the examples? What is Barry's PURPOSE in being (or pretending to be) so rigorous?

⟩⟩⟩⟩⟩⟩⟩⟩⟩⟩⟩⟩ WORDS AND FIGURES OF SPEECH ⟨⟨⟨⟨⟨⟨⟨⟨⟨⟨⟨⟨

1. How does Barry DEFINE "male" (2)? How about "manly" (2)? So, according to Barry's definitions, is "manly male" an OXYMORON? (Barry would probably make a joke here, one that would not be complimentary either to males or to oxen.)

2. How would you define "loons" (3)? How do they differ from "goobers" (3)?

3. Why does Barry capitalize "Big Trouble" in paragraph 26?

4. Translate the following Barry phrase into standard English: "one humongous and spectacularly gizmo-intensive item of hardware" (15).

⟩⟩⟩⟩⟩⟩⟩⟩⟩⟩⟩⟩⟩⟩⟩⟩⟩ FOR WRITING ⟨⟨⟨⟨⟨⟨⟨⟨⟨⟨⟨⟨⟨⟨⟨⟨⟨⟨

1. Rightly or wrongly, Barry has been called a humorist. How would you DEFINE one? Make a list of the distinguishing characteristics that make a good humorist in your view, and give EXAMPLES of humorists who you think represent these characteristics (you might want to use Barry as an example, or not).

2. How would you define "guys"? What characteristics does Barry leave out? Can a female be a "guy" (as in "When we go shopping, my grandmother is just one of the guys")? Write an essay setting forth your definition of "guys." Or choose another gender term (such as *men, women, girls,* or *girlfriends*), and write an essay that gives "another way to look" at gender through your definition of this term.

TANYA BARRIENTOS

Se Habla Español

Tanya Barrientos (b. 1960) is a novelist, a columnist for the *Philadelphia Inquirer*, and a writing teacher at Arcadia University. She is the author of *Frontera Street* (2002) and *Family Resemblance* (2003). "Se Habla Español" is from a 2004 issue of the bilingual magazine *Latina*. The title refers to the sign, often seen in store windows, announcing "Spanish is spoken" here. In this essay, Barrientos raises a basic question of self-definition and ethnic identity: Can a woman born in Guatemala who grew up in the United States speaking English instead of Spanish be legitimately considered a *Latina*?

XXXXXXXXXXXXXXXXXXXXXXXXXXXXXXXXXXXXXXXXXXXXXXXXXXXXXXXXXXX

The man on the other end of the phone line is telling me the classes I've called about are first-rate: native speakers in charge, no more than six students per group. I tell him that will be fine and yes, I've studied a bit of Spanish in the past. He asks for my name and I supply it, rolling the double "r" in "Barrientos" like a pro. That's when I hear the silent snag, the momentary hesitation I've come to expect at this part of the exchange. Should I go into it again? Should I explain, the way I have to half a dozen others, that I am Guatemalan by birth but *pura gringa*[1] by circumstance?

This will be the sixth time I've signed up to learn the language my parents speak to each other. It will be the sixth time I've bought work-books and notebooks and textbooks listing 501 conjugated verbs in alphabetical order, in hopes that the subjunctive tense will finally take root in my mind. In class I will sit across a table from the "native speaker," who will wonder what to make of me. "Look," I'll want to say

1. *Gringa*, which is the feminine form of *gringo*, is used to refer to someone of non-Latino background.

(but never do). "Forget the dark skin. Ignore the obsidian eyes. Pretend I'm a pink-cheeked, blue-eyed blonde whose name tag says 'Shannon.'" Because that is what a person who doesn't innately know the difference between *corre, corra,* and *corrí* is supposed to look like, isn't it?

3   I came to the United States in 1963 at age 3 with my family and immediately stopped speaking Spanish. College-educated and seamlessly bilingual when they settled in west Texas, my parents (a psychology professor and an artist) wholeheartedly embraced the notion of the American melting pot. They declared that their two children would speak nothing but *inglés.* They'd read in English, write in English, and fit into Angelo society beautifully.

4   It sounds politically incorrect now. But America was not a hyphenated nation back them. People who called themselves Mexican Americans or Afro-Americans were considered dangerous radicals, while law-abiding citizens were expected to drop their cultural baggage at the border and erase any lingering ethnic traits.

5   To be honest, for most of my childhood I liked being the brown girl who defined expectations. When I was 7, my mother returned my older brother and me to elementary school one week after the school year had already begun. We'd been on vacation in Washington, D.C., visiting the Smithsonian, the Capitol, and the home of Edgar Allan Poe. In the Volkswagen on the way home, I'd memorized "The Raven," and I would recite it with melodramatic flair to any poor soul duped into sitting through my performance. At the school's office, the registrar frowned when we arrived.

6   "You people. Your children are always behind, and you have the nerve to bring them in late?"

7   "My children," my mother answered in a clear, curt tone, "will be at the top of their classes in two weeks."

8   The registrar filed our cards, shaking her head.

9   I did not live in an neighborhood with other Latinos, and the public school I attended attracted very few. I saw the world through the clear, cruel vision of a child. To me, speaking Spanish translated into being poor. It meant waiting tables and cleaning hotel rooms. It meant being left off the cheerleading squad and receiving a condescending smile from the guidance counselor when you said you planned on

becoming a lawyer or a doctor. My best friends' names were Heidi and Leslie and Kim. They told me I didn't seem "Mexican" to them, and I took it a as compliment. I enjoyed looking into the faces of Latino store clerks and waitresses and, yes, even our maid and saying *"Yo no hablo español."* It made me feel superior. It made me feel American. It made me feel white. I thought if I stayed away from Spanish, stereotypes would stay away from me.

Then came the backlash. During the two decades when I'd   10 worked hard to isolate myself from the stereotype I'd constructed in my own head, society shifted. The nation changed its views on ethnic identity. College professors started teaching history through African American and Native American eyes. Children were told to forget about the melting pot and picture America as a multicolored quilt instead. Hyphens suddenly had muscle, and I was left wondering where I fit in.

The Spanish language was supposedly the glue that held the new   11 Latino community together. But in my case it was what kept me apart. I felt awkward among groups whose conversations flowed in and out of Spanish. I'd be asked a question in Spanish and I'd have to answer in English, knowing this raised a mountain of questions. I wanted to call myself Latina, to finally take pride, but it felt like a lie. So I set out to learn the language that people assumed I already knew.

After my first set of lessons, I could function in the present tense.   12 *"Hola, Paco. ¿Qué tal? ¿Qué color es tu cuaderno? El mío es azul."* My vocabulary built quickly, but when I spoke, my tongue felt thick inside my mouth—and if I needed to deal with anything in the future or the past, I was sunk. I enrolled in a three-month submersion program in Mexico and emerged able to speak like a sixth-grader with a solid C average. I could read Gabriel García Márquez[2] with a Spanish-English dictionary at my elbow, and I could follow 90 percent of the melodrama on any given telenovela.[3] But true speakers discover my limitations the moment I stumble over a difficult construction, and that is when I get

---

2. Columbian novelist and short-story writer (b. 1928).

3. Spanish-language TV soap opera.

the look. The one that raises the wall between us. The one that makes me think I'll never really belong. Spanish has become a litmus test showing how far from your roots you've strayed.

13   My bilingual friends say I make too much of it. They tell me that my Guatemalan heritage and unmistakable Mayan features are enough to legitimize my membership in the Latin American club. After all, not all Poles speak Polish. Not all Italians speak Italian. And as this nation grows more and more Hispanic, not all Latinos will share one language. But I don't believe them.

14   There must be other Latinas like me. But I haven't met any. Or, I should say, I haven't met any who have fessed up. Maybe they are secretly struggling to fit in, the same way I am. Maybe they are hiring tutors and listening to tapes behind locked doors, just like me. I wish we all had the courage to come out of our hiding places and claim our rightful spot in the broad Latino spectrum. Without being called hopeless gringas. Without having to offer apologies or show remorse.

15   If it will help, I will go first.

16   *Aquí estoy.* Spanish-challenged and *pura* Latina.

XXXXXXXXXXXXXXXXXX **For Discussion** XXXXXXXXXXXXXXXXXX

1. Tanya Barrientos is not a native speaker of Spanish, though both of her parents were. Why didn't they encourage her to learn the language as a child? Should they have? Why or why not?

2. According to Barrientos, how were "hyphenated" Americans in general DEFINED when she and her family first came to the United States from Guatemala in 1963 (4)? How did young Barrientos herself define Latinos who spoke Spanish?

3. In the decades following her arrival in the United States, says Barientos, societal views toward ethnic identity "shifted" (10). What are some of the more significant aspects of that shift, according to Barrientos?

4. In your opinion, is Barrientos a legitimate member of "the Latin American club" (13)? That is, can she and others with similar backgrounds rightfully define themselves as Latinas or Latinos? Why or why not?

XXXXXXXXXXXXX **STRATEGIES AND STRUCTURES** XXXXXXXXXXXXX

1. What is Barrientos's PURPOSE in "Se Habla Español": to explain why she does not speak Spanish with the fluency of a native speaker? to persuade readers that she is a true Latina? to DEFINE the ambiguous condition of being both "Spanish-challenged and *pura* Latina" (16)? Explain.

2. Is Barrientos's essay aimed mainly at a multilingual AUDIENCE or a largely English-speaking one? Why do you say so?

3. Throughout her essay, how does Barrientos use the Spanish language itself to help define who and what she is? Give several examples that you find particularly effective.

4. Where and how does Barrientos construct a stereotypical definition of "Latin American?" Where and how does she reveal the shortcomings of this definition?

5. Barrientos's essay includes many NARRATIVE elements. What are some of them, and how do they help her to define herself and her condition?

XXXXXXXXXXXX **WORDS AND FIGURES OF SPEECH** XXXXXXXXXXXX

1. Once defined as a "melting-pot," the United States, says Barrientos, is now a "multicolored quilt" (10). What are some of the implications of this shift in METAPHORS for national diversity?

2. When Barrientos refers to the Spanish language as "glue," is she avoiding CLICHÉS or getting stuck in one (11)? Explain.

3. In printing, a *stereotype* was a cast metal plate used to reproduce blocks of type or crude images. How does this early meaning of the term carry over into the modern definition as Barrientos uses it (10)?

4. Barrientos sometimes groups herself with other "Latinos," sometimes with other "Latinas" (9, 14). Why the difference?

XXXXXXXXXXXXXXXXXXX **FOR WRITING** XXXXXXXXXXXXXXXXXXXXXXX

1. Write a paragraph or two about an incident in which someone DEFINED you on the basis of your choice of words, your accent, or some other aspect of your speech or appearance.

2. Write an essay about your experience learning, or attempting to learn, a language other than your native tongue—and how that experience affected your own self-definition or cultural identity.

SALLY SATEL

ADDICTION DOESN'T DISCRIMINATE?

Sally Satel (b. 1956) is a psychiatrist, medical writer, and resident scholar at the American Enterprise Institute, a conservative think tank devoted to research in public policy. She studied at Cornell University and the University of Chicago before earning an M.D. from Brown University and completing her residency in psychiatry at Yale. In 2006, suffering from renal failure, she received a kidney from the writer Virginia Postrel. Satel is the author of several books, including *Drug Treatment: The Case for Coercion* (1999); *PC, M.D.: How Political Correctness Is Corrupting Medicine* (2001); and (with Jonathan Klick) *The Health Disparities Myth: Diagnosing the Treatment Gap* (2006). First published in the *New York Times* in 2008, "Addiction Doesn't Discriminate?" challenges those who would define addiction as a disease to which we are all equally vulnerable.

XXXXXXXXXXXXXXXXXXXXXXXXXXXXXXXXXXXXXXXXXXXXXXXXXXXXXXXXXX

1   We've heard it before. "Drug abuse is an equal opportunity destroyer." "Drug addition is a bipartisan illness." "Addiction does not discriminate; it doesn't care if you are rich or poor, famous or unknown, a man or woman, or even a child."

2   The phrase "addiction doesn't care" is not meant to remind us that addiction casts a long shadow—everyone knows that. Rather, it is supposed to suggest that any individual, no matter who, is vulnerable to the ravages of drugs and alcohol.

3   The same rhetoric has been applied to other problems, including child abuse, domestic violence, alcoholism—even suicide. Don't stigmatize the afflicted, it cautions; you could be next. Be kind, don't judge.

4   The democratization of addiction may be an appealing message, but it does not reflect reality. Teenagers with drug problems are not like

those who never develop them. Adults whose problems persist for decades manifest different traits from those who get clean.

So while anyone can theoretically become an addict, it is more likely the fate of some, among them women sexually abused as children; truant and aggressive young men; children of addicts; people with diagnosed depression and bipolar illness; and groups including American Indians and poor people.

Attitudes, values, and behaviors play a potent role as well.

Imagine two people trying cocaine, just to see what it is like. Both are 32-year-old men with jobs and families. One snorts a line, loves it and asks for more. The other also loves it but pushes it away, leaves the party, and never touches it again. Different values? Different tolerance for risk? Many factors may distinguish the two cocaine lovers, but only one is at risk for a problem.

Asking for more drug is no guarantee of being seduced into routine use. But what if it happens? Jacob Sullum, a senior editor at *Reason* magazine, has interviewed many users who became aware that they were sliding down the path to addiction.

"It undermined their sense of themselves as individuals in control of their own destinies," Mr. Sullum wrote in his 2003 book, *Saying Yes: In Defense of Drug Use*. "And so they stopped."

I only read about these people. Patients who come to our methadone clinic are there, obviously, because they're using. The typical patient is someone who has been off heroin for a while (maybe because life was good for a while, maybe because there was no access to drugs, maybe because the boss did urine testing) and then resumed.

But the road to resumption was not unmarked. There were signs and exit ramps all along the way. Instead of heeding them, our patients made small, deliberate choices many times a day—to be with other users, to cop drugs for friends, to allow themselves to become bored—and soon there was no turning back.

Addiction does indeed discriminate. It "selects" for people who are bad at delaying gratification and gauging consequences, who are impulsive, who think they have little to lose, have few competing interests, or are willing to lie to a spouse.

13   Though the National Institute on Drug Abuse describes addiction as a "chronic and relapsing disease," my patients, seeking help, are actually the exception. Addiction is not an equal opportunity destroyer even among addicts because, thankfully, most eventually extricate themselves from the worst of it.

14   Gene Heyman, a lecturer and research psychologist at Harvard Medical School and McLean Hospital, said in an interview that "between 60 and 80 percent of people who meet criteria for addiction in their teens and twenties are no longer heavy, problem users by their thirties." His analysis of large national surveys revealed that those who kept using were almost twice as likely to have a concurrent psychiatric illness.

15   None of this is to deny that brain physiology plays a meaningful role in becoming and staying addicted, but that is not the whole story.

16   "The culture of drink endures because it offers so many rewards: confidence for the shy, clarity for the uncertain, solace to the wounded and lonely," wrote Pete Hamill in his memoir, *A Drinking Life*. Heroin and speed helped the screenwriter Jerry Stahl, author of *Permanent Midnight*, attain the "the soothing hiss of oblivion."

17   If addiction were a random event, there would be no logic to it, no desperate reason to keep going back to the bottle or needle, no reason to avoid treatment.

18   The idea that addiction doesn't discriminate may be a useful story line for the public—if we are all under threat, then we all should urge our politicians to support more research and treatment for addiction. There are good reasons to campaign for those things, but not on the basis of a comforting fiction.

XXXXXXXXXXXXXXXXXXXX **FOR DISCUSSION** XXXXXXXXXXXXXXXXXXXX

1. As a psychiatrist, Sally Satel thinks the conventional wisdom that addiction is a disease that everyone is vulnerable to "does not reflect reality" (4). What is the reality of addiction, as Satel DEFINES it?

2. According to Satel, who is most likely to become an addict?

3. What particular "attitudes, values, and behaviors" also characterize addicts, in Satel's view (6)?

4. According to the research that Satel cites, what characteristic often distinguishes addicts who stay addicted from those who "extricate themselves from the worst of it" (13)?

XXXXXXXXXXXXX **STRATEGIES AND STRUCTURES** XXXXXXXXXXXXX

1. Before developing her own DEFINITION of addiction, Satel cites the common, opposing view that addiction is a condition or disease that "doesn't discriminate." Is this an effective strategy? Why or why not?

2. Satel's THESIS, or main point, in defining (or redefining) her subject is that addiction is a disease that "selects" for certain types of people (12). Satel is also making a point, however, about addiction research and treatment. What is that secondary point, and how does she make it?

3. Although Satel cites research in her field, her definition of what makes a true addict relies heavily on her personal experience at a methadone clinic. How compelling do you find this EVIDENCE? Why?

4. In paragraph 17, Satel refers to the "logic" of addiction. On what assumption, or premise, is her ARGUMENT based here? Explain.

5. Although Satel says "there are good reasons" to campaign for addiction research and treatment, she does not say what those reasons are (18). Should she have? Why or why not?

6. Compared to the view that addiction doesn't discriminate, Satel's way of defining addiction places more responsibility on the person who makes many "small, deliberate choices" along the way (11). What positive message does this imply? How might this message relate to Satel's PURPOSE for writing this essay? Explain.

7. Satel COMPARES AND CONTRASTS chronic addicts with those who recover. How and how well does she use this comparison to support her definition of addiction?

XXXXXXXXXXXXX **WORDS AND FIGURES OF SPEECH** XXXXXXXXXXXXX

1. What does Satel mean by the "democratization of addiction" (4)? Why might some people find this view of addiction to be "appealing" or "comforting" (4, 18)?

2. Explain the PUN in the phrase "road to resumption" (11).

3. In what sense does addiction "select" for certain types of victims (12)?

4. Why does Satel use terms like "story line" and "fiction"—rather than "falsehood" or "lie"—to characterize the common DEFINITION of addiction as a disease that doesn't discriminate (18)?

XXXXXXXXXXXXXXXXXXXX **FOR WRITING** XXXXXXXXXXXXXXXXXXXXXX

1. In a paragraph or two, DEFINE addiction as you understand it. Be sure to say whether you consider it to be a choice or a disease.

2. Do some research on the topic and, following the guidelines in the Appendix, write an essay defining some form of drug addiction, alcoholism, eating disorder, or other mental illness. Include in your definition suggestions for how the condition can be prevented and treated.

SEAN B. CARROLL

THE EVO DEVO REVOLUTION

Sean B. Carroll (b. 1960) is a professor of molecular biology and genetics at the University of Wisconsin, Madison, and an investigator at the Howard Hughes Medical Institute. Carroll specializes in the study of genes that control animal body patterns and that play major roles in the evolution of animal diversity. He is the author of *Endless Forms Most Beautiful: The New Science of Evo Devo* (2005) and *The Making of the Fittest* (2006). "The Evo Devo Revolution" is a complete section from the introduction to *Endless Forms Most Beautiful,* which takes its title from Charles Darwin's observation in *On the Origin of Species* (1859) that evolution produces "endless forms most beautiful and most wonderful." In this selection, Carroll defines a new field of scientific study and its importance as a source of genetic evidence for "the logic and order underlying the generation of animal form."

XXXXXXXXXXXXXXXXXXXXXXXXXXXXXXXXXXXXXXXXXXXXXXXXXXXXXXXXXXXXX

Everyone knew that genes must be at the center of the mysteries of both development and evolution. Zebras look like zebras, butterflies look like butterflies, and we look like we do because of the genes we carry. The problem was that there were very few clues as to which genes mattered for the development of any animal.

The long drought in embryology[1] was eventually broken by a few brilliant geneticists who, while working with the fruit fly, the workhorse of genetics for the past eighty years, devised schemes to find the genes that controlled fly development. The discovery of these genes and their study in the 1980s gave birth to an exciting new vista on development and revealed a logic and order underlying the generation of animal form.

1

2

---

1. The study of the development of living organisms immediately after conception.

3   Almost immediately after the first sets of fruit fly genes were characterized came a bombshell that triggered a new revolution in evolutionary biology. For more than a century, biologists had assumed that different types of animals were genetically constructed in completely different ways. The greater the disparity in animal form, the less (if anything) the development of two animals would have in common at the level of their genes. One of the architects of the Modern Synthesis, Ernst Mayr,[2] had written that "the search for homologous genes is quite futile except in very close relatives." But contrary to the expectations of *any* biologist, most of the genes first identified as governing major aspects of fruit fly body organization were found to have exact counterparts that did the same thing in most animals, including ourselves. This discovery was followed by the revelation that the development of various body parts such as eyes, limbs, and hearts, vastly different in structure among animals and long thought to have evolved in entirely different ways, was also governed by the same genes in different animals. The comparison of developmental genes between species became a new discipline at the interface of embryology and evolutionary biology—evolutionary developmental biology, or "Evo Devo" for short.

4   The first shots in the Evo Devo revolution revealed that despite their great differences in appearance and physiology, all complex animals—flies and flycatchers, dinosaurs and trilobites, butterflies and zebras and humans—share a common "tool kit" of "master" genes that govern the formation and patterning of their bodies and body parts. I'll describe the discovery of this tool kit and the remarkable properties of these genes in detail in chapter 3. The important point to appreciate from the outset is that its discovery shattered our previous notions of animal relationships and of what made animals different, and opened up a whole new way of looking at evolution.

2. One of the twentieth century's most important evolutionary biologists (1904–2005). Mayr's ideas contributed to the Modern Synthesis, which refers to the combination of the then-distant fields of evolution and genetics in the early twentieth century to create the current model of evolutionary biology.

We now know from sequencing the entire DNA of species (their   5
genomes) that not only do flies and humans share a large cohort of developmental genes, but that mice and humans have virtually identical sets
of about 29,000 genes, and that chimps and humans are nearly 99 percent identical at the DNA level. These facts and figures should be hum-
bling to those who wish to hold humans above the animal world and not
as an evolved part of it. I wish the view I heard expressed by Lewis
Black, the stand-up comedian, was more widely shared. He said he
won't even debate evolution's detractors because "we've got the fossils.
We win." Well put, Mr. Black, but there is far more to rely on than just
fossils.

Indeed, the new facts and insights from embryology and Evo   6
Devo devastate lingering remnants of stale anti-evolution rhetoric
about the utility of intermediate forms or the probability of evolving
complex structures. We now understand how complexity is constructed from a single cell into a whole animal. And we can see, with
an entirely new set of powerful methods, how modifications of development increase complexity and expand diversity. The discovery of
the ancient genetic tool kit is irrefutable evidence of the descent and
modification of animals, including humans, from a simple common
ancestor. Evo Devo can trace the modifications of structures through
vast periods of evolutionary time—to *see* how fish fins were modified
into limbs in terrestrial vertebrates, how successive rounds of innova-
tion and modification crafted mouthparts, poison claws, swimming
and feeding appendages, gills, and wings from a simple tubelike walking leg, and how many kinds of eyes have been constructed beginning
with a collection of photosensitive cells. The wealth of new data from
Evo Devo paints a vivid picture of how animal forms are made and
evolve.

XXXXXXXXXXXXXXXXXX **For Discussion** XXXXXXXXXXXXXXXXXXXX

1. What is "Evo Devo" as Sean B. Carroll DEFINES it?

2. What once universal assumption about how animals of "different types" are
formed does the new science of Evo Devo call into question (3)? Explain.

3. According to Carroll, what were the two most revolutionary discoveries of Evo Devo researchers? How and when were they made?

4. Carroll claims that the "wealth of new data" provided by Evo Devo research "devastates" "anti-evolution rhetoric" (6). Is he right? Explain.

XXXXXXXXXXXXXX **STRATEGIES AND STRUCTURES** XXXXXXXXXXXXXX

1. "The Evo Devo Revolution" is a section from the introduction to a book on a new field of science. For what PURPOSE would the author of such a study be likely to use the strategy of DEFINITION in his introduction?

2. Carroll defines Evo Devo but not such related fields as embryology or evolutionary biology. Why not? What assumptions is he making about his AUDIENCE?

3. Evo Devo, says Carroll, stands "at the interface of embryology and evolutionary biology" (3). What particular defining characteristics does he use to distinguish the new field of study from older fields? Aside from giving distinguishing characteristics, how else does Carroll extend his basic definition of Evo Devo?

4. Although Carroll defines Evo Devo in general terms, he does not define, in any detail, one of its most important elements—the genetic "tool kit." Why do you think he waits until a later chapter to specify the tool kit's "remarkable properties" (4)? Should he have specified them here? Why or why not?

5. Carroll's definition of Evo Devo traces a NARRATIVE of the field's development. Is this an effective strategy for defining a new scientific field? Why or why not?

XXXXXXXXXXXXX **WORDS AND FIGURES OF SPEECH** XXXXXXXXXXXXX

1. Is Carroll justified in referring to the emergence of Evo Devo as a "revolution"? Why or why not?

2. Point out several places in his introduction where Carroll develops the revolution METAPHOR.

3. Why does Carroll put "tool kit" and "master" genes in quotation marks (4)?

4. What are the implications of a scientist's characterizing evolutionary forms as "beautiful"—in addition to logical and orderly?

5. Look up any of the following words with which you're not on easy terms: "drought" (2), "disparity" (3), "futile" (3), "homologous" (3), "cohort" (5), "detractors" (5), "remnants" (6), "irrefutable" (6), "appendages" (6). Are these terms specific to Carroll's field? Or might they be commonly found in academic writing? Explain.

XXXXXXXXXXXXXXXXXXX **FOR WRITING** XXXXXXXXXXXXXXXXXXXX

1. In a paragraph or two, DEFINE the basic concept of biological evolution.

2. Write an essay defining an important "revolution" in science, industry, business, music, art, theater, or some other field. Be sure to research your topic thoroughly, following the guidelines in the Appendix at the end of this book.

GEETA KOTHARI

IF YOU ARE WHAT YOU EAT,
THEN WHAT AM I?

Geeta Kothari teaches writing at the University of Pittsburgh. She is
the editor of *Did My Mama Like to Dance? and Other Stories about
Mothers and Daughters* (1994). Her stories and essays have appeared in
various newspapers and journals, including the *Toronto South Asian
Review* and the *Kenyon Review*, from which these complete selections
of a longer article are taken. Kothari's essay (1999) presents a problem
in personal definition. The Indian food she eats, says Kothari, is not
really Indian like her mother's; nor is the American food she eats really
American like her husband's. So, Kothari wonders, if we are defined
by what we eat—and the culture it represents—how are she and her
culture to be defined?

XXXXXXXXXXXXXXXXXXXXXXXXXXXXXXXXXXXXXXXXXXXXXXXXXXXXXXX

> To belong is to understand the tacit codes of the people you
> live with.
>
> MICHAEL IGNATIEFF, *Blood and Belonging*

1   The first time my mother and I open a can of tuna, I am nine years
old. We stand in the doorway of the kitchen, in semidarkness, the
can tilted toward daylight. I want to eat what the kids at school eat:
bologna, hot dogs, salami—foods my parents find repugnant because
they contain pork and meat byproducts, crushed bone and hair glued
together by chemicals and fat. Although she has never been able to tolerate the smell of fish, my mother buys the tuna, hoping to satisfy my
longing for American food.

2   Indians, of course, do not eat such things.

The tuna smells fishy, which surprises me because I can't remem- 3
ber anyone's tuna sandwich actually smelling like fish. And the tuna in
those sandwiches doesn't look like this, pink and shiny, like an internal
organ. In fact, this looks similar to the bad foods my mother doesn't
want me to eat. She is silent, holding her face away from the can while
peering into it like a half-blind bird.

"What's wrong with it?" I ask. 4

She has no idea. My mother does not know that the tuna everyone 5
else's mothers made for them was tuna *salad*.

"Do you think it's botulism?" 6

I have never seen botulism, but I have read about it, just as I have 7
read about but never eaten steak and kidney pie.

There is so much my parents don't know. They are not like other 8
parents, and they disappoint me and my sister. They are supposed to
help us negotiate the world outside, teach us the signs, the clues to
proper behavior: what to eat and how to eat it.

We have expectations, and my parents fail to meet them, especially 9
my mother, who works full-time. I don't understand what it means, to
have a mother who works outside and inside the home; I notice only the
ways in which she disappoints me. She doesn't show up for school plays.
She doesn't make chocolate-frosted cupcakes for my class. At night, if I
want her attention, I have to sit in the kitchen and talk to her while she
cooks the evening meal, attentive to every third or fourth word I say.

We throw the tuna away. This time my mother is disappointed. I 10
go to school with tuna eaters. I see their sandwiches, yet cannot explain
the discrepancy between them and the stinking, oily fish in my mother's
hand. We do not understand so many things, my mother and I.

When we visit our relatives in India, food prepared outside the house is 11
carefully monitored. In the hot, sticky monsoon months in New Delhi
and Bombay, we cannot eat ice cream, salad, cold food, or any fruit that
can't be peeled. Definitely no meat. People die from amoebic dysentery,
unexplained fevers, strange boils on their bodies. We drink boiled water
only, no ice. No sweets except for jalebi, thin fried twists of dough in
dripping hot sugar syrup. If we're caught outside with nothing to drink,

Fanta, Limca, Thums Up (after Coca-Cola is thrown out by Mrs. Gandhi[1]) will do. Hot tea sweetened with sugar, served with thick creamy buffalo milk, is preferable. It should be boiled, to kill the germs on the cup.

12   My mother talks about "back home" as a safe place, a silk cocoon frozen in time where we are sheltered by family and friends. Back home, my sister and I do not argue about food with my parents. Home is where they know all the rules. We trust them to guide us safely through the maze of city streets for which they have no map, and we trust them to feed and take care of us, the way parents should.

13   Finally, though, one of us will get sick, hungry for the food we see our cousins and friends eating, too thirsty to ask for a straw, too polite to insist on properly boiled water.

14   At my uncle's diner in New Delhi, someone hands me a plate of aloo tikki, fried potato patties filled with mashed channa dal and served with a sweet and a sour chutney. The channa, mixed with hot chilies and spices, burns my tongue and throat. I reach for my Fanta, discard the paper straw, and gulp the sweet orange soda down, huge drafts that sting rather than soothe.

15   When I throw up later that day (or is it the next morning, when a stomachache wakes me from deep sleep?), I cry over the frustration of being singled out, not from the pain my mother assumes I'm feeling as she holds my hair back from my face. The taste of orange lingers in my mouth, and I remember my lips touching the cold glass of the Fanta bottle.

16   At that moment, more than anything, I want to be like my cousins.

17   In New York, at the first Indian restaurant in our neighborhood, my father orders with confidence, and my sister and I play with the silverware until the steaming plates of lamb biryani arrive.

---

1. Coca-Cola was banned in India for twenty years beginning in the mid-1970s, when Indira Gandhi was prime minister, because the company would not reveal its formula to the government. Fanta, Limca, and Thums Up are other soft drinks popular in India.

What is Indian food? my friends ask, their noses crinkling up.   18

Later, this restaurant is run out of business by the new Indo-Pak-   19
Bangladeshi combinations up and down the street, which serve similar
food. They use plastic cutlery and Styrofoam cups. They do not distinguish between North and South Indian cooking, or between Indian, Pakistani, and Bangladeshi cooking, and their customers do not care. The
food is fast, cheap, and tasty. Dosa, a rice flour crepe stuffed with masala
potato, appears on the same trays as chicken makhani.

Now my friends want to know, Do you eat curry at home?   20

One time my mother makes lamb vindaloo for guests. Like dosa,   21
this is a South Indian dish, one that my Punjabi[2] mother has to learn
from a cookbook. For us, she cooks everyday food—yellow dal, rice,
chapati, bhaji. Lentils, rice, bread, and vegetables. She has never
referred to anything on our table as "curry" or "curried," but I know
she has made chicken curry for guests. Vindaloo, she explains, is a curry
too. I understand then that curry is a dish created for guests, outsiders,
a food for people who eat in restaurants.

I look around my boyfriend's freezer one day and find meat: pork chops,   22
ground beef, chicken pieces, Italian sausage. Ham in the refrigerator,
next to the homemade bolognese sauce. Tupperware filled with chili
made from ground beef and pork.

He smells different from me. Foreign. Strange.   23

I marry him anyway.   24

He has inherited blue eyes that turn gray in bad weather, light   25
brown hair, a sharp pointy nose, and excellent teeth. He learns to make
chili with ground turkey and tofu, tomato sauce with red wine and por-
tobello mushrooms, roast chicken with rosemary and slivers of garlic
under the skin.

He eats steak when we are in separate cities, roast beef at his   26
mother's house, hamburgers at work. Sometimes I smell them on his
skin. I hope he doesn't notice me turning my face, a cheek instead of my
lips, my nose wrinkled at the unfamiliar, musky smell.

---

2. Native of the state of Punjab, in northern India.

27 I have inherited brown eyes, black hair, a long nose with a crooked bridge, and soft teeth with thin enamel. I am in my twenties, moving to a city far from my parents, before it occurs to me that jeera, the spice my sister avoids, must have an English name. I have to learn that haldi = turmeric, methi = fenugreek. What to make with fenugreek, I do not know. My grandmother used to make methi roti for our breakfast, cornbread with fresh fenugreek leaves served with a lump of homemade butter. No one makes it now that she's gone, though once in a while my mother will get a craving for it and produce a facsimile ("The cornmeal here is wrong") that only highlights what she's really missing: the smells and tastes of her mother's house.

28 I will never make my grandmother's methi roti or even my mother's unsatisfactory imitation of it. I attempt chapati; it takes six hours, three phone calls home, and leaves me with an aching back. I have to write translations down: jeera = cumin. My memory is unreliable. But I have always known garam = hot.

29 If I really want to make myself sick, I worry that my husband will one day leave me for a meat-eater, for someone familiar who doesn't sniff him suspiciously for signs of alimentary infidelity.

30 Indians eat lentils. I understand this as absolute, a decree from an unidentifiable authority that watches and judges me.

31 So what does it mean that I cannot replicate my mother's dal? She and my father show me repeatedly, in their kitchen, in my kitchen. They coach me over the phone, buy me the best cookbooks, and finally write down their secrets. Things I'm supposed to know but don't. Recipes that should be, by now, engraved on my heart.

32 Living far from the comfort of people who require no explanation for what I do and who I am, I crave the foods we have shared. My mother convinces me that moong is the easiest dal to prepare, and yet it fails me every time: bland, watery, a sickly greenish yellow mush. These imperfect imitations remind me only of what I'm missing.

33 But I have never been fond of moong dal. At my mother's table it is the last thing I reach for. Now I worry that this antipathy toward dal

signals something deeper, that somehow I am not my parents' daughter, not Indian, and because I cannot bear the touch and smell of raw meat, though I can eat it cooked (charred, dry, and overdone), I am not American either.

I worry about a lifetime purgatory in Indian restaurants where I will complain that all the food looks and tastes the same because they've used the same masala.

34

XXXXXXXXXXXXXXXXX **FOR DISCUSSION** XXXXXXXXXXXXXXXXX

1. How does Geeta Kothari DEFINE "meat byproducts" (1)? Why is she so concerned with different kinds of food? Who or what is she trying to define?

2. How do Kothari and her mother define "back home" in paragraph 12?

3. Why is Kothari angry with herself in paragraphs 15 and 16? What "rule" has she momentarily forgotten?

4. Kothari's friends ask for a definition of Indian food in paragraph 18. How does she answer them (and us)?

5. What's wrong, from Kothari's POINT OF VIEW, with the "Indo-Pak-Bangladeshi" restaurants that spring up in her neighborhood (19)?

6. Marriage is an important event in anyone's biography, but why is it especially central in Kothari's case?

XXXXXXXXXXXXX **STRATEGIES AND STRUCTURES** XXXXXXXXXXXX

1. How does Kothari go about answering the DEFINITION question that she raises in her title? Give specific examples of her strategy. What point is she making in answering this question?

2. Why does Kothari recall the tuna incident in paragraphs 1 through 10? What does this ANECDOTE illustrate about her relationship with her mother? About her "Americanness"?

3. Why does Kothari introduce the matter of heredity in paragraphs 25 and 27? How do these paragraphs anticipate the reference to "something deeper" in paragraph 33?

4. According to Kothari, is culture something we inherit or something we learn? How do paragraphs 31 and 32 contribute to her definition of culture?

5. Kothari's essay is largely made up of specific EXAMPLES, particularly culinary ones. How do they relate to the matters of personal and cultural identity she is defining? Should she have made these connections more explicit? Why?

XXXXXXXXXXXX **WORDS AND FIGURES OF SPEECH** XXXXXXXXXXXX

1. What is usually meant by the saying "You are what you eat"? How is Kothari interpreting this adage?

2. What does Kothari mean by "alimentary infidelity" (29)? What ANALOGY is she drawing here?

3. What is "purgatory" (34)? Why does Kothari end her essay with a reference to it?

4. *Synecdoche* is the FIGURE OF SPEECH that substitutes a part for the whole. What part does Kothari substitute for what whole when she uses the phrase "meat-eater" (29)? Can we say her entire essay works by means of synecdoche? Why or why not?

5. Kothari provides both the Indian word and its English equivalent for several terms in her essay—"garam" for "hot" in paragraph 28, for example. Why? What do these translations contribute to her DEFINITION of cultural identity? Point out several other examples in the text.

XXXXXXXXXXXXXXXXXXX **FOR WRITING** XXXXXXXXXXXXXXXXXXXX

1. Write an extended DEFINITION of your favorite type of food. Be sure to relate how your food and food customs help to define who you are.

2. Food and food customs are often regional, as Kothari points out. Write an essay in which you define one of the following: New England, Southern, or Midwestern cooking; California cuisine; Tex-Mex, French, or Chinese food; fast food; or some other distinctive cuisine.

3. Write an essay about food and eating in your neighborhood. Use the food customs of specific individuals and groups to help define them—personally, ethnically, socially, or in some other way.

CHAPTER NINE

CAUSE AND EFFECT

XXXXXXXXXXXXXXXXXXXXXXXXXXXXXXXXXXXXXXXXXXXXXXXXXXXXXXXXXXX

If you were at home on vacation and read in the morning paper that the physics building at your school had burned, your first questions would probably be about the *effects* of the fire: "How much damage was done? Was anyone hurt?" Once you knew what the effects were—the building burned to the ground, but the blaze broke out in the middle of the night when nobody was in it—your next questions would likely be about the *causes*: "What caused the fire? Lightning? A short circuit in the electrical system? An arsonist's match?"

If the newspaper went on to say that the fire was set by your old roommate, Larry, you would probably have some more questions, such as "Why did Larry do it? What will happen to Larry as a result of his action?" When you write a CAUSE AND EFFECT* essay, you answer fundamental questions like these about the *what* and *why* of an event or phenomenon. The questions may be simple, but answering them fully and adequately may require you to consider a variety of possible causes and effects—and to distinguish one type of cause from another.

In our example, Larry struck a match, which caused the building to catch fire. That effect in turn caused another effect—the building burned down. Larry's striking the match is the *immediate* cause of the fire—the one closest to the event in time. A *remote* cause, on the other hand, might be Larry's failure on a physics test two weeks earlier. But which cause is the *main* cause, the most important one, and which causes are less important or *contributing*? Was Larry depressed and angry before he took the physics test? What were his feelings toward his father, the physics professor? Often you will need to run through a whole chain of related causes and effects like these before deciding to emphasize one or two.

---

*Words printed in SMALL CAPITALS are defined in the Glossary.

How do you make sure that the causes you choose to emphasize actually account for the particular event or phenomenon you're analyzing? Two basic conditions have to be met to prove causation. A main cause has to be both *necessary* and *sufficient* to produce the effect in question. That is, it must be shown that (1) the alleged cause *always* accompanies the effect and (2) that the alleged cause (and only the alleged cause) has the power to produce the effect. Let's look at these conditions in the following passage from a 2009 article on statistics in the *New York Times*. The author is recalling a time before the Salk vaccine defeated polio:

> For example, in the late 1940s, before there was a polio vaccine, public health experts in America noted that polio cases increased in step with the consumption of ice cream and soft drinks. . . . Eliminating such treats was even recommended as part of an anti-polio diet. It turned out that polio outbreaks were most common in the hot months of summer, when people naturally ate more ice cream. . . .
>
> STEVE LOHR, "For Today's Graduates, Just One Word: Statistics"

The health experts who thought that ice cream and soft drinks *caused* polio failed to distinguish between causation and mere correlation. Although outbreaks of polio always seemed to be accompanied by an increase in the consumption of cool summer treats, ice cream and soft drinks did not actually have the power to cause the disease. And though the *heat* was the clear cause of the increased consumption of ice cream and soft drinks, Jonas Salk and his colleagues suspected that normal summer weather was not sufficiently harmful to produce the paralyzing disease. Eventually they isolated the *main* cause—the poliomyletis virus. This tiny killer met both tests for true causality: it appeared in every case, and it was the only factor capable of producing the dire effect ascribed to it. It was both necessary and sufficient.

As Dr. Salk knew from the beginning, mere sequences in time— cases of polio increase as, or immediately after, the consumption of ice cream and soft drinks increases—is not sufficient to prove causation. This mistake in causal analysis is commonly referred to as the *post hoc, ergo propter hoc* FALLACY, Latin for "after this, therefore because of this."

Salk understood the two conditions that must be met before causation may be accurately inferred.

These two conditions can be expressed as a simple formula:

B cannot have happened without A;
Whenever A happens, B must happen.

When we are dealing with psychological and social rather than purely physical factors, the main cause may defy simple analysis. Or it may turn out that there are a number of causes working together. Suppose we looked for an answer to the following question: Why does Maria smoke? This looks like a simple question, but it is a difficult one to answer because there are so many complicated reasons why a young woman like Maria might smoke. The best way for a writer to approach this kind of causal analysis might be to list as many of the contributing causes as he or she can turn up:

MARIA: I smoke because I need to do something with my hands.
MARIA'S BOYFRIEND: Maria smokes because she thinks it looks sophisticated.
MEDICAL DOCTOR: Because Maria has developed a physical addiction to tobacco.
PSYCHOLOGIST: Because of peer pressure.
SOCIOLOGIST: Because Maria is Hispanic; in recent years tobacco companies have spent billions in advertising to attract more Hispanic smokers.

When you list particular causes like this, be as specific as you can. When you list effects, be even more specific. Instead of saying "Smoking is bad for your health," be particular. In an essay on the evils of tobacco, for example, Erik Eckholm provides a grim effect. "The most potentially tragic victims," he writes, "are the infants of mothers who smoke. They are more likely than the babies of nonsmoking mothers to be born underweight and thus to encounter death or disease at birth or during the initial months of life."

In singling out the effects of smoking upon unwitting infants, Eckholm uses an EXAMPLE that might be just powerful enough to convince some smokers to quit. Though your examples may not be as dramatic as Eckholm's, they must be specific to be powerful. And they must be selected with your AUDIENCE in mind. In the previous example, Eckholm addresses young women who smoke. If he were writing for a middle-aged audience, however, he might point out that the incidence of cancer and heart disease is 70 percent higher among one-pack-a-day men and women than among nonsmokers.

Your audience needs to be taken into account when you analyze causes and effects because, among other reasons, you are usually making an ARGUMENT about the causes or effects of a phenomenon or event. Thus, you must carry the reader step by step through some kind of proof. Your explanation may be instructive, amusing, or startling; but if your analysis is to make the point you want it to make, it must also be persuasive.

A BRIEF GUIDE TO WRITING A CAUSE-AND-EFFECT ESSAY

When you analyze causes or effects, you explain why something happened or what its results are. So as you write a cause-and-effect essay, you need to identify your subject and indicate which you plan to emphasize—causes or effects. Malindi Corbel makes these basic moves at the beginning of her essay in this chapter:

> Smoking is on the defensive everywhere. . . . Nobody disputes anymore that it's deadly. Yet look around: Kids are lighting up! Why?
>
> MALINDI CORBEL, "The Deadly Allure of a Smoke"

Corbel identifies the subject of her analysis (smoking among kids) and indicates that she plans to emphasize the causes of this phenomenon ("Why?").

Whether you emphasize causes or effects, remember that the effect of one event may become the cause of a subsequent event, forming a CAUSAL CHAIN that you will need to follow link by link in order to fully analyze why something happened. For example: Two cars collide, killing the driver of the second car. The first driver's excessive speed is the cause; the death of the second driver is the effect. That effect, in turn, causes another dire effect—the children of the second driver grow up in an orphanage.

The following guidelines will help you make the basic moves of cause and effect as you draft an essay. They will also help you come up with your subject, explain why you're analyzing causes and effects, distinguish between different kinds of causes, and present your analysis in an organized way.

Coming Up with a Subject

To find a subject for an essay that analyzes cause and effect, start with your own curiosity—about the physical world or about history, sociology, or any other field that interests you. Look for specific phenomena or events—global warming, President Truman's decision to drop the atomic bomb on Japan in 1945, growing obesity among young children in the United States—that you find intriguing. In order to narrow your subject down into a topic that is specific enough to investigate within the time allotted by your instructor, begin by asking yourself what its main causes (or effects) are likely to be. You may need to do some research on your subject; you'll find guidelines for doing research in the Appendix of this book.

Considering Your Purpose and Audience

As you examine particular causes and effects, think about why you're analyzing them. Is your PURPOSE to inform your readers? Amuse them? ARGUE that one set of causes (or effects) is more likely than another? One writer, for example, may try to persuade readers that autism is caused by inherent biological factors, while another writer might argue for environmental causes.

You'll also need to consider the AUDIENCE you want to reach. Are your readers already familiar with the topic, or will you need to provide background information and DEFINE unfamiliar terms? Are they likely to be receptive to the point you're making, or opposed to it? An article on the causes of autism may have a very different slant depending on whether the intended readers are parents of autistic children, medical doctors, psychologists, or the general public.

Generating Ideas: Asking Why, What, and What If

When you want to figure out what caused something, the essential question to ask is *why*. Why does a curve ball drop as it crosses home plate? Why was Napoleon defeated in his march on Russia in 1812? If, on the other hand, you want to figure out what the effects of something are, or will be, then the basic question to ask is *what*, or *what if*. What will happen if the curve ball fails to drop? What effect did the weather have on Napoleon's campaign?

As you ask *why* or *what* about your subject, keep in mind that a single effect may have multiple causes, or vice versa. Be sure to write down as many causes or effects as you can think of. If you were to ask why the U.S. financial system almost collapsed in the fall of 2008, for example, you would need to consider a number of possible causes, including greed on Wall Street, vastly inflated real estate values, subprime mortgages offered to unqualified borrowers, and a widespread credit crunch. Similarly, if you were analyzing the effects of the financial crisis, you would need to consider several of them, such as widespread unemployment, falling stock prices, and the loss of consumer confidence.

Templates for Analyzing Causes and Effects

The following templates can help you to generate ideas for a cause-and-effect essay and then to start drafting. Don't take these as formulas where you just have to fill in the blanks. There are no easy formulas for good writing. But these templates can help you plot out some of the key moves of cause and effect and thus may serve as good starting points.

> ‣ The main cause/effect of X is _____.
>
> ‣ X would also seem to have a number of contributing causes, including _____, _____, and _____.

> ➤ One effect of X is _____, which in turn causes _____.

> ➤ Some additional effects of X are _____, _____, and _____.

> ➤ Although the causes of X are not known, we can speculate that a key factor is _____.

> ➤ X cannot be attributed to mere chance or coincidence because _____.

> ➤ Once we know what causes X, we are in a position to say that _____.

For more techniques to help you generate ideas and start writing, see Chapter 1.

Stating Your Point

As you draft an essay that analyzes cause and effect tell readers at the outset whether you are going to focus on causes or effects—or both. Also make clear what your main point, or THESIS, is. For example, if you are analyzing the causes of the financial meltdown in the United States in 2008, you might signal your main point in a THESIS STATE-MENT like this one:

> The main cause of the financial meltdown in the United States in 2008 was the freezing of credit, which made it impossible for anyone to borrow money.

Once you've stated your thesis, you're ready to present the analysis that supports it.

Distinguishing One Type of Cause from Another

To help your reader understand how a number of causes work together to produce a particular effect, you can distinguish among causes based on their relative importance in producing the effect and on their occurrence in time.

MAIN AND CONTRIBUTING CAUSES. The *main cause* is the one that has the greatest power to produce the effect. It must be both necessary to cause the effect and sufficient to do so. On August 1, 2007, a bridge collapsed on Interstate 35W in Minneapolis, Minnesota. Most investigators now agree that the main cause of the collapse was a flaw in the bridge's design. A *contributing cause* is a secondary cause—it helps to produce the effect but is not sufficient to do it alone. In the Minnesota bridge collapse, a contributing cause was the weight of construction supplies and equipment on the bridge at the time. Although it would have been wise to locate at least some of the construction equipment off the bridge, the added weight alone did not cause the collapse. As one investigator pointed out, "If the bridge had not been improperly designed, everybody says it would have held up that weight easily."

IMMEDIATE AND REMOTE CAUSES. The *immediate cause* is the one closest in time and most directly responsible for producing the effect, whereas *remote causes* are less apparent and more removed in time. The immediate cause of the financial meltdown of 2008 was the drying up of credit, but several remote causes were in play as well, such as subprime lending, the burst in the housing bubble, and recklessness on Wall Street.

Keep in mind, however, that these two ways of distinguishing causes aren't mutually exclusive. For example, the weight of the construction equipment on the bridge was both a contributing cause and an immediate one—though not the main cause, it immediately triggered the collapse of the bridge.

As you link together causes and effects, be careful not to confuse causation with coincidence. Just because one event (increased sales of soft drinks) comes before another (higher incidence of polio) does not mean the first event actually caused the second.

Organizing a Cause-and-Effect Essay

One way to present the effects of a given cause is by arranging them in chronological order. If you were tracing the effects of the credit crisis of 2008, for example, you would start with the crisis itself (the freezing of credit) and then proceed chronologically, detailing its effects in the order in which they occurred: first several investment banks collapsed, then the stock market plummeted, then the federal government stepped in with a massive bailout, and so on.

Reverse chronological order, in which you begin with a known effect and work backward through the possible causes, can also be effective. In the case of the 2007 Minnesota bridge collapse, you would start with the collapse itself (the known effect) and work backward in time through all of the possible causes: heavy construction equipment overloaded the bridge; the bridge structure was already weakened by corrosion; corrosion had not been discovered because of lack of inspections and maintenance; the capacity of the bridge was reduced at the outset by an error in design.

Often you will want to organize your analysis around various types of causes or effects. You might, for instance, explore the immediate cause before moving on to the remote causes, or vice versa. Or you might explore the contributing causes before the main cause, or vice versa. Whatever method you choose, be sure to organize your analysis in a way that makes the relationship between causes and effects clear to your reader.

EVERYDAY CAUSE AND EFFECT
A Poster

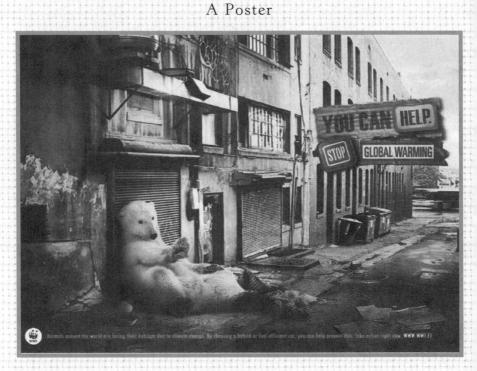

In this poster, sponsored by WWF, a world wildlife foundation, a polar bear sleeps on a seedy backstreet. The sign in the background suggests that one cause of his predicament is global warming. How has global warming left the bear on the skids? The fine print at the bottom of the poster explains: "Animals around the world are losing their habitats due to climate change. By choosing a hybrid or fuel efficient car, you can help prevent this. Take action right now." When you analyze causes and effects, follow the lead of the WWF: identify the particular effect you plan to look into (homeless polar bear) and the causes of this effect (loss of habitat due to global warming). You may also want to say how readers can prevent undesirable causes and their effects "right now"—so that polar bears and other animals can get back to their own neighborhoods.

RICHARD BERNSTEIN

THE GROWING COWARDICE
OF ONLINE ANONYMITY

Richard Bernstein (b. 1944) is a writer and book critic for the *New York Times*. He was *Time* magazine's first bureau chief to serve in Beijing, China. Bernstein is the author of numerous books, including *The Coming Conflict with China* (with Ross H. Monroe, 1997) and *Out of the Blue: The Story of September 11, 2001, from Jihad to Ground Zero* (2002). In "The Growing Cowardice of Online Anonymity," which appeared in the *International Herald Tribune* in 2008, Bernstein analyzes the effects, both personal and public, of ever more (and more slanderous) unsigned commentary on Internet sites like JuicyCampus.com.

XXXXXXXXXXXXXXXXXXXXXXXXXXXXXXXXXXXXXXXXXXXXXXXXXXXXXXXXXX

A nonymous sources are of course among the newspaper reporter's   1
best friends, without whom the cause of informing the public would
be severely set back.

But anonymity is also a tremendous aid to the resentful, the scan-   2
dalous and the cowardly, and the signs are that the tidal wave of anonymous comment made possible by the Internet is getting even bigger.

Or that, at any rate, is the impression that some recent reporting   3
on the rising vogue of college gossip Web sites would indicate.

One site, called JuicyCampus.com, which maintains message   4
boards on fifty-nine university campuses, has been attracting special
attention. As a recent article in *Radar* magazine put it, JuicyCampus.com is "a virtual bathroom wall upon which college students
across the country scrawl slurs, smears, and secrets, true or otherwise,
about their classmates."

In one feature, to take one modest example, the site asked for   5
replies to the question: Who are the sluttiest girls at Cornell? As of this

week, there were forty-seven postings in response, several of which gave names, apparently real ones.

6   All of the postings, needless to say, were anonymous, and that would appear to be the main point. It's bad enough to tarnish reputations and to publish insults, but if the people doing so identify themselves, there is at least a possibility of censure and accountability.

7   But the Internet not only makes the anonymous pejorative possible, it also bestows a certain techno glamour to what ought to be a guilty snicker. "C'mon, give us the juice," JuicyCampus.com says on its home page. "Posts are totally, 100 percent anonymous."

8   To be sure, there are often good reasons for anonymity: an employee of a corporation who uses a company intranet site to criticize senior management or to expose misbehavior at the top could fear for his job if he had to provide his name. In the news business, anonymous sources are ethically tricky, and the better papers handle them with care. But sources are commonly promised anonymity in exchange for information that would otherwise be kept secret.

9   But what the Internet and its cult of anonymity do is to provide a blanket sort of immunity for anybody who wants to say anything about anybody else, and it would be difficult in this sense to think of a more morally deformed exploitation of the concept of free speech.

10   An illustration, admittedly personal: Some time ago, I complained to Amazon.com about reviews posted on its site that offered what I felt were viciously negative and factually incorrect views of a book I had written.

11   Anybody of course is entitled to say what he or she wants about a book, including one written by me. It's the anonymity that Amazon grants to its reader-reviewers that I objected to, on the grounds that anybody who wants to say something nasty about somebody else's work ought to have the little bit of bravery needed to say it under his or her name.

12   When I wrote an e-mail to that effect to Jeffrey Bezos, Amazon's head and founder, I received a reply from Amazon's customer relations department saying that it allowed anonymous reviews as a way to encourage discussion. My reply was that, under the guise of encouraging free expression and unhindered debate, Amazon was really encouraging cowardice instead.

At the time I earned my living as a book critic for the *New York* 13
Times, which, needless to say, did not allow me to hide behind a shield
of anonymity in my own reviews. If I did have negative opinions about
a book—and I often did—I could be held responsible if, in fact, my
opinion was unjustified or unfair, or if I was avenging myself against
someone who had once written negatively about me.

Amazon's reader reviews are an old story. What is more recent is 14
the Internet's encouragement not just of scandalous and malignant personal commentary but of racist remarks of the sort that have for years
been branded outside the scope of acceptable discourse.

Reading JuicyCampus.com, for example, I found this remark, 15
anonymous of course: "Are there any black guys who aren't dumb
jocks?"

There was much worse stuff along these lines, unprintable here 16
even if only to illustrate how the grant of anonymity can lead to the
regression of public discourse. It almost makes one nostalgic for the days
when people who uttered racist slurs were all too happy to identify
themselves.

Concerned about the effect of JuicyCampus.com, prosecutors in 17
New Jersey have lately been investigating the site for consumer fraud—
on the grounds that it promises in its terms and conditions that no
offensive content will be allowed on the site even while it conspicuously
provides no enforcement of that promise.

In fact, to get JuicyCampus on the grounds of consumer fraud 18
would be a bit like the feds getting the gangster Al Capone[1] on tax evasion. But the law does make it very hard to hold Web sites legally
accountable, even for libelous opinions. This is because the U.S. government's Communications Decency Act grants immunity to Web site
operators for false or slanderous information they publish when that
information has been provided by third parties.

In other words, the law would seem to contain its own sort of 19
catch-22: the Web site itself can't be held legally responsible for defamatory statements, but neither can anybody else, since the defamatory
opinion was expressed anonymously.

---

1. Mafia leader (1899–1947) who was suspected, though never convicted, of racketeering
but did go to jail for tax evasion in 1931.

20   There have been other illustrations of the use of anonymity in recent years of questionable moral value. One was the decision of the publisher Random House a few years ago to publish the novel *Primary Colors*, the best-selling satire of Bill Clinton, by "Anonymous." It was a brilliant marketing ploy, the suggestion being that the author was an administration insider who could be harmed if his identity were known.

21   In fact, as it turned out, the book was written by Joe Klein, a very talented and worthy political journalist but one whose well-being did not require that his identity remain secret.

22   But that was in the days when there was a certain assumption that people who were anonymous needed to be so for some reason. Now that the Internet has made anonymity almost standard, it's unlikely that anybody would make that assumption anymore.

XXXXXXXXXXXXXXXXXXX **FOR DISCUSSION** XXXXXXXXXXXXXXXXXXX

1. According to Richard Bernstein, the Internet has made anonymity "almost standard" in online communication (22). Is this accurate? Why or why not?

2. In Bernstein's view, what are some "good reasons for anonymity" in the practice of journalism and elsewhere (8)? Why is Bernstein nonetheless dismayed by "the tidal wave of anonymous comment made possible by the Internet" (2)?

3. How does the federal Communications Decency Act, as Bernstein explains it, actually contribute to the problem of indecency in public communications (18)?

4. Do you agree with Bernstein that making anonymous comments that are "scandalous and malignant"—whether on the Internet or elsewhere—is an immoral act of cowardice (14)? Why or why not?

5. In military SLANG, a "catch-22" is a rule that prevents anyone from achieving the outcome that he or she has consulted the rules in order to achieve (19). What is the catch-22 in the law that Bernstein sites?

XXXXXXXXXXXXX **STRATEGIES AND STRUCTURES** XXXXXXXXXXXXX

1. Bernstein is writing for the general public, but what particular segment of that AUDIENCE is he appealing to when he analyzes JuicyCampus.com?

2. What is Bernstein's main point in analyzing the EFFECTS of websites such as JuicyCampus.com? Where does he state his THESIS most directly?

3. How and how effectively does Bernstein use the JuicyCampus.com EXAMPLE to illustrate the effects of online anonymity? How about the personal example of the "viciously negative" review of one of his books on Amazon.com (10)?

4. By suggesting that it is cowardly to make anonymous online comments that slander other people or their work, Bernstein makes a moral ARGUMENT. How effective is his use of CAUSE and effect in making this argument?

5. Except for suggesting that book reviews on Amazon.com be signed, Bernstein does not offer concrete solutions to the growing problem, as he sees it, of online anonymity. Would his essay be more effective if he had? Why or why not?

XXXXXXXXXXXX **WORDS AND FIGURES OF SPEECH** XXXXXXXXXXXX

1. Bernstein refers to the swelling volume of anonymous comments on the Internet as a "tidal wave" (2). Is this HYPERBOLE justified? Why or why not?

2. How accurate do you find Bernstein's ANALOGY, borrowed from *Radar* magazine, between the anonymous postings on JuicyCampus.com and the "slurs, smears, and secrets" scribbled on the wall of a public bathroom (4)?

3. In what way is calling "unprintable" racial and other slurs a "regression in public discourse" an UNDERSTATEMENT (16)? Why might Bernstein use this FIGURE OF SPEECH?

4. What is the TONE of Bernstein's essay? Approving? Angry? Sarcastic? Something else? Point to specific words and phrases that indicate the tone.

XXXXXXXXXXXXXXXXXXX **FOR WRITING** XXXXXXXXXXXXXXXXXXXXXXX

1. In a paragraph or two, analyze one or more of the EFFECTS that the right of freedom of speech has (or might have) on the daily life of someone living in the United States.

2. Aside from increased anonymity, what EFFECTS, positive and negative, has the increased power and presence of the Internet had on the ways we communicate? Write an essay analyzing one or more of these effects. Be sure to cite specific EXAMPLES, such as a particular website or bulletin board.

HENRY LOUIS GATES JR.

A Giant Step

Henry Louis Gates Jr. (b. 1950) is the director of the W. E. B. Du Bois
Institute for African and African American Research at Harvard. He is
the author or editor of many works on black literature and history and of
literary criticism, including *The Signifying Monkey: A Theory of Afro-
American Literary Criticism* (1988) and *The Norton Anthology of African
American Literature* (2nd ed., 2004). Gates grew up in Piedmont, West
Virginia, the small town depicted in this personal narrative from the
New York Times Magazine. He later incorporated this essay into *Colored
People: A Memoir* (1994), a book that tells of events and people in the
author's past from the standpoint of the present. But "A Giant Step" is
also an essay in cause and effect, playfully examining the social attitudes
that caused young Gates to be misdiagnosed as an "overachiever" and
showing how he sidestepped the potentially crippling effects of both
physical disability and racial prejudice on his way to becoming a distinguished scholar.

XXXXXXXXXXXXXXXXXXXXXXXXXXXXXXXXXXXXXXXXXXXXXXXXXXXXXXXXXX

1   "What's this?" the hospital janitor said to me as he stumbled over my
       right shoe.

2   "My shoes," I said.

3   "That's not a shoe, brother," he replied, holding it to the light.
       "That's a brick."

4   It *did* look like a brick, sort of.

5   "Well, we can throw these in the trash now," he said.

6   "I guess so."

7   We had been together since 1975, those shoes and I. They were
       orthopedic shoes built around molds of my feet, and they had a 2¼-inch
       lift. I had mixed feelings about them. On the one hand, they had given
       me a more or less even gait for the first time in 10 years. On the other

hand, they had marked me as a "handicapped person," complete with cane and special license plates. I went through a pair a year, but it was always the same shoe, black, wide, weighing about four pounds.

It all started 26 years ago in Piedmont, W. Va., a backwoods town   8
of 2,000 people. While playing a game of touch football at a Methodist summer camp, I incurred a hairline fracture. Thing is, I didn't know it yet. I was 14 and had finally lost the chubbiness of my youth. I was just learning tennis and beginning to date, and who knew where that might lead?

Not too far. A few weeks later, I was returning to school from   9
lunch when, out of the blue, the ball-and-socket joint of my hip sheared apart. It was instant agony, and from that time on nothing in my life would be quite the same.

I propped myself against the brick wall of the schoolhouse, where   10
the school delinquent found me. He was black as slate, twice my size, mean as the day was long and beat up kids just because he could. But the look on my face told him something was seriously wrong, and—bless him—he stayed by my side for the two hours it took to get me into a taxi.

"It's a torn ligament in your knee," the surgeon said. (One of the   11
signs of what I had—a "slipped epithysis"—is intense knee pain, I later learned.) So he scheduled me for a walking cast.

I was wheeled into surgery and placed on the operating table. As   12
the doctor wrapped my leg with wet plaster strips, he asked about my schoolwork.

"Boy," he said, "I understand you want to be a doctor."   13

I said, "Yessir." Where I came from, you always said "sir" to white   14
people, unless you were trying to make a statement.

Had I taken a lot of science courses?   15

"Yessir. I enjoy science."   16

"Are you good at it?"   17

"Yessir, I believe so."   18

"Tell me, who was the father of sterilization?"   19

"Oh, that's easy, Joseph Lister."   20

Then he asked who discovered penicillin.   21

22   Alexander Fleming.

23   And what about DNA?

24   Watson and Crick.

25   The interview went on like this, and I thought my answers might get me a pat on the head. Actually, they just confirmed the diagnosis he'd come to.

26   He stood me on my feet and insisted that I walked. When I tried, the joint ripped apart and I fell on the floor. It hurt like nothing I'd ever known.

27   The doctor shook his head. "Pauline," he said to my mother, his voice kindly but amused, "there's not a thing wrong with that child. The problem's psychosomatic. Your son's an overachiever."

28   Back then, the term didn't mean what it usually means today. In Appalachia,[1] in 1964, "overachiever" designated a sort of pathology: the overstraining of your natural capacity. A colored kid who thought he could be a doctor—just for instance—was headed for a breakdown.

29   What made the pain abate was my mother's reaction. I'd never, ever heard her talk back to a white person before. And doctors, well, their words were scripture.

30   Not this time. Pauline Gates stared at him for a moment. "Get his clothes, pack his bags—we're going to the University Medical Center," which was 60 miles away.

31   Not great news: the one thing I knew was that they only moved you to the University Medical Center when you were going to die. I had three operations that year. I gave my tennis racket to the delinquent, which he probably used to club little kids with. So I wasn't going to make it to Wimbledon.[2] But at least I wasn't going to die, though sometimes I wanted to. Following the last operation, which fitted me for a metal ball, I was confined to bed, flat on my back, immobilized by a complex system of weights and pulleys. It was six weeks of bondage—and bedpans. I spent

---

1. Rural area of the eastern United States that stretches from western New York to northern Alabama, Mississippi, and Georgia; named for the mountain range that passes through it.

2. The world's oldest tennis tournament, named for the London suburb in which it is held.

my time reading James Baldwin,[3] learning to play chess and quarreling daily with my mother, who had rented a small room—which we could ill afford—in a motel just down the hill from the hospital.

I think we both came to realize that our quarreling was a sort of   32
ritual. We'd argue about everything—what time of day it was—but the arguments kept me from thinking about that traction system.

I limped through the next decade—through Yale and Cambridge   33
. . . as far away from Piedmont as I could get. But I couldn't escape the pain, which increased as the joint calcified and began to fuse over the next 15 years. My leg grew shorter, as the muscles atrophied and the ball of the ball-and-socket joint migrated into my pelvis. Aspirin, then Motrin, heating pads and massages, became my traveling companions.

Most frustrating was passing store windows full of fine shoes. I   34
used to dream about walking into one of those stores and buying a pair of shoes. "Give me two pairs, one black, one cordovan," I'd say. "Wrap 'em up." No six-week wait as with the orthotics in which I was confined. These would be real shoes. Not bricks.

In the meantime, hip-joint technology progressed dramatically. But   35
no surgeon wanted to operate on me until I was significantly older, or until the pain was so great that surgery was unavoidable. After all, a new hip would last only for 15 years, and I'd already lost too much bone. It wasn't a procedure they were sure they'd be able to repeat.

This year, my 40th, the doctors decided the time had come.   36

I increased my life insurance and made the plunge.   37

The nights before my operations are the longest nights of my life—   38
but never long enough. Jerking awake, grabbing for my watch, I experience a delicious sense of relief as I discover that only a minute or two have passed. You never want 6 A.M. to come.

And then the door swings open. "Good morning, Mr. Gates," the   39
nurse says. "It's time."

The last thing I remember, just vaguely, was wondering where   40
amnesiac minutes go in one's consciousness, wondering if I experienced the pain and sounds, then forgot them, or if these were somehow blocked

3. African American novelist and essayist (1924–1987).

out, dividing the self on the operating table from the conscious self in the recovery room. I didn't like that idea very much. I was about to protest when I blinked.

41   "It's over, Mr. Gates," says a voice. But how could it be over? I had merely *blinked*. "You talked to us several times," the surgeon had told me, and that was the scariest part of all.

42   Twenty-four hours later, they get me out of bed and help me into a "walker." As they stand me on my feet, my wife bursts into tears. "Your foot is touching the ground!" I am afraid to look, but it is true: the surgeon has lengthened my leg with that gleaming titanium and chrome-cobalt alloy ball-and-socket-joint.

43   "You'll need new shoes," the surgeon says. "Get a pair of Dock-Sides; they have a secure grip. You'll need a ¾-inch lift in the heel, which can be as discreet as you want."

44   I can't help thinking about those window displays of shoes, those elegant shoes that, suddenly, I will be able to wear. Dock-Sides and sneakers, boots and loafers, sandals and brogues. I feel, at last, a furtive sympathy for Imelda Marcos,[4] the queen of soles.

45   The next day, I walk over to the trash can, and take a long look at the brick. I don't want to seem ungracious or unappreciative. We have walked long miles together. I feel disloyal, as if I am abandoning an old friend. I take a second look.

46   Maybe I'll have them bronzed.

4. Wife and government ambassador (b. 1929) of Philippine dictator Ferdinand Marcos. When his regime fell in 1986, evidence of the extravagance of Imelda Marcos's lifestyle included some 5,500 pairs of shoes.

XXXXXXXXXXXXXXXXXXX **For Discussion** XXXXXXXXXXXXXXXXXXXX

1. The doctor misdiagnoses Henry Louis Gates's injury in paragraph 11. What does he misdiagnose in paragraph 27? What CAUSES the doctor to make the first mistake? The second?

2. What EFFECTS did each misdiagnosis have on Gates? On his mother, Pauline?

3. "Where I came from," says Gates, "you always said 'sir' to white people, unless you were trying to make a statement" (14). What "statement," or point, is Gates making about race and "natural capacity" in this essay (28)?

4. Why does Gates think of having his old shoes "bronzed" (46)?

XXXXXXXXXXXXX **STRATEGIES AND STRUCTURES** XXXXXXXXXXXXX

1. What is the PURPOSE of Gates's essay? To inform? Persuade? Amuse? Something else? How do you know?

2. Gates takes a giant step when he gets a new hip. Up until then, however, his life story has been shaped around an earlier turning point. What is it? How do the two "steps" differ? What EFFECT does each have on his life?

3. Besides the effects of physical pain, young Gates also had to deal with the effects of racism. How does the incident involving his mother and the doctor who "interviews" him show both what he is up against and what strengths he has that will enable him to succeed (13–30)?

4. Gates begins his essay by relating the moment he threw away his orthopedic shoes—the end of the chain of events that begins with the incident he relates in paragraph 8. Is this an effective strategy for beginning this essay? Why or why not?

5. How much time elapses between when the "bricks" first go in the trash can and when Gates thinks of having them bronzed (5, 46)? How many distinct time periods does Gates identify? What do these elements of NARRATIVE contribute to Gates's essay?

XXXXXXXXXXXXX **WORDS AND FIGURES OF SPEECH** XXXXXXXXXXXXX

1. How, according to Gates, has the meaning of "overachiever" changed since 1964 (28)?

2. A "slipped epithysis" is a medical pathology (11). What kind of pathology is Gates referring to in paragraph 28?

3. What are the multiple meanings of each of the following words as Gates uses them here: "breakdown," "bondage," "limped" (28, 31, 33)?

4. Why does Gates profess to feel "disloyal" in paragraph 45? What does it mean to say to someone, "You've been a brick"?

XXXXXXXXXXXXXXXXXXXXX **For Writing** XXXXXXXXXXXXXXXXXXXXXX

1. Write a paragraph about an object you might like to have bronzed. Be sure to analyze the EFFECTS it has had on your life.

2. Write an essay that examines the effects of dealing with some kind of adversity. Those effects might be physical, psychological, or both. Give specific EXAMPLES, as Gates does when he tells about his mixed feelings toward his old shoes.

MALINDI CORBEL

THE DEADLY ALLURE OF A SMOKE

Malindi Corbel is a journalist working in Paris. A graduate of Bryn Mawr College, Corbel joined the editorial staff of the *International Herald Tribune* in 2004. She is also a researcher at France 24, an international news channel in Paris. Published in the *IHT* in 2007, "The Deadly Allure of a Smoke" examines Corbel's early addiction to tobacco—and the role in social survival that smoking played for her and her classmates. Analyzing the effects of her habit as well as the causes, Corbel also looks into ways of breaking it by "reinforcing an association" between smoking and "something very uncool."

XXXXXXXXXXXXXXXXXXXXXXXXXXXXXXXXXXXXXXXXXXXXXXXXXXXXXXXXXXXXX

S moking is on the defensive everywhere, even in places like France 1 where any restrictions on smoking only recently seemed laughable. Nobody disputes anymore that it's deadly. Yet look around: Kids are lighting up! Why?

I did it for one reason, and one reason only: to be cool. I'm not 2 sure it worked, but I'm relatively certain that it helped. I remember the first pack of smokes I bought. I felt like a criminal. I lit up and nearly stumbled from the headrush. It certainly wasn't the unacquired pleasure of, say, chocolate.

Feeling like a criminal was my goal, of course. As an adolescent, 3 confronted with so many insecurities, crises, and general angst, smoking was my banner. It was an act of rebellion against authority—parents above all. It showed that I was not afraid of taking risks, that I had an edge. I was above caring.

Conversely, before the health risks were established, kids probably 4 started smoking because their parents did, so it was the "grown-up" thing to do. I'm sure it was still regarded as cool.

5   And, of course, smoking is a social crutch. There was a huge difference for me between standing outside school by myself, feeling totally
vulnerable, or smoking a cigarette and being very clearly occupied.

6   For guys, smoking is proving they're macho, tough. No matter that
they start smoking precisely because they're too weak not to. The need
to be cool is nothing to trivialize. You do what you have to do for social
survival. The problem, of course, is that you're left with a dangerous
addiction.

7   In his book *The Tipping Point*, Malcolm Gladwell[1] argues that cool
kids are often smokers, so other teens emulate them. In other words, the
kids who really are cool—who are attractive, magnetic, and popular—
tend to smoke. So they become the connection between smoking
and cool.

8   That made me wonder, was I a cool person who smoked or a
smoker who wanted to be cool? Either way, the problem with the theory
is that it doesn't explain why the truly cool start to smoke.

9   I think the ultimate draw is that there really is something sexy
about smoking. I mean the simple physical act and motion of it. The
inhaling and exhaling. The drifting and curling and color of smoke.
Exploiting this is easy. Hollywood has obviously played a big role in creating and sustaining a glamorized image of smoking. From Humphrey
Bogart[2] to James Bond to Sharon Stone, the cigarette has long been one
of the cinema's favorite props.

10   Can smoking bans have an impact on teenage smoking rates? I
don't think so. They treat the symptom, not the cause. In fact, making a
bigger taboo of smoking might only make it more attractive. Bad things
will always have allure.

11   That's the problem. If the campaign against smoking is limited to
describing the evils of nicotine and restricting areas where it can be
done, it will likely remain cool.

1. Journalist (b. 1963) who writes about social behavior. *The Tipping Point* (2002) focuses
on the small changes that lead to major trends.

2. American film star (1899–1957) known for playing tough-guy roles. He died of
smoking-related cancer.

The real challenge is to convince kids—and adults—that smoking   12
is bad. Not bad as in good, but bad as in straight-up disgusting. This
can only be done by reinforcing an association with something very
uncool. My daily walk to the Metro,[3] when I pass my corner bar and see
who's already into a morning beer and butt, is helping me.

3. The Paris subway.

XXXXXXXXXXXXXXXXXXX **FOR DISCUSSION** XXXXXXXXXXXXXXXXXXXX

1. According to her analysis, why did Malindi Corbel become a smoker? Do
you think the CAUSES she cites for teenage smoking are sufficient to produce this
EFFECT? Explain.

2. Do you agree with Corbel that "there really is something sexy about smoking" (9)? Why or why not?

3. How is Corbel's daily walk past the corner bar "helping" her to deal with her
addiction (12)?

4. Corbel thinks that banning smoking will not affect "teenage smoking rates"
(10). Why not? Do you agree or disagree? Why?

XXXXXXXXXXXXX **STRATEGIES AND STRUCTURES** XXXXXXXXXXXXX

1. After announcing her topic (the CAUSES of teenage smoking) in the first paragraph of her essay, Corbel immediately identifies the main cause as she sees it.
Is this an effective organizational strategy, or should she have introduced the
main cause later in her analysis? Explain.

2. In paragraphs 7 and 8, how does Corbel address the possibility that what she
considers to be a cause may actually be an EFFECT? How does she resolve the
question she raises here?

3. In paragraph 10, Corbel concludes that the failure of anti-smoking campaigns
is due, in general, to an error in analyzing cause and effect. How accurate do
you find Corbel's analysis here? Explain.

4. What is Corbel's main point in analyzing what she considers to be the true
causes of smoking in teenagers? Where does she state her THESIS most directly?

5. Corbel's primary EVIDENCE in support of the ARGUMENT she makes in her
analysis is her own experience. How effective is this evidence in making her
case? Do you find her evidence persuasive? Why or why not?

XXXXXXXXXXXX **WORDS AND FIGURES OF SPEECH** XXXXXXXXXXXX

1. How does Corbel DEFINE *cool* (2, 4, 7, 8, 11)? How accurate is her definition?

2. In the case of addiction or disease, another name for effects is *symptoms*. How and where does Corbel use this SYNONYM?

3. The challenge, says Corbel, is to convince people "that smoking is bad. Not bad as in good, but bad as in straight-up disgusting" (12). What does this lesson in semantics say about the nature of Corbel's intended AUDIENCE?

XXXXXXXXXXXXXXXXXXXX **FOR WRITING** XXXXXXXXXXXXXXXXXXXXX

1. Make a list of all the potential CAUSES of smoking you can think of—that Corbel hasn't identified. Then choose one and write a brief paragraph analyzing how it leads to this effect.

2. At the end of her essay, Corbel asserts that "bad things will always have allure" (10). Identify another "bad" behavior besides smoking—perhaps drug abuse, binge drinking, or reckless driving—and write an essay that analyzes the causes and EFFECTS of this behavior among the people who engage in it.

MARISSA NUÑEZ

CLIMBING THE GOLDEN ARCHES

Marissa Nuñez (b. 1974) was nineteen when she wrote this essay about working for McDonald's. Nuñez started at the bottom (the "fried products" station) and worked her way up to management training. "Climbing the Golden Arches" not only tells the story of this ascent, it also analyzes the effects, personal and professional, of learning to do a job, dealing with the public, and being part of a team. An essay about making choices and becoming oneself, "Climbing the Golden Arches" originally appeared in 1997 in *New Youth Connections*, a magazine that publishes work by student authors.

XXXXXXXXXXXXXXXXXXXXXXXXXXXXXXXXXXXXXXXXXXXXXXXXXXXXXXXXX

Two years ago, while my cousin Susie and I were doing our Christmas shopping on Fourteenth Street, we decided to have lunch at McDonald's. 1

"Yo, check it out," Susie said. "They're hiring. Let's give it a try." I looked at her and said, "Are you serious?" She gave me this look that made it clear that she was. 2

After we ate our food, I went over to the counter and asked the manager for two applications. I took them back to our table and we filled them out. When we finished, we handed them in to the manager and he told us he'd be calling. 3

When Susie and I got home from school one day about a month later, my mother told us that McDonald's had called. They wanted to interview us both. We walked straight over there. They asked us why we wanted to work at McDonald's and how we felt about specific tasks, like cleaning the bathrooms. Then they told us to wait for a while. Finally the manager came out and said we had the job. 4

When we got outside, I looked over at Susie and laughed because I hadn't thought it would work. But I was happy to have a job. I would be 5 able to buy my own stuff and I wouldn't have to ask my mother for money anymore.

6   A week and a half later we went to pick up our uniforms (a blue and white striped shirt with blue pants or a blue skirt) and to find out what days we'd be working. We were also told the rules and regulations of the work place. "No stealing" was at the top of the list. A couple of the others were: "Leave all your problems at home" and "Respect everyone you work with."

7   Before you can officially start working, you have to get trained on every station. I started on "fried products," which are the chicken nuggets, chicken sandwiches, and Filet-o-Fish. Then I learned to work the grill, which is where we cook the burgers. Next was the assembly table where we put all the condiments (pickles, onions, lettuce, etc.) on the sandwiches. After all that, you have to learn the french fry station. Then finally you can learn to work the register. It was a month before I could be left alone at any station.

8   The most difficult thing was learning how to work the grill area. We use a grill called a clamshell which has a cover. It cooks the whole burger in forty-four seconds without having to flip it over. At first I didn't like doing this. Either I wouldn't lay the meat down right on the grill and it wouldn't cook all the way through or I would get burned. It took a few weeks of practicing before I got the hang of it. Now, after a lot more practice, I can do it with no problem.

9   My first real day at work was a lot of fun. The store had been closed for remodeling and it was the grand opening. A lot of people were outside waiting for the store to open. I walked around just to get the feel of things before we let the customers come in. I was working a register all by myself. My cousin was at the station next to me and we raced to see who could get the most customers and who could fill the orders in fifty-nine seconds. I really enjoyed myself.

10   Susie worked for only three months after our grand opening, but I stayed on. I liked having a job because I was learning how to be a responsible person. I was meeting all kinds of people and learning a lot about them. I started making friends with my co-workers and getting to know many of the customers on a first-name basis. And I was in charge of my own money for the first time. I didn't have to go asking

Mom for money when I wanted something anymore. I could just go and buy it.

Working at McDonald's does have its down side. The worst thing about the job is that the customers can be real jerks sometimes. They just don't seem to understand the pressure we're under. At times they will try to jerk you or make you look stupid. Or they will blame you for a mistake they made. If you don't watch and listen carefully, some of them will try to short-change you for some money.

The most obnoxious customer I ever had came in one day when it was really busy. She started saying that one of my co-workers had overcharged her. I knew that wasn't the case, so I asked her what the problem was. She told me to mind my own business, so I told her that she was my business. She started calling me a "Spanish b-tch" and kept on calling me names until I walked away to get the manager. If I had said anything back to her, I would have gotten in trouble.

Another time, a woman wanted to pay for a $2.99 Value Meal with a $100 bill. No problem, we changed it. She walked away from the counter with her food and then came back a few minutes later saying we had given her a counterfeit $20 bill in her change. We knew it was a lie. She wouldn't back down and even started yelling at the manager. He decided that we should call the cops and get them to settle it. That got her so mad that she threw her tray over the counter at us. Then she left. Of course, not all our customers are like this. Some are very nice and even take the time to tell the manager good things about me.

Sometimes we make up special events to make the job more fun for everyone. For example, we'll have what we call a "battle of the sexes." On those days, the women will work the grill area and the french fry station and all the other kitchen jobs and the men will work the registers. For some reason, the guys usually like to hide in the grill area. The only time they'll come up front and pretend they are working there is to see some female customer they are interested in. Still, they always act like working the grill is so much harder than working the register. I say the grill is no problem compared to working face-to-face with customers all day. After a battle of the sexes, the guys start to give the girls more respect because they see how much pressure we're under.

15   Every six months, our job performance is reviewed. If you get a good review, you get a raise and sometimes a promotion. After my first six months on the job I got a raise and was made a crew trainer. I became the one who would show new employees how to work the register, fry station, and yes, even the grill area.

16   When I made a year and a half, I was asked if I would like to become a manager-trainee. To move to that level, your performance has to be one hundred percent on all stations of the store. That means doing every job by the book with no shortcuts. The managers have to trust you, and you have to set a good example for your co-workers. I was so happy. Of course I said yes.

17   Now that I've been there two years, the managers trust me to run a shift by myself. I am working to get certified as a manager myself. To do that I have to attend a class and take an exam, and my manager and supervisor have to observe the way I work with everyone else and grade my performance. I have been in the program for nine months now and expect to get certified this month. I'm thinking about staying on full-time after I graduate from high school.

18   Working at McDonald's has taught me a lot. The most important thing I've learned is that you have to start at the bottom and work your way up. I've learned to take this seriously—if you're going to run a business, you need to know how to do all the other jobs. I also have more patience than ever and have learned how to control my emotions. I've learned to get along with all different kinds of people. I'd like to have my own business someday, and working at McDonald's is what showed me I could do that.

ⅩⅩⅩⅩⅩⅩⅩⅩⅩⅩⅩⅩⅩⅩⅩⅩⅩ **FOR DISCUSSION** ⅩⅩⅩⅩⅩⅩⅩⅩⅩⅩⅩⅩⅩⅩⅩⅩⅩⅩ

1. Marissa Nuñez had been working for McDonald's for two years when she wrote this essay. What EFFECTS did the experience have on her? What were some of the main CAUSES of those effects?

2. What particular work experiences did Nuñez find most instructive? How did they help bring about the personal changes she mentions?

3. What does Nuñez hope to become by working at McDonald's? How does she expect to accomplish that goal?

4. What do you think of Nuñez's response to the customer who calls her a name?

5. This essay was originally published in a magazine for teenagers. How does it appeal to the attitudes and values of that AUDIENCE?

XXXXXXXXXXXXX **STRATEGIES AND STRUCTURES** XXXXXXXXXXXXX

1. In paragraph 10, Nuñez sums up what she is learning in her new job. Where does she sum up what she *has* learned? If Nuñez had left out these two paragraphs, how would the focus and direction of her essay be changed?

2. How does the following sentence, which comes approximately halfway through her essay, help Nuñez to present different aspects of her work experience: "Working at McDonald's does have its down side" (11)? What sort of CAUSES is she analyzing now? What EFFECT do they have on her?

3. In addition to analyzing causes and effects, "Climbing the Golden Arches" tells a story. What is the role of the "most obnoxious customer" and of the woman who throws her tray (12–13)? What roles do these people play in her analysis of causes and effects?

4. Nuñez's essay covers a two-year work period that might be broken down into application, apprenticeship, "officially working," management training, future plans. Where does each stage begin and end? How effective do you find this strategy for organizing this analysis?

5. The phases of Nuñez's NARRATIVE resemble the steps or stages of much PROCESS ANALYSIS, or how-to writing (Chapter 6). Why is this? Besides examining the effects on her life of working at McDonald's, what process or processes does she analyze by telling her story?

XXXXXXXXXXXXX **WORDS AND FIGURES OF SPEECH** XXXXXXXXXXXXX

1. Why does Nuñez put "battle of the sexes" in quotation marks (14)?

2. What does the word "station" mean in connection with restaurant work (7)?

3. Explain the METAPHOR in Nuñez's title. What figurative meaning does the word "arches" take on in an account of someone's career goals? How about "golden" arches?

4. How does Nuñez DEFINE the word "fun" in this essay (9, 14)? What specific EXAMPLES does she give? What does her distinctive use of the word indicate about her attitude toward work?

XXXXXXXXXXXXXXXXXXX **For Writing** XXXXXXXXXXXXXXXXXXXX

1. Write a letter of application for your ideal job. Explain your qualifications, your career goals, and how you expect to achieve them.

2. Write a personal NARRATIVE of your work experience or some other experience that taught you a lot. Break it into phases, if appropriate, and explain how specific aspects and events of the experience caused you to become who you are. In other words, tell what happened to you, but also analyze the specific EFFECTS the experience had on you and your life.

MARJORIE AGOSÍN

ALWAYS LIVING IN SPANISH

Marjorie Agosín (b. 1955) is a poet and professor of Spanish at Wellesley College. Born in the United States, Agosín was raised in Chile, which she and her family fled in 1971, shortly before the military dictator Augusto Pinochet overthrew the socialist government of Salvador Allende. She is the author of seven books of poetry, including *Brujas y Aglo Más/Witches and Other Things* (1984), the first of her books to be published with English translations. In *A Cross and a Star* (1995), Agosín writes about her mother's childhood as a Jewish immigrant in a German community in Chile during World War II. "Always Living in Spanish," which first appeared in *Poets & Writers* magazine in 1999, is about the lasting effects of her own early life in a multilingual culture and her return to the United States. As she examines the causes and effects of her sense of isolation, she conveys the condition of being "an exile" living only "in translation."

XXXXXXXXXXXXXXXXXXXXXXXXXXXXXXXXXXXXXXXXXXXXXXXXXXXXXX

In the evenings in the northern hemisphere, I repeat the ancient ritual   1
that I observed as a child in the southern hemisphere: going out while
the night is still warm and trying to recognize the stars as it begins to
grow dark silently. In the sky of my country, Chile, that long and wide
stretch of land that the poets blessed and dictators abused, I could easily
name the stars: the three Marias, the Southern Cross, and the three
Lilies, names of beloved and courageous women.

But here in the United States, where I have lived since I was a   2
young girl, the solitude of exile makes me feel that so little is mine, that
not even the sky has the same constellations, the trees and the fauna the
same names or sounds, or the rubbish the same smell. How does one
recover the familiar? How does one name the unfamiliar? How can one

be another or live in a foreign language? These are the dilemmas of one who writes in Spanish and lives in translation.

3   Since my earliest childhood in Chile I lived with the tempos and the melodies of a multiplicity of tongues: German, Yiddish,[1] Russian, Turkish, and many Latin songs. Because everyone was from somewhere else, my relatives laughed, sang, and fought in a Babylon of languages. Spanish was reserved for matters of extreme seriousness, for commercial transactions, or for illnesses, but everyone's mother tongue was always associated with the memory of spaces inhabited in the past: the shtetl,[2] the flowering and vast Vienna avenues, the minarets of Turkey, and the Ladino[3] whispers of Toledo. When my paternal grandmother sang old songs in Turkish, her voice and body assumed the passion of one who was there in the city of Istanbul, gazing by turns toward the west and the east.

4   Destiny and the always ambiguous nature of history continued my family's enforced migration, and because of it I, too, became one who had to live and speak in translation. The disappearances, torture, and clandestine deaths in my country in the early seventies drove us to the United States, that other America that looked with suspicion at those who did not speak English and especially those who came from the supposedly uncivilized regions of Latin America. I had left a dangerous place that was my home, only to arrive in a dangerous place that was not: a high school in the same town of Athens, Georgia, where my poor English and my accent were the cause of ridicule and insult. The only way I could recover my usurped country and my Chilean childhood was by continuing to write in Spanish, the same way my grandparents had sung in their own tongues in diasporic[4] sites.

---

1. A Germanic language traditionally written in the Hebrew alphabet. It originated with the Ashkenazi Jews, who lived in the Rhineland valley in Germany and later spread through Europe and elsewhere.

2. Small town (Yiddish).

3. A nearly extinct language, based on archaic Spanish and spoken by Sephardic Jews who fled Spain and settled in North Africa, the Balkans, and the Middle East.

4. Relating to a diaspora, the spread or migration of a group of people away from a single geographic region.

The new and learned English language did not fit with the visceral emotions and themes that my poetry contained, but by writing in Spanish I could recover fragrances, spoken rhythms, and the passion of my own identity. Daily I felt the need to translate myself for the strangers living all around me, to tell them why we were in Georgia, why we ate differently, why we had fled, why my accent was so thick, and why I did not look Hispanic. Only at night, writing poems in Spanish, could I return to my senses, and soothe my own sorrow over what I had left behind.

This is how I became a Chilean poet who wrote in Spanish and lived in the southern United States. And then, one day, a poem of mine was translated and published in the English language. Finally, for the first time since I had left Chile, I felt I didn't have to explain myself. My poem, expressed in another language, spoke for itself . . . and for me.

Sometimes the austere sounds of English help me bear the solitude of knowing that I am foreign and so far away from those about whom I write. I must admit I would like more opportunities to read in Spanish to people whose language and culture is also mine, to join in our common heritage and in the feast of our sound. I would also like readers of English to understand the beauty of the spoken word in Spanish, that constant flow of oxytonic and paraoxytonic[5] syllables (*Verde que te quiero verde*),[6] the joy of writing—of dancing—in another language. I believe that many exiles share the unresolvable torment of not being able to live in the language of their childhood.

I miss that undulating and sensual language of mine, those baroque descriptions, the sense of being and feeling that Spanish gives me. It is perhaps for this reason that I have chosen and will always choose to write in Spanish. Nothing else from my childhood world remains. My country seems to be frozen in gestures of silence and oblivion. My relatives have died, and I have grown up not knowing a young generation of cousins and nieces and nephews. Many of my friends were disappeared,

5. Paraoxytonic: when the stress falls on the next to last syllable of a word. Oxytonic: when the stress falls on the last syllable of a word.

6. "Green, how I want you green" (Spanish). The opening line of a poem by Federico García Lorca; it illustrates oxytonic and paraoxytonic stress.

others were tortured, and the most fortunate, like me, became guardians of memory. For us, to write in Spanish is to always be in active pursuit of memory. I seek to recapture a world lost to me on that sorrowful afternoon when the blue electric sky and the Andean cordillera[7] bade me farewell. On that, my last Chilean day, I carried under my arm my innocence recorded in a little blue notebook I kept even then. Gradually that diary filled with memoranda, poems written in free verse, descriptions of dreams and of the thresholds of my house surrounded by cherry trees and gardenias. To write in Spanish is for me a gesture of survival. And because of translation, my memory has now become a part of the memory of many others.

9   Translators are not traitors, as the proverb says, but rather splendid friends in this great human community of language.

7. A mountain range (Spanish).

XXXXXXXXXXXXXXXXX **For Discussion** XXXXXXXXXXXXXXXXXXX

1. What were some of the circumstances that CAUSED Marjorie Agosín and her family to leave Chile and return to the United States to live permanently?

2. How did Agosín's experience of "enforced migration" relate to that of previous generations of her family (4)? How does she indicate this connection between the generations?

3. Although she has clearly mastered the English language, Agosín continues to write in her native Spanish. Why?

4. Agosín DESCRIBES English as an "austere" language (7). Do you think the characterization is justified? Why or why not?

5. What was Agosín's reaction when she discovered that one of her poems had been translated from Spanish into English? Why did she feel this way? What EFFECT did this event have upon her life?

XXXXXXXXXXXXX **Strategies and Structures** XXXXXXXXXXXXX

1. Agosín analyzes the EFFECTS of being moved, unwillingly, from one culture to another. What are some of those effects, and where does she identify them most clearly and directly?

2. Where and how does Agosín, a poet, show the effects that her experience had upon her use of language?

3. The main CAUSE of Agosín's sense of "exile" was her family's forced move, under an oppressive government, from Chile to the United States (2). What are some of the specific contributing causes of that sense of isolation? How do they contribute to this effect? Explain.

4. How and where does Agosín draw upon memory to help her examine the causes and effects of the events and feelings she is analyzing? How effective is this strategy? Explain.

5. Agosín ends her essay by celebrating the work of translators. What would be the effect if she left off this ending and concluded with paragraph 8 instead? Explain.

6. Point out specific places in the text where Agosín uses elements of NARRA-TIVE. In what way do these elements help to organize her analysis?

XXXXXXXXXXXX **WORDS AND FIGURES OF SPEECH** XXXXXXXXXXXX

1. In what sense does one live *in* a language? How does Agosín's use of the word "in" express her concerns with language in general?

2. *Translate* can refer to a move from one place to another as well as from one language to another. How and where does Agosín make use of this double meaning of the word and its related forms, such as *translation*?

3. Explain why "disappeared" as Agosín uses it in paragraph 8 is a *euphemism*, or polite phrase for a harsher term. How does she signal that she is using a euphemism here?

XXXXXXXXXXXXXXXXXXX **FOR WRITING** XXXXXXXXXXXXXXXXXXXX

1. Have you ever experienced a sense of exile or extreme isolation? Make a list of some of the most important CAUSES AND EFFECTS of this sense of exile.

2. Write an essay in which you analyze the causes and effects of someone's migration—yours, your family's, or that of a racial, ethnic, or political group. Draw on memory, if appropriate, but also do some research, including interviews with the people involved, if possible.

CHAPTER TEN

ARGUMENT

XXXXXXXXXXXXXXXXXXXXXXXXXXXXXXXXXXXXXXXXXXXXXXXXXXXXXXXX

A RGUMENT* is the strategic use of language to convince an AUDIENCE to agree with you on an issue or to act in a way that you think is right—or at least to hear you out, even if they disagree with you. You can convince people in three ways: (1) by appealing to their sense of reason, (2) by appealing to their emotions, and (3) by appealing to their sense of ethics (their standards of what constitutes proper behavior). The essays in this chapter illustrate all three appeals.

When you appeal to a reader's sense of reason, you don't simply declare, "Be reasonable; agree with what I say." You must supply solid EVIDENCE for your claim in the form of facts, examples, statistics, expert testimony, and personal experience. And you must use logical reasoning in presenting that evidence. There are basically two kinds of logical reasoning: INDUCTION and DEDUCTION. When we use induction, we reason from particulars to generalities: "You have a gun in your house; this whole neighborhood must be violent." When we deduce something, we reason from general premises to particular conclusions: "Guns are always dangerous; your family is in danger because you have one in your house." (A proposition can be logical, incidentally, without necessarily being true—as we shall see.)

Whether an argument uses induction or deduction, it must make an arguable statement or CLAIM. Take, for example, the idea that the world's leaders "should start an international campaign to promote imports from sweatshops." Nicholas D. Kristof argued in favor of this controversial proposition in an article published in the *New York Times* in 2002 entitled "Let Them Sweat." Kristof's essay is an instructive example of how all the techniques of argumentation can work together.

*Words printed in SMALL CAPITALS are defined in the Glossary.

Kristof knows that arguing in favor of sweatshops is likely to be an uphill battle. Like any writer with a point to make, especially a controversial one, he needs to win the reader's trust. One way to do this is to anticipate objections the reader might raise. So before anyone can accuse him of being totally out of his head for promoting sweatshops, Kristof writes: "The Gentle Reader will think I've been smoking Pakistani opium. But sweatshops are the only hope of kids like Ahmed Zia, 14, here in Attock, a gritty center for carpet weaving."

Right away, Kristof is hoping to convince his audience that they are hearing the words of an ethical person who deserves to be heeded. Next, he tugs at the readers' heartstrings:

> Ahmed earns $2 a day hunched over the loom, laboring over a rug that will adorn some American's living room. It is a pittance, but the American campaign against sweatshops could make his life much more wretched by inadvertently encouraging mechanization that could cost him his job.
>
> "Carpet-making is much better than farm work," Ahmed said. "This makes much more money and is more comfortable."

Underlying Kristof's emotional appeal in citing Ahmed's case is the logical claim that Ahmed's plight is representative of that of most factory workers in poor countries. "Indeed," writes Kristof, "talk to Third World factory workers and the whole idea of 'sweatshops' seems a misnomer. It is farmers and brick-makers who really sweat under the broiling sun, while sweatshop workers merely glow."

The same claim—that other cases are like this one—also lies behind Kristof's second example: "But before you spurn a shirt made by someone like Kamis Saboor, 8, an Afghan refugee whose father is dead and who is the sole breadwinner in the family, answer this question: How does shunning sweatshop products help Kamis? All the alternatives for him are worse." Kristof is appealing to the reader's emotions and sense of ethics, and he is using logical reasoning. If we grant Kristof's premise that in really poor countries "all the alternatives" to sweatshop labor are worse, we must logically concede his main point that, for these workers, "a sweatshop job is the first step on life's escalator" and, therefore, that sweatshops are to be supported.

Kristof has not finished marshaling his reasons and evidence yet. To strengthen his argument, he introduces another, broader example, one that Americans are more likely to be familiar with:

> Nike has 35 contract factories in Taiwan, 49 in South Korea, only three in Pakistan and none at all in Afghanistan—if it did, critics would immediately fulminate about low wages, glue vapors, the mistreatment of women.
>
> But the losers are the Afghans, and especially Afghan women. The country is full of starving widows who can find no jobs. If Nike hired them at 10 cents an hour to fill all-female sweatshops, they and their country would be hugely better off.
>
> Nike used to have two contract factories in impoverished Cambodia, among the neediest countries in the world. Then there was an outcry after BBC reported that three girls in one factory were under 15 years old. So Nike fled controversy by ceasing production in Cambodia.
>
> The result was that some of the 2,000 Cambodians (90 percent of them young women) who worked in three factories faced layoffs. Some who lost their jobs probably were ensnared in Cambodia's huge sex slave industry—which leaves many girls dead of AIDS by the end of their teenage years.

We can object to Kristof's premises. Can the widows of Afghanistan find no decent jobs whatsoever? Will they actually starve if they don't? Will some of the young women of Cambodia die of AIDS because Nike has pulled out of their impoverished country? (Notice that Kristof qualifies this assertion with "probably.") We can even dispute Kristof's reasoning based on statistics. In statistics, when it is not possible to poll every individual in the set being analyzed, sound practice requires at least a representative sampling. Has Kristof given us a truly representative sampling of *all* the workers in Third World sweatshops?

We can pick away at Kristof's logic—as have many of his critics since this article was first published. But with the exception of a court of law, a good argument does not have to prove its point beyond a shadow of a doubt. It only has to convince the reader. Whether or not you're convinced by Kristof's argument, you can learn from the tactics he uses to support his position.

A Brief Guide to Writing an Argument

When you construct an ARGUMENT, you take a position on an issue and then support that position, as Nicholas D. Kristof does in his argument in favor of sweatshops. So the first moves you need to make as you write an argument are to identify the subject or issue you are addressing and to state the claim you are making about it. Here's how Mark D. White and Robert Arp make these fundamental moves near the beginning of their argument in this chapter:

> Pop culture, such as the Batman comics and movies, provides an opportunity to think philosophically about issues and topics that parallel the real world. For instance, thinking about why Batman has never killed the Joker may help us reflect on the nation's issues with terror and torture, specifically their ethics.
>
> MARK D. WHITE AND ROBERT ARP, "Should Batman Kill the Joker?"

White and Arp identify the subject of their argument (pop culture) and state their claim about it ("provides an opportunity to think philosophically about issues and topics"). Next they narrow the broad field of pop culture to a specific topic ("why Batman has never killed the Joker") and a more limited claim ("may help us reflect on the nation's issues with terror and torture").

The following guidelines will help you make these basic moves as you draft an argument. They will also help you support your claim with reasoning and evidence, avoid logical fallacies, appeal to your readers' emotions and sense of ethics, and anticipate other arguments.

Coming Up with a Claim

Unlike a statement of fact (broccoli is a vegetable) or personal taste (I hate broccoli), a CLAIM is a statement that is debatable, that rational people can disagree with. We can all agree, for example, that pop culture has something to teach us. We might reasonably disagree, however, on what those lessons are. To come up with a claim, think of issues that are debatable: Batman is a sterling model of ethical behavior. Broccoli provides more health benefits than any other vegetable. Genetic factors are the main determiners of personality. The risks of global warming have been exaggerated by the scientific community. Before you decide on a particular claim, make sure it is one you actually care about enough to argue it persuasively. If you don't care much about your topic, your readers probably won't either.

Considering Your Purpose and Audience

The PURPOSE of an argument is to convince other people to listen thoughtfully to what you have to say—even if they don't completely accept your views. Whatever your claim, your argument is more likely to appeal to your AUDIENCE if it is tailored to their particular needs and interests. Suppose, for example, that you have a friend who habitually sends text messages while driving even though she knows it's dangerous. You think your friend should put down her phone while driving—or pull over when she needs to text. Your friend might be more likely to agree with you if, in addition to citing statistics on increased traffic deaths due to driving while texting, you also pointed out that she was setting a bad example for her younger sister.

So think about what your audience's views on the particular issue are likely to be. Of all the evidence you might present in support of your case, what kind would your intended readers most likely find reasonable and, thus, convincing?

Generating Ideas: Finding Effective Evidence

What EVIDENCE can you provide to convince your readers that your claim is true? Suppose you want to argue that the SAT is unfair because it is biased in favor of the wealthy. To support a claim like this effectively, you can use *facts, statistics, examples, expert testimony,* and *personal experience.*

FACTS. To argue that the SAT favors the wealthy, you might cite facts about the cost of tutors for the test: "In New York City, a company called Advantage charges $500 for 50 minutes of coaching with their most experienced tutors."

STATISTICS. You could cite statistics about income and text scores: "On the 2008 SAT, students with family incomes of more than $200,000 had an average math score of 570, while those with family incomes up to $20,000 had an average score of 456."

EXAMPLES. You could discuss a question from an actual SAT exam that might show SAT bias. The following question asks the test taker to select a pair of words whose relationship matches the relationship expressed by RUNNER : MARATHON. The choices are (A) envoy : embassy; (B) martyr : massacre; (C) oarsman : regatta; (D) referee : tournament; (E) horse : stable. The correct answer is C: an oarsman competes in a regatta, an organized boat race, in much the same way as a runner competes in a marathon. But because regattas are largely a pursuit of the wealthy, you could argue that the question favors the wealthy test taker.

EXPERT TESTIMONY. You might quote a statement like this one by Richard Atkinson, former president of the University of California: "Anyone involved in education should be concerned about how overemphasis on the SAT is distorting educational priorities and practices [and] how the test is perceived by many as unfair. . . ."

PERSONAL EXPERIENCE. The following anecdote reveals, in a personal way, how the SAT favors certain socioeconomic groups: "No one in my family ever participated in a regatta—as a high school student, I didn't even know the meaning of the word. So when I took the SAT and encountered analogy questions that referred to regattas and other unfamiliar things, I barely broke 600 on the verbal aptitude section."

No matter what type of evidence you present, it must be pertinent to your argument and sufficient to convince your audience that your claim is worth taking seriously. It should also be presented to the reader in a well-organized fashion that makes sense logically.

Templates for Arguing

The following templates can help you to generate ideas for an argument and then to start drafting. Don't take these as formulas where you just have to fill in the blanks. There are no easy formulas for good writing, though these templates can help you plot out some of the key moves of argumentation and thus may serve as good starting points.

> ➤ In this argument about X, the main point I want to make is _____.
>
> ➤ Others may say _____, but I would argue that _____.
>
> ➤ My contention about X is supported by the fact that _____.
>
> ➤ Additional facts that support this view of X are _____, _____, and _____.
>
> ➤ My own experience with X shows that _____ because _____.
>
> ➤ My view of X is supported by _____, who says that X is _____.
>
> ➤ What you should do about X is _____.

For more techniques to help you generate ideas and start writing, see Chapter 1.

Organizing an Argument

Any well-constructed argument is organized around a claim and support for that claim. Here is a straightforward plan that can be effective for most argument essays. You may, of course, need to supplement or modify this plan to fit a particular topic.

1. In your *introduction*, identify your topic and state your claim clearly. Indicate why you're making this claim and why the reader

should be interested in it. Make sure your topic is narrow enough to be covered in the time and space allotted.

2. In the main *body* of your argument, introduce an important example, or a solid piece of evidence, that is likely to catch your reader's attention; then use a clear, logical organization to present the rest of your support. For example, move from your weakest point to your strongest. Or vice versa.

3. Deal with *counterarguments* at appropriate points throughout your essay.

4. In the *conclusion*, restate your claim—and why you're making it—and sum up how the evidence supports that claim.

Narrowing and Stating Your Claim

State your claim clearly at the beginning of your argument—and take care not to claim more than you can possibly prove in one essay. "Sweatshops are acceptable," for example, is too broad to work as an arguable claim. Acceptable for whom, we might ask? Under what circumstances?

To narrow this claim, we could restate it as follows: "In very poor countries, sweatshops are acceptable." This claim could be still more restricted, however: "In very poor countries, sweatshops are acceptable *when the alternatives are even worse*." Because it is narrower, this is a more supportable claim than the one we started with.

Using Logical Reasoning: Induction and Deduction

In many writing situations, logical reasoning is indispensable for persuading others that your ideas and opinions are valid. As we noted in the introduction, there are two main kinds of logical reasoning, induction and deduction. INDUCTION is reasoning from particular evidence to a general conclusion. It is based on probability: drawing a conclusion from a limited number of specific cases. You reason inductively when you observe the cost of a gallon of gas at half a dozen service stations and conclude that the price of gas is uniformly high. In contrast to induction, DEDUCTION moves from general principles to a particular conclusion. You reason deductively when your car stops running and—knowing that cars need fuel, that you started with half a tank and have been driving all day—you conclude that you are out of gas.

Deductive arguments can be stated as SYLLOGISMS, which have a major premise, a minor premise, and a conclusion. For example:

> *Major premise:* All scientific theories should be taught in science classes.
> *Minor premise:* Intelligent design is a scientific theory.
> *Conclusion:* Intelligent design should be taught in science classes.

This is a valid syllogism, meaning that the conclusion follows logically from the premises. (As we will see shortly, however, *validity* in a syllogism is not always the same as *truth*.)

The great advantage of deduction over induction is that it deals with logical certainty rather than mere probability. As long as the premises you begin with are true and the syllogism is properly constructed, the conclusion must be true. But what if one or more of the premises are false?

> *Major premise:* Only people who have tattoos are cool.
> *Minor premise:* Robin got a tattoo on her shoulder last weekend.
> *Conclusion:* Robin is cool.

Advertisers use this kind of faulty reasoning all the time to try to convince you that you must buy their products if you want to be a cool person. Many people, however, would consider the major premise false; there are lots of cool people who don't have tattoos at all, so the reasoning is faulty.

You can also run into trouble when you know that some of your readers may disagree with your premises, but you still want to convince them. For example, look again at the syllogism about intelligent design. Some readers may not accept the minor premise—that intelligent design is a scientific theory—and thus they probably won't accept the conclusion. When you find yourself in this situation—but you still hope to win over your readers—you should provide strong evidence for those premises. As we saw in the introduction, this is what Kristof does to support his premise that in poor countries sweatshops are preferable to some other alternatives.

Avoiding Logical Fallacies

LOGICAL FALLACIES are errors in logical reasoning. Here are some of the most common logical fallacies to watch out for:

POST HOC, ERGO PROPTER HOC. Assuming that just because one event (such as rain) comes after another event (a rain dance), it occurs *because* of the first event: "From 1995 to 2005, as the Internet grew, the number of new babies named Jennifer grew by 30 percent." The increase in "Jennifers" may have followed the spread of the Internet, but the greater Internet use didn't necessarily CAUSE the increase.

NON SEQUITUR. A statement that has no logical connection to the preceding statement: "The early Egyptians were masters of architecture. Thus they created a vast network of trade throughout the ancient world." Since mastering architecture has little to do with expanding trade, this second statement is a non sequitur.

BEGGING THE QUESTION. Taking for granted what is supposed to be proved: "Americans should be required to carry ID cards because Americans need to be prepared to prove their identity." Instead of addressing the claim that Americans should be required to prove their identity by having an ID card that verifies it, the "because" statement takes it for granted.

APPEAL TO DOUBTFUL AUTHORITY. Citing as expert testimony the opinions of people who are not experts on the issue: "According to David Letterman, the candidate who takes Ohio will win the election." Letterman isn't an expert on politics.

AD HOMINEM. Attacking the person making an argument instead of addressing the actual issue: "She's too young to be head of the teachers' union, so why listen to her views on wages?" Saying she's too young focuses on her as a person rather than on her views on the issue.

EITHER/OR REASONING. Treating a complicated issue as if it had only two sides: "Either you believe that God created the universe, or you believe that the universe evolved randomly." This statement doesn't allow for beliefs outside of these two options.

HASTY GENERALIZATION. Drawing a conclusion based on far too little evidence: "In the four stories by Edgar Allan Poe that we read, the narrator is mentally ill. Poe himself must have been insane." There is not nearly enough evidence here to determine Poe's mental health.

FALSE ANALOGY. Making a faulty comparison: "Children are like dogs. A happy dog is a disciplined dog, and a happy child is one who knows the rules and is taught to obey them." Dogs and children aren't alike enough to assume that what is good for one is necessarily good for the other.

RED HERRING. Leading the reader off on a false scent, away from the main argument: "Sure, my paper is full of spelling errors. But English is not a very phonetic language. Now if we were writing in Spanish . . ."

OVERSIMPLIFICATION. Assigning insufficient causes to explain an EFFECT or justify a conclusion: "In a school budget crunch, art and music classes should be eliminated first because these subjects are not very practical." This argument is oversimplified because it doesn't admit that there are other reasons, besides practicality, for keeping a subject in the school curriculum.

Appealing to Your Readers' Emotions

Sound logical reasoning is hard to refute, but appealing to your readers' emotions can also be an effective way to convince them to accept—or at least listen to—your argument. In a January 2009 follow-up to his 2002 argument in favor of sweatshops, Nicholas D. Kristof writes:

> The miasma of toxic stink leaves you gasping, breezes batter you with filth, and even the rats look forlorn. Then the smoke parts and you come across a child ambling barefoot, searching for old plastic cups that recyclers will buy for five cents a pound.
>
> NICHOLAS D. KRISTOF, "Where Sweatshops Are a Dream"

Kristof is describing a gigantic garbage dump in Phnom Penh, Cambodia, where whole families try to eke out a living under inhumane conditions. Compared to this "Dante-like vision of hell," Kristof argues, "sweltering at a sewing machine" seems like an unattainable dream. By making us feel the desperation of the people he describes, Kristof is clearly tugging at the readers' heartstrings—before going on to supply more facts and examples to support his claim.

Establishing Your Own Credibility

When you construct an argument, you can demonstrate with irrefutable logic that what you have to say is valid and true. And you can appeal to your readers' emotions with genuine fervor. Your words may still fall on deaf ears, however, if your readers don't fully trust you. Here are a few tips to help you establish trust:

- *Present issues objectively.* Acknowledge opposing points of view, and treat them fairly and accurately. If you have experience or expertise in your subject, let your readers know. For example, Kristof tells his readers, "My views on sweatshops are shaped by years living in East Asia, watching as living standards soared—including those in my wife's ancestral village in southern China—because of sweatshop jobs."

- *Pay close attention to the* TONE *of your argument.* Whether you come across as calm and reasonable or full of righteous anger, your tone will say much about your own values and motives for writing—and about you as a person.

- *Convince your readers* that they are listening to the words of a moral and ethical person who shares their values and understands their concerns.

Anticipating Other Arguments

As you construct an argument, it's important to consider viewpoints other than your own, including objections that others might raise. Anticipating other arguments, in fact, is yet another way to establish your credibility. Readers are more likely to see you as trustworthy if, instead of ignoring an opposing argument, you state it fairly and accurately and then refute it. Kristof knows that many readers will disagree with his position on sweatshops, so he acknowledges the opposition up front before going on to give his evidence for his position:

> When I defend sweatshops, people always ask me: But would you want to work in a sweatshop? No, of course not. But I would want even less to pull a rickshaw. . . . I often hear the argument: Labor standards can improve wages and working conditions, without greatly affecting the eventual retail cost of goods. That's true. But . . .
>
> NICHOLAS D. KRISTOF, "Where Sweatshops Are a Dream"

You still may not agree with Kristof's position that sweatshops are a good idea. But you're more likely to listen to what he, or any other writer, has to say if you think that person has thought carefully about all aspects of the issue, including points of view opposed to his or her own.

EVERYDAY ARGUMENT
A Sign on an Old House

When you make an argument, you ask those you're addressing to hear you out and take your message seriously. "Three weeks after Sept. 11," said Don Jones of Delhi, New York, owner of the frame house pictured here, "I bought a 4-by-6 American flag and wrote those words on the house. I still have people stopping by to take pictures of it." Jones's message is plain. It is the underlying message inscribed on much loftier monuments: Never forget. To convince readers to accept such a message, you can appeal to their rational side by using logical reasoning. Or you can appeal to your readers' emotions and to their sense of ethics and fair play—as Jones did by displaying the American flag, symbol of patriotism and resolve, above his words.

BARACK OBAMA

Inaugural Address

Barack Obama (b. 1961) is the forty-fourth president of the United States. The son of a father from Kenya and a mother from Kansas, Obama grew up mostly in Hawaii. Prior to being elected president in 2008, Obama served three terms in the Illinois State Senate, taught constitutional law at the University of Chicago, and served in the United States Senate. He is the author of *Dreams from My Father: A Story of Race and Inheritance* (1995) and *The Audacity of Hope* (2006). He delivered this inaugural address on January 20, 2009; the following text gives his speech as it was published that day in *The Washington Post*. Calmly and confidently, the new president addresses a nation in "crisis."

XXXXXXXXXXXXXXXXXXXXXXXXXXXXXXXXXXXXXXXXXXXXXXXXXXXXXXXXXXX

1   My fellow citizens: I stand here today humbled by the task before us, grateful for the trust you have bestowed, mindful of the sacrifices borne by our ancestors. I thank President Bush for his service to our nation, as well as the generosity and cooperation he has shown throughout this transition.

2   Forty-four Americans have now taken the presidential oath. The words have been spoken during rising tides of prosperity and the still waters of peace. Yet, every so often the oath is taken amidst gathering clouds and raging storms. At these moments, America has carried on not simply because of the skill or vision of those in high office, but because We the People have remained faithful to the ideals of our forbearers, and true to our founding documents.

3   So it has been. So it must be with this generation of Americans.

4   That we are in the midst of crisis is now well understood. Our nation is at war, against a far-reaching network of violence and hatred. Our economy is badly weakened, a consequence of greed and irresponsibility on the part of some, but also our collective failure to make hard

choices and prepare the nation for a new age. Homes have been lost; jobs shed; businesses shuttered. Our health care is too costly; our schools fail too many; and each day brings further evidence that the ways we use energy strengthen our adversaries and threaten our planet.

These are the indicators of crisis, subject to data and statistics. Less measurable but no less profound is a sapping of confidence across our land—a nagging fear that America's decline is inevitable, and that the next generation must lower its sights.   5

Today I say to you that the challenges we face are real. They are serious and they are many. They will not be met easily or in a short span of time. But know this, America—they will be met.   6

On this day, we gather because we have chosen hope over fear, unity of purpose over conflict and discord.   7

On this day, we come to proclaim an end to the petty grievances and false promises, the recriminations and worn-out dogmas, that for far too long have strangled our politics.   8

We remain a young nation, but in the words of Scripture, the time has come to set aside childish things.[1] The time has come to reaffirm our enduring spirit; to choose our better history; to carry forward that precious gift, that noble idea, passed on from generation to generation: the God-given promise that all are equal, all are free, and all deserve a chance to pursue their full measure of happiness.   9

In reaffirming the greatness of our nation, we understand that greatness is never a given. It must be earned. Our journey has never been one of short-cuts or settling for less. It has not been the path for the faint-hearted—for those who prefer leisure over work, or seek only the pleasures of riches and fame. Rather, it has been the risk-takers, the doers, the makers of things—some celebrated but more often men and women obscure in their labor, who have carried us up the long, rugged path towards prosperity and freedom.   10

For us, they packed up their few worldly possessions and traveled across oceans in search of a new life.   11

1. In 1 Corinthians 13:11, the apostle Paul writes, "When I was a child, I spake as a child, I understood as a child, I thought as a child: but when I became a man, I put away childish things."

12   For us, they toiled in sweatshops and settled the West; endured the lash of the whip and plowed the hard earth.

13   For us, they fought and died, in places like Concord and Gettysburg; Normandy and Khe Sahn.[2]

14   Time and again these men and women struggled and sacrificed and worked till their hands were raw so that we might live a better life. They saw America as bigger than the sum of our individual ambitions; greater than all the differences of birth or wealth or faction.

15   This is the journey we continue today. We remain the most prosperous, powerful nation on Earth. Our workers are no less productive than when this crisis began. Our minds are no less inventive, our goods and services no less needed than they were last week or last month or last year. Our capacity remains undiminished. But our time of standing pat, of protecting narrow interests and putting off unpleasant decisions—that time has surely passed. Starting today, we must pick ourselves up, dust ourselves off, and begin again the work of remaking America.

16   For everywhere we look, there is work to be done. The state of the economy calls for action, bold and swift, and we will act—not only to create new jobs, but to lay a new foundation for growth. We will build the roads and bridges, the electric grids and digital lines that feed our commerce and bind us together. We will restore science to its rightful place, and wield technology's wonders to raise health care's quality and lower its cost. We will harness the sun and the winds and the soil to fuel our cars and run our factories. And we will transform our schools and colleges and universities to meet the demands of a new age. All this we can do. And all this we will do.

17   Now, there are some who question the scale of our ambitions—who suggest that our system cannot tolerate too many big plans. Their mem-

---

2. The Battle of Khe Sahn during the Vietnam War (1968) provided an important tactical victory for the United States. The Battle of Concord, Massachusetts (1775), a victory for the colonists, was among the first conflicts of the American Revolution. The Union victory in the Battle of Gettysburg, Pennsylvania (1863), was one of the turning points of the American Civil War. Near the close of World War II in 1944, U.S. and allied troops stormed the beaches at Normandy, France, then occupied by the Nazis.

ories are short. For they have forgotten what this country has already done; what free men and women can achieve when imagination is joined to common purpose, and necessity to courage.

What the cynics fail to understand is that the ground has shifted beneath them—that the stale political arguments that have consumed us for so long no longer apply. The question we ask today is not whether our government is too big or too small, but whether it works—whether it helps families find jobs at a decent wage, care they can afford, a retirement that is dignified. Where the answer is yes, we intend to move forward. Where the answer is no, programs will end. And those of us who manage the public's dollars will be held to account—to spend wisely, reform bad habits, and do our business in the light of day—because only then can we restore the vital trust between a people and their government.

Nor is the question before us whether the market is a force for good or ill. Its power to generate wealth and expand freedom is unmatched, but this crisis has reminded us that without a watchful eye, the market can spin out of control—and that a nation cannot prosper long when it favors only the prosperous. The success of our economy has always depended not just on the size of our Gross Domestic Product, but on the reach of our prosperity; on our ability to extend opportunity to every willing heart—not out of charity, but because it is the surest route to our common good.

As for our common defense, we reject as false the choice between our safety and our ideals. Our Founding Fathers, faced with perils we can scarcely imagine, drafted a charter to assure the rule of law and the rights of man, a charter expanded by the blood of generations.[3] Those ideals still light the world, and we will not give them up for expedience's sake. And so to all other peoples and governments who are watching today, from the grandest capitals to the small village where my father was born: know that America is a friend of each nation and every man, woman, and child who seeks a future of peace and dignity, and that we are ready to lead once more.

18

19

20

---

3. The U.S. Constitution, completed in 1787 and fully ratified in 1789. Twenty-seven amendments have been added since it was first ratified.

21   Recall that earlier generations faced down fascism and communism not just with missiles and tanks, but with sturdy alliances and enduring convictions. They understood that our power alone cannot protect us, nor does it entitle us to do as we please. Instead, they knew that our power grows through its prudent use; our security emanates from the justness of our cause, the force of our example, the tempering qualities of humility and restraint.

22   We are the keepers of this legacy. Guided by these principles once more, we can meet those new threats that demand even greater effort— even greater cooperation and understanding between nations. We will begin to responsibly leave Iraq to its people, and forge a hard-earned peace in Afghanistan. With old friends and former foes, we will work tirelessly to lessen the nuclear threat, and roll back the specter of a warming planet. We will not apologize for our way of life, nor will we waver in its defense, and for those who seek to advance their aims by inducing terror and slaughtering innocents, we say to you now that our spirit is stronger and cannot be broken; you cannot outlast us, and we will defeat you.

23   For we know that our patchwork heritage is a strength, not a weakness. We are a nation of Christians and Muslims, Jews and Hindus—and nonbelievers. We are shaped by every language and culture, drawn from every end of this Earth; and because we have tasted the bitter swill of civil war and segregation, and emerged from that dark chapter stronger and more united, we cannot help but believe that the old hatreds shall someday pass; that the lines of tribe shall soon dissolve; that as the world grows smaller, our common humanity shall reveal itself; and that America must play its role in ushering in a new era of peace.

24   To the Muslim world, we seek a new way forward, based on mutual interest and mutual respect. To those leaders around the globe who seek to sow conflict, or blame their society's ills on the West—know that your people will judge you on what you can build, not what you destroy. To those who cling to power through corruption and deceit and the silencing of dissent, know that you are on the wrong side of history; but that we will extend a hand if you are willing to unclench your fist.

25   To the people of poor nations, we pledge to work alongside you to make your farms flourish and let clean waters flow; to nourish starved

bodies and feed hungry minds. And to those nations like ours that enjoy relative plenty, we say we can no longer afford indifference to suffering outside our borders; nor can we consume the world's resources without regard to effect. For the world has changed, and we must change with it.

As we consider the road that unfolds before us, we remember with humble gratitude those brave Americans who, at this very hour, patrol far-off deserts and distant mountains. They have something to tell us today, just as the fallen heroes who lie in Arlington[4] whisper through the ages. We honor them not only because they are guardians of our liberty, but because they embody the spirit of service; a willingness to find meaning in something greater than themselves. And yet, at this moment—a moment that will define a generation—it is precisely this spirit that must inhabit us all. 26

For as much as government can do and must do, it is ultimately the faith and determination of the American people upon which this nation relies. It is the kindness to take in a stranger when the levees break, the selflessness of workers who would rather cut their hours than see a friend lose their job which sees us through our darkest hours. It is the firefighter's courage to storm a stairway filled with smoke, but also a parent's willingness to nurture a child, that finally decides our fate. 27

Our challenges may be new. The instruments with which we meet them may be new. But those values upon which our success depends— hard work and honesty, courage and fair play, tolerance and curiosity, loyalty and patriotism—these things are old. These things are true. They have been the quiet force of progress throughout our history. What is demanded then is a return to these truths. What is required of us now is a new era of responsibility—a recognition, on the part of every American, that we have duties to ourselves, our nation, and the world, duties that we do not grudgingly accept but rather seize gladly, firm in the knowledge that there is nothing so satisfying to the spirit, so defining of our character, than giving our all to a difficult task. 28

This is the price and the promise of citizenship. 29

---

4. Arlington National Cemetery in Virginia has been the burial site of combat veterans since the Civil War.

30   This is the source of our confidence—the knowledge that God calls on us to shape an uncertain destiny.

31   This is the meaning of our liberty and our creed—why men and women and children of every race and every faith can join in celebration across this magnificent mall, and why a man whose father less than sixty years ago might not have been served at a local restaurant can now stand before you to take a most sacred oath.

32   So let us mark this day with remembrance, of who we are and how far we have traveled. In the year of America's birth, in the coldest of months, a small band of patriots huddled by dying campfires on the shores of an icy river. The capital was abandoned. The enemy was advancing. The snow was stained with blood. At a moment when the outcome of our revolution was most in doubt, the father of our nation ordered these words be read to the people:

33   "Let it be told to the future world . . . that in the depth of winter, when nothing but hope and virtue could survive . . . that the city and the country, alarmed at one common danger, came forth to meet [it]."[5]

34   America, in the face of our common dangers, in this winter of our hardship, let us remember these timeless words. With hope and virtue, let us brave once more the icy currents, and endure what storms may come. Let it be said by our children's children that when we were tested we refused to let this journey end, that we did not turn back nor did we falter; and with eyes fixed on the horizon and God's grace upon us, we carried forth that great gift of freedom and delivered it safely to future generations.

5. Thomas Paine, *The American Crisis*, I, December 23, 1776. George Washington ordered this pamphlet, which begins "These are the times that try men's souls," to be read aloud to his troops on the night before the Battle of Trenton, December 26, 1776. Washington's victory revived the country's morale and proved to be a turning point in the war.

XXXXXXXXXXXXXXXXXXX **FOR DISCUSSION** XXXXXXXXXXXXXXXXXXXX

1. Toward the beginning of his inaugural address, the forty-fourth president of the United States declares that "we are in the midst of crisis" (4). What is the nature of that crisis as he DEFINES it?

2. According to Barack Obama, who is chiefly responsible for ensuring that the nation will endure and prosper despite the "gathering clouds and raging storms" (2)?

3. How confident is the new president that "the challenges we face" will be met (6)? What ideals and principles, in his view, will be our best guides and support for dealing with the tasks ahead?

4. What is Obama's message to other nations and to future generations concerning the ability and the willingness of the American people to "endure what storms may come" (34)?

XXXXXXXXXXXXXX **STRATEGIES AND STRUCTURES** XXXXXXXXXXXXXX

1. One of Obama's techniques as an orator is repetition with variation, as when he says, "So it has been. So it must be . . ." (3). Where else in his speech does he use this technique? What PURPOSE does this technique serve, and how effective is it? Cite specific examples from the text.

2. A speaker can move an AUDIENCE to accept his or her views by appealing to their logical faculties, their emotions, or their sense of ethics. Which of these appeals does Obama rely upon most heavily? Support your answer with specific passages from his address.

3. How and how well does Obama establish his credibility as a trustworthy speaker? Point to specific passages to support your answer.

4. Obama COMPARES the state of the nation "in this winter of our hardship" with that of George Washington and the "small band of patriots" who held on in the darkest days of the American Revolution (34, 32). What ARGUMENT is he making with this ANALOGY? What is the purpose of this argument by analogy, and how well does it serve that purpose?

5. "For as much as government can do and must do," says Obama, "it is ultimately the faith and determination of the American people upon which this nation relies" (27). In an inaugural address, how appropriate is it for Obama to evoke such ABSTRACT principles and virtues to support his CLAIM of confidence in the American people? Should he have provided a more specific program of action to support his argument about the ability of the United States to prevail?

6. How and where does Obama use elements of NARRATIVE to provide a history of the United States? How does this narrative support the argument he is making in this address?

XXXXXXXXXXXXX **WORDS AND FIGURES OF SPEECH** XXXXXXXXXXXXX

1. Throughout his inaugural address, Obama seldom uses the personal pronoun *I*. What pronoun does he use? Why?

2. In the second paragraph of his address, Obama speaks of "rising tides" and "gathering clouds and raging storms." Where else in his address does he use such figurative language? For what PURPOSE?

3. Why does Obama capitalize the phrase "We the People" (2)? To what document is he referring? Why the ALLUSION?

4. How does your dictionary DEFINE *cynic*? Why is Obama concerned, especially on this occasion, with anticipating the objections of "cynics" (18)?

5. To whom is Obama speaking when he says, "we will extend a hand if you are willing to unclench your fist" (24)? What is his message here, and how is it supported by this METAPHOR?

XXXXXXXXXXXXXXXXXXX **FOR WRITING** XXXXXXXXXXXXXXXXXXXXX

1. Make a list of the challenges that the United States faces today in addition to those cited by President Obama. Then list the resources it can draw on to meet them.

2. Write a letter of encouragement and support to a friend or family member who has fallen upon hard times. Without minimizing the challenges ahead, convince your reader to summon the resources necessary to go forth and meet those challenges.

JOHNSON C. MONTGOMERY

THE ISLAND OF PLENTY

Johnson C. Montgomery (1934–1974) was a California attorney and an early member of the organization Zero Population Growth. Montgomery's "The Island of Plenty," which first appeared as a "My Turn" column in *Newsweek* in 1974, is an argument in favor of American social isolationism. Until we have enough food to feed all Americans plentifully, Montgomery reasons, Americans should not share their material resources with other countries of the world.

XXXXXXXXXXXXXXXXXXXXXXXXXXXXXXXXXXXXXXXXXXXXXXXXXXXXXXXXXXXXXX

The United States should remain an island of plenty in a sea of hunger. The future of mankind is at stake. We are not responsible for the rest of humanity. We should not accept responsibility for all humanity. We owe more to the hundreds of billions of *Homo futurans* than we do to the hungry millions—soon to be billions—of our own generations.

Ample food and resources exist to nourish man and all other creatures indefinitely into the future. This planet is indeed an Eden—to date our only Eden. Admittedly our Eden is plagued by pollution. Some of us have polluted the planet by reproducing too many of us. Too many people have made excessive demands on the long-range carrying capacity of our garden; and during the last 200 years there has been dramatic, ever-increasing destruction of the web of life on earth. If we try to save the starving millions today, we will simply destroy what's left of Eden.

The problem is not that there is too little food. The problem is there are too many people—many too many. It is not that the children should never have been born. It is simply that we have mindlessly tried to cram too many of us into too short a time span. Four billion humans are fine—but they should have been spread over several hundred years.

But the billions are already here. What should we do about them? Should we send food, knowing that each child saved in Southeast Asia,

India or Africa will probably live to reproduce and thereby bring more people into the world to live even more miserably? Should we eat the last tuna fish, the last ear of corn and utterly destroy the garden? That is what we have been doing for a long time and all the misguided efforts have merely increased the number who go to bed hungry each night. There have never been more miserable, deprived people in the world than there are right now.

5   It was obvious even in the late 1950s that the famine the world now faces was coming unless people immediately began exercising responsibility for reducing population levels. It was also obvious that too many people contributed to the risk of nuclear war, global pestilence, illiteracy and even to many problems that are usually classified as purely economic. For example, unemployment is having too many people for the available jobs. Inflation is in part the result of too much demand from too many people. But in the 1950s, population control was taboo and those who warned of impending disasters received a cool reception.

6   By the time Zero Population Growth, Inc.,[1] was formed, those of us who wanted to do something useful decided to concentrate our initial efforts on our own families and friends and then on the white American middle and upper classes. Our belief was that by setting an example, we could later insist that others pay attention to our proposals.

7   I think I was the first in the original ZPG group to have had a vasectomy. Nancy and I had two children—each doing superbly well and each getting all the advantages of the best nutrition, education, attention, love and other resources available. I think Paul Ehrlich[2] (one child) was the next. Now don't ask me to cut my children back to the same number of calories that children from large families eat. In fact, don't ask me to cut my children back on anything. I won't do it without a fight; and in today's world, power is in knowledge, not numbers. Nancy and I made a conscious decision to limit the number of our children so each child could have a larger share of whatever we could make available. We intend to keep the best for them.

1. International movement founded in 1968; its original goal was to limit the birth rate in the United States and other developed countries.
2. Biology professor at Stanford, founder and past-president of Zero Population Growth.

The future of mankind is indeed with the children. But it is with the nourished, educated and loved children. It is not with the starving, uneducated and ignored. This is of course a highly elitist point of view. But that doesn't make the view incorrect. As a matter of fact, the lowest reproductive rate in the nation is that of one of the most elite groups in the world—black, female Ph.D.'s. They had to be smart and effective to make it. Having made it, they are smart enough not to wreck it with too many kids.

8

We in the United States have made great progress in lowering our birth rates. But now, because we have been responsible, it seems to some that we have a great surplus. There is, indeed, waste that should be eliminated, but there is not as much fat in our system as most people think. Yet we are being asked to share our resources with the hungry peoples of the world. But why should we share? The nations having the greatest needs are those that have been the least responsible in cutting down on births. Famine is one of nature's ways of telling profligate peoples that they have been irresponsible in their breeding habits.

9

Naturally, we would like to help; and if we could, perhaps we should. But we can't be of any use in the long run—particularly if we weaken ourselves.

10

Until we have at least a couple of years' supply of food and other resources on hand to take care of our own people and until those asking for handouts are doing at least as well as we are at reducing existing excessive population-growth rates, we should not give away our resources—not so much as one bushel of wheat. Certainly we should not participate in any programs that will increase the burden that mankind is already placing on the earth. We should not deplete our own soils to save those who will only die equally miserably a decade or so down the line—and in many cases only after reproducing more children who are inevitably doomed to live and die in misery.

11

We know the world is finite. There is only so much pie. We may be able to expand the pie, but at any point in time, the pie is finite. How big a piece each person gets depends in part on how many people there are. At least for the foreseeable future, the fewer of us there are, the more there will be for each. That is true on a family, community, state, national and global basis.

12

At the moment, the future of mankind seems to depend on our maintaining the island of plenty in a sea of deprivation. If everyone

13

shared equally, we would all be suffering from protein-deficiency brain damage—and that would probably be true even if we ate every last animal on earth.

14   As compassionate human beings, we grieve for the condition of mankind. But our grief must not interfere with our perception of reality and our planning for a better future for those who will come after us. Someone must protect the material and intellectual seed grain for the future. It seems to me that that someone is the U.S. We owe it to our children—and to their children's children's children's children.

15   These conclusions will be attacked, as they have been within Zero Population Growth, as simplistic and inhumane. But truth is often very simple and reality often inhumane.

XXXXXXXXXXXXXXXXXX **For Discussion** XXXXXXXXXXXXXXXXXX

1. What is Johnson C. Montgomery's main CLAIM?

2. Which of Montgomery's reasons for his position do you find most persuasive? Why? What counterarguments would you make?

3. In paragraph 4, what is the last sentence intended to prove? Why do you think Montgomery includes it?

4. Montgomery warns us not to ask him "to cut my children back on anything" (7). How is this position consistent with what he says about there not being enough food to go around?

XXXXXXXXXXXXX **Strategies and Structures** XXXXXXXXXXXXX

1. The logic of Montgomery's basic ARGUMENT can be represented by a SYLLOGISM:

> *Major premise:* To provide undamaged human stock for the future, some people must remain healthy.
>
> *Minor premise:* All will suffer if all share equally in the world's limited bounty.
>
> *Conclusion:* Therefore, some must not share what they have.

How sound is this logic? Do you think Montgomery's premises are true? Why or why not? Do they affect the validity of his argument?

2. Montgomery's hard-headed realism intends not only to show us the "truth" of the human condition, but also to convince us to act (15). What would Montgomery have us do?

3. Logic is only part of Montgomery's persuasive arsenal. Where does he appeal more to emotion and ethics than to logic? Give examples from the text.

4. Montgomery seems to be speaking from a position of authority. Where does he get his authority, and how much weight does it carry, in your opinion?

5. Montgomery admits that his position is elitist (8). How does he anticipate the objection that it is racist?

6. Montgomery's argument is based on a COMPARISON. What is he comparing to what? Which points of his comparison do you find most convincing? Why?

XXXXXXXXXXXXX **WORDS AND FIGURES OF SPEECH** XXXXXXXXXXXXX

1. How does the METAPHOR of the island contribute to Montgomery's ARGUMENT?

2. For the sake of the future, he says we must save "material and intellectual seed grain" (14). Explain this metaphor. What does he COMPARE to what?

3. *Homo futurans*, meaning "man of the future," is modeled after such scientific terms as *Homo erectus* ("upright man") and *Homo sapiens* ("thinking man"). Why do you think Montgomery uses the language of science at the beginning of his argument?

4. How does Montgomery's use of the word "mindlessly" epitomize his entire argument (3)?

5. What is the meaning of "profligate" (9)? Why does Montgomery use this term?

XXXXXXXXXXXXXXXXXXX **FOR WRITING** XXXXXXXXXXXXXXXXXXXXX

1. Write an essay agreeing or disagreeing with Montgomery's position, particularly his assumption that "the future of mankind seems to depend on our maintaining the island of plenty in a sea of deprivation" (13).

2. Read Jonathan Swift's "A Modest Proposal" in the next chapter, and write a "modest proposal" of your own in which you ARGUE for a way to solve one of the world's great problems—such as feeding the masses, sharing the world's wealth, regulating human breeding habits, reversing global warming, or eliminating terrorism.

MARK D. WHITE AND ROBERT ARP

SHOULD BATMAN KILL THE JOKER?

Mark D. White is a professor of political science, economics, and philosophy at the College of Staten Island of the City University of New York. He is the co-editor with Irene van Staveren of *Ethics and Economics* (2009). Robert Arp is a specialist in biomedical ethics and the philosophy of biology and an associate of the Analysis Group of Falls Church, Virginia, a company that provides technical and operational support for national security clients. He is the author of *Scenario Visualization: An Evolutionary Account of Creative Problem Solving* (2008). Together, White and Arp have edited a collection of essays, *Batman and Philosophy: The Dark Knight of the Soul* (2008). In "Should Batman Kill the Joker?" first published in the *Boston Globe* in 2008, they argue for the value of pop culture in helping us explore ethical approaches to real-world issues.

XXXXXXXXXXXXXXXXXXXXXXXXXXXXXXXXXXXXXXXXXXXXXXXXXXXXXXXXXXXXX

1   Batman should kill the Joker. How many of us would agree with that? Quite a few, we'd wager. Even Heath Ledger's Joker in *The Dark Knight* marvels at Batman's refusal to kill him. After all, the Joker is a murderous psychopath, and Batman could save countless innocent lives by ending his miserable existence once and for all.

2   Of course, there are plenty of masked loonies ready to take the Joker's place, but none of them has ever shown the same twisted devotion to chaos and tragedy as the Clown Prince of Crime.

3   But if we say that Batman should kill the Joker, doesn't that imply that we should torture terror suspects if there's a chance of getting information that could save innocent lives? Of course, terror is all too present in the real world, and Batman only exists in the comics and movies. So maybe we're just too detached from the Dark Knight and the problems of Gotham City, so we can say "go ahead, kill him." But, if anything, that detachment implies that there's more at stake in the real world—so

404

why aren't we tougher on actual terrorists than we are on the make-believe Joker?

Pop culture, such as the Batman comics and movies, provides an [4] opportunity to think philosophically about issues and topics that parallel the real world. For instance, thinking about why Batman has never killed the Joker may help us reflect on the nation's issues with terror and torture, specifically their ethics.

Three major schools of ethics provide some perspective on Batman's quandary. [5]

Utilitarianism, based on the work of Jeremy Bentham and John [6] Stuart Mill,[1] would probably endorse killing the Joker, based on comparing the many lives saved against the one life lost.

Deontology, stemming largely from the writings of Immanuel Kant,[2] [7] would focus on the act of murder itself, rather than the consequences. Kant's position would be more ambiguous than the utilitarian's: While it may be preferable for the Joker to be dead, it may not be morally right for any person (such as Batman) to kill him. If the Joker is to be punished, it should be through official procedures, not vigilante justice. More generally, while the Joker is evil, he is still a human being, and is thus deserving of at least a minimal level of respect and humanity.

Finally, virtue ethics, dating back to the ancient Greeks (such as [8] Aristotle[3]), would highlight the character of the person who kills the Joker. Does Batman want to be the kind of person that takes his enemies' lives? If he killed the Joker, would he be able to stop there, or would every two-bit thug get the same treatment?

Taking these three ethical perspectives together, we see that while [9] there are good reasons to kill the Joker, in terms of innocent lives saved, there are also good reasons not to kill him, based on what killing him would mean about Batman and his motives, mission, and character.

---

1. Mill (1806–1873) and Bentham (1748–1832) were British philosophers and social reformers.

2. German philosopher (1724–1804) whose works include treatises on reason and ethics.

3. Classical Greek philosopher (384–322 B.C.E.) whose work was foundational for Western philosophy and culture.

10   The same arguments apply to the debate over torture: While there are good reasons to do it, based on the positive consequences that may come from it, there are also good reasons not to, especially those based on our national character. Many Americans who oppose torture explain their position by saying, "It's not who we are" or "We don't want to turn into them." Batman often says the same thing when asked why he hasn't killed the Joker: "I don't want to become that which I hate."

11   Applying philosophy to Batman, *South Park*, or other pop culture phenomena may seem silly or frivolous, but philosophers have used fanciful examples and thought experiments for centuries. The point is making philosophy accessible, and helping us think through difficult topics by casting them in a different light.

12   Regardless of your position, torture is an uncomfortable and emotional topic. If translating the core issue to another venue, such as Batman and the Joker, helps us focus on the key aspects of the problem, that can only help refine our thinking. And Batman would definitely approve of that.

✕✕✕✕✕✕✕✕✕✕✕✕✕✕✕✕✕✕ FOR DISCUSSION ✕✕✕✕✕✕✕✕✕✕✕✕✕✕✕✕✕✕

1. Mark D. White and Robert Arp do not give a final answer to the question posed in their title. Should they have? Why or why not?

2. Of the three schools of philosophy cited by White and Arp, which one(s) best support Batman's CLAIM that if he kills the Joker he will become "that which I hate" (10)? Explain your answer.

3. Are White and Arp being "silly or frivolous" when they take Batman's adventures as a serious guide to moral and ethical behavior (11)? Why or why not?

4. So *is* Batman morally and ethically right to let the Joker live? Or should he kill the Joker at the first opportunity? Why do you think so?

✕✕✕✕✕✕✕✕✕✕✕✕✕ STRATEGIES AND STRUCTURES ✕✕✕✕✕✕✕✕✕✕✕✕✕

1. What AUDIENCE in particular do White and Arp have in mind when they use pop culture to examine complex ethical and philosophical questions?

2. What is White and Arp's main CLAIM in COMPARING the actions and decisions of a comic book character to those that real-life leaders must make in government and society? Where in the text is that claim directly stated?

3. Throughout their ARGUMENT, White and Arp rely heavily on logical reasoning, both INDUCTIVE and DEDUCTIVE. Where in their argument do they reason inductively? Where is their reasoning more deductive? Point to specific instances of each type of reasoning.

4. "Should Batman Kill the Joker?" is primarily a moral and ethical argument. How and how well do White and Arp present themselves as knowledgeable and ethical people who deserve to be heard? Point to specific passages in the text where they establish (or fail to establish) their credibility.

5. Is it logical to say that a person who condones torture is in danger of becoming that which he or she hates? Or does such reasoning introduce a red herring, or some other LOGICAL FALLACY? Explain.

6. Arguments by ANALOGY draw COMPARISONS, as White and Arp do in comparing Batman's dilemma to the debate over torture and terrorism. The PURPOSE of such arguments, as they say, is to help us "think through difficult topics by casting them in a different light" (11). How effective is this strategy in helping White and Arp to clarify the difficult issue of torture?

7. In general, arguments by analogy are only as strong as the analogy, or likeness between the terms being compared, is close. How close is the analogy—and, thus, how strong is the argument—in "Should Batman Kill the Joker?" Explain.

8. How do the DEFINITIONS that White and Arp provide in paragraphs 6–8 support their argument about the value of pop culture for understanding ethical and philosophical issues?

XXXXXXXXXXXXXX **WORDS AND FIGURES OF SPEECH** XXXXXXXXXXXXXX

1. A "psychopath" is someone who is antisocial and self-centered to the point of having no regard for the rules of society or the needs of other people (1). In what ways does the Joker, as White and Arp DESCRIBE him, exhibit the behavior of a psychopath?

2. "Utilitarianism" stresses the welfare of the majority over the special interests of the few (6). How and how well does White and Arp's summary of this philosophy fit this DEFINITION?

3. "Deontology" takes its name from the Greek word for *obligation* or *duty* (7). How does this root meaning apply to the school of ethics by that name as White and Arp define it?

4. Look up the root meanings of *ethics* and *ethnic* in your dictionary. What do the two terms have in common? What does their ETYMOLOGY tell you about the nature of *ethical* arguments, as opposed to *emotional* argument and arguments that appeal to the reader's sense of logic?

XXXXXXXXXXXXXXXXXXXX **FOR WRITING** XXXXXXXXXXXXXXXXXXXX

1. Choose a pop culture icon whose adventures you find particularly enlightening. Write an ARGUMENT for why that figure's deeds and moral standards (or lack thereof) can teach us moral, ethical, or practical lessons.

2. Write an argument condemning (or justifying) the use of torture when dealing with terrorists. Consider applying one or more of the schools of philosophy outlined by White and Arp—or any other that you choose—to make your argument.

What's Wrong with Performance-Enhancing Drugs in Sports?

*I*n September 2003, federal agents raided a laboratory in the Bay Area of California that supplied its clients with special food supplements—and, it turned out, steroids and human growth hormone, drugs frequently used by athletes to enhance performance. Among the star athletes whose names appeared on BALCO's ledgers were the sprinter Marion Jones, cyclist Tammy Thomas, and—biggest fish of all—San Francisco Giants slugger Barry Bonds, whose lifetime record of 762 home runs would surpass those of Hank Aaron (755) and Babe Ruth (714). Aaron and Ruth belonged to the hallowed ranks of sports heroes who set their records using the bodies they were born with, enhanced only by training and such natural foods as, in Ruth's case, beer and hot dogs. But Bonds's records were set, according to federal prosecutors, with the aid of performance-enhancing drugs: "the cream" (testosterone ointment) and "the clear" (anabolic steroids). Should Barry Bonds go down in the record books with an asterisk beside his name, along with other "cheaters" in baseball, track, tennis, and almost all other modern sports? Particularly hard hit by doping and allegations of doping in recent years is the sport of professional cycling. Floyd Landis, for example, was stripped of his title as winner of the 2006 Tour de France because he tested positive for high levels of testosterone after his "miraculous" come-back near the end of the race. Sometimes drug test are wrong. Should Landis have been considered innocent until proven guilty in a court of law? Or is it acceptable to hold organizations that regulate doping in sports to a lesser standard of proof? Are athletes who cheat criminals or victims? Should tougher, more accurate tests be developed to catch them? Or should fans look the other way?

The following essays by **William Moller, Brian Alexander, Michael Shermer,** and **Andy Borowitz** address these and other aspects of the increasing use of performance-enhancing drugs in sports.

WILLIAM MOLLER

THOSE WHO LIVE IN GLASS HOUSES

William Moller (b. 1983) graduated from Kenyon College in 2006 and lives in New York City, where he works as an analyst in the financial industry. An avid baseball fan, he regularly writes for *It's About the Money*, a blog about his hometown team, the New York Yankees. In the following May 2009 post to the blog *The Yankees Dollar*, Moller addresses the media's response to the news that Yankees slugger Alex Rodriguez had admitted to using "banned substances" while playing for the Texas Rangers. In his original post, Moller used hyperlinks to other websites to show the sources that support his conclusions; he has replaced those links with footnotes for this book.

XXXXXXXXXXXXXXXXXXXXXXXXXXXXXXXXXXXXXXXXXXXXXXXXXXXXXXXXXXX

1   I spent my high school years at a boarding school hidden among the apple orchards of Massachusetts. Known for a spartan philosophy regarding the adolescent need for sleep, the school worked us to the bone, regularly slamming us with six hours of homework. I pulled a lot more all-nighters (of the scholastic sort) in my years there than I ever did in college. When we weren't in class, the library, study hall, or formal sit-down meals, we were likely found on a sports field. We also had school on Saturday, beginning at 8 AM just like every other non-Sunday morning.

2   Adding kindling to the fire, the students were not your laid-back types; everyone wanted that spot at the top of the class, and social life was rife with competition. The type A's that fill the investment banking, legal, and political worlds—those are the kids I spent my high school years with.

3   And so it was that midway through my sophomore year, I found myself on my third all-nighter in a row, attempting to memorize historically significant pieces of art out of E. H. Gombrich's *The Story of Art*.

I had finished a calculus exam the day before, and the day before that had been devoted to world history. And on that one cold night in February, I had had enough. I had hit that point where you've had so little sleep over such a long time that you start seeing spots, as if you'd been staring at a bright light for too long. The grade I would compete for the next day suddenly slipped in importance, and I began daydreaming about how easy the real world would be compared to the hell I was going through.

But there was hope. A friend who I was taking occasional study   4
breaks with read the story in the bags beneath my eyes, in the slump of my shoulders, the nervous drumming of my fingers on the chair as we sipped flat, warm Coke in the common room. My personal *deus ex machina*,[1] he handed me a small white pill.

I was very innocent. I matured way after most of my peers, and   5
was probably best known for being the kid who took all the soprano solos away from the girls in the choir as a first-year student. I don't think I had ever been buzzed, much less drunk. I'd certainly never smoked a cigarette. And knowing full well that what I was doing could be nothing better than against the rules (and *less* importantly, illegal) I did what I felt I needed to do, to accomplish what was demanded of me. And it worked. I woke up and regained focus like nothing I'd ever experienced. Unfortunately, it also came with serious side effects: I was a hypersensitized, stuffed-up, sweaty, wide-eyed mess, but I studied until the birds started chirping. And I aced my test.

Later I found out the pill was Ritalin, and it was classified as a class   6
3 drug.[2] I did it again, too—only a handful of times, as the side effects were so awful. But every time it was still illegal, still against the rules. And as emphasized above, I was much more worried about the scholastic consequences if I were discovered abusing a prescription drug than the fact that I was breaking the law. Though I was using it in a far different manner than the baseball players who would later get caught with it in their systems, it was still very clearly a "performance-enhancing drug."

1. Term from ancient Greek drama (literally, "god from the machine"), referring to an actor playing a god who was mechanically lowered onto the stage in order to intervene on a character's behalf.

2. Drugs it is illegal to possess without a prescription.

7   Just like every other person on this planet, I was giving in to the incentive scheme that was presented to me. The negative of doing poorly on the test was far greater than the negative of getting caught, discounted by the anesthetic of low probability.

8   I imagine that the same dilemma must have occurred in Alex Rodriguez's subconscious before he made the decision to start taking steroids. Alex has been a phenom in every sense of the word since he was old enough to be labeled an athlete. Who knows if he took steroids in high school—and who cares, really? He did take them in the major leagues, he almost certainly took them before moving to Texas, and there's really no compelling argument that he hasn't been taking them since he moved to New York.

9   What it really comes down to is that the reason Alex did steroids is you and me. We, the public, place the best athletes on pedestals, gods on high. And Alex is a prime candidate for such treatment. He's an archetype, carrying the look of someone who will one day he cast in bronze. He's a physical monstrosity, capable of knocking the ball out of Yankee Stadium with only one hand on the bat. And at the deepest level Alex Rodriguez wants, *craves*, fame. More than that, really, he wants to be loved. He came to New York wanting to erase the memories of Mantle and DiMaggio and Berra.[3] He wanted to be beautiful and powerful and funny and philanthropic and every other positive adjective he could find.

10   Really, it was no question whether Alex would take steroids once they were offered. They promised wealth and fame above his wildest dreams. Let's be clear: A-Rod could have been a good player without steroids, maybe even a great player. But he didn't want that. He wanted to be *A-Rod*.

11   And now the cat is out of the bag. Now that we have a test showing us that A-Rod used, we finally stop turning a blind eye to what was patently obvious before. But only for Alex.

12   The entire steroid outcry is pure hypocrisy. Look, you and I both understand that the majority of the best players in baseball are steroid users. And so are a good portion of the less-than-best. And when I say

---

3. Yogi Berra (b. 1925), Mickey Mantle (1931–1995), and Joe DiMaggio (1914–1999), all record-breaking Yankees players.

that, I do so without adding the negative connotation added by the self-righteous media types who make a living by drumming up indignation from the masses. If it came out that Mariano Rivera and Derek Jeter[4] were on some sort of designer steroid, I'd be surprised and disappointed, but by no means amazed.

It's why I wasn't surprised in the slightest when Andy Pettitte 13 admitted to using HGH.[5] My only disgust with that situation is that he certainly didn't use it once and then get rid of it, as he said. When Pettitte used HGH (which isn't proven to do anything for athletes, by the way) he did it because he didn't think he'd get caught, not because he thought it was acceptable. And there's no reason to believe he really would have stopped after one use.

This all reeks of the attitude taken toward marijuana by politicians 14 until Barack Obama came around. When asked about marijuana use, Bill Clinton's response was typical: "I didn't inhale." When later asked about marijuana in the context of Clinton's response, Obama replied, "Yes, I did . . . The point was to inhale, that was the point."

Just as the vast majority of people try marijuana at some point in 15 their lives, the vast majority of baseball players have used steroids, be it HGH, Stanozolol, the cream, the clear, or any other BALCO creation.[6] This game is all about getting an edge—whether it be the front offices using BABIP[7] to pick the right players, Sammy Sosa corking a bat, Johnny Damon using maple instead of ash bats, K-Rod putting resin on his baseball cap, Pete Rose mixing Adderall in with a cup of

---

4. Jeter (b. 1974) and Rivera (b. 1969) are both current Yankees stars.

5. In 2007, after allegations were leaked to the press following a federal investigation, Yankees pitcher Andy Pettitte (b. 1972) admitted to using human growth hormone (HGH) to enhance his athletic performance.

6. The Bay Area Laboratory Cooperative (BALCO) is a San Francisco-based company that was at the center of the MLB drug scandal. Stanozolol is an anabolic steroid (see http://en.wikipedia.org/wiki/Stanozolol). The cream and the clear are steroids created and distributed by BALCO (see http://en.wikipedia.org/wiki/BALCO_Scandal) [Moller's note].

7. Batting average on balls in play, one statistic used to gauge a player's abilities.

coffee,[8] or Mark McGwire's unabashed andro use. Heck, after Ritalin was outlawed in MLB, the number of baseball players being diagnosed with ADD[9] (for which Ritalin happens to be prescribed) jumped significantly! Is it okay, since they have a doctor's scrip? There's a lot of money and fame at stake, and it skews that all-important incentive scheme.

16   Each and every general manager in the game shares at least three attributes: They're very smart, and they know exactly what's going on—but act as if they don't. And we the public let ourselves be fooled. What's worse, when enough information comes out that we can no longer ignore that a player used, we demonize them relative to their "untainted" peers. By all accounts, Barry Bonds is a real jerk—which is plenty of reason to dislike him. But don't hate him because he's a "cheater." In that sense, he's just one of the gang.

17   Back in February of 2000, I got to choose between breaking the rules and breaking my grades. I chose the rules, and it wasn't a tough decision. And I'd wager that the lure of being A-Rod is a bit more seductive than an A on that art history test.

8. Until 2006, no rules existed to prevent players from using amphetamines such as Adderall to cause a spike in focus and energy level, and such use was rampant. "Corking a bat": hollowing out a bat and replacing the core with a lighter material, to bring the bat beneath regulation weight and gain an advantage. "Maple instead of ash bats": In 2008, the use of maple bats, which tend to shatter rather than splinter, came under scrutiny for the danger they posed to fielders and fans alike. "Resin": Pitchers are known to sometimes use the brim of their baseball caps to hide banned substances such as pine tar, vasoline, or resin, which affect the movement of the ball [Moller's note].

9. Attention deficit disorder; symptoms include difficulty with staying focused and controlling one's behavior.

XXXXXXXXXXXXXXX **Understanding the Essay** XXXXXXXXXXXXXXX

1. When he took Ritalin to stay alert while studying for exams in high school, says William Moller, he "was giving in to the incentive scheme that was presented to me" (7). What "scheme" is he talking about? Is he right to say that "every other person on this planet" is subject to such incentives (7)? Explain.

2. Why does Moller think it is "pure hypocrisy" to criticize athletes for taking performance-enhancing drugs (12)? Do you agree or disagree? Why?

3. What EVIDENCE does Moller provide to support his CLAIM that no one should seriously fault Alex Rodriguez and other star athletes for taking steroids? Is that evidence sufficient to make his case? If not, what additional evidence should he have—or could he have—included? Would your answer be different if Moller's piece were a term paper instead of a blog post? Why or why not?

4. Moller argues by ANALOGY, drawing a COMPARISON between his actions and those of athletes who take performance-enhancing drugs. Such arguments are only as strong as the analogy is close. By this measure, how strong do you find his argument? Explain.

5. Why does Moller refer to the low probability of getting caught as an "anesthetic" (7)? How and how well does this METAPHOR support his general argument?

6. The root meaning of *hypocrisy* is "play acting" (12). How and how well does this basic sense of the word apply to sports fans and the media as Moller characterizes them?

BRIAN ALEXANDER

Tour de Farce

Brian Alexander (b. 1959) is a journalist who writes about biotechnology and drugs in sports for *Outside* magazine and other publications. In "Tour de Farce," posted in 2006 in the web magazine *Slate*, Alexander focuses on the case of Floyd Landis, who was stripped of his win in the Tour de France by a drug-testing system that, according to Alexander, "is not fair to athletes, science, and sports consumers."

XXXXXXXXXXXXXXXXXXXXXXXXXXXXXXXXXXXXXXXXXXXXXXXXXXXXXXXXXXXXX

1   Like much of the rest of the world, I was thrilled by Floyd Landis's startling comeback in Stage 17 of the Tour de France. But since I write about doping and sports, I've learned to be suspicious of miracles. The real tragedy of doping is the way it tarnishes everything and everybody and forbids us from giving in to the wonder of sports. And now the news comes out that Floyd Landis tested positive for high testosterone levels following that very same miracle stage. There is a disheartening feeling of inevitability about the whole thing.

2   It is certainly possible that Landis did nothing wrong. The test the Tour de France uses for testosterone does not actually detect the use of a drug; it detects a ratio of testosterone to another hormone called epitestosterone. There are vagaries, the science can be imprecise, and it is known that massive athletic effort can fog the test. Innocent until proven guilty and all that.

3   Regardless of Landis's fate, this episode, and the banning of a group of top riders before this year's Tour began, illustrates why the current system of doping detection and "justice" does not work. The main reason why it doesn't work is that the world, and especially the American sports-consuming public, is not ready to embrace the changes necessary to leech drugs from sports. Sure, Congress holds hearings on steroid use in baseball. Sports officials make earnest statements, and athletes

decry those among them who dope. Fans and editorial writers demand action. But do they realize what they are asking for?

That the current testing regimen does not work to prevent doping 4 is painfully obvious. True enough, Landis's "A" sample—the first of two needed to confirm that he broke the rules—turned up positive. So, you could argue that the testing worked in this case. But if his testosterone was low, what does that mean about the value of the test? You might point to Tyler Hamilton,[1] who was caught using somebody else's blood to boost his own endurance by a new test that detects foreign blood cells. He was banned for two years, sure. But how long had he been using that technique before he was found out by a brand-new procedure? Cyclists are always figuring out new ways to dope, and the testers will always be playing catch-up. For example, there is still no urine test for human growth hormone, a commonly used performance booster. There's also no test for a new drug called Increlex, which gives athletes more insulin-like growth factor 1—a protein that does essentially the same thing as growth hormone.

If a test won't stop doping, what will? The biggest crackdowns of 5 recent times have been the result of law enforcement action, not testing. The BALCO case blew up because the feds started investigating the BALCO lab and because a track coach, Trevor Graham, blew the whistle by sending a syringe of a previously undetectable steroid to testing authorities. The scandal that wiped out the cream of this year's Tour crop was the result of an investigation by Spanish police. During the last Winter Olympics in Italy, the Italian police raided the quarters of the Austrian ski team. Nobody tested positive in either the Spanish or the Austrian scandals.

When cyclists and track athletes get caught doping these days, 6 their punishment gets meted out by the World Anti-Doping Agency.[2]

---

1. Former professional bicycle racer and Olympic gold medalist (b. 1971).

2. An independent Swiss foundation created in 1999 through an initiative set up by the International Olympic Committee. It develops and helps to implement international policies governing doping in sports.

This odd parallel justice system is not fair to athletes, science, and sports consumers. In order to stamp out doping, WADA must be backed by real law enforcement.

7   Italy has already taken a step in that direction. Athletes there could face jail for "fraud"—competing under false pretenses. The Italian government treats doping as a criminal matter, not something to be dealt with from the cosseted confines of sports. Now, a doper must weigh the potential for enormous wealth and prestige that a victory would bring against the possibility of a temporary ban from competition for a first offense. In the Italian model, he must also weigh a stint behind bars or a substantial financial penalty.

8   We are faced, then, with a proposal to criminalize sports doping. There would be raids by the feds, trials, and law enforcement resources burned in the pursuit of multi-millionaire druggies. I'm not so sure we have the stomach for this. Barry Bonds is still a hero in San Francisco.[3] There are no boycotts of Giants games. And remember that if Bonds goes down, it will be for perjury or tax evasion—none of the athletes involved in the BALCO case will ever see jail time for taking performance-enhancing drugs.

9   Major League Baseball insists that it is taking care of its own drug problems, and the sports-consuming public seems content to believe it. Only aficionados can recall who was banned from track and field because of the BALCO case. Lance Armstrong,[4] who has struggled through years of accusations but has never officially tested positive for performance-enhancing drugs, remains an American icon. And if it would be hard to muster support for a federal justice role here, think about the difficulty of mounting an international effort. Just imagine the outcry the first time French police pick up a star American tennis player during the French Open.

---

3. In 2007, San Francisco Giants slugger Barry Bonds (b. 1964) was charged with perjury and obstruction of justice relating to his testimony about his use of performance-enhancing drugs.

4. Professional bicycle racer (b. 1971) who won the Tour de France seven times consecutively and came in third in 2009.

This is what American consumers have to ask themselves: If we   10
really want doping to stop, we have to be prepared to see our heroes do
hard time. Do we care that much?

XXXXXXXXXXXXXX **UNDERSTANDING THE ESSAY** XXXXXXXXXXXXXX

1. According to Brian Alexander, the present system for testing for banned substances in cycling and other sports is unfair and often inaccurate. Why does
Alexander think so? How convincing do you find his ARGUMENT in support of
this CLAIM? Explain.

2. What standard of proof would be required, in Alexander's view, in a testing
system that *was* fair and accurate? What objections to such a system does
Alexander raise?

3. The "tragedy" of doping, says Alexander, is that it prevents fans "from giving in to the wonder of sports" (1). Upon what premise does Alexander base
this conclusion? Is that premise valid? Why or why not?

4. When Alexander argues that drug testing cannot be relied upon to prevent
doping because cyclists "are always figuring out new ways to dope," is his logic
valid, or is he committing the fallacy of either/or reasoning (4)? Explain.

5. Alexander characterizes the disillusionment of sports fans due to widespread
doping as a "tragedy" (1). Is this HYPERBOLE justified? Why or why not?

6. Alexander ends his argument with a question. To what extent is it a RHETOR-
ICAL QUESTION?

MICHAEL SHERMER

The Doping Dilemma

Michael Shermer (b. 1954) is the editor of *Skeptic* magazine and a monthly columnist for *Scientific American*. He is the author of several books that debunk superstitions and other forms of irrational thinking, including *Why People Believe Weird Things* (1998), *How We Believe* (1999), *Why Darwin Matters* (2006), and *The Mind of the Market* (2007). A serious amateur cyclist who cofounded the Race Across America, Shermer considers how best to address the doping "arms race" in sports in the following essay, which he adapted for *The Norton Sampler* from a longer article published in *Scientific American* in 2008.

XXXXXXXXXXXXXXXXXXXXXXXXXXXXXXXXXXXXXXXXXXXXXXXXXXXXXXXXXX

1   For a competitive cyclist, there is nothing more physically crushing and psychologically demoralizing than getting dropped by your competitors on a climb. With searing lungs and burning legs, your body hunches over the handlebars as you struggle to stay with the leader. You know all too well that once you come off the back of the pack the drive to push harder is gone—and with it any hope for victory.

2   I know the feeling because it happened to me in 1985 on the long climb out of Albuquerque during the 3,000-mile, nonstop transcontinental Race Across America. On the outskirts of town I had caught up with the second-place rider (and eventual winner), Jonathan Boyer, a svelte road racer who was the first American to compete in the Tour de France. About halfway up the leg-breaking climb, that familiar wave of crushing fatigue swept through my legs as I gulped for oxygen in my struggle to hang on.

3   To no avail. By the top of the climb Boyer was a tiny dot on the shimmering blacktop, and I didn't see him again until the finish line in Atlantic City. Later that night Jim Lampley, the commentator for ABC's Wide World of Sports, asked what else I might have done to go faster.

"I should have picked better parents," I deadpanned. We all have   4
certain genetic limitations, I went on, that normal training cannot overcome. What else could I have done?

Plenty, and I knew it. Cyclists on the 1984 U.S. Olympic cycling   5
team had told me how they had injected themselves with extra blood
before races, either their own—drawn earlier in the season—or that of
someone else with the same blood type. "Blood doping," as the practice
is called, was not banned at the time, and on a sliding moral scale it
seemed only marginally distinguishable from training at high altitude.
Either way, you increase the number of oxygen-carrying red blood cells
in your body. Still, I was already thirty years old and had an academic
career to fall back on. I was racing bikes mostly to see how far I could
push my body before it gave out. Enhancing my performance artificially
didn't mesh well with my reasons for racing.

But suppose I had been twenty and earning my living through   6
cycling, my one true passion, with no prospects for some other career.
Imagine that my team had made performance-enhancing drugs part of
its "medical program" and that I knew I could be cut if I was not competitive. Finally, assume I believed that most of my competitors were
doping and that the ones who were tested almost never got caught.

That scenario, in substance, is what many competitive cyclists say   7
they have been facing since the early 1990s. And although the details
differ for other sports such as baseball, the overall doping circumstances
are not dissimilar. Many players are convinced that "everyone else"
takes drugs and so have come to believe that they cannot remain competitive if they do not participate. On the governance side, the failure of
Major League Baseball to make the rules clear, much less to enforce
them with extensive drug testing throughout the season, coupled with its
historical tendency to look the other way, has created an environment
conducive to doping.

Naturally, most of us do not want to believe that any of these stel-   8
lar athletes are guilty of doping. But the convergence of evidence leads
me to conclude that in cycling, as well as in baseball, football, and track
and field, most of the top competitors of the past two decades have been
using performance-enhancing drugs. The time has come to ask not if but
why. The reasons are threefold: first, better drugs, drug cocktails, and

drug-training regimens; second, an arms race consistently won by drug takers over drug testers; and third, a shift in many professional sports that has tipped the balance of incentives in favor of cheating and away from playing by the rules.

* * *

9   Cycling, like all sports, is a game with rules and players. The rules today clearly prohibit the use of performance-enhancing drugs. But because the drugs are extremely effective and the payoffs for success are so high, and because most of the drugs are difficult if not impossible to detect, the incentive to use them is powerful. Once a few elite riders "defect" to gain an advantage over their cooperating competitors, [those competitors] too must defect (even if they only *think* others are cheating), leading to a cascade of defection down through the ranks; the doping leaders need strong supportive team members, who are then tempted to dope in order to do their job, leading amateur athletes to dope in order to even compete, and before long the entire system breaks down. Because the rules are clear, however, a code of silence prevents any open communication and cooperation between competitors and teams in order to reverse the defection trend.

10   Just as in evolution there is an arms race between predators and prey that drives both to greater levels of fitness, in sports there is an arms race between the drug takers and the drug testers. In my opinion the testers are five years away from catching the takers . . . and always will be. Those who stand to benefit the most from defecting on the rules of the game will always be more creative than those enforcing the rules, unless the latter have equivalent incentives.

11   In game theory, when players reach a point where none have anything to gain by unilaterally changing strategies, this is called *Nash equilibrium*, a concept identified by the Nobel laureate mathematician John Forbes Nash Jr. and immortalized in the film *A Beautiful Mind*. To end doping in sports we need to structure the game so that competing clean is in a Nash equilibrium. That is, in a hypothetical game matrix, we need to change the rules of enforcement so that the temptation to "defect" by cheating is of a lower utility value than cooperating, especially so that the players do not feel like suckers for following the rules.

Here are my recommendations for how cycling (and other sports)   12
can reach a Nash equilibrium in which no one has any incentive to cheat
by doping:

1. Grant immunity to all athletes for past (pre-2008) cheating. Because
   the entire system is corrupt and most competitors have been doping, it
   accomplishes nothing to strip the winner of a title after the fact when
   it is almost certain that the runners-up were also doping. With immunity, retired athletes may help to improve the antidoping system.

2. Increase the number of competitors tested—in competition, out of
   competition, and especially immediately before or after a race—to
   thwart countermeasures. Testing should be done by independent
   drug agencies not affiliated with any sanctioning bodies, riders,
   sponsors, or teams. Teams should also employ independent drug-
   testing companies to test their own riders, starting with a preseason
   performance test on each athlete to create a baseline profile. Corporate sponsors should provide additional financial support to make
   sure the testing is rigorous.

3. Establish a reward, modeled on the X prizes (cash awards offered
   for a variety of technical achievements), for scientists to develop
   tests that can detect currently undetectable doping agents. The
   incentive for drug testers must be equal to or greater than that for
   drug takers.

4. Increase substantially the penalty for getting caught: one strike and
   you're out—forever. To protect the athlete from false positive
   results or inept drug testers (both exist), the system of arbitration
   and appeals must be fair and trusted. Once a decision is made,
   however, it must be substantive and final.

5. Disqualify all team members from an event if any member of the
   team tests positive for doping. Compel the convicted athlete to
   return all salary paid and prize monies earned to the team sponsors.
   The threat of this penalty will bring the substantial social pressures
   of "band of brothers" psychology to bear on all the team members,
   giving them a strong incentive to enforce their own antidoping rules.

13   That may sound utopian. But it can work. [Jonathan] Vaughters, who is now director of the U.S. cycling team Slipstream/Chipotle, has already started a program of extensive and regular in-house drug testing. "Remember, most of these guys are athletes, not criminals," he says. "If they believe the rest are stopping [the doping] and feel it in the speed of the peloton,[1] they will stop, too, with a great sigh of relief."

14   Hope springs eternal. But with these changes I believe the psychology of the game can be shifted from defection to cooperation. If so, sports can return to the tradition of rewarding and celebrating excellence in performance, enhanced only by an athlete's will to win.

1. The main pack of riders maintaining a similar speed in a bicycle race.

XXXXXXXXXXXXXX **UNDERSTANDING THE ESSAY** XXXXXXXXXXXXXX

1. What reasons does Michael Shermer identify for the use of performance-enhancing drugs in sports? How does his five-point plan for combating drugs in sports address each of those reasons?

2. If Shermer's plan were adopted, how successful do you think it would be? Explain.

3. "I know the feeling," says Shermer, "because it happened to me" (2). In the first part of his essay, why does Shermer refer to his own experience as a competitive cyclist? Is this an effective strategy? Why or why not?

4. "The time has come to ask not if" many top athletes are using performance-enhancing drugs, says Shermer, "but why" (8). Is Shermer begging the question here, or is his logic valid? Explain.

5. Shermer says that the "convergence of evidence leads [him] to conclude that . . . most of the top competitors" in major league sports in the past two decades have used drugs (8). What EVIDENCE is he referring to here? How valid do you find his conclusion? Does he use INDUCTION or DEDUCTION to reach it? Explain.

6. What are the implications of referring to the struggle between athletes who take drugs and those who test for them as an "arms race" (8)?

7. Strictly speaking, how many (usually unpleasant) choices does a "dilemma" have to offer? How appropriate is Alexander's use of the word to characterize doping in sports? Explain.

ANDY BOROWITZ

ANGRY CLEVELAND INDIANS FANS DEMAND TEAM TAKE STEROIDS

Andy Borowitz (b. 1958) is a humorist and founder of the satiric website *Borowitz Report*. Born and raised in Cleveland, Borowitz has seen his home team lose so many baseball games that he can think of only one way to improve their performance. Borowitz's satiric article was first posted in 2009 on *The Huffington Post*, a news and multi-blog website.

XXXXXXXXXXXXXXXXXXXXXXXXXXXXXXXXXXXXXXXXXXXXXXXXXXXXXXX

The national pastime suffered another black eye last night when a mob of irate Cleveland Indians fans poured onto the diamond at Progressive Field[1] to demand that their team take steroids.

Displeasure with the championship-starved squad reached a boiling point with the news that slugger Manny Ramirez took performance-enhancing drugs—but only after leaving the Indians.

When asked by ESPN if he ingested the banned medication while playing for Cleveland, Mr. Ramirez shrugged his shoulders and replied, "What would be the point of that?"

Mr. Ramirez is just the latest in a long line of baseball players who have refused to take steroids while playing for the Indians, says fan Chuck Goulardi, forty-nine, the leader of last night's protest.

"Manny's comment was the straw that broke the proverbial camel's back," says Mr. Goulardi, who has seen his 'roid-free Tribe fall to their juiced-up competition more times than he can recall. "These players are paid good money, and all we're asking them to do is take one measly shot in the ass."

---

1. Baseball park that is home to the Cleveland Indians.

6   But getting the Indians to start taking steroids may be easier said than done, says former slugger Jose Canseco,[2] the author of the controversial tell-all book *Juiced.*

7   "On more than forty occasions I sneaked into the Cleveland clubhouse, offering to shoot those guys up with 'roids," says Mr. Canseco. "No takers."

8   Last night's melee was only the latest display of dissatisfaction on the part of Cleveland fans, who earlier this season demanded that the giant TV screen on the outfield scoreboard show a different game.

2. Retired baseball player (b. 1964) who admitted to steroid use in his 2007 book *Juiced: Wild Times, Rampant 'Roids, Smash Hits, and How Baseball Got Big.* He also claimed that 85 percent of major league players use steroids.

XXXXXXXXXXXXXX **UNDERSTANDING THE ESSAY** XXXXXXXXXXXXXX

1. According to Andy Borowitz, why are the fans of the Cleveland Indians so "irate" (1)?

2. Not only do Indians fans not object to their team using steroids, they (the fans) are so desperate, Borowitz claims, that they will actually "demand" that their team use steroids. How logical is Borowitz's CLAIM—in the case of chronically disappointed Cleveland fans?

3. One serious ARGUMENT for condoning (or, at least, not condemning) the use of drugs in sports is that professional athletes are entertainers and entertainers have often used performance-enhancing substances. Why should baseball players be held to a higher standard than, say, rock musicians? To what extent (however humorously) does Borowitz's "report" imply that they shouldn't?

4. Borowitz's SATIRIC commentary on sports fans and doping takes the form of a news article. Is this an effective strategy for making an argument about doping in sports? Why or why not?

5. What is a "melee" (8), and what does Borowitz's use of this term imply about the behavior of mobs in general? What about sports fans?

WHAT'S WRONG WITH PERFORMANCE-ENHANCING DRUGS IN SPORTS?

The following questions refer to the arguments on pp. 410–26.

XXXXXXXXXXXXX **ANALYZING THE ARGUMENTS** XXXXXXXXXXXXX

1. Among the four writers in this debate on the use of performance-enhancing drugs in sports, only Brian Alexander and Michael Shermer actually propose solutions to the problem. What solutions do they propose? Which solution seems more reasonable? Why?

2. William Moller ARGUES that sports fans should not throw stones at their heroes for taking banned substances because fans create incentives to take drugs by demanding superhuman performance from mere mortals. How does Andy Borowitz use the image of an angry mob to make essentially the same point?

3. Of the four writers in this debate, only Shermer has been a serious athlete. To what extent does his experience as a cyclist give Shermer an authority that the others lack? How, and how effectively, do the other writers establish their credibility? Explain.

4. "If we really want doping to stop," Alexander concludes, "we have to be prepared to see our heroes do hard time. Do we care that much?" (10). How would the other three writers in this debate respond to this question?

XXXXXXXXXXXXXXXXXXX **FOR WRITING** XXXXXXXXXXXXXXXXXXXXXX

1. Write a paragraph or two about the potential EFFECTS of using alcohol, barbiturates, or some other mood-altering substance to "enhance performance" on an academic task, such as writing a term paper, preparing for an exam, or giving a speech.

2. Write an essay about a time you witnessed someone cheating—in school, sports, business, or some other arena. Explain what the incentives to cheat were, or might have been; but ARGUE that the act was morally wrong anyway—and explain why.

3. Focusing on the sport (or sports) you know best, write an argument about the use of performance-enhancing drugs by athletes. Try to propose a solution to the problem. If you don't see a solution—or, for that matter, a problem—explain why. Be sure to support your CLAIM with solid EVIDENCE.

What Language(s) Do You Speak
If You're an American?

In America today, more than three hundred languages are commonly spoken. They include Spanish, Chinese, Korean, Navajo—and, of course, English. English is an official national language in India, Ireland, New Zealand, Canada, the Philippines, and a host of other countries. It is also the official language of California, Florida, Illinois, and more than half of the other states in the union. But the English language is not—nor has it ever been—the official national language of the United States. Almost every year some members of Congress introduce "English only" legislation. Every year that legislation fails—so far. Is speaking English a prerequisite for participating fully in American society? The traditional "melting pot" view of America argues that Americans have achieved a national identity in part by speaking a common language. In the past, most American immigrants learned to speak English, and today some immigrant parents are opposed to bilingual programs in the schools. They want their children to learn English, which they see as a condition of success in America. Many Americans, however, want to honor their cultural and linguistic heritage by speaking the family's native language at home and, at times, in public. Like many other Americans, these multilingual Americans see the country not as a melting pot but as a "quilt"—a patchwork society held together by its tolerance for diversity, including linguistic diversity. Speaking other languages besides English, they feel, does not make them any less "American," though English is usually one of their languages.

In a nation so diverse, how do we reconcile multicultural values and linguistic diversity with the need for common cultural ground? In the following essays, **Myriam Marquez, Chang-Rae Lee, Greg Lewis,** *and* **Dennis Baron** *offer a range of views on the extent to which our identity and our success—as individuals and as a nation—are tied to the use of the English language.*

MYRIAM MARQUEZ

WHY AND WHEN WE SPEAK SPANISH IN PUBLIC

Myriam Marquez is in charge of the editorial pages of the *Miami Herald*. Born in Cuba, she fled to the United States with her parents in 1959. In "Why and When We Speak Spanish in Public," first published in *Orlando Sentinel* in 1999, Marquez considers why she and her family "haven't adopted English as our official family language."

XXXXXXXXXXXXXXXXXXXXXXXXXXXXXXXXXXXXXXXXXXXXXXXXXXXXXXXXX

W hen I'm shopping with my mother or standing in line with my stepdad to order fast food or anywhere else we might be together, we're going to speak to one another in Spanish.   1

That may appear rude to those who don't understand Spanish and overhear us in public places.   2

Those around us may get the impression that we're talking about them. They may wonder why we would insist on speaking in a foreign tongue, especially if they knew that my family has lived in the United States for forty years and that my parents do understand English and speak it, albeit with difficulty and a heavy accent.   3

Let me explain why we haven't adopted English as our official family language. For me and most of the bilingual people I know, it's a matter of respect for our parents and comfort in our cultural roots.   4

It's not meant to be rude to others. It's not meant to alienate anyone or to Balkanize America.   5

It's certainly not meant to be un-American—what constitutes an "American" being defined by English speakers from North America.   6

Being an American has very little to do with what language we use during our free time in a free country. From its inception, this country was careful not to promote a government-mandated official language.   7

8   We understand that English is the common language of this country and the one most often heard in international-business circles from Peru to Norway. We know that, to get ahead here, one must learn English.

9   But that ought not mean that somehow we must stop speaking in our native tongue whenever we're in a public area, as if we were ashamed of who we are, where we're from. As if talking in Spanish—or any other language, for that matter—is some sort of litmus test used to gauge American patriotism.

10   Throughout this nation's history, most immigrants—whether from Poland or Finland or Italy or wherever else—kept their language through the first generation and, often, the second. I suspect that they spoke among themselves in their native tongue—in public. Pennsylvania even provided voting ballots written in German during much of the 1800s for those who weren't fluent in English.

11   In this century, Latin American immigrants and others have fought for this country in U.S.-led wars. They have participated fully in this nation's democracy by voting, holding political office and paying taxes. And they have watched their children and grandchildren become so "American" that they resist speaking in Spanish.

12   You know what's rude?

13   When there are two or more people who are bilingual and another person who speaks only English and the bilingual folks all of a sudden start speaking Spanish, which effectively leaves out the English-only speaker. I don't tolerate that.

14   One thing's for sure. If I'm ever in a public place with my mom or dad and bump into an acquaintance who doesn't speak Spanish, I will switch to English and introduce that person to my parents. They will respond in English and do so with respect.

XXXXXXXXXXXXXX **Understanding the Essay** XXXXXXXXXXXXXX

1. Even though they speak English and have lived in the United States for forty years, Myriam Marquez and her parents have not adopted English as their "official family language" (4). Should they have? Would the "patriotism" of the family be stronger if they did (9)? Why or why not?

2. Why, according to Marquez, do she and her family and "most of the bilingual people" she knows continue to speak their native language (4)? How valid are her reasons for claiming they should? Explain.

3. If Marquez speaks Spanish with her family, why does she think it "rude" to continue to speak her native language in the presence of people who speak only English (12)? How does this attitude affect her credibility? Why?

4. Why does Marquez cite Polish, Finnish, Italian, and German immigrants in paragraph 10? How does this support her CLAIM that she and her family should continue to speak Spanish in public?

5. To "Balkanize" a region is to divide it into small, powerless states that are constantly in conflict with each other (5). Where does this meaning of the word come from? How appropriate is this word in an essay about using different languages in the United States?

6. A "litmus test" is used to test whether a solution is or is not acidic (9). Is it logical to apply such an either/or test to a person's character or patriotism? Why or why not?

CHANG-RAE LEE

MUTE IN AN ENGLISH-ONLY WORLD

Chang-Rae Lee (b. 1965) is a novelist and writing teacher at Princeton. Born in Korea, Lee emigrated to the United States with his family at the age of three. His novels include *Native Speaker* (1995), *Aloft* (2004), and *The Surrendered* (2008). In "Mute in an English-Only World," published in 1996 on the Op-Ed page of the *New York Times*, Lee considers what his mother would think of laws requiring that at least half of any commercial sign in Korean neighborhoods in New Jersey be translated into English.

XXXXXXXXXXXXXXXXXXXXXXXXXXXXXXXXXXXXXXXXXXXXXXXXXXXXXXXXXXXXXX

1   When I read of the troubles in Palisades Park, N.J., over the proliferation of Korean-language signs along its main commercial strip, I unexpectedly sympathized with the frustrations, resentments and fears of the longtime residents. They clearly felt alienated and even unwelcome in a vital part of their community. The town, like seven others in New Jersey, has passed laws requiring that half of any commercial sign in a foreign language be in English.

2   Now I certainly would never tolerate any exclusionary ideas about who could rightfully settle and belong in the town. But having been raised in a Korean immigrant family, I saw every day the exacting price and power of language, especially with my mother, who was an outsider in an English-only world.

3   In the first years we lived in America, my mother could speak only the most basic English, and she often encountered great difficulty whenever she went out.

4   We lived in New Rochelle, N.Y., in the early '70s, and most of the local businesses were run by the descendants of immigrants who, generations ago, had come to the suburbs from New York City. Proudly dotting Main Street and North Avenue were Italian pastry and cheese

shops, Jewish tailors and cleaners, and Polish and German butchers and bakers. If my mother's marketing couldn't wait until the weekend, when my father had free time, she would often hold off until I came home from school to buy the groceries.

Though I was only six or seven years old, she insisted that I go out   5
shopping with her and my younger sister. I mostly loathed the task, partly because it meant I couldn't spend the afternoon playing catch with my friends but also because I knew our errands would inevitably lead to an awkward scene, and that I would have to speak up to help my mother.

I was just learning the language myself, but I was a quick study, as   6
children are with new tongues. I had spent kindergarten in almost complete silence, hearing only the high nasality of my teacher and comprehending little but the cranky wails and cries of my classmates. But soon, seemingly mere months later, I had already become a terrible ham and mimic, and I would crack up my father with impressions of teachers, his friends and even himself. My mother scolded for me for aping his speech, and the one time I attempted to make light of hers I rated a roundhouse smack on my bottom.

For her, the English language was not very funny. It usually meant   7
trouble and a good dose of shame, and sometimes real hurt. Although she had a good reading knowledge of the language from university classes in South Korea, she had never practiced actual conversation. So in America, she used English flashcards and phrase books and watched television with us kids. And she faithfully carried a pocket workbook illustrated with stick-figure people and compound sentences to be filled in.

But none of it seemed to do her much good. Staying mostly at   8
home to care for us, she didn't have many chances to try out sundry words and phrases. When she did, say, at the window of the post office, her readied speech would stall, freeze, sometimes altogether collapse.

One day was unusually harrowing. We ventured downtown in the   9
new Ford Country Squire my father had bought her, an enormous station wagon that seemed as long—and deft—as an ocean liner. We were shopping for a special meal for guests visiting that weekend, and my mother had heard that a particular butcher carried fresh oxtails—which she needed for a traditional soup.

10   We'd never been inside the shop, but my mother would pause before its window, which was always lined with whole hams, crown roasts and ropes of plump handmade sausages. She greatly esteemed the bounty with her eyes, and my sister and I did also, but despite our desirous cries she'd turn us away and instead buy the packaged links at the Finast supermarket, where she felt comfortable looking them over and could easily spot the price. And, of course, not have to talk.

11   But that day she was resolved. The butcher store was crowded, and as we stepped inside the door jingled a welcome. No one seemed to notice. We waited for some time, and people who entered after us were now being served. Finally, an old woman nudged my mother and waved a little ticket, which we hadn't taken. We patiently waited again, until one of the beefy men behind the glass display hollered our number.

12   My mother pulled us forward and began searching the cases, but the oxtails were nowhere to be found. The man, his big arms crossed, sharply said, "Come on, lady, whaddya want?" This unnerved her, and she somehow blurted the Korean word for oxtail, *soggori*.

13   The butcher looked as if my mother had put something sour in his mouth, and he glanced back at the lighted board and called the next number.

14   Before I knew it, she had rushed us outside and back in the wagon, which she had double-parked because of the crowd. She was furious, almost vibrating with fear and grief, and I could see she was about to cry.

15   She wanted to go back inside, but now the driver of the car we were blocking wanted to pull out. She was shooing us away. My mother, who had just earned her driver's license, started furiously working the pedals. But in her haste she must have flooded the engine, for it wouldn't turn over. The driver started honking and then another car began honking as well, and soon it seemed the entire street was shrieking at us.

16   In the following years, my mother grew steadily more comfortable with English. In Korean, she could be fiery, stern, deeply funny, and ironic; in English, just slightly less so. If she was never quite fluent, she gained enough confidence to make herself clearly known to anyone, and particularly to me.

Five years ago, she died of cancer, and some months after we 17
buried her I found myself in the driveway of my father's house, washing
her sedan. I liked taking care of her things; it made me feel close to her.
While I was cleaning out the glove compartment, I found her pocket
English workbook, the one with the silly illustrations. I hadn't seen it in
nearly twenty years. The yellowed pages were brittle and dogeared. She
had fashioned a plain-paper wrapping for it, and I wondered whether
she meant to protect the book or hide it.

I don't doubt that she would have appreciated doing the family 18
shopping on the new Broad Avenue of Palisades Park. But I like to
think, too, that she would have understood those who now complain
about the Korean-only signs.

I wonder what these same people would have done if they had seen 19
my mother studying her English workbook—or lost in a store. Would
they have nodded gently at her? Would they have lent a kind word?

XXXXXXXXXXXXXXX **UNDERSTANDING THE ESSAY** XXXXXXXXXXXXXXX

1. His mother, says Chang-Rae Lee, had studied English in South Korea and
could read it well. So why did she have trouble with "actual conversation" (7)?
How did she eventually overcome her difficulties with speaking English?

2. If commercial signs written in Korean would have been useful to Lee's
mother when doing her shopping, why does Lee think she would approve of
new laws requiring that signs in some New Jersey towns be written at least half
in English? What is Lee suggesting about his mother's character?

3. In addition to telling a story about his mother, Lee is making an ARGUMENT
about language and immigration. What is the central CLAIM of Lee's argument,
and where does he state it most directly?

4. How and well does Lee's ANECDOTE about going to the butcher support his
argument about the challenges of adjusting to a new culture? Explain.

5. In the anecdote of the butcher shop, Lee includes a single line of DIALOGUE,
"Come on, lady, whaddya want?" (12). Is this an accurate EXAMPLE of spoken English? Should Lee have included other examples of direct speech? Why or why not?

6. Lee not only tells us that his mother forgot the English word for oxtail, he
supplies the Korean word, "sogorri" (12). How and how well does this example
help Lee show why adults like his mother may have more difficulties learning a
new language than their children do?

GREG LEWIS

AN OPEN LETTER
TO DIVERSITY'S VICTIMS

Greg Lewis (b. 1942), a former teacher and businessman, is a writer and frequent contributor to the news website washingtondispatch.com. He is the co-author of *End Your Addiction Now* (2002). In "An Open Letter to Diversity's Victims," published on washingtondispatch.com in 2003, Lewis makes an argument about the effectiveness of bilingual education in preparing students to make their way "in the broader culture."

✗✗✗

1   Those who promote what they call "diversity" have insisted that American schools provide instruction in both English and Spanish so that Hispanic children will not have to learn English. As near as I can determine, the reasoning is that Hispanic people living in the United States are at risk for losing their cultural identity if they learn the language spoken by the overwhelming majority of their fellow citizens.

2   Until 1998, California's liberal educators and administrators managed to buck common sense and the wishes of 85 percent of the state's Hispanic population to perpetuate their "separate but equal" doctrine of bilingual education. Proposition 227, which passed with a landslide majority in that year, effectively put an end to the practice in California. By August of 2000, the average reading scores of the sate's more than one million Hispanic elementary students had improved more than 20 points across the board, confounding liberal educational segregationists.

3   In fact, because children who don't learn to speak "Standard" English have a much more difficult time achieving job and career success, liberals who still blindly support bilingual education are condemning a significant portion of Spanish-speaking children to second-class economic citizenship. One can only hope that in the near future Hispanics

taught in their native language will claim victim status and bring a class-action lawsuit against the arrogant, agenda-driven educators who still hold out for bilingual education for not giving them the linguistic tools they needed to take advantage of the wonderful economic opportunities that would have been available to them had they been "forced" to learn English. This is one of the few instances I can think of in which the American legal profession might actually distinguish itself through class-action litigation.

California, you will recall, was also the state which tried to railroad 4 its citizens into recognizing Ebonics (that is, so-called African American English) as a language, and to give credit to (primarily) inner-city students for having been raised to speak a dialect which is inadequate to the demands of the world beyond the circumscribed confines of their neighborhoods. How much better off would everyone involved be if the same effort had been put into teaching African American children English as a second language?

Simply put, bilingual education doesn't provide students whose first 5 language is not Standard English with the single most important skill they need for making their way in the broader culture. The fact that that broader culture is what its adversaries denigrate as "white" culture begs the question. To succeed in America—with a number of relatively minor although often highly visible exceptions—it's important to speak, read, and understand English as most Americans speak it. There's nothing cruel or unfair in that; it's just the way it is. And when liberals try to downplay that fact in the name of diversity or multiculturalism (or whatever the liberal buzzword *du jour* happens to be at the time), they're cynically appealing to a kind of cultural vanity that almost every one of us possesses. People don't want to be told that the way they speak (or dress or behave) won't gain them credence with a majority of Americans.

In this case, however, the appeal to cultural vanity is destructive. It 6 results in a kind of collective blind spot among the blacks and Hispanics who allow themselves to be hoodwinked into believing that when they walk into a job interview for a responsible position and say, "Yo, 's up?" the person sitting across the desk from them—whether black or white, male or female—is going to throw some internal Ebonics switch and reply, "You got it."

7   I'm not talking about a McJob. I'm talking about a position for which there might be some competition, one whose pay starts in the high twenties or low thirties. I'm talking about a job for which the company that hires you is going to invest as much as $5,000.00 or more in instructors' salaries and the infrastructure necessary to support a good corporate entry-level management training function and to compensate you for the weeks you spend in training; that is, in order to provide you with everything you'll need to take advantage of an opportunity they want to see you succeed in.

8   Because we need to get something straight. Companies want to see their employees succeed. They don't care what color your skin is. They don't care if your first name is Lakeesha or your surname is Gonzales. (Well, they wouldn't if there weren't Federal regulations telling them they had to.) They want to see you do well, no matter your ethnicity or skin color. Corporate success is a win-win proposition. If you do well, you help the company you work for do well. If the company you work for does well, then there are expanding opportunities for you to move up to positions of increasing responsibility for which you will be rewarded with higher salaries and greater benefits.

9   And I can tell you: By the time you get to be regional Vice President of Sales overseeing a fifteen-state territory, or are appointed Corporate Head of Creative Development, or are chosen as one of the four key team members charged with opening your company's new European headquarters in London, England . . . you're going to be damn glad you listened to all those teachers who, while respecting who you were and your ethnicity and your cultural heritage, nonetheless insisted that you learn your way around the English language, that you learn to communicate not just with your homeboys and homegirls but with other English-speaking human beings in the broader culture.

10   And it doesn't really have anything to do with someone's respecting or not respecting who you are or where you came from, anyway. It does have to do with something that has very deep roots in the American soul. It has to do with a set of fundamental human values that we Americans hold sacred. Among the most important of those values is that every young person be given the opportunity to prosper through the exercise of his or her talents and skills. You may have heard the words "life, liberty, and the pursuit of happiness."

If it seems as though you have to compromise your identity or your integrity to accomplish these things, let me say this: It is actually those who promote "diversity" who ask you to deny your individuality and your humanity by insisting that you assume a collective identity as a member of a racial or ethnic or cultural group. Membership in these groups is reductive; it restricts your horizons and diminishes the likelihood that you'll be successful even in articulating your own personal aspirations, let alone achieving them. 11

Make no mistake about it: The values on which this country was founded are universal values which transcend culture and history and race and nationality. And no concept as flimsy and restrictive and, ultimately, indefensible as diversity should be enough to sway you from your chance to use your talents in the service of truly positive and universal values. Don't let diversity destroy your soul and rob you of the chance to be who you truly are. 12

✕✕✕✕✕✕✕✕✕✕✕✕✕✕ UNDERSTANDING THE ESSAY ✕✕✕✕✕✕✕✕✕✕✕✕✕✕

1. Greg Lewis ARGUES that you should "learn your way around the English language" so that you can "communicate not just with your homeboys and homegirls but with other English-speaking human beings in the broader culture" (9). Is Lewis right about the importance of learning Standard English? Why or why not?

2. Why is Lewis so opposed to bilingual education? Is he summarizing the opposing point of view fairly and accurately when he says that some schools teach in both English and Spanish "so that Hispanic children will not have to learn English" (1)? Why or why not?

3. What LOGICAL FALLACY does Lewis attribute to his adversaries in paragraph 5? How valid is Lewis's reasoning here? How effective is this as a strategy for anticipating objections to his argument?

4. Lewis ends his argument by imploring, "Don't let diversity destroy your soul and rob you of the chance to be who you truly are" (12). Why do you think Lewis follows up his logical argument with an emotional appeal like this? How effective do you find this strategy? Explain.

5. How does Lewis DEFINE "Standard English" (5)? How would you change or refine his definition?

6. How and how well does the phrase "diversity's victims" summarize Lewis's entire argument?

DENNIS BARON

DON'T MAKE ENGLISH OFFICIAL—
BAN IT INSTEAD

Dennis Baron (b. 1944) is a professor of English and linguistics at the University of Illinois at Urbana-Champaign. He is the author of, among other books on society and language, *The English-Only Question: An Official Language for Americans?* (1992). On his website, *The Web of Language*, Baron says that "we don't need an official language" because "if the government doesn't give immigrants the English classes they demand, they will sue." In the following essay, first published in the *Washington Post* in 1996, he makes a modest proposal for changing the status of the unofficial language of the United States.

XXXXXXXXXXXXXXXXXXXXXXXXXXXXXXXXXXXXXXXXXXXXXXXXXXXXXXXXXXX

1   Congress is considering, and may soon pass, legislation making English the official language of the United States. Supporters of the measure say that English forms the glue that keeps America together. They deplore the dollars wasted translating English into other languages. And they fear a horde of illegal aliens adamantly refusing to acquire the most powerful language on earth.

2   On the other hand, opponents of official English remind us that without legislation we have managed to get over 97 percent of the residents of this country to speak the national language. No country with an official language law even comes close. Opponents also point out that today's non-English-speaking immigrants are picking up English faster than earlier generations of immigrants did, so instead of official English, they favor "English Plus," encouraging everyone to speak both English and another language.

3   I would like to offer a modest proposal to resolve the language impasse in Congress. Don't make English official—ban it instead.

That may sound too radical, but proposals to ban English first surfaced in the heady days after the American Revolution. Anti-British sentiment was so strong in the new United States that a few superpatriots wanted to get rid of English altogether. They suggested replacing English with Hebrew, thought by many in the eighteenth century to be the world's first language, the one spoken in the garden of Eden. French was also considered, because it was thought at the time, and especially by the French, to be the language of pure reason. And of course there was Greek, the language of Athens, the world's first democracy. It's not clear how serious any of these proposals were, though Roger Sherman[1] of Connecticut supposedly remarked that it would be better to keep English for ourselves and make the British speak Greek.

Even if the British are now our allies, there may be some benefit to banning English today. A common language can often be the cause of strife and misunderstanding. Look at Ireland and Northern Ireland, the two Koreas, or the Union and the Confederacy. Banning English would prevent that kind of divisiveness in America today.

Also, if we banned English, we wouldn't have to worry about whose English to make official: the English of England or America? of Chicago or New York? of Ross Perot or William F. Buckley?[2]

We might as well ban English, too, because no one seems to read it much lately, few can spell it, and fewer still can parse it. Even English teachers have come to rely on computer spell checkers.

Another reason to ban English: it's hardly even English anymore. English started its decline in 1066, with the unfortunate incident at Hastings.[3] Since then it has become a polyglot conglomeration of French, Latin, Italian, Scandinavian, Arabic, Sanskrit, Celtic, Yiddish and Chinese, with an occasional smiley face thrown in.

1. Early American lawyer and leader in the Revolutionary War (1721–1793).

2. Buckley (1925–2008) was a conservative author and commentator born into the upper class of Manhattan whose speech was markedly refined; Perot (b. 1930) is a Texas businessman and one-time presidential candidate who speaks with a regional twang.

3. The Battle of Hastings, won by the invading Norman forces, was the decisive victory in their conquest of Britain, which brought speakers of French to power.

9   More important, we should ban English because it has become a world language. Remember what happened to all the other world languages: Latin, Greek, Indo-European? One day they're on everybody's tongue; the next day they're dead. Banning English now would save us that inevitable disappointment.

10   Although we shouldn't ban English without designating a replacement for it, there is no obvious candidate. The French blew their chance when they sold Louisiana. It doesn't look like the Russians are going to take over this country anytime soon—they're having enough trouble taking over Russia. German, the largest minority language in the U.S. until recently, lost much of its prestige after two world wars. Chinese is too hard to write, especially if you're not Chinese. There's always Esperanto, a language made up a hundred years ago that is supposed to bring about world unity. We're still waiting for that. And if you took Spanish in high school you can see that it's not easy to get large numbers of people to speak another language fluently.

11   In the end, though, it doesn't matter what replacement language we pick, just so long as we ban English instead of making it official. Prohibiting English will do for the language what Prohibition did for liquor. Those who already use it will continue to do so, and those who don't will want to try out what has been forbidden. This negative psychology works with children. It works with speed limits. It even worked in the Garden of Eden.

XXXXXXXXXXXXXX UNDERSTANDING THE ESSAY XXXXXXXXXXXXXX

1. Dennis Baron ARGUES that Congress should ban English instead of making it the official national language. What does this "modest proposal" have in common with Jonathan Swift's "A Modest Proposal" (3)? What is Baron's PURPOSE in writing this proposal, and who is his intended AUDIENCE? (See Chapter 11 for the full text of Swift's proposal.)

2. If Congress were to take Baron's suggestion and ban English, what replacement language do you think would be the best choice? Why?

3. Even if Congress does ban English, says Baron, "it doesn't matter what replacement language we pick" (11). Why not? Do you think Baron is right or wrong about the staying power of English? Why?

4. What reasons does Baron give to support his CLAIM that Congress should ban English? What EVIDENCE does he provide to support each reason?

5. Baron uses the EXAMPLES of civil wars or conflicts in Ireland, Korea, and the United States to support his point that a "common language can often be the cause of strife and misunderstanding" (5). Is his logic here INDUCTIVE or DEDUCTIVE? How valid is this logic? How valid is it meant to be?

6. Baron says supporters of legislation making English the official language of the United States "fear a horde of illegal aliens adamantly refusing to acquire the most powerful language on earth" (1). What is the point of this HYPERBOLE?

7. Baron says his proposal to ban English is an example of "negative psychology" (11). What does he mean by this term? What does he mean when he says that it "worked in the Garden of Eden" (11)?

What Language(s) Do You Speak If You're an American?

The following questions refer to the arguments on pp. 429–43.

XXXXXXXXXXXXXX **Analyzing the Arguments** XXXXXXXXXXXXX

1. Among the four writers in this debate, which one(s) make the strongest ARGUMENT for the importance of speaking English? For the value of linguistic diversity? What makes those arguments particularly convincing?

2. In what ways might Dennis Baron's essay be seen as an answer to Greg Lewis's? COMPARE the strategies each writer uses to make his argument. Which approach do you find more effective? Why?

3. Both Myriam Marquez and Chang-Rae Lee make their arguments in part by telling illustrative stories. Which of the two essays has the more elaborate PLOT? Point out other NARRATIVE elements in these essays (and the other two in this cluster), and explain how these narratives support the main CLAIM that each author is making.

4. Regardless of whether you agree with their conclusions, which of these writers do you find most credible? Why? What strategies do they use to establish their credibility? For example, how well do they anticipate opposing arguments? Refer to particular passages.

XXXXXXXXXXXXXXXXXX **For Writing** XXXXXXXXXXXXXXXXXXXX

1. Choose a CLAIM from one of these four ARGUMENTS that you think could use more support. Write a paragraph providing additional EVIDENCE to support that claim—or to refute it.

2. Write an argument that either supports or opposes the claim that learning "Standard English" is vitally important for non-native speakers who hope to make their way in the broader culture. Feel free to cite your own experience or that of your family or friends to support your argument.

3. Although English is the unofficial national language in America, many other languages are spoken. Write a "modest proposal" suggesting that some other language, for example Spanish or Japanese, should be the official national language—or that there should be no common language at all. Be sure to cite all the advantages of your proposal.

CHAPTER ELEVEN

CLASSIC ESSAYS AND SPEECHES

XXXXXXXXXXXXXXXXXXXXXXXXXXXXXXXXXXXXXXXXXXXXXXXXXXXXX

The essays and speeches in this chapter are "classics"—timeless EXAMPLES* of good writing across the centuries. What makes them timeless? Jonathan Swift's "A Modest Proposal," for instance, is nearly 300 years old, and the speaker is a "projector," a word we don't even use anymore in the sense that Swift used it, of a person who is full of foolish projects. However, the moral and economic issues that Swift addresses are as timely today as they were in the eighteenth century. His greedy countrymen, Swift charges—not to mention English landlords and "a very knowing American of my acquaintance"—will do anything for money (9).

E. B. White's nostalgic "Once More to the Lake," written on the eve of World War II, is explicitly about time—or, rather, timelessness. When White takes his young son fishing at the quiet lake where he himself had spent so many summers as a boy, a dragonfly lands on the tip of White's rod, and time seems to stand still: "It was the arrival of this fly that convinced me beyond any doubt that everything was as it always had been, that the years were a mirage and that there had been no years" (5). The suspension of time is an illusion, of course, and White's essay ends with the shock we all feel when waking up from a dream that is better than life.

This sense of recognition—the feeling that what the writer has to say applies directly to us and our time—is one measure of a "classic."

---

*Words printed in SMALL CAPITALS are defined in the Glossary.

We feel it with all the essays and speeches in this chapter, including the Declaration of Independence, Abraham Lincoln's Second Inaugural Address, Virginia Woolf's "The Death of the Moth," and Martin Luther King Jr.'s "I Have a Dream."

In addition to their timeless themes, the works in this chapter are classics because the writer of each one has a brilliant command of language and of the fundamental forms and patterns of written or spoken discourse. By taking apart these great essays and speeches, you will find that they are constructed using the same basic strategies and techniques of writing you have been studying throughout this book. All the MODES OF WRITING are here—NARRATION, DESCRIPTION, EXPOSITION, and ARGUMENT—but interwoven as seamlessly as the layers of time in White's essay.

Let's look more closely at Virginia Woolf's influential "The Death of the Moth" as an example of how a great writer combines the basic patterns of writing into a unified whole. These patterns are all the more tightly woven because Woolf's essay not only makes connections, it is *about* the connectedness of all living things.

As in Annie Dillard's essay on the same subject at the beginning of this book, the eponymous moth gives Woolf's essay a visual and thematic focal point. (*Eponymous*, meaning "name-giving," is not a word you get to use every day.) Thus much of her essay is devoted to a detailed description of "the present specimen, with his narrow haycoloured wings, fringed with a tassel" (1). The moth's little world is so limited that we wonder, at first, why Woolf is bothering to show it to us: "He flew vigorously to one corner" of the surrounding windowpane and, "after waiting there a second, flew across to the other. What remained for him," Woolf wonders, "but to fly to a third corner and then to a fourth?" (2).

This question is soon answered, and we discover that the physical SETTING Woolf describes here is the framework of a narrative. All that remains for the moth is to die. Just when the NARRATOR, deeply absorbed in her book, has forgotten the moth, it catches her attention again: "He was trying to resume his dancing, but seemed either so stiff or so awkward that he could only flutter to the bottom of the windowpane; and when he tried to fly across it he failed" (4).

At first, Woolf's narrator does not realize the significance of what she sees. "Being intent on other matters," she says, "I watched these futile attempts for a time without thinking, unconsciously waiting for him to resume his flight, as one waits for a machine, that has stopped momentarily, to start again without considering the reason for its failure" (4).

Here is the basic PLOT of Woolf's narrative: not the death of a moth but the writer's sympathetic *observation* of the creature's death—and her inability to stop it. The writer can only chronicle death; she cannot conquer it. "But, as I stretched out a pencil, meaning to help him to right himself," says the writer at her desk, "it came over me that the failure and awkwardness were the approach of death. I laid the pencil down again" (4). The real story here is in the writer's mind. To explain the significance of that story, Woolf draws on common techniques of exposition; in particular, she uses COMPARISON AND CONTRAST and DEFINITION.

The writer's window looks out onto the nearby fields and the rolling hills beyond. The earth is gleaming from the plough, and the birds are rising and falling "as if a vast net with thousands of black knots in it has been cast up into the air" (1). What could the frail moth possibly have to do with all this "vigour," the writer wonders, even as her celebrated description of the "net" of blackbirds captures the interconnectedness of life?

As the thought of connections rises in the writer's mind, she makes a direct comparison between the moth and the scene outside her window: "The same energy which inspired the rooks, the ploughmen, the horses, and even, it seemed, the lean bare-backed downs, sent the moth fluttering from side to side of his square of the window-pane" (2).

That energy is "pure life" (3). But what is life, essentially? Woolf can now answer this momentous question because she has made the connection between the moth and the scene outside her window: "It was as if someone had taken a tiny bead of pure life and decking it as lightly as possible with down and feathers, had set it dancing and zigzagging to show us the true nature of life" (3).

Life is to be defined, at bottom, as motion, animation, and when that motion ceases, that is death: "One could only watch the extraordinary efforts made by those tiny legs against an oncoming doom which could, had it chosen, have submerged an entire city, not merely a city, but masses of human beings; nothing, I knew, had any chance against death" (5). (This essay was written shortly before Woolf's suicide by drowning.)

Woolf's essay, then, is a description of the moth and the downs, a narrative about the woman watching them, and an exposition on the nature of life and death. It is also an ARGUMENT. Having defined life, Woolf subtly makes the case for how it should be lived. If a mere moth, a "tiny bead of pure life," expends its little energy "dancing and zigzagging" to the fullest extent that its meager compass will allow (3), then the woman musing aloud to herself on this "pleasant morning, mid-September, mild, benignant, yet with a keener breath than that of the summer months" (1), should perhaps convince herself (and us) to do likewise.

To reduce Woolf's subtle essay to another moth-to-the-flame message about being inspired by life or making hay while the sun shines, however, would kill it. The meaning of a complex piece of writing is not to be extracted like pulling a thread from a tapestry. We can dissect a great essay into its constituent parts, but its meaning derives from the essay as a whole—from all the modes of writing working together. Keep this lesson in mind as you study the other fine specimens in this chapter.

THOMAS JEFFERSON

THE DECLARATION OF INDEPENDENCE

Thomas Jefferson (1743–1826) was the third president of the United States. A lawyer by training, he was also a philosopher and man of letters. Charged with drafting the Declaration of Independence (1776), he was assisted by Benjamin Franklin, John Adams, and the Continental Congress at large. A model of the rational thinking of the Enlightenment, the Declaration is as much a timeless essay on tyranny and human rights as a legal document announcing the colonies' break with England. The version reprinted here is that published on the website of the United States National Archives, www.archives.gov.

XXXXXXXXXXXXXXXXXXXXXXXXXXXXXXXXXXXXXXXXXXXXXXXXXXXXXXXXXXX

When in the Course of human events, it becomes necessary for one people to dissolve the political bands which have connected them with another, and to assume among the powers of the earth, the separate and equal station to which the Laws of Nature and of Nature's God entitle them, a decent respect to the opinions of mankind requires that they should declare the causes which impel them to the separation. 1

We hold these truths to be self-evident, that all men are created equal, that they are endowed by their Creator with certain unalienable Rights, that among these are Life, Liberty and the pursuit of Happiness. That to secure these rights, Governments are instituted among Men, deriving their just powers from the consent of the governed. That whenever any Form of Government becomes destructive of these ends, it is the Right of the People to alter or to abolish it, and to institute new Government, laying its foundation on such principles and organizing its powers in such form, as to them shall seem most likely to effect their Safety and Happiness. Prudence, indeed, will dictate that Governments long established should not be changed for light and transient causes; and accordingly all experience hath shewn, that mankind are more dis- 2 posed to suffer, while evils are sufferable, than to right themselves by abolishing the forms to which they are accustomed. But when a long train of abuses and usurpations pursuing invariably the same Object evinces a design to reduce them under absolute Despotism, it is their right, it is their duty, to throw off such Government, and to provide new Guards for their future security. Such has been the patient sufferance of these Colonies; and such is now the necessity which constrains them to alter their former Systems of Government. The history of the present King of Great Britain[1] is a history of repeated injuries and usurpations, all having in direct object the establishment of absolute Tyranny over these States. To prove this, let Facts be submitted to a candid world.

3   He has refused his Assent to Laws, the most wholesome and necessary for the public good.

4   He has forbidden his Governors to pass Laws of immediate and pressing importance, unless suspended in their operation till his Assent should be obtained; and when so suspended, he has utterly neglected to attend to them.

5   He has refused to pass other Laws for the accommodation of large districts of people, unless those people would relinquish the right of Representation in the Legislature, a right inestimable to them and formidable to tyrants only.

6   He has called together legislative bodies at places unusual, uncomfortable, and distant from the depository of their public Records, for the sole purpose of fatiguing them into compliance with his measures.

7   He has dissolved Representative Houses repeatedly, for opposing with manly firmness his invasions on the rights of the people.

8   He has refused for a long time, after such dissolutions, to cause others to be elected; whereby the Legislative powers, incapable of Annihilation, have returned to the People at large for their exercise; the State remaining in the mean time exposed to all the dangers of invasion from without, and convulsions within.

9   He has endeavoured to prevent the population of these States; for that purpose obstructing the Laws of Naturalization of Foreigners; refus-

---

1. George III (ruled 1760–1820).

ing to pass others to encourage their migration hither, and raising the conditions of new Appropriations of Lands.

He has obstructed the Administration of Justice, by refusing his 10 Assent to Laws for establishing Judiciary powers.

He has made Judges dependent on his Will alone, for the tenure of 11 their offices, and the amount and payment of their salaries.

He has erected a multitude of New Offices, and sent hither swarms 12 of Officers to harass our people, and eat out their substance.

He has kept among us, in time of peace, Standing Armies without 13 the Consent of our legislatures.

He has affected to render the Military independent of and superior 14 to the Civil power.

He has combined with others to subject us to a jurisdiction foreign 15 to our constitution, and unacknowledged by our laws; giving his Assent to their acts of pretended Legislation:

For Quartering large bodies of armed troops among us: 16

For protecting them, by a mock Trial, from punishment for any 17 Murders which they should commit on the Inhabitants of these States:

For cutting off our Trade with all parts of the world: 18

For imposing Taxes on us without our Consent: 19

For depriving us in many cases, of the benefits of Trial by Jury: 20

For transporting us beyond the Seas to be tried for pretended 21 offenses:

For abolishing the free System of English Laws in a neighbouring 22 Province, establishing therein an Arbitrary government, and enlarging its Boundaries so as to render it at once an example and fit instrument for introducing the same absolute rule into these Colonies:

For taking away our Charters, abolishing our most valuable Laws, 23 and altering fundamentally the Forms of our Governments:

For suspending our own Legislatures, and declaring themselves 24 invested with power to legislate for us in all cases whatsoever.

He has abdicated Government here, by declaring us out of his Pro- 25 tection and waging War against us.

He has plundered our seas, ravaged our Coasts, burnt our towns 26 and destroyed the lives of our people.

27   He is at this time transporting large Armies of foreign Mercenaries to compleat the works of death, desolation and tyranny, already begun with circumstances of Cruelty & perfidy scarcely paralleled in the most barbarous ages, and totally unworthy the Head of a civilized nation.

28   He has constrained our fellow Citizens taken Captive on the high Seas to bear Arms against their Country, to become the executioners of their friends and Brethren, or to fall themselves by their Hands.

29   He has excited domestic insurrections amongst us, and has endeavoured to bring on the inhabitants of our frontiers, the merciless Indian Savages, whose known rule of warfare, is an undistinguished destruction of all ages, sexes and conditions.

30   In every stage of these Oppressions We have Petitioned for Redress in the most humble terms: Our repeated Petitions have been answered only by repeated injury. A Prince whose character is thus marked by every act which may define a Tyrant, is unfit to be the ruler of a free people.

31   Nor have We been wanting in attentions to our British brethren. We have warned them from time to time of attempts by their legislature to extend an unwarrantable jurisdiction over us. We have reminded them of the circumstances of our emigration and settlement here. We have appealed to their native justice and magnanimity, and we have conjured them by the ties of our common kindred to disavow these usurpations, which would inevitably interrupt our connections and correspondence. They too have been deaf to the voice of justice and of consanguinity. We must, therefore acquiesce in the necessity, which denounces our Separation, and hold them, as we hold the rest of mankind, Enemies in War, in Peace Friends.

32   We, therefore, the Representatives of the United States of America, in General Congress, Assembled, appealing to the Supreme Judge of the world for the rectitude of our intentions, do, in the Name, and by Authority of the good People of these Colonies, solemnly publish and declare, That these United Colonies are, and of Right ought to be Free and Independent States; that they are Absolved from all Allegiance to the British Crown, and that all political connection between them and the State of Great Britain, is and ought to be totally dissolved; and that

as Free and Independent States, they have full Power to levy War, conclude Peace, contract Alliances, establish Commerce, and to do all other Acts and Things which Independent States may of right do. And for the support of this Declaration, with a firm reliance on the protection of divine Providence, we mutually pledge to each other our Lives, our Fortunes and our sacred Honor.

XXXXXXXXXXXXXXX **UNDERSTANDING THE ESSAY** XXXXXXXXXXXXXXX

1. Thomas Jefferson's main PURPOSE in the Declaration of Independence is to declare the sovereignty of the United States. How and where does he use CAUSE AND EFFECT to help achieve this purpose?

2. How does Jefferson DEFINE what it means to be a tyrant? In what way does this definition help him achieve his main purpose?

3. Above all, the Declaration of Independence is a logical ARGUMENT. How and where does Jefferson use INDUCTION (reasoning from specific instances to a general conclusion) to make the point that King George is indeed a tyrant?

4. Once Jefferson reaches this conclusion about King George, he uses it as the minor (or narrower) premise of a DEDUCTIVE argument (from general principles to specific conclusions). The conclusion of that argument is that "these United Colonies are, and of Right ought to be Free and Independent States" (32). What is the major (or broader) premise of this deductive argument? Explain.

5. Jefferson refers to the British people as "our British brethren" (31). Why? What AUDIENCE does he have in mind here, and why would he need to convince them that his cause is just?

6. According to Jefferson and the other signers of the Declaration, what is the purpose of government, and where does a government get its authority? What form of government do they envision for the states, and how well does the Declaration make the case for this form of government? Explain.

JONATHAN SWIFT

A MODEST PROPOSAL

Jonathan Swift (1667–1745) was born in Ireland and educated at Trinity College, Dublin, where he was censured for breaking the rules of discipline, graduating only by "special grace." He was ordained as a clergyman in the Anglican Church in 1694 and became dean of St. Patrick's, Dublin, in 1713. Swift's satires in prose and verse, including *Gulliver's Travels* (1726), addressed three main issues: political relations between England and Ireland; Irish social questions; and matters of church doctrine. Swift's best-known essay was published in 1729 under the full title "A Modest Proposal For Preventing the Children of poor People in Ireland, from being a Burden to their Parents or Country; and for making them beneficial to the Publick." Using irony as his weapon, Swift pours into the essay his deep contempt for materialism and for logic without compassion.

XXXXXXXXXXXXXXXXXXXXXXXXXXXXXXXXXXXXXXXXXXXXXXXXXXXXXXXXX

1　　It is a melancholy object to those who walk through this great town[1] or travel in the country, when they see the streets, the roads, and cabin doors, crowded with beggars of the female sex, followed by three, four, or six children, all in rags and importuning every passenger for an alms. These mothers, instead of being able to work for their honest livelihood, are forced to employ all their time in strolling to beg sustenance for their helpless infants, who, as they grow up, either turn thieves for want of work, or leave their dear native country to fight for the Pretender in Spain, or sell themselves to the Barbadoes.[2]

1. Dublin, capital city of Ireland.

2. Barbados is an island in the West Indies. The pretender to the throne of England was James Francis Edward Stuart (1688–1766), son of the deposed James II.

I think it is agreed by all parties that this prodigious number of children in the arms, or on the backs, or at the heels of their mothers, and frequently of their fathers, is in the present deplorable state of the kingdom a very great additional grievance; and therefore whoever could find out a fair, cheap, and easy method of making these children sound, useful members of the commonwealth would deserve so well of the public as to have his statue set up for a preserver of the nation.

But my intention is very far from being confined to provide only for the children of professed beggars; it is of a much greater extent, and shall take in the whole number of infants at a certain age who are born of parents in effect as little able to support them as those who demand our charity in the streets.

As to my own part, having turned my thoughts for many years upon this important subject and maturely weighed the several schemes of other projectors,[3] I have always found them grossly mistaken in their computation. It is true, a child just dropped from its dam may be supported by her milk for a solar year, with little other nourishment; at most not above the value of two shillings,[4] which the mother may certainly get, or the value in scraps, by her lawful occupation of begging; and it is exactly at one year old that I propose to provide for them in such a manner as instead of being a charge upon their parents or the parish, or wanting food and raiment for the rest of their lives, they shall on the contrary contribute to the feeding, and partly to the clothing, of many thousands.

There is likewise another great advantage in my scheme, that it will prevent those voluntary abortions, and that horrid practice of women murdering their bastard children, alas, too frequent among us, sacrificing the poor innocent babes, I doubt, more to avoid the expense than the shame, which would move tears and pity in the most savage and inhuman breast.

The number of souls in this kingdom being usually reckoned one million and a half, of these I calculate there may be about two hundred

3. Men whose heads were full of foolish schemes or projects.

4. The British pound sterling was made up of twenty shillings; five shillings made a crown.

thousand couple whose wives are breeders; from which number I subtract thirty thousand couples who are able to maintain their own children, although I apprehend there cannot be so many under the present distress of the kingdom; but this being granted, there will remain an hundred and seventy thousand breeders. I again subtract fifty thousand for those women who miscarry, or whose children die by accident or disease within the year. There only remain an hundred and twenty thousand children of poor parents annually born. The question therefore is, how this number shall be reared and provided for, which, as I have already said, under the present situation of affairs, is utterly impossible by all the methods hitherto proposed. For we can neither employ them in handicraft or agriculture; we neither build houses (I mean in the country) nor cultivate land. They can very seldom pick up a livelihood by stealing till they arrive at six years old, except where they are of towardly parts,[5] although I confess they learn the rudiments much earlier, during which time they can however be looked upon only as probationers, as I have been informed by a principal gentleman in the county of Cavan,[6] who protested to me that he never knew above one or two instances under the age of six, even in a part of the kingdom so renowned for the quickest proficiency in that art.

7   I am assured by our merchants that a boy or a girl before twelve years old is no salable commodity; and even when they come to this age they will not yield above three pounds, or three pounds and half a crown at most on the Exchange; which cannot turn to account either to the parents or the kingdom, the charge of nutriment and rags having been at least four times that value.

8   I shall now therefore humbly propose my own thoughts, which I hope will not be liable to the least objection.

9   I have been assured by a very knowing American of my acquaintance in London, that a young healthy child well nursed is at a year old a most delicious, nourishing, and wholesome food, whether stewed, roasted, baked, or boiled; and I make no doubt that it will equally serve in a fricassee or a ragout.

---

5. Having natural ability.

6. A county in northeast Ireland.

I do therefore humbly offer it to public consideration that of the   10
hundred and twenty thousand children, already computed, twenty thousand may be reserved for breed, whereof only one fourth part to be
males, which is more than we allow to sheep, black cattle, or swine; and
my reason is that these children are seldom the fruits of marriage, a circumstance not much regarded by our savages, therefore one male will be
sufficient to serve four females. That the remaining hundred thousand
may at a year old be offered in sale to the persons of quality and fortune
through the kingdom, always advising the mother to let them suck plentifully in the last month, so as to render them plump and fat for a good
table. A child will make two dishes at an entertainment for friends; and
when the family dines alone, the fore or hind quarter will make a reasonable dish, and seasoned with a little pepper or salt will be very good
boiled on the fourth day, especially in winter.

I have reckoned upon a medium that a child just born will weigh   11
twelve pounds, and in a solar year if tolerably nursed increaseth to
twenty-eight pounds.

I grant this food will be somewhat dear, and therefore very proper   12
for landlords, who, as they have already devoured most of the parents,
seem to have the best title to the children.

Infant's flesh will be in season throughout the year, but more plen-   13
tiful in March, and a little before and after. For we are told by a grave
author, an eminent French physician,[7] that fish being a prolific diet,
there are more children born in Roman Catholic countries about nine
months after Lent than at any other season; therefore, reckoning a year
after Lent, the markets will be more glutted than usual, because the
number of popish infants is at least three to one in this kingdom; and
therefore it will have one other collateral advantage, by lessening the
number of Papists[8] among us.

---

7. François Rabelais (1494?–1553), French satirist.

8. Roman Catholics, called Papists because of their allegiance to the pope. Though
Catholics made up the majority of the Irish population in this period, English Protestants controlled the government, and Catholics were subject to discrimination and
oppressive policies.

14   I have already computed the charge of nursing a beggar's child (in which list I reckon all cottagers, laborers, and four fifths of the farmers) to be about two shillings per annum, rags included; and I believe no gentleman would repine to give ten shillings for the carcass of a good fat child, which, as I have said, will make four dishes of excellent nutritive meat, when he hath only some particular friend or his own family to dine with him. Thus the squire will learn to be a good landlord, and grow popular among the tenants; the mother will have eight shillings net profit, and be fit for work till she produces another child.

15   Those who are more thrifty (as I must confess the times require) may flay the carcass; the skin of which artificially[9] dressed will make admirable gloves for ladies, and summer boots for fine gentlemen.

16   As to our city of Dublin, shambles[10] may be appointed for this purpose in the most convenient parts of it, and butchers we may be assured will not be wanting; although I rather recommend buying the children alive, and dressing them hot from the knife as we do roasting pigs.

17   A very worthy person, a true lover of his country, and whose virtues I highly esteem, was lately pleased in discoursing on this matter to offer a refinement upon my scheme. He said that many gentlemen of this kingdom, having of late destroyed their deer, he conceived that the want of venison might be well supplied by the bodies of young lads and maidens, not exceeding fourteen years of age nor under twelve, so great a number of both sexes in every country being now ready to starve for want of work and service; and these to be disposed of by their parents, if alive, or otherwise by their nearest relations. But with due deference to so excellent a friend and so deserving a patriot, I cannot be altogether in his sentiments; for as to the males, my American acquaintance assured me from frequent experience that their flesh was generally tough and lean, like that of our schoolboys, by continual exercise, and their taste disagreeable; and to fatten them would not answer the charge. Then as to the females, it would, I think with humble submission, be a loss to the public, because they soon would become breeders themselves: and

9. Skillfully, artfully.

10. Slaughterhouses.

besides, it is not improbable that some scrupulous people might be apt to censure such a practice (although indeed very unjustly) as a little bordering upon cruelty; which, I confess, hath always been with me the strongest objection against any project, how well 'soever intended.

But in order to justify my friend, he confessed that this expedient was put into his head by the famous Psalmanazar, a native of the island Formosa,[11] who came from thence to London above twenty years ago, and in conversation told my friend that in his country when any young person happened to be put to death, the executioner sold the carcass to persons of quality as a prime dainty; and that in his time the body of a plump girl of fifteen, who was crucified for an attempt to poison the emperor, was sold to his Imperial Majesty's prime minister of state, and other great mandarins of the court, in joints from the gibbet,[12] at four hundred crowns. Neither indeed can I deny that if the same use were made of several plump young girls in this town, who without one single groat[13] to their fortunes cannot stir abroad without a chair, and appear at the playhouse and assemblies in foreign fineries which they never will pay for, the kingdom would not be the worse. 18

Some persons of a desponding spirit are in great concern about that vast number of poor people who are aged, diseased, or maimed, and I have been desired to employ my thoughts what course may be taken to ease the nation of so grievous an encumbrance. But I am not in the least pain upon that matter, because it is very well known that they are every day dying and rotting by cold and famine, and filth and vermin, as fast as can be reasonably expected. And as to the younger laborers, they are now in almost as hopeful a condition. They cannot get work, and consequently pine away for want of nourishment to a degree that if at any time they are accidentally hired to common labor, they have not strength to perform it; and thus the country and themselves are happily delivered from the evils to come. 19

---

11. Former name of Taiwan. George Psalmanazar (1679?–1763), a Frenchman, fooled British society for several years by masquerading as a pagan Formosan.

12. A structure for hanging a felon.

13. An British coin of the time, worth the equivalent of four cents.

20   I have too long digressed, and therefore shall return to my subject. I think the advantages by the proposal which I have made are obvious and many, as well as of the highest importance.

21   For first, as I have already observed, it would greatly lessen the number of Papists, with whom we are yearly overrun, being the principal breeders of the nation as well as our most dangerous enemies; and who stay at home on purpose to deliver the kingdom to the Pretender, hoping to take their advantage by the absence of so many good Protestants, who have chosen rather to leave their country than stay at home and pay tithes against their conscience to an Episcopal curate.[14]

22   Secondly, the poorer tenants will have something valuable of their own, which by law may be made liable to distress, and help to pay their landlord's rent, their corn and cattle being already seized and money a thing unknown.

23   Thirdly, whereas the maintenance of an hundred thousand children, from two years old and upward, cannot be computed at less than ten shillings a piece per annum, the nation's stock will be thereby increased fifty thousand pounds per annum, besides the profit of a new dish introduced to the tables of all gentlemen of fortune in the kingdom who have any refinement in taste. And the money will circulate among ourselves, the goods being entirely of our own growth and manufacture.

24   Fourthly, the constant breeders, besides the gain of eight shillings sterling per annum by the sale of their children, will be rid of the charge of maintaining them after the first year.

25   Fifthly, this food would likewise bring great custom to taverns, where the vintners will certainly be so prudent as to procure the best receipts for dressing it to perfection, and consequently have their houses frequented by all the fine gentlemen, who justly value themselves upon their knowledge in good eating; and a skillful cook, who understands how to oblige his guests, will contrive to make it as expensive as they please.

14. Tithes are taxes or levys, traditionally 10 percent of one's income, paid to the church or other authority. Swift blamed much of Ireland's poverty upon large landowners who avoided church tithes by living (and spending their money) abroad.

Sixthly, this would be a great inducement to marriage, which all 26
wise nations have either encouraged by rewards or enforced by laws and
penalties. It would increase the care and tenderness of mothers toward
their children, when they were sure of a settlement for life to the poor
babes, provided in some sort by the public, to their annual profit instead
of expense. We should see an honest emulation among the married
women, which of them could bring the fattest child to the market. Men
would become as fond of their wifes during the time of their pregnancy
as they are now of their mares in foal, their cows in calf, or sows when
they are ready to farrow; nor offer to beat or kick them (as is too frequent a practice) for fear of a miscarriage.

Many other advantages might be enumerated. For instance, the 27
addition of some thousand carcasses in our exportation of barreled beef,
the propagation of swine's flesh, and improvement in the art of making
good bacon, so much wanted among us by the great destruction of pigs,
too frequent at our tables, which are no way comparable in taste or mag-
nificence to a well-grown, fat, yearling child, which roasted whole will
make a considerable figure at a lord mayor's feast or any other public
entertainment. But this and many others I omit, being studious of
brevity.

Supposing that one thousand families in this city would be constant 28
customers for infants' flesh, besides others who might have it at merry
meetings, particularly weddings and christenings, I compute that Dublin
would take off annually about twenty thousand carcasses, and the rest of
the kingdom (where probably they will be sold somewhat cheaper) the
remaining eighty thousand.

I can think of no one objection that will possibly be raised against 29
this proposal, unless it should be urged that the number of people will
be thereby much lessened in the kingdom. This I freely own, and it was
indeed one principal design in offering it to the world. I desire the
reader will observe, that I calculate my remedy for this one individual
kingdom of Ireland and for no other that ever was, is, or I think ever can
be upon earth. Therefore let no man talk to me of other expedients:[15] of

---

15. The following are all measures that Swift himself proposed in various pamphlets.

taxing our absentees at five shillings a pound: of using neither clothes nor household furniture except what is of our own growth and manufacture: of utterly rejecting the materials and instruments that promote foreign luxury: of curing the expensiveness of pride, vanity, idleness, and gaming in our women: of introducing a vein of parsimony, prudence, and temperance: of learning to love our country, in the want of which we differ even from Laplanders and the inhabitants of Topinamboo:[16] of quitting our animosities and factions, nor acting any longer like the Jews, who were murdering one another at the very moment their city[17] was taken: of being a little cautious not to sell our country and conscience for nothing: of teaching landlords to have at least one degree of mercy toward their tenants: lastly, of putting a spirit of honesty, industry, and skill into our shopkeepers; who, if a resolution could now be taken to buy only our native goods, would immediately unite to cheat and exact upon us in the price, the measure, and the goodness, nor could ever yet be brought to make one fair proposal of just dealing, though often and earnestly invited to it.

30   Therefore I repeat, let no man talk to me of these and the like expedients, till he hath at least some glimpse of hope that there will ever be some hearty and sincere attempt to put them in practice.

31   But as to myself, having been wearied out for many years with offering vain, idle, visionary thoughts, and at length utterly despairing of success, I fortunately fell upon this proposal, which, as it is wholly new, so it hath something solid and real, of no expense and little trouble, full in our own power, and whereby we can incur no danger in disobliging England. For this kind of commodity will not bear exportation, the flesh being of too tender a consistence to admit a long continuance in salt, although perhaps I could name a country[18] which would be glad to eat up our whole nation without it.

---

16. The British of Swift's time would have considered the inhabitants of Lapland (region in northern Europe) and Topinamboo (area in the jungles of Brazil) highly uncivilized.

17. Jerusalem, sacked by the Romans in 70 C.E.

18. England.

After all, I am not so violently bent upon my own opinion as to reject any offer proposed by wise men, which shall be found equally innocent, cheap, easy, and effectual. But before something of that kind shall be advanced in contradiction to my scheme, and offering a better, I desire the author or authors will be pleased maturely to consider two points. First, as things now stand, how they will be able to find food and raiment for an hundred thousand useless mouths and backs. And secondly, there being a round million of creatures in human figure throughout this kingdom, whose sole subsistence put into a common stock would leave them in debt two millions of pounds sterling, adding those who are beggars by profession to the bulk of farmers, cottagers, and laborers, with their wives and children who are beggars in effect; I desire those politicians who dislike my overture, and may perhaps be so bold to attempt an answer, that they will first ask the parents of these mortals whether they would not at this day think it a great happiness to have been sold for food at a year old in the manner I prescribe, and thereby have avoided such a perpetual scene of misfortunes as they have since gone through by the oppression of landlords, the impossibility of paying rent without money or trade, the want of common sustenance, with neither house nor clothes to cover them from the inclemencies of the weather, and the most inevitable prospect of entailing the like or greater miseries upon their breed forever.

I profess, in the sincerity of my heart, that I have not the least personal interest in endeavoring to promote this necessary work, having no other motive than the public good of my country, by advancing our trade, providing for infants, relieving the poor, and giving some pleasure to the rich. I have no children by which I can propose to get a single penny; the youngest being nine years old, and my wife past childbearing.

XXXXXXXXXXXXXXX **UNDERSTANDING THE ESSAY** XXXXXXXXXXXXXX

1. Jonathan Swift's essay is celebrated for its IRONY, which is sometimes misdefined as saying the opposite of what is meant. But Swift is not really arguing that the people of Ireland should not eat children. What is he ARGUING? (Clue: see paragraph 29.) How would you define irony based on this example?

2. SATIRE is writing that exposes vice and wrongdoing to ridicule for the PURPOSE of correcting them. Who are the wrongdoers addressed in Swift's great satire?

3. Swift's projector offers what he considers a serious solution to a serious problem. How would you DESCRIBE the projector's personality and TONE of voice? How does using the persona of the projector contribute to Swift's irony throughout the essay? Give specific examples from the text.

4. In "A Modest Proposal," the projector uses both PROCESS ANALYSIS (how to solve Ireland's economic woes) and CAUSE AND EFFECT (the causes of Ireland's poverty and moral condition; the effects of the proposed "improvements"). How do these two MODES OF WRITING work together to support the projector's logical ARGUMENT?

5. Swift's persona is the soul of reason, yet what he proposes is so horrible and bizarre that any reader, except perhaps Hannibal Lecter, would reject it. Why do you think Swift resorts to the METAPHOR of cannibalism? How does it help him to critique arguments that depend on pure reason, even when the situations they address are truly desperate?

ABRAHAM LINCOLN

Second Inaugural Address

Abraham Lincoln (1809–1865) was the sixteenth president of the United States. Largely self-taught, Lincoln studied law as a young man and spent eight years in the Illinois state legislature before being elected president in 1860. By the time Lincoln took office, seven states had seceded from the Union, and his first inaugural address was a conciliatory speech calling for national unity. Four years later, slavery had been abolished and the Civil War was drawing to a close. Lincoln's Second Inaugural Address was delivered on March 4, 1865; several weeks after delivering these words, he was assassinated.

XXXXXXXXXXXXXXXXXXXXXXXXXXXXXXXXXXXXXXXXXXXXXXXXXXXXXX

A t this second appearing to take the oath of the presidential office, there is less occasion for an extended address than there was at the first. Then a statement, somewhat in detail, of a course to be pursued, seemed fitting and proper. Now, at the expiration of four years, during which public declarations have been constantly called forth on every point and phase of the great contest which still absorbs the attention, and engrosses the energies of the nation, little that is new could be presented. The progress of our arms, upon which all else chiefly depends, is as well known to the public as to myself; and it is, I trust, reasonably satisfactory and encouraging to all. With high hope for the future, no prediction in regard to it is ventured. 1

On the occasion corresponding to this four years ago, all thoughts were anxiously directed to an impending civil war. All dreaded it—all sought to avert it. While the inaugural address was being delivered from this place, devoted altogether to *saving* the Union without war, insurgent agents were in the city seeking to *destroy* it without war—seeking to dis- 2

solve the Union, and divide effects, by negotiation.[1] Both parties depre-
cated war; but one of them would *make* war rather than let the nation
survive; and the other would *accept* war rather than let it perish. And
the war came.

3   One-eighth of the whole population were colored slaves, not distributed generally over the Union, but localized in the Southern part of
it. These slaves constituted a peculiar and powerful interest. All knew
that this interest was, somehow, the cause of the war. To strengthen,
perpetuate, and extend this interest was the object for which the insur-
gents would rend the Union, even by war; while the government
claimed no right to do more than to restrict the territorial enlargement of
it. Neither party expected for the war, the magnitude, or the duration,
which it has already attained. Neither anticipated that the *cause* of the
conflict might cease with, or even before, the conflict itself should cease.
Each looked for an easier triumph, and a result less fundamental and
astounding. Both read the same Bible, and pray to the same God; and
each invokes His aid against the other. It may seem strange that any
men should dare to ask a just God's assistance in wringing their bread
from the sweat of other men's faces; but let us judge not that we be not
judged.[2] The prayers of both could not be answered; that of neither has
been answered fully. The Almighty has His own purposes. "Woe unto
the world because of offenses! for it must needs be that offenses come;
but woe to that man by whom the offense cometh!"[3] If we shall suppose
that American slavery is one of those offenses which, in the providence
of God, must needs come, but which, having continued through His
appointed time, He now wills to remove, and that He gives to both

1. Prior to the start of the Civil War, representatives from the slave-holding states
attempted to convince the federal government to allow them to secede and form their
own union.

2. "Let us judge not" alludes to Jesus' Sermon on the Mount ("Judge not, that ye be not
judged") in Matthew 7:1; "wringing their bread from the sweat of other men's faces"
alludes to God's curse on Adam ("In the sweat of thy face shalt thou eat bread") in Gen-
esis 3:19.

3. From Matthew 18:7, Jesus' speech to his disciples.

North and South, this terrible war, as the woe due to those by whom the offense came, shall we discern therein any departure from those divine attributes which the believers in a Living God always ascribe to Him? Fondly do we hope—fervently do we pray—that this mighty scourge of war may speedily pass away. Yet, if God wills that it continue, until all the wealth piled by the bondman's two hundred and fifty years of unrequited toil shall be sunk, and until every drop of blood drawn with the lash, shall be paid by another drawn with the sword, as was said three thousand years ago, so still it must be said, "the judgments of the Lord are true and righteous altogether."[4]

  With malice toward none; with charity for all; with firmness in the right, as God gives us to see the right, let us strive on to finish the work we are in; to bind up the nation's wounds; to care for him who shall have borne the battle, and for his widow, and his orphan—to do all which may achieve and cherish a just, and a lasting peace, among ourselves, and with all nations.

4

4. From Psalms 19:9.

XXXXXXXXXXXXXX **Understanding the Essay** XXXXXXXXXXXXXX

1. Compared to the inaugural speeches of most presidents, Abraham Lincoln's Second Inaugural Address is remarkably short. Why? What is the main PURPOSE of his speech, and what knowledge (and sentiment) does he assume on the part of his AUDIENCE in order to accomplish that purpose in so few words?

2. Lincoln calls for action "with malice toward none; with charity for all," including the people of the vanquished Southern states (4). Unlike his first inaugural address, this second one is delivered from a position of strength. How and where, then, does the author counterbalance conciliatory language like this "with firmness" (4)?

3. As he contemplates the opposing sides in the war, Lincoln reasons that "[n]either anticipated that the *cause* of the conflict might cease with, or even before, the conflict itself should cease" (3). If the still-continuing conflict is the effect, what is the great *cause* to which Lincoln refers? For what purpose does Lincoln use CAUSE AND EFFECT in this speech? What point is he making here?

4. Toward the end of paragraph 3 ("If we shall suppose . . ."), Lincoln uses logical reasoning to make the ARGUMENT that the Civil War and all its woes are, in some measure, the will of God. How valid is his reasoning here? Explain.

5. COMPARE AND CONTRAST Lincoln's Second Inaugural Address with the Inaugural Address of Barack Obama (in Chapter 10) as direct appeals to the people of the nation in time of crisis. How are the challenges currently faced by the United States similar to those of Lincoln's day? How are they different? Compare the strategies each president uses to lay out those challenges and motivate the nation to address them.

VIRGINIA WOOLF

THE DEATH OF THE MOTH

Virginia Woolf (1882–1941) was a distinguished novelist and essayist, the center of the "Bloomsbury Group" of writers and artists that flourished in London from about 1907 to 1930. Suffering from recurrent depression, she drowned herself in the river Ouse near her home at Rodmell, England. *The Voyage Out* (1915), *Mrs. Dalloway* (1925), *To the Lighthouse* (1927), *Orlando* (1928), and *The Waves* (1931) are among her works that helped to alter the course of the novel in English. Today she is recognized as a psychological novelist especially gifted at exploring the minds of her female characters. "The Death of the Moth" is the title essay of a collection published in 1942, soon after her suicide. It is a personal narrative in which she depicts herself at her desk, being distracted by a moth that expires on her windowsill. This "tiny bead of pure life" causes her to reflect on the life force infusing the natural world beyond her study (3).

XXXXXXXXXXXXXXXXXXXXXXXXXXXXXXXXXXXXXXXXXXXXXXXXXXXXXXX

Moths that fly by day are not properly to be called moths; they do   1
not excite that pleasant sense of dark autumn nights and ivy-blossom which the commonest yellow underwing asleep in the shadow of the curtain never fails to rouse in us. They are hybrid creatures, neither gay like butterflies nor sombre like their own species. Nevertheless the present specimen, with his narrow hay-coloured wings, fringed with a tassel of the same colour, seemed to be content with life. It was a pleasant morning, mid-September, mild, benignant, yet with a keener breath than that of the summer months. The plough was already scoring the field opposite the window, and where the share had been, the earth was pressed flat and gleamed with moisture. Such vigour came rolling in from the fields and the down beyond that it was difficult to keep the eyes strictly turned upon the book. The rooks too were keeping one of their annual festivities; soaring round the tree-tops until it looked as if a

vast net with thousands of black knots in it has been cast up into the air; which, after a few moments sank slowly down upon the trees until every twig seemed to have a knot at the end of it. Then, suddenly, the net would be thrown into the air again in a wider circle this time, with the utmost clamour and vociferation, as though to be thrown into the air and settle slowly down upon the tree-tops were a tremendously exciting experience.

2   The same energy which inspired the rooks, the ploughmen, the horses, and even, it seemed, the lean bare-backed downs, sent the moth fluttering from side to side of his square of the window-pane. One could not help watching him. One was, indeed, conscious of a queer feeling of pity for him. The possibilities of pleasure seemed that morning so enormous and so various that to have only a moth's part in life, and a day moth's at that, appeared a hard fate, and his zest in enjoying his meagre opportunities to the full, pathetic. He flew vigorously to one corner of his compartment, and, after waiting there a second, flew across to the other. What remained for him but to fly to a third corner and then to a fourth? That was all he could do, in spite of the size of the downs, the width of the sky, the far-off smoke of houses, and the romantic voice, now and then, of a steamer out at sea. What he could do he did. Watching him, it seemed as if a fiber, very thin but pure, of the enormous energy of the world had been thrust into his frail and diminutive body. As often as he crossed the pane, I could fancy that a thread of vital light became visible. He was little or nothing but life.

3   Yet, because he was so small, and so simple a form of the energy that was rolling in at the open window and driving its way through so many narrow and intricate corridors in my own brain and in those of other human beings, there was something marvelous as well as pathetic about him. It was as if someone had taken a tiny bead of pure life and decking it as lightly as possible with down and feathers, had set it dancing and zigzagging to show us the true nature of life. Thus displayed one could not get over the strangeness of it. One is apt to forget all about life, seeing it humped and bossed and garnished and cumbered so that it has to move with the greatest circumspection and dignity. Again, the thought of all that life might have been had he been born in any other shape caused one to view his simple activities with a kind of pity.

After a time, tired by his dancing apparently, he settled on the win-   4
dow ledge in the sun, and the queer spectacle being at an end, I forgot
about him. Then, looking up, my eye was caught by him. He was trying
to resume his dancing, but seemed either so stiff or so awkward that he
could only flutter to the bottom of the window-pane; and when he tried
to fly across it he failed. Being intent on other matters I watched these
futile attempts for a time without thinking, unconsciously waiting for
him to resume his flight, as one waits for a machine, that has stopped
momentarily, to start again without considering the reason for its failure.
After perhaps a seventh attempt he slipped from the wooden ledge and
fell, fluttering his wings, on to his back on the window-sill. The help-
lessness of his attitude roused me. It flashed upon me that he was in difficulties; he could no longer raise himself; his legs struggled vainly. But,
as I stretched out a pencil, meaning to help him to right himself, it came
over me that the failure and awkwardness were the approach of death. I
laid the pencil down again.

The legs agitated themselves once more. I looked as if for the   5
enemy against which he struggled. I looked out of doors. What had happened there? Presumably it was midday, and work in the fields had
stopped. Stillness and quiet had replaced the previous animation. The
birds had taken themselves off to feed in the brooks. The horses stood
still. Yet the power was there all the same, massed outside indifferent,
impersonal, not attending to anything in particular. Somehow it was
opposed to the little hay-coloured moth. It was useless to try to do anything. One could only watch the extraordinary efforts made by those
tiny legs against an oncoming doom which could, had it chosen, have
submerged an entire city, not merely a city, but masses of human beings;
nothing, I knew, had any chance against death. Nevertheless after a
pause of exhaustion the legs fluttered again. It was superb this last
protest, and so frantic that he succeeded at last in righting himself.
One's sympathies, of course, were all on the side of life. Also, when
there was nobody to care or to know, this gigantic effort on the part of
an insignificant little moth, against a power of such magnitude, to retain
what no one else valued or desired to keep, moved one strangely. Again,
somehow, one saw life, a pure bead. I lifted the pencil again, useless
though I knew it to be. But even as I did so, the unmistakable tokens of

death showed themselves. The body relaxed, and instantly grew stiff. The struggle was over. The insignificant little creature now knew death. As I looked at the dead moth, this minute wayside triumph of so great a force over so mean an antagonist filled me with wonder. Just as life had been strange a few minutes before, so death was now as strange. The moth having righted himself now lay most decently and uncomplainingly composed. O yes, he seemed to say, death is stronger than I am.

XXXXXXXXXXXXXX **UNDERSTANDING THE ESSAY** XXXXXXXXXXXXXX

1. In this personal NARRATIVE, Virginia Woolf presents herself with pencil in hand, perhaps sitting alone in her study or workroom reading and writing. Why are there no other people in the room? What is the significance of Woolf's keeping a window open to the world outside?

2. Woolf DESCRIBES the moth in considerable detail. Why do you think she tells us so little about what she herself and her room look like? What does this CONTRAST achieve in the essay?

3. Woolf seems to have trouble concentrating on her work. Why? How does she show us that this is the case?

4. How would you describe Woolf's general state of mind in the essay? How does it COMPARE with the "vigour" of the scene outside (1)? What is the significance of her finding both life and death to be "strange" (5)?

5. Published posthumously in 1942, "The Death of the Moth" was written shortly before Woolf experienced a mental breakdown and committed suicide. Are these facts relevant to a reading of the essay? Why or why not?

E. B. WHITE

Once More to the Lake

Elwyn Brooks White (1899–1985) was considered by many to be the leading American essayist of his day. For more than fifty years, White contributed regularly to the *New Yorker, Harper's,* and other magazines. He also wrote books for children, among them *Charlotte's Web* (1952). "Once More to the Lake" originally appeared in *Harper's* in 1941; it is a personal narrative about time and the generations. When asked about the process of composing this American classic, White responded: "The 'process' is probably every bit as mysterious to me as it is to some of your students—if that will make them feel any better. As for the revising I did, it was probably quite a lot. I always revise the hell out of everything. It's the only way I know how to write."

XXXXXXXXXXXXXXXXXXXXXXXXXXXXXXXXXXXXXXXXXXXXXXXXXXXXX

One summer, along about 1904, my father rented a camp on a lake in Maine and took us all there for the month of August. We all got ringworm from some kittens and had to rub Pond's Extract on our arms and legs night and morning, and my father rolled over in a canoe with all his clothes on; but outside of that the vacation was a success and from then on none of us ever thought there was any place in the world like that lake in Maine. We returned summer after summer—always on August 1 for one month. I have since become a salt-water man, but sometimes in summer there are days when the restlessness of the tides and the fearful cold of the sea water and the incessant wind that blows across the afternoon and into the evening make me wish for the placidity of a lake in the woods. A few weeks ago this feeling got so strong I bought myself a couple of bass hooks and a spinner and returned to the lake where we used to go, for a week's fishing and to revisit old haunts.

I took along my son, who had never had any fresh water up his nose and who had seen lily pads only from train windows. On the jour-

ney over to the lake I began to wonder what it would be like. I wondered how the time would have marred this unique, this holy spot—the
coves and streams, the hills that the sun set behind, the camps and the
paths behind the camps. I was sure that the tarred road would have
found it out, and I wondered in what other ways it would be desolated.
It is strange how much you can remember about places like that once
you allow your mind to return into the grooves that lead back. You
remember one thing, and that suddenly reminds you of another thing. I
guess I remembered clearest of all the early mornings, when the lake was
cool and motionless, remembered how the bedroom smelled of the lum-
ber it was made of and of the wet woods whose scent entered through
the screen. The partitions in the camp were thin and did not extend
clear to the top of the rooms, and as I was always the first up I would
dress softly so as not to wake the others, and sneak out into the sweet
outdoors and start out in the canoe, keeping close along the shore in the
long shadows of the pines. I remembered being very careful never to rub
my paddle against the gunwale for fear of disturbing the stillness of the
cathedral.

3   The lake had never been what you would call a wild lake. There
were cottages sprinkled around the shores, and it was in farming country
although the shores of the lake were quite heavily wooded. Some of the
cottages were owned by nearby farmers, and you would live at the shore
and eat your meals at the farmhouse. That's what our family did. But
although it wasn't wild, it was a fairly large and undisturbed lake and
there were places in it that, to a child at least, seemed infinitely remote
and primeval.

4   I was right about the tar: it led to within half a mile of the shore.
But when I got back there, with my boy, and we settled into a camp near
a farmhouse and into the kind of summertime I had known, I could tell
that it was going to be pretty much the same as it had been before—I
knew it, lying in bed the first morning, smelling the bedroom and hearing the boy sneak quietly out and go off along the shore in a boat. I
began to sustain the illusion that he was I, and therefore, by simple
transposition, that I was my father. This sensation persisted, kept crop-
ping up all the time we were there. It was not an entirely new feeling,
but in this setting, it grew much stronger. I seemed to be living a dual

existence. I would be in the middle of some simple act, I would be picking up a bait box or laying down a table fork, or I would be saying something, and suddenly it would be not I but my father who was saying the words or making the gesture. It gave me a creepy sensation.

We went fishing the first morning. I felt the same damp moss covering the worms in the bait can, and saw the dragonfly alight on the tip of my rod as it hovered a few inches from the surface of the water. It was the arrival of this fly that convinced me beyond any doubt that everything was as it always had been, that the years were a mirage and that there had been no years. The small waves were the same, chucking the rowboat under the chin as we fished at anchor, and the boat was the same boat, the same color green and the ribs broken in the same places, and under the floorboards the same freshwater leavings and débris—the dead helgramite, the wisps of moss, the rusty discarded fishhook, the dried blood from yesterday's catch. We stared silently at the tips of our rods, at the dragonflies that came and went. I lowered the tip of mine into the water, tentatively, pensively dislodging the fly, which darted two feet away, poised, darted two feet back, and came to rest again a little farther up the rod. There had been no years between the ducking of this dragonfly and the other one—the one that was part of memory. I looked at the boy, who was silently watching his fly, and it was my hands that held his rod, my eyes watching. I felt dizzy and didn't know which rod I was at the end of.

We caught two bass, hauling them in briskly as though they were mackerel, pulling them over the side of the boat in a businesslike manner without any landing net, and stunning them with a blow on the back of the head. When we got back for a swim before lunch, the lake was exactly where we had left it, the same number of inches from the dock, and there was only the merest suggestion of a breeze. This seemed an utterly enchanted sea, this lake you could leave to its own devices for a few hours and come back to, and find that it had not stirred, this constant and trustworthy body of water. In the shallows, the dark, water-soaked sticks and twigs, smooth and old, were undulating in clusters on the bottom against the clean ribbed sand, and the track of the mussel was plain. A school of minnows swam by, each minnow with its small individual shadow, doubling the attendance, so clear and sharp in the sunlight. Some of the other campers were in swimming, along the shore, one of them with a cake of soap, and the water felt thin and clear and unsubstantial. Over the years there had been this person with the cake of soap, this cultist, and here he was. There had been no years.

7   Up to the farmhouse to dinner through the teeming, dusty field, the road under our sneakers was only a two-track road. The middle track was missing, the one with the marks of the hooves and the splotches of dried, flaky manure. There had always been three tracks to choose from in choosing which track to walk in; now the choice was narrowed down to two. For a moment I missed terribly the middle alternative. But the way led past the tennis court, and something about the way it lay there in the sun reassured me; the tape had loosened along the backline, the alleys were green with plantains and other weeds, and the net (installed in June and removed in September) sagged in the dry noon, and the whole place steamed with midday heat and hunger and emptiness. There was a choice of pie for dessert, and one was blueberry and one was apple, and the waitresses were the same country girls, there having been no passage of time, only the illusion of it as in a dropped curtain—the waitresses were still fifteen; their hair had been washed, that was the only difference—they had been to the movies and seen the pretty girls with the clean hair.

8   Summertime, oh, summertime, pattern of life indelible, the fade-proof lake, the woods unshatterable, the pasture with the sweetfern and the juniper forever and ever, summer without end; this was the background, and the life along the shore was the design, the cottages with their innocent and tranquil design, their tiny docks with the flagpole and the American flag floating against the white clouds in the blue sky, the little paths over the roots of the trees leading from camp to camp and the paths leading back to the outhouses and the can of lime for sprinkling, and at the souvenir counters at the store the miniature birch-bark canoes and the postcards that showed things looking a little better than they looked. This was the American family at play, escaping the city heat, wondering whether the newcomers in the camp at the head of the cove were "common" or "nice," wondering whether it was true that the people who drove up for Sunday dinner at the farmhouse were turned away because there wasn't enough chicken.

It seemed to me, as I kept remembering all this, that those times and those summers had been infinitely precious and worth saving. There had been jollity and peace and goodness. The arriving (at the beginning of August) had been so big a business in itself, at the railway station the farm wagon drawn up, the first smell of the pine-laden air, the first glimpse of the smiling farmer, and the great importance of the trunks and your father's enormous authority in such matters, and the feel of the wagon under you for the long ten-mile haul, and at the top of the last long hill catching the first view of the lake after eleven months of not seeing this cherished body of water. The shouts and cries of the other campers when they saw you, and the trunks to be unpacked, to give up their rich burden. (Arriving was less exciting nowadays, when you sneaked up in your car and parked it under a tree near the camp and took out the bags and in five minutes it was all over, no fuss, no loud wonderful fuss about trunks.)

Peace and goodness and jollity. The only thing that was wrong now, really, was the sound of the place, an unfamiliar nervous sound of the outboard motors. This was the note that jarred, the one thing that would sometimes break the illusion and set the years moving. In those other summertimes all motors were inboard; and when they were at a little distance, the noise they made was a sedative, an ingredient of summer sleep. They were one-cylinder and two-cylinder engines, and some were make-and-break and some were jump-spark, but they all made a sleepy sound across the lake. The one-lungers throbbed and fluttered, and the twin-cylinder ones purred and purred, and that was a quiet sound, too. But now the campers all had outboards. In the daytime, in the hot mornings, these motors made a petulant, irritable sound; at night, in the still evening when the afterglow lit the water, they whined about one's ears like mosquitoes. My boy loved our rented outboard, and his great desire was to achieve single-handed mastery over it, and authority, and he soon learned the trick of choking it a little (but not too much), and the adjustment of the needle valve. Watching him I would remember the things you could do with the old one-cylinder engine with the heavy flywheel, how you could have it eating out of your hand if you got really close to it spiritually. Motorboats in those days didn't have clutches, and you would make a landing by shutting off the motor at the proper time and coasting in with a dead rudder. But there was a way of reversing them, if you learned the trick, by cutting the switch and putting it on again exactly on the final dying revolution of the flywheel, so that it would kick back against compression and begin reversing. Approaching a dock in a strong following breeze, it was difficult to slow up sufficiently by the ordinary coasting method, and if a boy felt he had complete mastery over his motor, he was tempted to keep it running beyond its time and then reverse it a few feet from the dock. It took a cool nerve, because if you threw the switch a twentieth of a second too soon you would catch the flywheel when it still had speed enough to go up past center, and the boat would leap ahead, charging bull-fashion at the dock.

11   We had a good week at the camp. The bass were biting well and the sun shone endlessly, day after day. We would be tired at night and lie down in the accumulated heat of the little bedrooms after the long hot day and the breeze would stir almost imperceptibly outside and the smell of the swamp drift in through the rusty screens. Sleep would come easily and in the morning the red squirrel would be on the roof, tapping out his gay routine. I kept remembering everything, lying in bed in the mornings—the small steamboat that had a long rounded stern like the lip of a Ubangi, and how quietly she ran on the moonlight sails, when the older boys played their mandolins and the girls sang and we ate doughnuts dipped in sugar, and how sweet the music was on the water in the shining night, and what it had felt like to think about girls then. After breakfast, we would go up to the store and the things were in the same place—the minnows in a bottle, the plugs and spinners disarranged and pawed over by the youngsters from the boys' camp, the Fig Newtons and the Beeman's gum. Outside, the road was tarred and cars stood in front of the store. Inside, all was just as it had always been, except there was more Coca-Cola and not so much Moxie[1] and root beer and birch beer and sarsaparilla. We would walk out with the bottle of pop apiece and sometimes the pop would backfire up our noses and hurt. We explored the streams, quietly, where the turtles slid off logs and dug

---

1. Brand name of an old-fashioned soft drink.

their way into the soft bottom; and we lay on the town wharf and fed worms to the tame bass. Everywhere we went I had trouble making out which was I, the one walking at my side, the one walking in my pants.

One afternoon while we were there at that lake a thunderstorm   12
came up. It was like the revival of an old melodrama that I had seen long ago with childish awe. The second-act climax of the drama of the electrical disturbance over a lake in America has not changed in any important respect. This was the big scene, still the big scene. The whole thing was so familiar, the first feeling of oppression and heat and a general air around camp of not wanting to go very far away. In midafternoon (it was all the same) a curious darkening of the sky, and a lull in everything that had made life tick; and then the way the boats suddenly swung the other way at their moorings with the coming of a breeze out of the new quarter, and the premonitory rumble. Then the kettle drum, then the snare, then the bass drum and cymbals, then crackling light against the dark, and the gods grinning and licking their chops in the hills. Afterward the calm, the rain steadily rustling in the calm lake, the return of light and hope and spirits, and the campers running out in joy and relief to go swimming in the rain, their bright cries perpetuating the deathless joke about how they were getting simply drenched, and the children screaming with delight at the new sensation of bathing in the rain, and the joke about getting drenched linking the generations in a strong indestructible chain. And the comedian who waded in carrying an umbrella.

When the others went swimming, my son said he was going in,   13
too. He pulled his dripping trunks from the line where they had hung all through the shower and wrung them out. Languidly, and with no thought of going in, I watched him, his hard little body, skinny and bare, saw him wince slightly as he pulled up around his vitals the small, soggy, icy garment. As he buckled the swollen belt, suddenly my groin felt the chill of death.

XXXXXXXXXXXXXX **UNDERSTANDING THE ESSAY** XXXXXXXXXXXXXX

1. "Once More to the Lake" combines many MODES OF WRITING: it is a personal NARRATIVE; it DESCRIBES the lake and its environs in detail; and it gives EXAMPLES of what the NARRATOR and his son find there. If the basic PLOT of E. B. White's narrative is the return to youth, how do the description and exemplification contribute to that plot?

2. White's narrative is told from the POINT OF VIEW of the father; and even though he at times "becomes" the boy, he always speaks from the older man's perspective. What does he know that his young son cannot? How does White reveal this?

3. His son, White says, "loved our rented outboard, and his great desire was to achieve single-handed mastery over it, and authority" (10). How does he relate this statement to the earlier one about "the great importance of the trunks and your father's enormous authority in such matters" (9)?

4. When he and his son first journey to the lake, White speaks of returning "into the grooves that lead back" (2). And later, when they go to eat at the farmhouse, he is disturbed because the middle "track" in the old road is missing (7). How are the two events (or musings) related? Where are these "grooves" and "tracks" located? How do they relate to the theme of time and timelessness as White explores it?

5. White's lake is said to be "utterly enchanted," and much of his essay has the air of a reverie or dream (6). How does White's treatment of time throughout contribute to this dreamlike quality?

6. White often speaks of the natural peace and placidity of the lake, broken only by the whine of the outboard motors. How does White's "theatrical" presentation of the noisy thunderstorm in paragraph 12 keep it from posing any real threat to the peace or safety of the campers? How is that tranquility broken permanently by the last line of the essay?

7. "This was the American family at play," says White (8). What, according to White, are the typical attributes of this (mythical?) institution? In your opinion, has the passage of time altered its portrait since 1941? If so, how?

MARTIN LUTHER KING JR.

I Have a Dream

Martin Luther King Jr. (1929–1968) was a clergyman and civil rights activist known for his doctrine of nonviolent protest. A graduate of Morehouse College and Crozer Theological Seminary, he was awarded a Ph.D. in theology from Boston University in 1955. That same year, as a member of the executive committee of the NAACP, King led a boycott of the segregated bus system in Montgomery, Alabama. The boycott resulted in a Supreme Court ruling banning racial segregation on the city's buses. After this landmark case, King spoke and demonstrated tirelessly in the cause of civil rights. His efforts culminated in the peaceful march on Washington D.C. in 1963 of more than a quarter of a million protesters, to whom he delivered his "I Have a Dream" address from the steps of the Lincoln Memorial. The next year King received the Noble Peace Prize. He was assassinated on April 4, 1968, in Memphis, Tennessee.

XXXXXXXXXXXXXXXXXXXXXXXXXXXXXXXXXXXXXXXXXXXXXXXXXXXXXXXXXX

Five score years ago, a great American, in whose symbolic shadow we stand, signed the Emancipation Proclamation.[1] This momentous decree came as a great beacon light of hope to millions of Negro slaves who had been seared in the flames of withering injustice. It came as a joyous daybreak to end the long night of captivity.

But one hundred years later, we must face the tragic fact that the Negro is still not free. One hundred years later, the life of the Negro is still sadly crippled by the manacles of segregation and the chains of discrimination. One hundred years later, the Negro lives on a lonely island of poverty in the midst of a vast ocean of material prosperity. One hun-

1. In 1863, President Abraham Lincoln signed a decree declaring that "all persons held as slaves within any States . . . shall be then, thenceforward, and forever free."

dred years later, the Negro is still languishing in the corners of American society and finds himself an exile in his own land. So we have come here today to dramatize an appalling condition.

3   In a sense we have come to our nation's capital to cash a check. When the architects of our republic wrote the magnificent words of the Constitution and the Declaration of Independence, they were signing a promissory note to which every American was to fall heir. This note was a promise that all men would be guaranteed the inalienable rights of life, liberty, and the pursuit of happiness.

4   It is obvious today that America has defaulted on this promissory note insofar as her citizens of color are concerned. Instead of honoring this sacred obligation, America has given the Negro people a bad check which has come back marked "insufficient funds." But we refuse to believe that the bank of justice is bankrupt. We refuse to believe that there are insufficient funds in the great vaults of opportunity of this nation. So we have come to cash this check—a check that will give us upon demand the riches of freedom and the security of justice. We have also come to this hallowed spot to remind America of the fierce urgency of *now*. This is no time to engage in the luxury of cooling off or to take the tranquilizing drug of gradualism. *Now* is the time to rise from the dark and desolate valley of segregation to the sunlit path of racial justice. *Now* is the time to open the doors of opportunity to all of God's children. *Now* is the time to lift our nation from the quicksands of racial injustice to the solid rock of brotherhood.

5   It would be fatal for the nation to overlook the urgency of the moment and to underestimate the determination of the Negro. This sweltering summer of the Negro's legitimate discontent will not pass until there is an invigorating autumn of freedom and equality. Nineteen sixty-three is not an end, but a beginning. Those who hope that the Negro needed to blow off steam and will now be content will have a rude awakening if the nation returns to business as usual. There will be neither rest nor tranquility in America until the Negro is granted his citizenship rights. The whirlwinds of revolt will continue to shake the foundations of our nation until the bright day of justice emerges.

6   But there is something that I must say to my people who stand on the warm threshold which leads into the palace of justice. In the process

of gaining our rightful place we must not be guilty of wrongful deeds. Let us not seek to satisfy our thirst for freedom by drinking from the cup of bitterness and hatred.

We must forever conduct our struggle on the high plane of dignity and discipline. We must not allow our creative protest to degenerate into physical violence. Again and again we must rise to the majestic heights of meeting physical force with soul force. The marvelous new militancy which has engulfed the Negro community must not lead us to distrust of all white people, for many of our white brothers, as evidenced by their presence here today, have come to realize that their destiny is tied up with our destiny and their freedom is inextricably bound to our freedom. We cannot walk alone.

And as we walk, we must make the pledge that we shall march ahead. We cannot turn back. There are those who are asking the devotees of civil rights, "When will you be satisfied?" We can never be satisfied as long as our bodies, heavy with the fatigue of travel, cannot gain lodging in the motels of the highways and the hotels of the cities. We cannot be satisfied as long as the Negro's basic mobility is from a smaller ghetto to a larger one. We can never be satisfied as long as a Negro in Mississippi cannot vote and a Negro in New York believes he has nothing for which to vote. No, no, we are not satisfied, and we will not be satisfied until justice rolls down like waters and righteousness like a mighty stream.

I am not unmindful that some of you have come here out of great trials and tribulations. Some of you have come fresh from narrow cells. Some of you have come from areas where your quest for freedom left you battered by the storms of persecution and staggered by the winds of police brutality. You have been the veterans of creative suffering. Continue to work with the faith that unearned suffering is redemptive.

Go back to Mississippi, go back to Alabama, go back to Georgia, go back to Louisiana, go back to the slums and ghettos of our northern cities, knowing that somehow this situation can and will be changed. Let us not wallow in the valley of despair.

I say to you today, my friends, that in spite of the difficulties and frustrations of the moment, I still have a dream. It is a dream deeply rooted in the American dream.

12   I have a dream that one day this nation will rise up and live out the true meaning of its creed: "We hold these truths to be self-evident: that all men are created equal."

13   I have a dream that one day on the red hills of Georgia the sons of former slaves and the sons of former slaveowners will be able to sit down together at a table of brotherhood.

14   I have a dream that one day even the state of Mississippi, a desert state, sweltering with the heat of injustice and oppression, will be transformed into an oasis of freedom and justice.

15   I have a dream that my four children will one day live in a nation where they will not be judged by the color of their skin but by the content of their character.

16   I have a dream today.

17   I have a dream that one day the state of Alabama, whose governor's lips are presently dripping with the words of interposition and nullification,[2] will be transformed into a situation where little black boys and black girls will be able to join hands with little white boys and white girls and walk together as sisters and brothers.

18   I have a dream today.

19   I have a dream that one day every valley shall be exalted, every hill and mountain shall be made low, the rough places will be made plain, and the crooked places will be made straight, and the glory of the Lord shall be revealed, and all flesh shall see it together.[3]

20   This is our hope. This is the faith with which I return to the South. With this faith we will be able to hew out of the mountain of despair a stone of hope. With this faith we will be able to transform the jangling discords of our nation into a beautiful symphony of brotherhood. With this faith we will be able to work together, to pray together, to struggle together, to go to jail together, to stand up for freedom together, knowing that we will be free one day.

2. George Wallace (1919–1998), four-time governor of Alabama, was a fierce opponent of the civil rights movement. In 1963 he defied U.S. law and mounted a campaign against the integration of Alabama public schools.

3. King is quoting a famous passage from the book of Isaiah (40:4–5).

This will be the day when all of God's children will be able to sing 21
with a new meaning, "My country, 'tis of thee, sweet land of liberty, of
thee I sing. Land where my fathers died, land of the pilgrim's pride,
from every mountainside, let freedom ring."

And if America is to be a great nation this must become true. So 22
let freedom ring from the prodigious hilltops of New Hampshire. Let
freedom ring from the mighty mountains of New York. Let freedom ring
from the heightening Alleghenies of Pennsylvania!

Let freedom ring from the snowcapped Rockies of Colorado! 23

Let freedom ring from the curvaceous peaks of California! 24

But not only that; let freedom ring from Stone Mountain of 25
Georgia![4]

Let freedom ring from Lookout Mountain of Tennessee![5] 26

Let freedom ring from every hill and every molehill of Mississippi. 27
From every mountainside, let freedom ring.

When we let freedom ring, when we let it ring from every village 28
and every hamlet, from every state and every city, we will be able to
speed up that day when all of God's children, black men and white men,
Jews and Gentiles, Protestants and Catholics, will be able to join hands
and sing in the words of the old Negro spiritual, "Free at last! free at
last! thank God Almighty, we are free at last!"

4. The figures of three leaders of the Confederacy are carved onto the face of Stone
Mountain, near Atlanta.

5. Site of a major battle during the Civil War in 1863.

XXXXXXXXXXXXX **UNDERSTANDING THE SPEECH** XXXXXXXXXXXXX

1. Speaking in 1963, a hundred years after slavery was abolished by President
Lincoln's Emancipation Proclamation, Martin Luther King Jr. tells his vast
AUDIENCE that African Americans still are "not free" (2). Why not? How and
where does he DESCRIBE this "appalling condition" (2)?

2. King uses his description of segregation as the basis for an ARGUMENT. What
is the central CLAIM of that argument? What does King ask his audience to do
about the situation he describes?

3. What does King mean by "the tranquilizing drug of gradualism"(4)? Why does he warn his audience to resist it?

4. King does not DESCRIBE his "dream" until almost midway through his speech (11). Why? How does the first half of King's address help to prepare his audience for the vision of the future he presents in the second half?

5. In King's vision, the oppressed do not rise up and crush their oppressors. Why not? How do the details by which he DEFINES his dream fit in with what King tells his audience in paragraphs 6–7 and with his general philosophy of nonviolence?

6. King relies heavily on FIGURES OF SPEECH throughout his address, particularly METAPHOR: the nation has given its black citizens a "bad check" (4); racial injustice is "quicksands" (4); brotherhood is a "table" (13); freedom is a bell that rings from the "hilltops" (22). Choose several of these figures that you find particularly effective, and explain how they help King to COMPARE AND CONTRAST the "appalling condition" of the past and present with his brighter vision for the future.

USING SOURCES
IN YOUR WRITING

XXXXXXXXXXXXXXXXXXXXXXXXXXXXXXXXXXXXXXXXXXXXXXXXXXX

In much of the writing you do, you will need to draw on the work of other writers. This appendix will show you how to do research and use what you find in your own writing, and how to document your sources accurately.

FINDING SOURCES

To analyze the 2009 debate about health care reform, you examine news stories and blogs published at the time. To write an essay interpreting "A Modest Proposal," you study the essay and read several critical interpretations in literary journals. You might also find out something about the situation in Ireland at the time that Swift wrote his piece. In both of these cases, you go beyond your own knowledge to consult additional sources of information.

The following section gives you some tips for finding a range of sources—print and online, general and specialized, published and first-hand. Keep in mind that as you do research, finding and evaluating sources are two activities that usually take place simultaneously. So this section and the next one go hand in hand.

Primary and Secondary Sources

Your research will likely lead you to both primary and secondary sources. Primary sources include historical documents, literary works, eyewitness accounts, field reports, diaries, letters, and lab studies. Secondary sources include scholarly books and articles, reviews, biographies, textbooks, and other works that interpret or discuss primary sources. Novels and poems are primary sources; articles interpreting them are secondary sources. The Declaration of Independence is a primary historical document; a historian's account of the events surrounding the Declaration's writing is secondary.

Print and Online Sources

Some sources are available only in print; some are available only online. But many print sources are also available on the Web. When it comes to finding sources, it's likely that you'll search for most sources online, through the library's website. In general, there are four kinds of sources you'll want to consult: reference works, books, periodicals, and material on the Web.

- *Reference works.* The reference section of your school's library is the place to find encyclopedias, dictionaries, atlases, almanacs, bibliographies, and other reference works in print. Many of these sources are also online. Remember, though, that reference works are only a starting point, a place where you can get an overview of your topic or basic facts about it. Some reference works are *general*, such as *The New Encyclopaedia Britannica* or the *Statistical Abstract of the United States*. Others are *specialized*, providing in-depth information on a single field or topic.

- *Books.* The library catalog is your primary source for finding books. Most library catalogs are computerized and can be accessed through the library's website. You can search by author, title, subject, or keyword. When you click on a specific source, you'll find bibliographic data about author, title, and publication; the call number (which identifies the book's location on the library's shelves); related subject headings (which may lead to other useful materials in the library)—and more.

- *Periodicals.* To find journal and magazine articles, you will need to search periodical indexes and databases, many of which are online. Indexes (such as the *New York Times Index*) provide listings of articles organized by topics; databases (such as LexisNexis) provide the full texts. Although some databases are available for free, many are available only by subscription and so must be accessed through a library.

- *The Web.* The Web provides access to countless sites containing information posted by governments, educational institutions, organizations, businesses, and individuals. Websites are different from other sources in several ways: (1) they often provide entire texts, not just citations of texts, (2) their content varies greatly in its reliability, and (3) they are not stable: what you see on a site today may be different (or gone) tomorrow. Anyone who wants to can post texts on the Web, so you need to evaluate carefully what you find there.

Searching Electronically

Whether you're searching for books, articles in periodicals, or material available on the Web, chances are you'll conduct much of your search electronically. In each case, you can search for authors, titles, or subjects.

The key to searching efficiently is to come up with keywords that focus on the information you need. Most search engines have "advanced search" options that will help you focus your research. Keep in mind that specific commands vary among search engines and within databases. Here are some common ones to try:

- Type quotation marks around words to search for an exact phrase—"Thomas Jefferson."
- Type AND to find sources that include more than one keyword: Jefferson AND Adams.
- Type OR if you're looking for sources that include one of several terms: Jefferson OR Adams OR Madison.
- Type NOT to find sources *without* a certain word: Jefferson NOT Adams.
- Type an asterisk—or some other symbol—to search for words in different forms—*teach** will yield sources containing *teacher* and

teaching, for example. Check the search engine's search tips to find out what symbol to use.

- Some search engines allow you to ask questions in conversational language: What did Thomas Jefferson write about slavery?

- If you don't get results with one set of keywords, substitute SYN-ONYMS (if *folk medicine* doesn't generate much information, try *home remedy*).

EVALUATING SOURCES

Searching the *MasterFILE Premier* database for information on the debate over health care reform, you find almost seven hundred articles. How do you decide which sources to read? This section helps you determine whether a source is reliable and useful for your PURPOSE.

First, think about your purpose. Are you trying to persuade readers to believe or do something? To inform them about something? If the former, try to find sources representing various stances; if the latter, you may need sources that are more factual or informative. Reconsider your AUDIENCE. What kinds of sources will they find persuasive? Following are some questions that can help you select reliable and useful sources:

- *Is it relevant?* How does the source relate to your purpose? What will it add to your work? Look at the title and at any introductory material—a preface, abstract, or introduction—to see what it covers.

- *What are the author's credentials?* What are the author's qualifications to write on the subject? Is he or she associated with a particular position on the issue? You might do a Web search to see what else you can learn about the author.

- *What is the stance?* Does the source cover various POINTS OF VIEW or advocate one particular point of view? Does its title suggest a certain slant?

- *Who is the publisher?* If it's a book, what kind of company published it? If it's an article, what kind of periodical did it appear in? University presses and scholarly journals review books or articles by experts before they are published, but that is typically not the case for other kinds of publications.

- *If it's a website, who is the sponsor?* Is the site maintained by an organization? An interest group? A government agency? An individual? What is the sponsor's purpose—to sell a product, for example, or to convey objective information?

- *What is the level?* Texts written for a general audience might be easier to understand but not authoritative enough. Texts written for scholars will be more authoritative but may be hard to comprehend.

- *When was it published?* See when books and articles were published and when websites were last updated. (If the site lists no date, see if links to other sites still work.) Recent does not necessarily mean better—some topics require current information whereas others call for older sources.

QUOTING, PARAPHRASING, AND SUMMARIZING

In an essay about the writings of Virginia Woolf, you quote a memorable line from "The Death of the Moth." For an essay on the use of torture on terrorism suspects, you summarize some key debates about the issue. Like all writers, you work with the ideas and words of others. This section will help you with the specifics of quoting, paraphrasing, and summarizing source materials.

Taking Notes

When you find material you think will be useful, take careful notes. Write down enough information so that when you refer to it later, you will be reminded of the main points, and keep a precise record of where the information comes from.

- *Use index cards, a computer file, or a notebook,* labeling each entry with the information that will allow you to keep track of where it comes from—author, title, the pages or the URL, and for online sources, the date of access.

- *Take notes in your own words, and use your own sentence patterns.* If you make a note that is a detailed paraphrase, label it as such as that you'll know to provide appropriate documentation if you use it.
- *If you find wording that you'd like to quote,* be sure to enclose the exact words in quotation marks to distinguish your source's words from your own.
- *Label each note with a subject heading.*

Deciding Whether to Quote, Paraphrase, or Summarize

When it comes time to draft, you'll need to decide how to use the sources you've found—in other words, whether to quote, paraphrase, or summarize. You might follow this rule of thumb: quote texts when the wording is worth repeating or makes a point so well that no rewording will do it justice, when you want to cite the exact words of a known authority on your topic, when his or her opinions challenge or disagree with those of others, or when the source is one you want to emphasize. Paraphrase sources that are not worth quoting but contain details you need to include. Summarize longer passages whose main points are important but whose details are not. In all of these instances, you need to identify the source and use proper documentation (see p. 497).

Quoting

When you use someone else's exact words, you need to reproduce the source exactly, though you can modify it to omit unnecessary details (with ellipses).

> Journalist David Brooks makes this assertion: "If Asia's success reopens the debate between individualism and collectivism . . . then it's unlikely that the forces of individualism will sweep the field or even gain an edge" (A21).

> Bruce Catton notes that General Robert E. Lee "saw himself in relation to his own region. He lived in a static society which could endure almost anything except change" (203).

Paraphrasing

When you paraphrase, you restate information from a source *in your own words,* using *your own sentence structures.* Paraphrase when the source material is important but the original wording is not. Because it includes all the main points of the source, a paraphrase is usually about the same length as the original.

Here is a paragraph from Deborah Tannen's essay "Gender in the Classroom." It is followed by two example paraphrases. The first demonstrates some of the challenges of paraphrasing:

ORIGINAL SOURCE

The research of sociologists and anthropologists such as Janet Lever, Marjorie Harness Goodwin, and Donna Eder has shown that girls and boys learn to use language differently in their sex-separate peer groups. Typically, a girl has a best friend with whom she sits and talks, frequently telling secrets. It's the telling of secrets, the fact and the way that they talk to each other, that makes them best friends. For boys, activities are central: Their best friends are the ones they do things with. Boys also tend to play in larger groups that are hierarchical. High-status boys give orders and push low-status boys around. So boys are expected to use language to seize center stage: by exhibiting their skills, displaying their knowledge, and challenging and resisting challenges.

UNACCEPTABLE PARAPHRASE

According to Tannen, sociological and anthropological researchers such as Marjorie Harness Goodwin, Janet Lever, and Donna Eder have revealed that girls and boys use language distinctly when in same-sex groups of peers. Girls usually have a best friend whom they talk and tell secrets to, and that's what makes them best friends. But for boys, it is activities that are at the center of their friendships—they do things with their best buddies. When boys play, it is in bigger, hierarchical groups, and those who are high-status bully those who are low-status. So it's expected that boys will use language to show abilities, reveal their knowledge, and take on challenges, all in order to seize the spotlight (B1).

This paraphrase borrows too much of the language of the original or changes it only slightly. It also follows the original sentence structure too closely. This acceptable paraphrase avoids both of these pitfalls:

ACCEPTABLE PARAPHRASE

According to Tannen, differences in how boys and girls use language among their peers of the same sex have been revealed through the anthropological and sociological work of researchers such as Donna Eder, Janet Lever, and Marjorie Harness Goodwin. As Tannen explains, girls tend to talk in pairs, using language to develop close friendships through telling secrets and other intimate conversation. Boys, by contrast, do not sit and talk in pairs; rather, they make friends by doing things together in hierarchically structured groups. They use language to negotiate their status in the group—to demonstrate skills and knowledge and to establish their rank in the pecking order (B1).

Summarizing

A summary states the main ideas found in a source concisely and in your own words. Unlike a paraphrase, a summary does not present all the details, so it is generally as brief as possible. Summaries may boil down an entire book or essay into a single sentence, or they may take a paragraph or more to present the main ideas. Here, for example, is a summary of the Tannen paragraph:

As Tannen explains, girls and boys differ in their use of language in social groups; whereas girls talk and share secrets in order to bond, boys bond through sharing activities and use language to assert their positions in the hierarchy of the group (B1).

Incorporating Source Materials into Your Text

You need to introduce quotations, paraphrases, and summaries clearly, letting readers know who the author is—and, if need be, something about his or her credentials. Consider this sentence:

Professor and textbook author Elaine Tyler May claims that many high school history books are too bland to interest young readers (531).

The beginning ("Professor and textbook author Elaine Tyler May claims") functions as a signal phrase, telling readers who is making the assertion and why she has the authority to speak on the topic. The verb you use in a signal phrase can be neutral (*says* or *thinks*) or it can suggest something about the stance—the source's or your own. The preceding example about the textbook author uses the verb *claims*, suggesting that what she says is arguable (or that the writer believes it is). How would it change your understanding if the signal verb were *observes* or *suggests*?

ACKNOWLEDGING SOURCES AND AVOIDING PLAGIARISM

Whenever you do research-based writing, you are entering a conversation—"putting in your oar," as the rhetorician Kenneth Burke once wrote. As a writer, you need to acknowledge any words and ideas that come from others—to give credit where credit is due, to recognize the various authorities and many perspectives you have considered, to show readers where they can find your sources, and to situate your own ideas in the ongoing conversation. Using other people's words and ideas without acknowledgment is plagiarism, a serious academic and ethical offense. This section will give you some tips on acknowledging the materials you use and avoiding plagiarism.

Acknowledging Sources

Your reader needs to know where your source's words or ideas begin and end. Therefore, you should introduce a source by naming the author in a signal phrase, and then include a brief parenthetical in-text citation following the words or ideas you are citing. Or you might choose to name the author in a parenthetical citation (see pp. 498–99).

SOURCES THAT NEED ACKNOWLEDGMENT

- Direct quotations, paraphrases, and summaries.
- Arguable statements and any information that is not commonly known.
- The opinions and assertions of others.

- Visuals that you did not create yourself (charts, photographs, and so on).
- Collaborative help that you received from others.

SOURCES THAT DON'T NEED ACKNOWLEDGMENT

- Information that most readers are likely to know or that can be found in many sources, such as the name of the current president of the United States.
- Well-known quotations, such as John F. Kennedy's "Ask not what your country can do for you; ask what you can do for your country."
- Material that you created or gathered yourself, as long as the data are yours as well. A graph that you devised from someone else's research would require acknowledgment.

Avoiding Plagiarism

When you use the words, ideas, or visual images of others, you need to acknowledge who and where the material came from; if you don't credit those sources, you are guilty of plagiarism. Plagiarism is often committed unintentionally—as when a writer paraphrases someone else's ideas in language that is close to the original. It is essential, therefore, to know what constitutes plagiarism: (1) using another writer's words or ideas without in-text citation and documentation, (2) using another writer's exact words without quotation marks, and (3) paraphrasing or summarizing someone else's ideas using language or sentence structures that are too close to theirs.

To avoid plagiarizing, take careful notes as you do your research, clearly labeling as quotations any words you quote directly and being careful to use your own words and sentence structures in paraphrases and summaries. Be sure you know what source material you must document, and give credit to your sources. Be especially careful with material found online—copying written or visual material right into a document you are writing is all too easy to do. You must acknowledge information you find on the Web just as you do all other source materials.

And you must recognize that plagiarism has consequences. A scholar's work will be discredited if it too closely resembles another's. Journalists found to have plagiarized lose their jobs, and students routinely fail courses or are dismissed from their school when they are caught cheating—all too often by submitting as their own essays that they have purchased from online "research" sites. If you're having trouble completing an assignment, seek assistance. Talk with your instructor, or if your school has a writing center, go there for advice on all aspects of your writing, including acknowledging sources and avoiding plagiarism.

DOCUMENTATION

When you write up the results of a research project, you need to cite the sources you use and tell readers where the ideas came from. The information you give about sources is called documentation.

The documentation style of the Modern Language Association (MLA) is a two-part system, consisting of (1) brief in-text parenthetical documentation for quotations, paraphrases, or summaries and (2) more-detailed documentation in a list of sources at the end of the text. MLA requires that the end-of-text documentation provide the following basic information about each source you cite: author, editor, or organization providing the information; title of work; place of publication; publisher; date of publication; medium of publication; and, for online sources, date when you accessed the source.

MLA is by no means the only documentation style. Many other publishers and organizations have their own style, among them the American Psychological Association (APA), the University of Chicago Press, and the Council of Science Editors. We focus on MLA here because it's one of the styles that college students are often required to use.

Following is an example of how the two parts—the brief parenthetical documentation in your text and the more detailed information at the end—correspond. As the example shows, when you cite a work in your text, you can name the author either in a signal phrase or in parentheses. If you name the author in a signal phrase, give the page number(s) in parentheses; when the author's name is not given in a signal phrase, include it in parentheses. Citing a source appropriately in your text enables readers to locate that source in your works-cited list.

IN-TEXT DOCUMENTATION

As Lester Faigley puts it, "The world has become a bazaar from which to shop for an individual 'lifestyle'" (12).

As one observer suggests, "The world has become a bazaar from which to shop for an individual 'lifestyle'" (Faigley 12).

WORKS-CITED DOCUMENTATION

Faigley, Lester. *Fragments of Rationality: Postmodernity and the Subject of Composition.* Pittsburgh: U of Pittsburgh P, 1992. Print.

MLA In-Text Documentation

In your text, you have three options for citing a source: quoting, paraphrasing, and summarizing. As you cite each source, you will need to decide whether or not to name the author in a signal phrase—"as Toni Morrison writes"—or in parentheses—"(Morrison 24)."

1. AUTHOR NAMED IN A SIGNAL PHRASE

If you mention the author in a signal phrase, put only the page number(s) in parentheses. Do not write *page* or *p.* When citing a direct quotation, note that the parenthetical reference comes after the closing quotation marks but before the period at the end of the sentence.

McCullough describes John Adams as having "the hands of a man accustomed to pruning his own trees, cutting his own hay, and splitting his own firewood" (18).

2. AUTHOR NAMED IN PARENTHESES

If you do not mention the author in a signal phrase, put his or her last name in parentheses along with the page number(s).

> One biographer describes John Adams as someone who was not a stranger to manual labor (McCullough 18).

For either style of reference, try to put the parenthetical citation at the end of the sentence or as close as possible to the material you've cited without awkwardly interrupting the sentence.

3. AFTER A BLOCK QUOTATION

When quoting more than three lines of poetry, more than four lines of prose, or DIALOGUE from a drama, set off the quotation from the rest of your text, indenting it one inch (or ten spaces) from the left margin. Do not use quotation marks. Place any parenthetical documentation after the final punctuation.

> In *Eastward to Tartary*, Kaplan captures ancient and contemporary Antioch for us:
>
>> At the height of its glory in the Roman-Byzantine age, when it had an amphitheater, public baths, aqueducts, and sewage pipes, half a million people lived in Antioch. Today the population is only 125,000. With sour relations between Turkey and Syria, and unstable politics throughout the Middle East, Antioch is now a backwater—seedy and tumbledown, with relatively few tourists. I found it altogether charming. (123)

4. TWO OR MORE AUTHORS

For a work by two or three authors, name all the authors.

> Some educators strive to introduce Julio Cortázar, Marjorie Agosín, and other Latin American writers to an audience of English-speaking adolescents (Carlson and Ventura 5).

For a work with four or more authors, you can mention all their names *or* just the name of the first author followed by *et al.*, which is Latin for "and others."

> One popular survey of American literature breaks the contents into sixteen thematic groupings (Anderson, Brinnin, Leggett, Arpin, and Toth 19–24).

> One popular survey of American literature breaks the contents into sixteen thematic groupings (Anderson et al. 19–24).

5. ORGANIZATION OR GOVERNMENT AS AUTHOR

If the author is an organization, cite the organization. It's acceptable to shorten long names.

> The U.S. government can be direct when it wants to be. For example, it sternly warns, "If you are overpaid, we will recover any payments not due you" (Social Security Administration 12).

6. AUTHOR UNKNOWN

Use the work's title or a shortened version of the title.

> A powerful editorial in last week's paper asserts that healthy liver donor Mike Hurewitz died because of "frightening" faulty postoperative care ("Every Patient's Nightmare").

7. LITERARY WORKS

When referring to literary works that are available in many different editions, you need to cite additional information so that readers of any edition can locate the text you are citing.

Novels: Give the page and chapter number.

> In *Pride and Prejudice*, Mrs. Bennet shows no warmth toward Jane and Elizabeth when they return from Netherfield (105; ch. 12).

Verse plays: Instead of page numbers, give the act, scene, and line numbers; separate them with periods.

Macbeth develops the vision theme when he addresses the Ghost
with "Thou hast no speculation in those eyes / Which thou dost
glare with" (3.3.96–97).

Poems: Instead of page numbers, give the part and line numbers (separated by periods). If the poem has only line numbers, use the word
line(s) in the first reference.

> Whitman includes not only opposing adjectives but also opposing
> nouns in "Song of Myself" when he says, "I am of old and young,
> of the foolish as much as the wise, / . . . a child as well as a man"
> (16.330–32).

> The mere in *Beowulf* is described as "not a pleasant place!" (line
> 1372). Later, it is called "the awful place" (1378).

8. TWO OR MORE WORKS CITED TOGETHER

If you cite two or more works in the same parentheses, separate the references with a semicolon.

> Critics have looked at both *Pride and Prejudice* and *Frankenstein*
> from a cultural perspective (Tanner 7; Smith viii).

9. SOURCE QUOTED IN ANOTHER SOURCE

When you are quoting text that you found quoted in another source, use
the abbreviation *qtd. in* in the parenthetical reference.

> Charlotte Brontë wrote to G. H. Lewes: "Why do you like Miss
> Austen so very much? I am puzzled on that point" (qtd. in
> Tanner 7).

10. SOURCES WITHOUT PAGE NUMBERS

For works without page numbers, give paragraph or section numbers,
using the abbreviation *par.* or *sec.* If you include the author's name in
the parenthetical reference, add a comma. If a work has no dividing
numbers at all, follow the model for an entire work (see number 11).

Russell's dismissals from Trinity College at Cambridge and from City College in New York City are seen as examples of the controversy that marked the philosopher's life (Irvine, par. 2).

11. AN ENTIRE WORK

If you refer to an entire work rather than a part of it, there's no need to include page numbers.

At least one observer considers Turkey and Central Asia explosive (Kaplan).

MLA List of Works Cited

A works-cited list provides full bibliographic information for every source cited in your text. Following is some general advice to help you prepare such a list:

GENERAL FORMAT

- Start the list on a new page, and center the title (Works Cited) one inch from the top of the page.
- Double-space the whole list.
- Put the entries in alphabetical order by the author's last name. If a work has no identifiable author, alphabetize it by the first major word of the title.
- Type the first line of each entry flush with the left-hand margin. Indent subsequent lines one-half inch or five spaces.

INDIVIDUAL ENTRIES

- *Authors*: List the authors by last name first, and include any middle name or initial after the first name. List additional authors, if any, first name before last. When citing the work of an editor, compiler, director, narrator, or translator, follow the name with the appropriate abbreviation (*ed., comp., narr., trans.*).

- *Titles*: Capitalize the first and last words of titles and subtitles and all principal words, including short verbs such as *is* and *are*. Do not capitalize *a, an, the, to,* or any preposition or conjunction unless they begin a title or subtitle. For periodical titles, omit any initial *A, An,* or *The.* The titles of books and periodicals should be italicized, but put quotation marks around titles of articles and short works.

- *Dates*: In entries for periodicals or electronic sources, abbreviate the names of months except for May, June, and July: Jan., Feb., Mar., Apr., Aug., Sept., Oct., Nov., Dec.

- *Medium*: For books and periodicals, use *Print.* For online sources, use *Web.* For other media, use *Film, Radio, Email, MP3 file, JPEG file,* and so on.

Books

For most books, you'll need to list the author; the title and any subtitle; and the place of publication, publisher, date, and the medium—*Print.* Note that MLA style requires you to use a shortened form of the publisher's name (Norton for W. W. Norton & Company, Princeton UP for Princeton University Press).

1. ONE AUTHOR

> Miller, Susan. *Assuming the Positions: Cultural Pedagogy and the Politics of Commonplace Writing.* Pittsburgh: U of Pittsburgh P, 1998. Print.

2. TWO OR MORE WORKS BY THE SAME AUTHOR(S)

Give the author's name in the first entry, and then use three hyphens in the author slot for each of the subsequent works, listing them alphabetically by the first important word of each title.

> Kaplan, Robert D. *The Coming Anarchy: Shattering the Dreams of the Post Cold War.* New York: Random, 2000. Print.

> - - -. *Eastward to Tartary: Travels in the Balkans, the Middle East, and the Caucasus.* New York: Random, 2000. Print.

3. TWO OR THREE AUTHORS

Follow the order of names on the book's title page.

> Malless, Stanley, and Jeffrey McQuain. *Coined by God: Words and Phrases That First Appear in the English Translations of the Bible.* New York: Norton, 2003. Print.

> Sebranek, Patrick, Verne Meyer, and Dave Kemper. *Writers INC: A Guide to Writing, Thinking, and Learning.* Burlington: Write Source, 1990. Print.

4. FOUR OR MORE AUTHORS

You may give each author's name or the name of the first author only, followed by *et al.* (and others).

> Anderson, Robert, et al. *Elements of Literature: Literature of the United States.* Austin: Holt, 1993. Print.

5. ORGANIZATION OR GOVERNMENT AS AUTHOR

> Diagram Group. *The Macmillan Visual Desk Reference.* New York: Macmillan, 1993. Print.

6. ANTHOLOGY

Use this model only when you are citing the whole anthology or the contributions of the editor(s).

> Kitchen, Judith, and Mary Paumier Jones, eds. *In Short: A Collection of Brief Creative Nonfiction.* New York: Norton, 1996. Print.

7. WORK(S) IN AN ANTHOLOGY

Give the inclusive page numbers of the selection you are citing.

> Achebe, Chinua. "Uncle Ben's Choice." *The Seagull Reader: Literature.* Ed. Joseph Kelly. New York: Norton, 2005. 23–27. Print.

To document two or more selections from one anthology, list each selection by author and title, followed by a cross-reference to the anthology. In addition, include in your works-cited list an entry for the anthology itself (see previous entry).

> Hiestand, Emily. "Afternoon Tea." Kitchen and Jones 65–67.

> Ozick, Cynthia. "The Shock of Teapots." Kitchen and Jones 68–71.

8. AUTHOR AND EDITOR

Start with the author if you've cited the text itself.

> Austen, Jane. *Emma*. Ed. Stephen M. Parrish. New York: Norton, 2000. Print.

Start with the editor if you've cited his or her work.

> Parrish, Stephen M., ed. *Emma*. By Jane Austen. New York: Norton, 2000. Print.

9. TRANSLATION

> Dostoevsky, Fyodor. *Crime and Punishment*. Trans. Richard Pevear and Larissa Volokhonsky. New York: Vintage, 1993. Print.

10. FOREWORD, INTRODUCTION, PREFACE, OR AFTERWORD

> Tanner, Tony. Introduction. *Pride and Prejudice*. By Jane Austen. London: Penguin, 1972. 7–46. Print.

11. MULTIVOLUME WORK

If you cite all the volumes, give the number of volumes after the title.

> Sandburg, Carl. *Abraham Lincoln: The War Years*. 4 vols. New York: Harcourt, 1939. Print.

If you cite only one volume, give the volume number after the title.

> Sandburg, Carl. *Abraham Lincoln: The War Years*. Vol. 2. New York: Harcourt, 1939. Print.

12. EDITION OTHER THAN THE FIRST

> Strunk, William, Jr., and E. B. White. *The Elements of Style.* 4th ed.
> Boston: Allyn and Bacon, 1999.

13. ARTICLE IN A REFERENCE BOOK

If a reference book is well known, list only the edition, if available, and the year of publication.

> "Iraq." *The New Encyclopædia Brittanica.* 15th ed. 2007. Print.

If a reference book is less familiar, give complete publication information.

> Benton-Cohen, Katherine. "Women in the Reform and Progressive
> Era." *A History of Women in the United States.* Ed. Doris
> Weatherford. 4 vols. Danbury, CT: Grolier, 2004. Print.

Periodicals

For most articles, you'll need to list the author, the article title and any subtitle, the periodical title, any volume and issue number, the date, inclusive page numbers, and the medium—*Print*. A few details to note:

- *Periodical titles*: Omit any initial *A, An,* or *The.*
- *Dates*: Abbreviate the names of months except for May, June, or July.
- *Pages*: If an article does not fall on consecutive pages, give the first page with a plus sign (55+).

14. ARTICLE IN A JOURNAL

> Bartley, William. "Imagining the Future in *The Awakening*." *College English* 62.6 (2000): 719–46. Print.

15. ARTICLE IN A JOURNAL NUMBERED BY ISSUE

For journals that do not have volume numbers, give the issue number after the title, followed by the year of publication and inclusive page numbers.

> Flynn, Kevin. "The Railway in Canadian Poetry." *Canadian Literature* 174 (2002): 70–95. Print.

16. ARTICLE IN A MONTHLY MAGAZINE

> Fellman, Bruce. "Leading the Libraries." *Yale Alumni Magazine* Feb. 2002: 26–31. Print.

17. ARTICLE IN A WEEKLY MAGAZINE

> Cloud, John. "Should SATs Matter?" *Time* 12 Mar. 2001: 62+. Print.

18. ARTICLE IN A DAILY NEWSPAPER

> Springer, Shira. "Celtics Reserves Are Whizzes vs. Wizards." *Boston Globe* 14 Mar. 2005: D4+. Print.

If you are documenting a particular edition of a newspaper, specify the edition (late ed., natl. ed., and so on) in between the date and the section and page reference. The following citation shows that the article begins on page 1 of section G of the late edition.

> Margulius, David L. "Smarter Call Centers: At Your Service?" *New York Times* 14 Mar. 2002, late ed.: G1+. Print.

19. UNSIGNED ARTICLE

> "Coal Mine Inspections Fall Short." *Atlanta Journal-Constitution* 18 Nov. 2007: A7. Print.

20. EDITORIAL OR LETTER TO THE EDITOR

"Gas, Cigarettes Are Safe to Tax." Editorial. *Lakeville Journal* 17 Feb. 2005: A10. Print.

Festa, Roger. "Social Security: Another Phony Crisis." Letter. *Lakeville Journal* 17 Feb. 2005: A10. Print.

21. REVIEW

Lahr, John. "Night for Day." Rev. of *The Crucible,* by Arthur Miller. *New Yorker* 18 Mar. 2002: 149–51. Print.

Electronic Sources

When you cite electronic sources, your goal, as with print sources, is to give readers all the information they need to find the particular source you used. If possible, your citation should include at least the following: (1) author's name; (2) title; (3) name of online site; (4) publisher or sponsoring institution; (5) date of first electronic publication and/or most recent revision; (6) the medium, e.g., *Web*; (7) date you accessed the source. Here is an example of a citation that includes all this information:

Johnson, Charles W. "How Our Laws Are Made." *Thomas: Legislative Information on the Internet.* Lib. of Congress, 31 Jan. 2000. Web. 21 June 2008.

A few details to note:

- *Basic information*: Some citations for electronic sources are based on the style you would follow for a print version, so you may need to consult the previous sections on books and periodicals. Note that the titles of websites and databases are italicized.

- *Dates*: Although MLA asks for the date when materials were first posted or most recently updated, you won't always be able to find that information; if it is unavailable, use *n.d.* ("no date"). The date you *must* include is the date on which you accessed the electronic source.

- *Publisher*: If the name of the publisher or sponsoring institution is unavailable, use *N.p.* ("no publisher").
- *URL*: This is required only if your reader will probably be unable to find the source without it. In such cases, give the address of the website at the end of the citation, enclosed in angle brackets. When a URL will not fit on one line, break it only after a slash (and do not add a hyphen).

22. ENTIRE WEBSITE

Zalta, Edward N., ed. *Stanford Encyclopedia of Philosophy*. Metaphysics Research Lab, Center for the Study of Language and Information, Stanford U, 2007. Web. 2 Jan. 2008.

23. PERSONAL WEBSITE

Chomsky, Noam. Home page. N.p., 2006. Web. 12 Dec. 2007.

24. WORK WITHIN A WEBSITE

"Medications: Using Them Safely." *KidsHealth*. Nemours Foundation, 2005.

25. ONLINE BOOK OR PART OF A BOOK

To cite part of an online book, list the short work before the book title.

Anderson, Sherwood. "The Philosopher." *Winesburg, Ohio*. New York: B. W. Huebsch, 1919. N. pag. *Bartleby.com*. Web. 2 Dec. 2007.

26. ARTICLE IN AN ONLINE JOURNAL

Cite the volume, issue, and year as you would for a print journal. If a journal does not number pages or if it numbers each article separately, use *n. pag.* in place of page numbers.

Moore, Greggory. "The Process of Life in *2001: A Space Odyssey*." *Images: A Journal of Film and Popular Culture* 9 (2000): n. pag. Web. 12 May 2009.

27. ARTICLE IN AN ONLINE MAGAZINE

> Landsburg, Steven E. "Putting All Your Potatoes in One Basket: The
> Economic Lessons of the Great Famine." *Slate.com.* Washington
> Post–Newsweek Interactive, 13 Mar. 2001. Web. 8 Dec. 2007.

28. ARTICLE FROM AN ONLINE DATABASE

Include any information about print publication as well as the name of
the database (in this example, *Academic Search Premier*).

> Bowman, James. "Moody Blues." *American Spectator* June 1999:
> 64–65. *Academic Search Premier.* Web. 15 Mar. 2005.

29. ARTICLE IN AN ONLINE NEWSPAPER

> Mitchell, Dan. "Being Skeptical of Green." *New York Times.* New
> York Times, 24 Nov. 2007. Web. 26 Nov. 2007.

30. ONLINE EDITORIAL

> "Outsourcing Your Life." Editorial. *Chicagotribune.com.* Chicago
> Tribune, 24 Nov. 2004. Web. 3 Jan. 2008.

31. EMAIL

> Smith, William. "Teaching Grammar—Some Thoughts." Message to
> the author. 15 Feb. 2008. Email.

32. POSTING TO AN ELECTRONIC FORUM

> Mintz, Stephen H. "Manumission During the Revolution." *H-Net List
> on Slavery.* Michigan State U, 14 Sept. 2006. Web. 18 Apr. 2009.

33. CD-ROM OR DVD-ROM

Cite like a book, but indicate any pertinent information about the edition or version.

> *Othello.* Princeton: Films for the Humanities and Sciences, 1998. CD-
> ROM.

Other Kinds of Sources

This section shows how to prepare works-cited entries for categories other than books, periodicals, and writing found on the Web and CD-ROMs. Many of these categories cover works that can be found both on and off the Web. Author (or performer) names, titles, and dates should be styled as in print versions.

34. ART (PRINT AND ONLINE)

Van Gogh, Vincent. *The Potato Eaters.* 1885. Oil on canvas. Van Gogh Museum, Amsterdam.

Warhol, Andy. *Self-Portrait.* 1979. J. Paul Getty Museum, Los Angeles. *The Getty.* Web. 5 Jan. 2008.

35. CARTOON OR COMIC STRIP (PRINT AND ONLINE)

Chast, Roz. "The Three Wise Men of Thanksgiving." Cartoon. *New Yorker* 1 Dec. 2003: 174. Print.

Adams, Scott. "Dilbert." Comic strip. *Dilbert.com.* United Features Syndicate, 9 Nov. 2007. Web. 26 Nov. 2007.

36. FILM, VIDEO, OR DVD

Casablanca. Dir. Michael Curtiz. Perf. Humphrey Bogart, Ingrid Bergman, and Claude Rains. Warner, 1942. Film.

Easter Parade. Dir. Charles Walters. Perf. Judy Garland and Fred Astaire. MGM, 1948. DVD.

37. BROADCAST, PUBLISHED, AND PERSONAL INTERVIEW

Gates, Henry Louis, Jr. Interview. *Fresh Air.* NPR. WNYC, New York. 9 Apr. 2002. Radio.

Brzezinski, Zbigniew. "Against the Neocons." *American Prospect* Mar. 2005: 26–27. Print.

Berra, Yogi. Personal interview. 17 June 2001.

38. PUBLISHED LETTER

> White, E. B. Letter to Carol Angell. 28 May 1970. *Letters of E. B. White.* Ed. Dorothy Lobarno Guth. New York: Harper, 1976. 600. Print.

39. MAP (PRINT AND ONLINE)

> *Toscana.* Map. Milan: Touring Club Italiano, 1987. Print.

> "Portland, Oregon." Map. *Google Maps.* Google, 25 Apr. 2009. Web. 25 Apr. 2009.

40. MUSICAL SCORE

> Beethoven, Ludwig van. *String Quartet No. 13 in B Flat, Op. 130.* 1825. New York: Dover, 1970. Print.

41. SOUND RECORDING (WITH ONLINE VERSION)

Whether you list the composer, conductor, or performer first depends on where you want to place the emphasis.

> Beethoven, Ludwig van. *Missa Solemnis.* Perf. Westminster Choir and New York Philharmonic. Cond. Leonard Bernstein. Sony, 1992. CD.

> The Beatles. "Can't Buy Me Love." *A Hard Day's Night.* United Artists, 1964. MP3 file.

> Davis, Miles. "So What." *Birth of the Cool.* Columbia, 1959. *Miles Davis.* Web. 14 Feb. 2009.

42. TELEVISION OR RADIO PROGRAM (WITH ONLINE VERSION)

> "Stirred." *The West Wing.* Writ. Aaron Sorkin, Dir. Jeremy Kagan. Perf. Martin Sheen. NBC. WPTV, West Palm Beach, 3 Apr. 2002. Television.

> "Bush's War." *Frontline.* Writ. and Dir. Michael Kirk. PBS, 24 Mar. 2008. *PBS.org.* Web. 10 Apr. 2009.

Dylan Borchers wrote the following research paper for a first-year writing class. He used MLA style for his essay, but documentation styles vary from discipline to discipline, so ask your instructor if you're not sure which style you should use.

Dylan Borchers

Professor Bullock

English 102, Section 4

20 April 2009

Against the Odds:

Harry S. Truman and the Election of 1948

"Thomas E. Dewey's Election as President Is a Foregone

Conclusion," read a headline in the *New York Times* during the

presidential election race between incumbent Democrat Harry S.

Truman and his Republican challenger, Thomas E. Dewey. Earlier, *Life*

magazine had put Dewey on its cover with the caption "The Next

President of the United States" (qtd. in "1948 Truman-Dewey

Election"). In a *Newsweek* survey of fifty prominent political writers,

each one predicted Truman's defeat, and *Time* correspondents

declared that Dewey would carry 39 of the 48 states (Donaldson 210).

Nearly every major media outlet across the United States endorsed

Dewey and lambasted Truman. As historian Robert H. Ferrell

observes, even Truman's wife, Bess, thought he would be beaten

(270).

The results of an election are not so easily predicted, as the

famous photograph on page 2 shows. Not only did Truman win the

election, but he won by a significant margin, with 303 electoral

votes and 24,179,259 popular votes, compared to Dewey's 189

electoral votes and 21,991,291 popular votes (Donaldson 204-07). In

fact, many historians and political analysts argue that Truman

Fig. 1. President Harry S. Truman holds up an Election Day edition of the *Chicago Daily Tribune*, which mistakenly announced "Dewey Defeats Truman." St. Louis, 4 Nov. 1948 (Rollins).

Put illustrations close to the text they relate to. Label with figure number, caption, and parenthetical source citation.

would have won by an even greater margin had third-party Progressive candidate Henry A. Wallace not split the Democratic vote in New York State and Dixiecrat Strom Thurmond not won four states in the South (McCullough 711). Although Truman's defeat was heavily predicted, those predictions themselves, Dewey's passiveness as a campaigner, and Truman's zeal turned the tide for a Truman victory.

   In the months preceding the election, public opinion polls predicted that Dewey would win by a large margin. Pollster Elmo Roper stopped polling in September, believing there was no reason to continue, given a seemingly inevitable Dewey landslide. Although the margin narrowed as the election drew near, the other pollsters

Indent paragraphs 5 spaces or $\frac{1}{2}$ inch.

Give the author and page in parentheses when there's no signal phrase.

predicted a Dewey win by at least 5 percent (Donaldson 209). Many historians believe that these predictions aided the president in the long run. First, surveys showing Dewey in the lead may have prompted some of Dewey's supporters to feel overconfident about their candidate's chances and therefore to stay home from the polls on Election Day. Second, these same surveys may have energized Democrats to mount late get-out-the-vote efforts ("1948 Truman-Dewey Election"). Other analysts believe that the overwhelming predictions of a Truman loss also kept at home some Democrats who approved of Truman's policies but saw a Truman loss as inevitable. According to political analyst Samuel Lubell, those Democrats may have saved Dewey from an even greater defeat (Hamby, *Man of the People* 465). Whatever the impact on the voters, the polling numbers had a decided effect on Dewey.

Historians and political analysts alike cite Dewey's overly cautious campaign as one of the main reasons Truman was able to achieve victory. Dewey firmly believed in public opinion polls. With all indications pointing to an easy victory, Dewey and his staff believed that all he had to do was bide his time and make no foolish mistakes. Dewey himself said, "When you're leading, don't talk"

If you quote text that's quoted in another source, cite that source in a parenthetical reference.

(qtd. in McCullough 672). Each of Dewey's speeches was well-crafted and well-rehearsed. As the leader in the race, he kept his remarks faultlessly positive, with the result that he failed to deliver a solid message or even mention Truman or any of Truman's policies. Eventually, Dewey began to be perceived as aloof and stuffy. One observer compared him to the plastic groom on top of a wedding cake (Hamby, "Harry S. Truman"), and others noted his stiff, cold demeanor (McCullough 671-74).

If you cite 2 or more works closely together, give a parenthetical citation for each one.

As his campaign continued, observers noted that Dewey seemed uncomfortable in crowds, unable to connect with ordinary people. And he made a number of blunders. One took place at a train stop when the candidate, commenting on the number of children in the crowd, said he was glad they had been let out of school for his arrival. Unfortunately for Dewey, it was a Saturday ("1948: The Great Truman Surprise"). Such gaffes gave voters the feeling that Dewey was out of touch with the public.

Again and again through the autumn of 1948, Dewey's campaign speeches failed to address the issues, with the candidate declaring that he did not want to "get down in the gutter" (qtd. in McCullough 701). When told by fellow Republicans that he was losing ground, Dewey insisted that his campaign not alter its course. Even *Time* magazine, though it endorsed and praised him, conceded that his speeches were dull (McCullough 696). According to historian Zachary Karabell, they were "notable only for taking place, not for any specific message" (244). Dewey's numbers in the polls slipped in the weeks before the election, but he still held a comfortable lead over Truman. It would take Truman's famous whistle-stop campaign to make the difference.

Few candidates in U.S. history have campaigned for the presidency with more passion and faith than Harry Truman. In the autumn of 1948, he wrote to his sister, "It will be the greatest campaign any President ever made. Win, lose, or draw, people will know where I stand" (91). For thirty-three days, Truman traveled the nation, giving hundreds of speeches from the back of the *Ferdinand Magellan* railroad car. In the same letter, he described the pace: "We made about 140 stops and I spoke over 147 times, shook hands with at least 30,000 and am in good condition to start out again tomorrow for Wilmington, Philadelphia, Jersey City, Newark, Albany and Buffalo" (91). McCullough writes of Truman's campaign:

> No President in history had ever gone so far in quest of support from the people, or with less cause for the effort, to judge by informed opinion. . . . As a test of his skills and judgment as a professional politician, not to say his stamina and disposition at age sixty-four, it would be like no other experience in his long, often difficult career, as he himself understood perfectly. More than any other event in his public life, or in his presidency thus far, it would reveal the kind of man he was. (655)

He spoke in large cities and small towns, defending his policies and attacking Republicans. As a former farmer and relatively late bloomer, Truman was able to connect with the public. He developed an energetic style, usually speaking from notes rather than from a prepared speech, and often mingled with the crowds that met his train. These crowds grew larger as the campaign

Set off quotations of 4 or more lines by indenting 1 inch (or 10 spaces).

Put parenthetical references after final punctuation in block quotations.

progressed. In Chicago, over half a million people lined the streets as he passed, and in St. Paul the crowd numbered over 25,000. When Dewey entered St. Paul two days later, he was greeted by only 7,000 supporters ("1948 Truman-Dewey Election"). Reporters brushed off the large crowds as mere curiosity seekers wanting to see a president (McCullough 682). Yet Truman persisted, even if he often seemed to be the only one who thought he could win. By going directly to the American people and connecting with them, Truman built the momentum needed to surpass Dewey and win the election.

The legacy and lessons of Truman's whistle-stop campaign continue to be studied by political analysts, and politicians today often mimic his campaign methods by scheduling multiple visits to key states, as Truman did. He visited California, Illinois, and Ohio 48 times, compared with 6 visits to those states by Dewey. Political scientist Thomas M. Holbrook concludes that his strategic campaigning in those states and others gave Truman the electoral votes he needed to win (61, 65).

The 1948 election also had an effect on pollsters, who, as Elmo Roper admitted, "couldn't have been more wrong" (qtd. in Karabell 255). *Life* magazine's editors concluded that pollsters as well as reporters and commentators were too convinced of a Dewey victory to analyze the polls seriously, especially the opinions of undecided voters (Karabell 256). Pollsters assumed that undecided voters would vote in the same proportion as decided voters -- and that

If you cite a work with no known author, use the title in your parenthetical reference.

turned out to be a false assumption (Karabell 258). In fact, the lopsidedness of the polls might have led voters who supported Truman to call themselves undecided out of an unwillingness to associate themselves with the losing side, further skewing the polls' results (McDonald, Glynn, Kim, and Ostman 152). Such errors led pollsters to change their methods significantly after the 1948 election.

In a work by 4 or more authors, either cite them all or name the first one followed by et al.

After the election, many political analysts, journalists, and historians concluded that the Truman upset was in fact a victory for the American people, who, the *New Republic* noted, "couldn't be ticketed by the polls, knew its own mind and had picked the rather unlikely but courageous figure of Truman to carry its banner" (qtd. in McCullough 715). How "unlikely" is unclear, however; Truman biographer Alonzo Hamby notes that "polls of scholars consistently rank Truman among the top eight presidents in American history" (*Man of the People* 641). But despite Truman's high standing, and despite the fact that the whistle-stop campaign is now part of our political landscape, politicians have increasingly imitated the style of the Dewey campaign, with its "packaged candidate who ran so as not to lose, who steered clear of controversy, and who made a good show of appearing presidential" (Karabell 266). The election of 1948 shows that voters are not necessarily swayed by polls, but it may have presaged the packaging of candidates by public relations experts, to the detriment of public debate on the issues in future presidential elections.

Works Cited

Donaldson, Gary A. *Truman Defeats Dewey*. Lexington: UP of
    Kentucky, 1999. Print.

Ferrell, Robert H. *Harry S. Truman: A Life*. Columbia: U of Missouri P,
    1994. Print.

Hamby, Alonzo L., ed. "Harry S. Truman (1945-1953)."
    AmericanPresident.org. 11 Dec. 2003. Miller Center of Public
    Affairs, U of Virginia, 11 Dec. 2003. Web. 10 Apr. 2009.

---. *Man of the People: A Life of Harry S. Truman*. New York: Oxford UP,
    1995. Print.

Holbrook, Thomas M. "Did the Whistle-Stop Campaign Matter?" *PS:
    Political Science and Politics* 35.1 (2002): 59-66. Print.

Karabell, Zachary. *The Last Campaign: How Harry Truman Won the 1948
    Election*. New York: Knopf, 2000. Print.

McCullough, David. *Truman*. New York: Simon & Schuster, 1992. Print.

McDonald, Daniel G., Carroll J. Glynn, Sei-Hill Kim, and Ronald E.
    Ostman. "The Spiral of Silence in the 1948 Presidential
    Election." *Communication Research* 28.2 (2001): 139-55. Print.

"1948: The Great Truman Surprise." *Media and Politics Online
    Projects: Media Coverage of Presidential Campaigns*. Dept. of
    Political Science and International Affairs, Kennesaw State U.
    29 Oct. 2003. Web. 10 Apr. 2009.

"1948 Truman-Dewey Election." *Electronic Government Project: Eagleton
    Digital Archive of American Politics*. Eagleton Inst. of Politics,
    Rutgers, State U of New Jersey, 2004. Web. 17 Apr. 2009.

1"

Center the
heading.

Double-space
throughout.

Alphabetize the
list by authors'
last names or by
title for works
with no author.

Begin each entry
at the left mar-
gin; indent sub-
sequent lines
$\frac{1}{2}$ inch or 5
spaces.

If you cite more
than one work
by a single
author, list them
alphabetically by
title, and use 3
hyphens instead
of repeating the
author's name
after the first
entry.

Rollins, Byron. Untitled photograph. "The First 150 Years: 1948." *AP History*. Associated Press. n.d. Web. 31 Mar. 2009.

Truman, Harry S. "Campaigning, Letter, October 5, 1948." *Harry S. Truman*. Ed. Robert H. Ferrell. Washington: CQ P, 2003. 91. Print.

Check to be sure that every source you use is on the list of works cited.

GLOSSARY

ABSTRACT General, having to do with essences and ideas: Liberty, truth, and beauty are abstract concepts. Most writers depend upon abstractions to some degree; however, abstractions that are not fleshed out with vivid particulars are not likely to hold a reader's interest. See also CONCRETE.

ALLUSION A passing reference, especially to a work of literature. When feminist Lindsy Van Gelder put forth the "modest proposal" that words of feminine gender be used whenever English traditionally uses masculine words, she had in mind Jonathan Swift's essay by that title (reprinted here in Chapter 11). This single brief reference carries the weight of Swift's entire essay behind it, humorously implying that the idea being advanced is about as modest as Swift's tongue-in-cheek proposal that Ireland eat its children as a ready food supply for a poor country. Allusions, therefore, are an efficient means of enlarging the scope and implications of a statement. They work best, of course, when they refer to works most readers are likely to know.

ANALOGY A comparison that explains aspects of something unfamiliar by likening it to something that is more familiar. In expository writing, analogies are used as aids to explanation and as organizing devices. In a persuasive essay, a writer may argue that what is true in one case is also true in the similar case that he or she is advancing. An argument "by analogy" is only as strong as the terms of the analogy are close.

ANECDOTE A brief narrative or humorous story, often told for the purpose of exemplifying or explaining a larger point. Anecdotal evidence is proof based on such stories rather than on rigorous statistical or scientific inquiry.

ARGUMENT An argument makes a case or proves a point. It seeks to convince someone to act in a certain way or to believe in the truth or validity of a statement or claim. According to traditional definitions of argumentation and persuasion, a writer can convince a reader in one of three ways: by appealing to reason, by appealing to the reader's emotions, or by appealing to the reader's sense of ethics.

AUDIENCE The people to whom a piece of writing is addressed. Writers are more likely to achieve their purpose in writing if they keep the needs and expectations of their audience in mind throughout the writing process when making choices about topics, diction, support, and so on. For example, an essay written for athletes that attacks the use of performance-enhancing drugs in sports might emphasize the hazards of taking steroids. On the other hand, an essay with the same purpose but written for an audience of sports fans might focus more on the value of fair play and of having heroes who are drug-free.

CAUSAL CHAIN A series of circumstances or events in which one circumstance or event causes another, which in turn causes another and so on—all leading to an ultimate effect. A row of dominoes on end is a classic example: The fall of one domino causes another to tip over, which in turn pushes over another domino, until the entire row of dominoes has been toppled.

CAUSE AND EFFECT A strategy of exposition. Cause and effect essays analyze why an event occurred and/or trace its consequences. See the introduction to Chapter 9 for further discussion of this strategy.

CLAIM The main point that an argument is intended to prove or support; a statement that is debatable, that rational people can disagree with.

CLASSIFICATION A strategy of exposition that puts people or things into categories based on their distinguishing characteristics. Strictly speaking, classification assigns individuals to categories (*This coin is an Indian-Head penny*), and division separates individuals in a group according to a given trait or traits (*Put the pennies in this box, the nickels in this one, and give me the quarters and half dollars*). Classification is a mode of organizing an essay as well as a means of obtaining knowledge. See Chapter 5 for further discussion of this strategy.

CLICHÉ A tired expression that has lost its original power to surprise because of overuse: *We'll have to go back to the drawing board. The quarterback turned the tables and saved the day.*

CLIMAX An aspect of plot in narrative writing. The climax is the moment when the action of a narrative is most intense—the culmination, after which the dramatic tension is released.

COMPARISON AND CONTRAST A strategy of expository writing that explores the similarities and differences between two persons, places, things, or ideas. See Chapter 7 for a more detailed explanation.

CONCRETE Definite, particular, capable of being perceived directly. Opposed to ABSTRACT. *Rose, Mississippi, pinch* are more concrete words than *flower, river, touch. Five-miles-per-hour* is a more concrete idea than *slowness*. It is a good practice to make your essays as concrete as possible, even when you are writing on a general topic. If you are defining an ideal wife or husband, cite specific wives or husbands you have known or heard about.

CONNOTATIONS The implied meanings of a word; its overtones and associations over and above its literal meaning. The strict meaning of *home*, for example, is "the place where one lives"; but the word connotes comfort, security, and love.

DEDUCTION A form of logical reasoning that proceeds from general premises to specific conclusions. See also SYLLOGISM.

DEFINITION A basic strategy of expository writing. Definitions give the essential meaning of something. Extended definitions enlarge upon that basic meaning by analyzing the qualities, recalling the history, explaining the purpose, or giving synonyms of whatever is being defined. See the introduction to Chapter 8 for further discussion of this strategy.

DESCRIPTION One of the four modes of writing. Description appeals to the senses: it tells how something looks, feels, sounds, smells, or tastes. An *objective* description focuses on verifiable facts and the observable physical details of a subject, whereas a *subjective* description conveys the writer's thoughts and feelings about a subject, in addition to its physical characteristics. See the introduction to Chapter 2 for further discussion of the descriptive mode.

DIALOGUE Direct speech, especially between two or more speakers, quoted word for word.

DICTION Word choice. Mark Twain was talking about diction when he said that the difference between the almost right word and the right word is the difference "between the lightning bug and the lightning." "Standard" diction is defined by dictionaries and other authorities as the language taught in schools and used in the national media. "Nonstandard" diction includes words like *ain't* that are generally not used in formal writing. *Slang* includes the figurative language of a group (*moll, gat, heist*) or fashionable, coined words (*bonkers, weirdo*) and extended meanings (*dough* for money; *garbage* for nonsense). Slang words often pass quickly into the standard language or just as quickly fade away. *Colloquial diction* is the language of informal speech or writing: *I'm crazy about you, Virginia. Regional* language is that spoken in certain geographic areas—for example, *remuda*, a word for a herd of riding horses, is used in the Southwest. *Obsolete* language includes terms like *pantaloons* and *palfrey* (saddle horse) that were once standard but are no longer used.

DIVISION See CLASSIFICATION.

DOMINANT IMPRESSION In descriptive writing, the main impression of a subject that a writer creates through the use of carefully selected details.

EVIDENCE Proof; the facts and figures, examples, expert testimony, personal experience, and other support that a writer provides in order to make a point.

ETYMOLOGY A word history or the practice of tracing such histories. The modern English word *march*, for example, is derived from the French *marcher* ("to walk"), which in turn is derived from the Latin word *marcus* ("a hammer"). The etymological definition of *march* is thus "to walk with a measured tread, like the rhythmic pounding of a hammer." In most dictionaries, the derivation, or etymology, of a word is explained in parentheses or brackets before the first definition is given.

EXAMPLE A specific instance of a general group or idea. Among "things that have given males a bad name," for example, humorist Dave Barry cites "violent crime, war, spitting, and ice hockey." See the introduction to Chapter 3 for more on using examples in writing.

EXPOSITION One of the four modes of writing. Expository writing is informative writing. It explains or gives directions. All the items in this glossary are written in the expository mode; and most of the practical prose that you write in the coming years will be—e.g., papers and examinations, job applications, business reports, insurance claims, your last will and testament. See the Introduction for a discussion of how exposition is related to the other modes of writing.

FIGURES OF SPEECH Colorful words and phrases used in a nonliteral sense. Some common figures of speech: *Simile:* A stated comparison, usually with *like* or *as: He stood like a rock. Metaphor:* A comparison that equates two objects without the use of a stated connecting word: *Throughout the battle, Sergeant Phillips was a rock. Metonymy:* The use of one word or name in place of another commonly associated with it: *The White House* [for the president] *awarded the sergeant a medal. Personification:* The assignment of human traits to nonhuman objects: *The very walls have ears. Hyperbole:* Conscious exaggeration: *The mountain reached to the sky. Understatement:* The opposite of hyperbole, a conscious playing down: *After forty days of climbing the mountain, we felt that we had made a start. Rhetorical Question:* A question to which the author expects no answer or that he answers himself: *Why climb the mountain? Because it is there.*

FLASHBACK The narrative technique of interrupting the main plot of a story to show the reader an incident that occurred earlier in time.

FLASH-FORWARD The narrative technique of interrupting the main plot of a story to show the reader an incident that occurs at some time in the future.

HYPERBOLE Exaggeration. See FIGURES OF SPEECH.

INDUCTION A form of logical reasoning that proceeds from specific examples to general principles. As a rule, an inductive argument is only as valid as its examples are representative. See the introduction to Chapter 10.

IRONY A statement that implies something other than what the words generally mean. For example, when Russell Baker writes that New Yorkers find Toronto "hopelessly bogged down in civilization," what he implies is that New Yorkers define "civilization" in an uncivilized way. Irony of situation, as opposed to verbal irony, occurs when events turn out differently than expected. It was ironic that Hitler, with his dream of world domination, committed suicide in the end.

LOGICAL FALLACY An error in logical reasoning. Common logical fallacies include reasoning *post hoc, ergo propter hoc; non sequiturs*; begging the question; arguing *ad hominem*; and false analogies. See the introduction to Chapter 10 for further discussion of logical fallacies.

METAPHOR A direct comparison that identifies one thing with another. See FIGURES OF SPEECH.

METONYMY A form of verbal association. See FIGURES OF SPEECH.

MODES OF WRITING Basic patterns of writing, including description, narration, exposition, and argumentation. Description is explained in detail in Chapter 2; narration, in Chapter 3; exposition, in Chapters 4–9; and argumentation, in Chapter 10.

NARRATION One of the four modes of writing. An account of actions and events that have befallen someone or something. Because narration is essentially story-telling, it is the mode most often used in fiction; however, it is also an important element in almost all writing and speaking. The opening of Lincoln's *Gettysburg Address,* for example, is in the narrative mode: "Fourscore and seven years ago our fathers brought forth on this continent a new nation . . . "

NARRATOR In a narrative, the person who is telling the story. The narrator can participate directly in the events of the story—or serve mainly as an observer reporting on those events.

ONOMATOPOEIA The use of words that sound like what they refer to: *What's the buzz?* or *The cat purred, the dog barked, and the clock ticked.*

OXYMORON An apparent contradiction or bringing together of opposites for rhetorical or humorous effect, as in *eloquent silence, mournful optimist,* or (some would say) *military intelligence, civic organization.*

PERSONIFICATION Assigning human characteristics to inanimate objects. See FIGURES OF SPEECH.

PERSUASION The art of moving an audience to action or belief. According to traditional definitions, a writer can persuade a reader in one of three ways: by appealing to the reader's reason, emotions, or sense of ethics.

PLOT The sequence of events in a story arranged in such a way that they have a beginning, middle, and an end.

POINT OF VIEW The perspective from which a story is told or an account given. Point of view is often described according to the grammatical person of a narrative. An "I" narrative, for example, is told from the "first-person" point of view. A narrative that refers to "he" or "she" is told from the "third-person" point of view. If the speaker of a third-person narrative seems to know everything about his or her subject, including their thoughts, the point of view is "omniscient"; if the speaker's knowledge is incomplete, the point of view is third-person "limited."

PROCESS ANALYSIS A form of expository writing that breaks a process into its component operations or that gives directions. Most "how to" essays are essays in process analysis: how to write an essay; how to operate a fork lift; how to avoid a shark bite. Process analyses are usually divided into stages or steps arranged in chronological order. They differ from narratives in that they tell how something functions rather than what happens to something or someone. See the introduction to Chapter 6 for further discussion of this expository strategy.

PUN A play on words, usually involving different words that sound alike, or different meanings of the same word (*The undertaker was a grave man*).

PURPOSE A writer's goal, or reason for writing. For example, the purpose may be to *inform* readers by explaining an important subject, such as global warming; to *persuade* readers to act, such as to combat climate change by buying more fuel-efficient cars; to *entertain* readers, such as by telling them a heart-warming story of an animal that successfully adapted to the loss of its natural habitat; or simply to *express* the writer's feelings, for example his or her indignation about environmental damage or waste.

RHETORIC The art of using language effectively in speech and in writing. The term originally belonged to oratory, and it implies the presence of both a speaker (or writer) and a listener (or reader). This book is a collection of the rhetorical techniques and strategies that some successful writers have found helpful for communicating effectively with an audience.

RHETORICAL QUESTION A question that is really a statement. See FIGURES OF SPEECH.

SATIRE A form of writing that attacks a person or practice in hopes of improving either. For example, in "A Modest Proposal" (Chapter 11), Jonathan Swift satirizes the materialism that had reduced his native Ireland to extreme poverty. His intent was to point out the greed of many of his countrymen and thereby shame them all into looking out for the public welfare. This desire to correct vices and follies distinguishes *satire* from *sarcasm*, which is intended primarily to wound. See also IRONY.

SETTING The physical place or scene in which an action or event takes place, especially in narrative and descriptive writing.

SIMILE A comparison that likens one thing to another, usually with *like* or *as*. See FIGURES OF SPEECH.

SYLLOGISM The basic form of deductive reasoning, in which a conclusion is drawn from a major (or wider) premise or assumption and a minor (or narrower) premise. For example: *Major premise:* All men are mortal. *Minor premise:* Socrates is a man. *Conclusion:* Socrates is mortal.

SYNONYM A word or phrase that has essentially the same meaning as another word or phrase: for example, *make do* or *get by* for *cope*.

THESIS The main point that a paragraph or an essay is intended to make or prove. A *thesis statement* is a direct statement of that point.

TONE An author's attitude toward his or her subject or audience: sympathy, longing, amusement, shock, sarcasm—the range is endless. When analyzing the tone of a passage, consider what quality of voice you would use in reading it aloud.

TRANSITIONS Connecting words and phrases—such as *next, by contrast, nevertheless, therefore, on the other hand*—that link sentences, paragraphs, and ideas in a piece of writing.

UNDERSTATEMENT A verbal playing down or softening for humorous or ironic effect. See FIGURES OF SPEECH.

VANTAGE POINT In a description, the physical perspective from which a subject is described. See the introduction to Chapter 2 for further discussion of vantage point.

PERMISSIONS
ACKNOWLEDGMENTS

XXXXXXXXXXXXXXXXXXXXXXXXXXXXXXXXXXXXXXXXXXXXXXXXXXXXXXXXXX

TEXT

Marjorie Agosín: "Always Living in Spanish," *The Literary Life*, p. 25. Reprinted by permission of the author.

Brian Alexander: "Tour de Farce: Floyd Landis' positive test shows why drug testing will never work," *Slate Magazine*, www.slate.com, July 27, 2006. © 2006 Washington Post, Newsweek Interactive, LLC and Slate. Reprinted by permission.

Isaac Asimov: "What Do You Call a Platypus?" *National Wildlife*, March/April 1971. Copyright © by Isaac Asimov. Reprinted by permission of the Estate of Isaac Asimov.

Dennis Baron: "Don't Make English Official – Ban It Instead." Dennis Baron is Professor of English and Linguistics at the University of Illinois. Reprinted by permission of the author.

Tanya Barrientos: "Se Habla Español," *Latina* Magazine, August 2004, pp. 64–66. Reprinted with permission.

Dan Barry: "Death in the Chair, Step By Remorseless Step," from *The New York Times*, September 16, 2007. © 2007 The New York Times. All rights reserved. Used by permission and protected by the copyright laws of the United States. The printing, copying, redistribution, or retransmission of the material without express written permission is prohibited.

Dave Barry: "Introduction: Guys vs. Men," from *Dave Barry's Complete Guide to Guys*, copyright © 1995 by Dave Barry. Used by permission of Random House, Inc.

Thomas Beller: "The Ashen Guy: Lower Broadway, September 11, 2001," *Before and After: Stories from New York* (Mr. Beller's Neighborhood Books, 2002), edited by Thomas Beller. Reprinted by permission.

INDEX